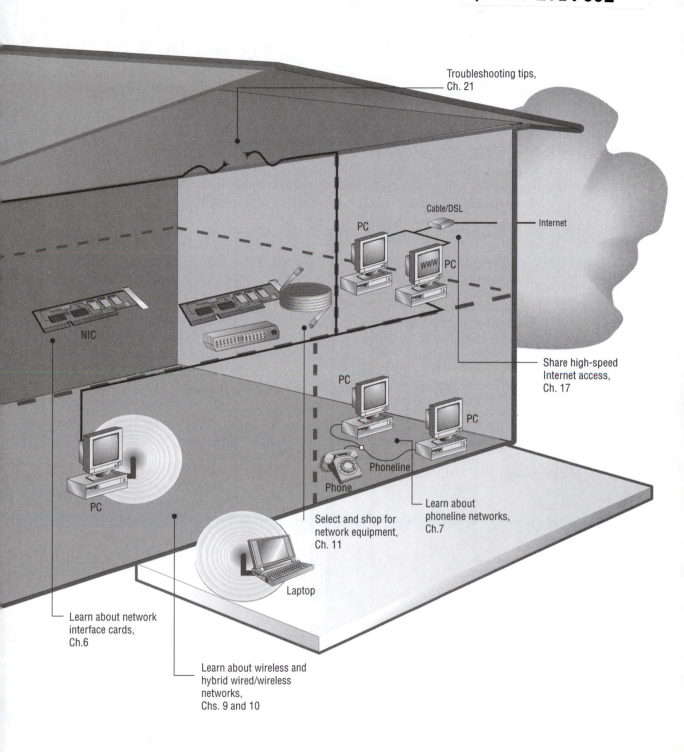

W9-BKA-092

Troubleshooting tips, Ch. 21

Cable/DSL

Internet

PC

PC

www

NIC

Share high-speed Internet access, Ch. 17

PC

PC

Phoneline

Phone

Select and shop for network equipment, Ch. 11

Learn about phoneline networks, Ch.7

PC

Laptop

Learn about network interface cards, Ch.6

Learn about wireless and hybrid wired/wireless networks, Chs. 9 and 10

MASTERING

HOME NETWORKING

MASTERING™
HOME NETWORKING

Mark Henricks

SYBEX®

San Francisco • Paris • Düsseldorf • Soest • London

Associate Publisher: Guy Hart-Davis
Contracts and Licensing Manager:
    Kristine O'Callaghan
Acquisitions & Developmental Editor: Linda Lee
Editor: Jill Schlessinger
Technical Editor: Donald Fuller
Book Designers: Patrick Dintino, Catalin Dulfu,
    Franz Baumhackl
Graphic Illustrators: Tony Jonick, Jerry Williams!
Electronic Publishing Specialist: Adrian Woolhouse
Project Team Leader: Leslie Higbee
Proofreader: Molly Glover
Indexer: Lynnzee Elze
CD Technician: Ginger Warner
CD Coordinator: Kara Schwartz
Cover Designer: Design Site
Cover Illustrator: Sergie Lobkoff

Software License Agreement:
Terms and Conditions

The media and/or any online materials accompanying this book that are available now or in the future contain programs and/or text files (the "Software") to be used in connection with the book. SYBEX hereby grants to you a license to use the Software, subject to the terms that follow. Your purchase, acceptance, or use of the Software will constitute your acceptance of such terms.

The Software compilation is the property of SYBEX unless otherwise indicated and is protected by copyright to SYBEX or other copyright owner(s) as indicated in the media files (the "Owner(s)"). You are hereby granted a single-user license to use the Software for your personal, noncommercial use only. You may not reproduce, sell, distribute, publish, circulate, or commercially exploit the Software, or any portion thereof, without the written consent of SYBEX and the specific copyright owner(s) of any component software included on this media.

In the event that the Software or components include specific license requirements or end-user agreements, statements of condition, disclaimers, limitations or warranties ("End-User License"), those End-User Licenses supersede the terms and conditions herein as to that particular Software component. Your purchase, acceptance, or use of the Software will constitute your acceptance of such End-User Licenses.

By purchase, use or acceptance of the Software you further agree to comply with all export laws and regulations of the United States as such laws and regulations may exist from time to time.

Software Support

Components of the supplemental Software and any offers associated with them may be supported by the specific Owner(s) of that material but they are not supported by SYBEX. Information regarding any available support may be obtained from the Owner(s) using the information provided in the appropriate read.me files or listed elsewhere on the media.

Should the manufacturer(s) or other Owner(s) cease to offer support or decline to honor any offer, SYBEX bears no responsibility. This notice concerning support for the Software is provided for your information only. SYBEX is not the agent or principal of the Owner(s), and SYBEX is in no way responsible for providing any support for the Software, nor is it liable or responsible for any support provided, or not provided, by the Owner(s).

Warranty

SYBEX warrants the enclosed media to be free of physical defects for a period of ninety (90) days after purchase. The Software is not available from SYBEX in any other form or media than that enclosed herein or posted to www.sybex.com. If you discover a defect in the media during this warranty period, you may obtain a replacement of identical format at no charge by sending the defective media, postage prepaid, with proof of purchase to:

SYBEX Inc.
Customer Service Department
1151 Marina Village Parkway
Alameda, CA 94501

(510) 523-8233
Fax: (510) 523-2373
e-mail: info@sybex.com
WEB: HTTP://WWW.SYBEX.COM

After the 90-day period, you can obtain replacement media of identical format by sending us the defective disk, proof of purchase, and a check or money order for $10, payable to SYBEX.

Disclaimer

SYBEX makes no warranty or representation, either expressed or implied, with respect to the Software or its contents, quality, performance, merchantability, or fitness for a particular purpose. In no event will SYBEX, its distributors, or dealers be liable to you or any other party for direct, indirect, special, incidental, consequential, or other damages arising out of the use of or inability to use the Software or its contents even if advised of the possibility of such damage. In the event that the Software includes an online update feature, SYBEX further disclaims any obligation to provide this feature for any specific duration other than the initial posting.

The exclusion of implied warranties is not permitted by some states. Therefore, the above exclusion may not apply to you. This warranty provides you with specific legal rights; there may be other rights that you may have that vary from state to state. The pricing of the book with the Software by SYBEX reflects the allocation of risk and limitations on liability contained in this agreement of Terms and Conditions.

Shareware Distribution

This Software may contain various programs that are distributed as shareware. Copyright laws apply to both shareware and ordinary commercial software, and the copyright Owner(s) retains all rights. If you try a shareware program and continue using it, you are expected to register it. Individual programs differ on details of trial periods, registration, and payment. Please observe the requirements stated in appropriate files.

Copy Protection

The Software in whole or in part may or may not be copy-protected or encrypted. However, in all cases, reselling or redistributing these files without authorization is expressly forbidden except as specifically provided for by the Owner(s) therein.

This book is dedicated to Barbara, Kathryn, and Corinne.

ACKNOWLEDGMENTS

Sybex Acquisitions and Developmental Editor Linda Lee believed in this book and this author enough to start the project and see it through. Sybex Editor Jill Schlessinger exhibited patience, optimism, and understanding through the details of the creative process itself. Kara Schwartz compiled the material for the CD and Heather O'Connor tracked down the permissions. Donald Fuller, the Technical Editor, displayed an impressive combination of forbearance and expertise.

Many networking equipment manufacturers and software publishers contributed evaluation units and review copies of their products. The public relations departments of Compaq Computer, Intelogis, Netgear, Intel, Diamond Multimedia, and Linksys stand out for their responsiveness and willingness to help.

To adequately describe the contributions to this book of the many Web sites, frequently asked questions, newsgroup posts, and other online resources on networking is an impossibility. A couple of the online authors who stand out for their technical savvy, clear presentation, and helpful viewpoints are Steve Gibson of the Gibson Research Corporation and Chase DuBois of Cablesense.com. Among authors whose work appears in traditional print volumes, particular thanks goes to Robert Cowart, Christa Anderson, Peter Dyson, Viktor Toth, and Robin Williams.

The mistakes are mine.

CONTENTS AT A GLANCE

TABLE OF CONTENTS

PART III · NETWORK SOFTWARE

PART IV • USING YOUR NETWORK

APPENDICES

INTRODUCTION

The time may come when networking home computers is as easy and everyday as driving a car with automatic transmission. That day has not arrived, however. In fact, to continue the metaphor, we are still in the days when you have to use muscle power to crank the machine to get it to start, and manually advance the spark to keep it going at speed. Until the day when networking home computers is automatic, you need the guidance provided in this book.

Mastering Home Networking covers all the hardware and software you will use in almost any conceivable network of home computers. It does this in a way that provides the technical detail needed to accomplish the job, along with enough background information to help you understand why things are this way, a touch of human interest, and—occasionally—humor to lighten the task.

Part I

Part I begins with defining a computer network. It explains where networks came from, what types of networks exist, and how they are physically laid out—their topologies. The discussion of network types includes, of course, the grandaddy of all networks, the Internet. This part also includes overviews of the many parts of a network, from the cables and adapter cards to the software and protocols that provide the real intelligence in any network. Since you're interested in networking (or you wouldn't be reading this book) you may not need to know what motivates networkers. But this part covers the topic so extensively—including resource sharing of all kinds, as well as communicating and gaming via network—that even a dedicated networker is likely to find new reasons to appreciate the subject. Networkers, who may tend to think they labor alone, will appreciate that this part defines home networkers precisely. You might be surprised at how many home networkers there are and how fast our numbers are growing.

Part II

Part II of the book is where you begin to really know your networks. It covers the different options of home networks, including Ethernet, wireless, phoneline, powerline, and hybrids. Reasons for choosing one over another are explained in detail. The advantages of Ethernet—chiefly, reliability and performance—are compared to the convenience of no-new-wires networking offered by phoneline, powerline, and wireless technologies.

Beginning with selecting the equipment for an Ethernet network and continuing through siting antennas for a wireless home network, this part lays out the nitty-gritty of networking. You'll learn in detail how to configure network adapter cards, install hubs, and connect cables. It also covers shopping for network equipment, including tips for making the most of offerings from online stores.

Part III

Network software is covered in Part III. Special aspects of Windows 95 and Windows 98, naturally, get the bulk of the coverage here. However, you will also learn to network your home computers using other major software environments, including the Macintosh OS, Windows 2000, Novell NetWare, and Linux/Unix. The information includes tips on how and why you might choose one software environment over another in a networking context.

Part IV

Building a network is only half the battle, however. In Part IV, you will learn about the many ways you can use your network. A network makes it easy to allocate and manage resources, such as printers, modems, hard drives, and scanners. You'll also learn how to share software, such as Word and PhotoShop, and data files, such as financial records and gift wish lists. This part tells you how to do all that, as well as how to save money through shared modems, including cable and DSL modems, and shared Internet access.

This part also covers the essential network administrator's task of setting up new users, selecting usernames, and using passwords. Finally, you will learn advanced networking skills, including how to use remote control software and set up personal Web servers to extend the reach of your network beyond your home.

Part V

Only if you can use your network day in and day out can you call a home network a success. That operational challenge is addressed in Part V, which covers topics including disaster prevention, network security, and troubleshooting. The networked housekeeper has some new chores to do, including backing up data, protecting against power surges and outages, and keeping out hackers and viruses. You'll also learn tips and techniques on controlling access to the Internet by minors in your household. This book will show you how to employ effective and easy-to-use filter software to make sure that young children are only exposed to the Web sites and other Internet resources that you choose.

Last but not least, you'll receive a primer in troubleshooting network problems. You'll learn how to diagnose trouble spots from loose connectors to incorrectly configured software, figure out how to fix the problem, and then make repairs.

Appendices

The Appendices provide valuable information in the form of guides to online home networking resources, tips on using home networking consultants, leads for pursuing formal education in networking, and a guide to the CD accompanying this book. This CD contains more than a dozen useful networking-related software programs. Moreover, the appendices give you descriptions and Web site addresses for the online resources most likely to handle general and specific networking questions. You'll learn how to select and deal with a networking expert-for-hire. And you'll get guidelines for pursuing additional instructional opportunities in networking. Finally, at the end of the book is a glossary of networking terms and an extensive index, which will allow you to turn to the most appropriate section for dealing with whatever home networking question is at hand.

Home networking is a fast-changing technology. The only way to keep up with it and all it has to offer is to do it. Now is the time to get started. Enjoy.

PART I

Networking Now

LEARN:

- *What a Network Is*

- *What Networks Are Good For*

- *Who Is Networking Their Homes*

CHAPTER 1

Understanding Computer Networks

Overview

I n its broadest sense, a network is anything that resembles a loosely woven fabric, with strands that cross each other and connect every part to every other part. So fishing nets as well as telephone systems, like AT&T's long distance operation, are networks. Broadcasters, such as television and radio stations, have networks, too. So do railroads, although their networks consist of steel rails strong enough to carry boxcars. Many companies have networks of suppliers. Anybody who has helped put together a school or family reunion knows how essential a network of acquaintances is when it comes to tracking down far-flung groups of people. Networks are everywhere.

What's a Computer Network?

Computers are everywhere too, of course, and they often come in groups. But not every group is a network, any more than the group of PCs in your home is networked—as you're probably aware since you're reading this book. The distinguishing feature of any network, compared to another type of group, is that all the members of a network are connected to each other. As you can see in Figure 1.1, like a chain-link fence, all points of a network are connected somehow to all other points. When it comes to computers, that connection is for the purpose of sharing information and resources.

FIGURE 1.1

Strands connect all points of a network.

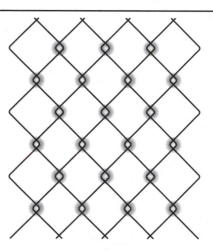

In the computer world, a network is a system of computers connected by wires or some other means, and set up to share information and other resources. Networks can be as small as two computers, or as large as several million computers. They may span a few feet or cross oceans. In addition to computers, networks may—and usually do—include peripheral devices such as printers, modems, and scanners. These peripherals, along with things like disk drives and DVD-ROM or CD-ROM drives, comprise the resources that may be shared over a network. The information that can be shared over a network includes application programs, utilities, and other software, in addition to data files such as word processing documents, spreadsheets, databases, images, and the like.

NOTE Non-networked PCs are called *standalone PCs.* Most PCs these days are networked, because most businesses are networked and most PCs are owned by businesses. But there's nothing inherently inferior about a standalone PC, whether in a home or business environment. Sometimes, as in the case where extremely sensitive information is stored on the computer, you're better off not connecting to a network where someone might get access to those files.

Computer networks are as ubiquitous as computers themselves. The computer networks you are likely to encounter as part of your daily routine include the following:

- A network of point-of-sale computers used as cash registers at your local bookstore or grocery.

- A network of computer workstations at your business or place of employment.

- A network of order-entry computers on the other end of your phone call to make a purchase from a catalog retailer.

- A network of computers containing a telephone calling database and being used by a telemarketer to pester you during dinner (not all computer networks are helpful).

One of the biggest topics in the news recently has to do with a computer network or, rather, the network of computer networks known as the Internet. What you're going to learn in this book won't turn your home into a mini-Internet, but it will allow you to make better use of any existing Internet connections you have. And it will give you, on a domestic scale, many of the information-sharing abilities that make the Internet such a significant global presence.

NOTE   If you have a modem on your computer, you may be able to contact an online service, the Internet, or another network. Does this mean you're networked? Not really. Among other things, a network connection is generally considered to be constantly connected, or always on, as opposed to a modem connection you reach by dialing up another modem on the telephone. Dial-up networking can provide some of the same information- and resource-sharing capabilities as more traditional networking. But it's nowhere as fast and flexible as a home network.

A Home Network is a Local Area Network

The kind of network we're going to be talking about is a *Local Area Network*, or LAN (rhymes with "can"). It's called a Local Area Network because it's restricted to a relatively small area compared to some of the other networking technologies. Having said that, LANs can get pretty large. Some cover campus-size areas and join hundreds of PCs in several buildings together. Usually this type of network is called a *Campus Area Network*, or CAN. A more common definition of a LAN is a small network, restricted to a single floor or a single building. You can join LANs together to make still larger networks.

For our purposes, a LAN is going to generally mean a network that is no bigger than your house. There will be some interesting exceptions to that rule, though. For instance, we'll be talking about wireless networks that will allow you to be on the network while using a laptop computer out in the backyard. Or up on the roof, if the mood strikes you.

All networking schemes have specific limitations concerning the distance that can separate the computers that are connected to the network. That just means they can't get too far apart. Don't worry, however. These distances are pretty large, ranging up to hundreds of meters for some commonly used wiring types. Unless your home rivals Bill Gates's in size, you can almost certainly find a networking plan that will hook up computers located in its farthest reaches.

There are numerous other types of networks, including Wide Area Networks, Metropolitan Area Networks, intranets, and Virtual Private Networks. Home networkers generally don't have to concern themselves with these. They can get the basic advantages of a network—including printer sharing, Internet access sharing, file sharing, and online gaming—from a local area network that doesn't extend past the walls of home. A LAN is about all the network you'll need.

Origins of Local Area Networks

If you go back 20 years or more, practically all computers were networked. Most of them were large mainframes or minicomputers that controlled groups of networked terminals. The advent of the personal computer, starting in the mid-1970s, was something of a reaction to the universality of networking. Early PCs were designed specifically as standalone machines, not connected to each other or any other computer.

The so-called "one man, one machine" approach gave PC users a lot of freedom. They could run any software they wanted. They could create their own files of information and store it right there on the desktop. The PC users themselves, thanks to the simplicity of running a desktop machine, weren't as dependent on the technicians and information specialists that ran things in the mainframe era.

This freedom was a breath of fresh air and was fine as far as it went. But before long, PC users began wishing they could exchange information more easily with their colleagues. They began feeling the pinch of having to have an entire printer devoted exclusively to each desktop machine. To remedy this situation, the industry developed the LAN, a networking technology well suited to efficiently tie together groups of personal computers.

LANs have been standard issue in many businesses for well over a decade. However, they're only now beginning to penetrate into the home environment. One reason is that, until recently, not very many homes had more than one PC. Another reason is that networking equipment and software has just now begun to become simple, reliable, and inexpensive enough to attract home networkers.

Now, however, home networking is here. It works well, doesn't cost much, and provides major benefits to the millions of homes with more than one PC. For these reasons, it seems likely that the next really interesting episode in the networking saga will take place primarily in the home.

Other Types of Networks

One networker's meat is another one's poison and, accordingly, there have been many different types of networks set up to meet the varying needs of network users. Some networks are great for spanning huge distances; others for making networks that will be used only by people within a single company. With the great interest in networking today, you can be sure that many more varieties of network will be invented to help fulfill the burgeoning needs of networkers. Following are a few of the more popular network niches.

Networking with Your Sneakers

One of the most popular ways to network computers consists of loading information onto a floppy disk and carrying it to another machine by walking: *SneakerNet*. If you have more than one computer, you've quite likely used a SneakerNet at one time or another. Aside from the cost in shoe leather, SneakerNet has serious deficiencies in speed, flexibility, and power compared to the other forms of networking we'll be discussing here. SneakerNet is almost, but not quite, a joke among networkers. Sometimes it is the only thing that works and, like that old manual typewriter I keep under my desk for emergencies, it's nice to know that SneakerNet is around as a backup.

The Internet

One of the first networks many people think of today when the term network is mentioned is the global computer community known as the Internet. And, sure enough, the Internet is a network. It's a special kind of network with some particular distinguishing characteristics.

When computer networks are connected together, they are said to be *internetworked*. The Internet is just such a network of networks. In fact, the name *Internet* is an abbreviation of *internetwork*. Before the Internet became so important and well known, a lot of people referred to all sorts of networks as *the Net* in shorthand. Today, however, when you say the Net it's generally understood to mean the Internet.

It's worth knowing that the Internet, which some enthusiasts claim is the most important communication innovation since the printing press, was developed for much the same reason you are now considering networking your home computers. More than 20 years ago, the government wanted to find a way to help connect the computers used by scientists and researchers. The idea was that by sharing information across a network of networks, the researchers would be more effective and efficient and help push back the boundaries of knowledge. This idea, as you've probably noticed, worked amazingly well. We can't claim that you, the home networker, are going to push Gutenberg out of the history books. You can, however, confidently expect a very positive result from networking your home computers. And you don't need congressional budget approval to go ahead with it.

The Internet of the Future: Internet II

Today, many of the original users of the Internet, including academics and government researchers, are migrating off the Internet to another, faster, less-crowded computer communications system called Internet II. This new internetwork will, like the first Internet, most likely eventually become the Internet for everybody after the bugs get worked out. And down the road, there will almost certainly be an Internet III.

Wide Area Networks (WANs)

A *Wide Area Network*, or WAN, is a network that goes beyond a single building. WANs may connect computers scattered across several buildings in a campus environment, or they may extend much further, such as across a whole city or even a continent. WANs are basically used to extend the reach of local area networks.

WANS use a lot of the same technology and terminology as LANs, and they also offer the same type of information- and resource-sharing advantages as local area networks. In addition to the expanded geographic scope, there are some other significant differences. For instance, it's often too costly to run a high-speed cable between all the nodes on a WAN. So WANs often rely on slower connections, such as dial-up telephone connections.

You may need a WAN-type solution if you're trying to connect two buildings that are too widely separated to incorporate in a LAN, or if you want to use, even intermittently, a computer at your work location as part of your home network. Generally, however, WANs are business tools while home networkers can be satisfied with a local network.

Intranets

An *intranet* is a private network that uses the same technology as the Internet. Many companies have intranets that they use for communicating with employees, keeping everyone up to date with sales or inventory information, and the like. Many people find it convenient to be able to get this type of information using the same browser they rely on for World Wide Web surfing. Intranets allow companies to use Internet-style technology for internal purposes by setting up a corporate Web.

Virtual Private Networks

Virtual Private Networks are another type of network that is becoming more common. Like an intranet, a VPN is a private network that works like the Internet, using the same suite of protocols (computer communication languages) and, usually, the same browsers and other software tools. However, a VPN reaches out beyond a single company to share information with suppliers, vendors, partners, and customers. VPNs are handy ways to extend the benefits of Internet communication to a select group of pen pals. VPNs have to use security and privacy tools such as firewalls and passwords to make sure outsiders don't get a peek at more information than they're supposed to see.

Understanding Network Elements

Not all LANs are the same. Various kinds of LANs are distinguished by features such as the types of computers on the network, the type of software, and the basic design, or architecture, of the network. Most of this book deals with Windows 95/98 computers, since that's the kind most of you have. We'll also discuss, in somewhat less detail, other popular systems including Apple Macintosh and Linux/Unix systems. In this section, you'll learn about the various types of physical and logical network topologies—the design of the network itself—as well as about peer-to-peer and client-server networking architectures.

Topology is the term used to describe a network's layout. Although there are a number of different topologies, they come in just two basic types: physical and logical. *Physical topology* is the way the actual wires are laid out. *Logical topology* refers to the way the information travels over those wires.

 WARNING Physical and logical topologies can be confusing at times. For instance, there is a bus physical topology and a bus logical topology. However, a network with a bus logical topology doesn't have to have the bus physical topology. It's important to keep straight which type of topology you're talking about.

Physical Network Topologies

The physical topology you pick for your network may be determined by such factors as how far apart your computers are and how your home is laid out. For a one-room network, for instance, a simple bus physical topology might be indicated. The physical topology you pick will, in turn, play a role in determining what type of cable you use to connect the nodes on the network, and whether or not you need a central hub or server. In the same way that all the computers on a network can work together, the decisions you make regarding your network's topology must work together.

Star Physical Topology

The most popular physical network topology, especially for home networking, is called a *star network*. In a star network, the computers are connected to a central hub or, in some cases, another computer called a server, as in Figure 1.2. One of the key traits of a star network is that all the computers on the network have their own connection to the hub. This means that, if one computer or connection isn't working properly, it won't necessarily affect the rest of the computers on the network.

FIGURE 1.2

A star physical topology connects computers to a central hub.

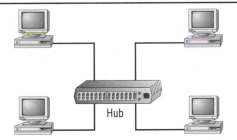

Hub

Bus Physical Topology

A network built on a *bus physical topology* has a cable that connects network nodes or computers directly to each other. The result is that each computer is like a link on a chain, as in Figure 1.3. This type of topology doesn't require a hub, but has the disadvantage that if one of the computers in the chain stops working properly, or loses its connection to the network for some reason, the network won't work either. Another oddity of a bus network is that the ends of the cable must be capped or terminated in a particular way or, again, the network won't work right.

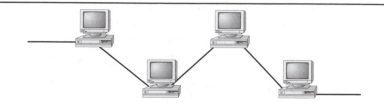

Ring Physical Topology

Networks using the *ring physical topology* connect all the PCs and other networked machines in a loop. Double cables run between each machine, as shown in Figure 1.4. Ring physical topologies are uncommon because of the significant added cost and hassle involved in running double cables.

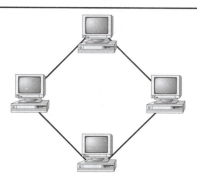

Mesh Physical Topology

Networks using the *mesh physical topology* have redundant links between the computers and other devices connected to the network, as shown in Figure 1.5. Strictly speaking, every computer (or other device on a network) with a mesh physical topology should be connected to every other device. This is rarely the case, however, because the task of installing and configuring a mesh physical topology quickly gets too complicated if there are more than a handful of devices on the network. On the plus side, they're highly reliable.

FIGURE 1.5

A mesh physical topology connects computers with multiple redundant links.

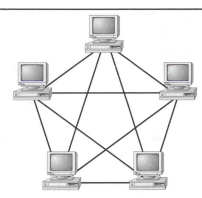

Logical Network Topologies

A network's logical topology describes the way it transmits information from one device to another. Notice the difference from physical topology, which describes the way the network looks. A network may look one way and transmit information in another. For instance, your network may physically look like a star, with nodes connected to a central hub, but logically work like a ring, with all data being broadcast to the entire network at once. The idea of a logical network topology is important to understand because your network's logical topology decides what type of network adapters and cables you will need to use.

Bus Logical Topology

The *bus logical topology* is the most popular type of logical topology because it's the one *Ethernet* uses, and Ethernet is the most popular type of LAN. The distinguishing feature of a network with a bus logical topology is that any time a node on the network has a message for another node, that message is broadcast to the entire network. This message may be part of an e-mail message, a file being sent to a network printer, or any other information sent over the network. Each time a message is sent, the computers and other devices on the network scan the message to see if it is intended for them. If it is, they accept the data. If not, they ignore it.

The bus logical topology is often compared to telephone party lines, which had a bunch of people who shared one phone number. Anytime one phone rang, they all rang and anybody could listen to any call. People on the party line could tell if a call was for them by the unique pattern of rings, such as two longs and one short, that signified a call was intended for their particular phone.

In a computer network, the nodes know whose message is whose by using identifying numbers in the network card. Each Ethernet card has a unique identifying number. This identifying number is used to direct any message to the appropriate network device. Since no two Ethernet cards have the same number, only the right network device will accept the message.

NOTE People talking on a phone use sentences that can be of any length. When computers communicate on a network, they send information in the form of *packets*. These packets consist of chunks of the whole message, which are broken down, sent, and reassembled at the other end. For this procedure to work, packets have to conform to a strict format, including a limitation on the length of each package. In Ethernet networks, for instance, packets can be no more than 1,518 bytes long. A sentence with 1,518 characters would take a couple of minutes for a person to speak. Luckily, computers are a lot faster than that, so each packet of information only requires milliseconds to send. This allows many computers to use the network effectively.

One of the most significant features of the bus logical topology is that nodes cannot be set too far apart. If there's too much distance between them, they can't hear each other's messages, and so they might try to use the network at the same time. If this happens, the messages collide and fail to reach their destinations. In practice, nodes on an Ethernet network can be separated by no more than 185 meters (600 feet) before the signal has to be boosted. Since this distance is more than adequate to span almost all households, the limitation is usually not a major concern for home networkers.

Ring Logical Topology

Unlike the bus logical topology, the *ring logical topology* does not broadcast messages to every node on the network. Instead, each workstation with a message only sends it to one other workstation. That workstation looks at the message and either accepts it or passes it on to the next workstation, as shown in Figure 1.6.

FIGURE 1.6

Data sent with the ring logical topology goes from one workstation to the next.

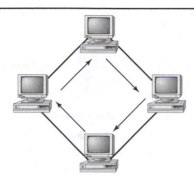

Network Architectures

In addition to its topology, a network has a particular architecture. Most home networks are *peer-to-peer* or, simply, *peer networks. Client-server networks* are more likely to be found in businesses.

Peer-to-Peer Networks

In a peer network, everybody's computer shares resources with everybody else. There is no centralized machine, or server, that serves as a main file storage space or resource manager. Instead, everyone keeps their files on their own machines or, sometimes, on each other's. They don't require a centralized network administrator, either. Everyone is responsible for running his or her own node on the network.

For small networks, peer networks are usually the way to go. For one thing, they're less expensive than the other option, client-server networks. Peer networking comes built into Windows 95/98, so you don't even have to buy a network operating system to get going with a peer network. Also, because users are responsible for taking care of themselves, peer networks don't require a dedicated network administrator to take care of everyone, as client-server networks do.

On the downside, peer networks typically don't have much security, meaning that your data may be more vulnerable to prying eyes than with a client-server setup. They don't usually offer helpful network management tools like remote administration. For the most part, however, these negatives don't overly concern home networkers. The upshot is that peer networking is the most popular form of networking for home users.

Client-server Networks

In a client-server network, one or more of the computers connected to the network is used to provide services to the others. The service-providing computers are, appropriately, called *servers*. The other computers, the ones who use the services, are *clients*. The services include providing disk space for centralized file storage, sharing printers, and handling communications such as electronic mail. Print servers, file servers, mail servers, and the like are useful on big, busy networks, but few home networks require dedicating machines to server duty.

 TIP Even though you're building a peer network for your home, don't rule out the possibility that you may want some kind of servers on the network. A firewall server, for instance, is practically essential if you want the best protection from hackers who may invade your network via the Internet. You may also want a dedicated PC to serve as a web server for your home network. In addition, some inexpensive but powerful servers for handling printing, file storage, and other tasks are also being introduced to the home networking market.

What's in a Network?

There's more to a network than a few PCs strung together with wires. In addition to the computers and wires (or cables, as they're commonly referred to in networking circles), you must have devices that connect the wires to and from the PCs. You also need more gadgets to hook together the wires, software to control and manage the flow of information, and, depending on the type and uses of your network, a good bit more.

In this section, you'll learn about what types of components make up a network. This section will provide a brief introduction to the different kinds of hardware and software you'll need to network your computers, and later chapters will go into more detail about the differences between these devices.

 NOTE For more detailed information about networking hardware, see Part 2, "Networking Nuts and Bolts." To learn more about networking software, see Part 3, "Network Software."

Computers to Connect on a Network

Just about any kind of computer can be networked. Mainframe computers, with their many different channels for receiving and sending information, are especially well suited to networking. As you will see in a later chapter, you can also network a device as small as a Personal Digital Assistant that will fit in a purse or pocket. In the future, all sorts of additional devices, from video cameras to home security and automation systems, may commonly be connected to home computer networks.

Although the focus of this book is on networking PCs running Windows 95 or Windows 98, we'll also address the networking of all sorts of computers and some other devices, including Apple Macintoshes, PCs running the Unix/Linux operating system, and laptop computers.

Cables to Connect Network Devices

Without some kind of connection tying them together, a bunch of PCs is not a network. Generally, this connection consists of copper wires, in any of several different varieties. These physically connect the PCs together in a network that is distinguished by speed and reliability. However, you can also use radio waves and infrared waves to connect PCs into a wireless network.

Networking cables range from cords that look just like the ones that go from your telephone to the wall jack, all the way up to python-thick coaxial and fiber-optic cables. The former are the ones you're likely to use in home networking, while the latter would be your choice if you were wiring a network to join two countries together.

Networking cables are pretty finicky about how they are connected, too. There are a number of different ways you can hook them together, as well as to computers and other network equipment. Some of the connectors look, again, just like the ones on your telephone. Others resemble cable television connectors. You'll learn which types of connectors go with which cable setups, and how to use them.

 NOTE   See Chapter 6, "Ethernet Networks," for more information on the differences between types of cables.

Cards to Connect Devices to the Cable

You generally need to have something called a *Network Interface Card* or NIC (pronounced "nick") to connect a device to the network. The NIC, which is also called a *network adapter* or *network board*, is an add-in card that you plug into the motherboard of your computer. It provides a place to plug your cable into the back of your computer. In addition to giving you a jack to attach your cable to, the NIC controls the movement of information between your computer and the rest of the network.

Physically, a network adapter is a printed circuit board that installs into one of the empty expansion slots on your PC's motherboard. Some computers, such as Apple Macintoshes and some newer Windows PCs, come with network interfaces built into the computer's motherboard. Other machines you may run across, especially new machines intended for business users, or older models you may have purchased used from a business—or gotten from your own work—are likely to already have NICs installed. In addition, if you're buying a new computer from a build-to-suit company such as Dell Computer or Gateway Computer, you can order it with a NIC installed. Generally, however, you'll need to install a NIC in an older PC.

 NOTE   See Chapter 6, "Ethernet Networks," for more information on the differences between types of NICs.

Hubs for Connecting Devices to Each Other

Hubs, also called concentrators, are where it all comes together in most types of networks. Hubs sit in the center of the network, providing a central location for all devices connected to the network to reach each other. If you think of the hub of a wheel, with spokes radiating out in all directions (and computers on the ends of those spokes), you'll get a good idea of the place a hub occupies in a network. There are active hubs, passive hubs, and intelligent hubs. But, basically, a hub has a bunch of places to plug cables into, and some software and chips inside that direct the traffic on the network.

Not all types of networks have hubs. Some networks have more than one hub. For your home network, you'll probably be using a small hub, with connectors for four to eight computers. Hubs aren't the most complicated of network equipment. You only have to pick the right one and install it properly.

Specialty Networking Hardware Devices

The most visible pieces of hardware in a network are, of course, the computers, followed most likely by the cables. But there are all sorts of other devices that can be attached to a network to make it do different things, or to help people on the network swap information and resources more efficiently.

Routers

A *router* is like a network doorkeeper. It doesn't have much to do with what goes on inside the network. It controls what comes in to and out of the network from the outside, including data from other networks. Another way to put it is that routers let networks talk to each other. As the name suggests, one of the things routers do is determine the best path by which to send information.

A router may be a regular computer equipped with special software, or a special-purpose black box device that does nothing but routing. You're not likely to be using a router unless, say, you want to internetwork with your neighbor's home network.

Repeaters and Bridges

If you envision a very large home network, you may need a *repeater* or *bridge* to make it work. All networks have limits on the distance between workstations, hubs, and other network devices. Signals fade over distance, and when workstations lose touch with each other on the network, things don't work well. If your network extends beyond the specified limits, it may function poorly or not at all.

A repeater is a black box-type device that takes information-carrying signals off the network, strengthens them, and sends them on their way. It's a way to get around the distance limits. A bridge is a type of repeater that, rather than just repeating information indiscriminately, also detects where that information is supposed to be going. The bridge only passes on information that needs to be going to the next segment (length of cable) of the network. Repeaters and bridges are commonly found in large and busy networks, but yours is unlikely to need so much horsepower.

Network Software

As in most areas of computing, the software is at least as important for networking as the hardware. Networks require software for several purposes, including

- Sending and receiving information
- Allocating resources like printers and shared hard drives
- Managing and maintaining the network
- Playing games (at least on home networks)

Your selection of software is a crucial one, especially your selection of your *Networking Operating Software* or NOS. And there are lots of different kinds of NOSs, not to mention messaging software, games, and the like. It could get confusing pretty quickly, especially considering that a lot of the software won't work with a lot of the other software. Luckily, a lot of these decisions have, in effect, been made for you, based on your existing computer systems.

If you have Windows 95 or 98 personal computers, for instance, you will have a range of network operating systems to choose from, including Windows' built-in networking support. Likewise, if you have Apple Macintoshes, you're likely to want to use the built-in networking software that comes with Macs. And if, by chance, you run the Linux operating system, you'll also have built-in networking that works just like the Internet.

 NOTE   See Chapter 6, "Ethernet Networks," for more information on selecting and using the right software for your home network.

Networking Operating Systems

An *operating system* is a program, or set of programs, that provides a foundation upon which the applications software will run. Along with operating systems such as Windows that run on single computers, there is a network operating system, or NOS, that makes the network function. Understand that NOS is installed on, and runs on, individual computers. The NOS makes sure that each computer it's installed on is able to respond to orders from the network. Without the NOS, a computer can be physically connected to the network, but it isn't going to be able to do much with that connection.

There are a number of NOSs in popular use. They range from Windows 95/98, which is on almost any computer running an operating system from Microsoft, up to business-class NOSs like NetWare, Windows NT Server, Windows 2000 Server, and others.

Other Software

Just as you have many applications that run on your computer's operating system, home networkers can choose from a wide variety of utilities, tools, and applications to help them run their networks. These include:

- Backup utilities
- Diagnostic tools
- Messaging software
- Network management software
- Shared productivity application software
- Games

Which ones of these you use, or whether you use any of them, will be decided by what you want from your network. Some of them, such as backup software, are highly recommended. Others, like games, may be something you'd rather do without—especially if you have an addictive personality and find yourself spending too much time playing them! But it's a good idea to take a look at some of the network software that is available, much of it for little or no cost. To a degree, your network is only as good as the software that's running on it.

 NOTE See Chapter 6, "Ethernet Networks," for more information on the software available for your home network.

Network Protocols

For diplomats, protocol is the set of conventions and traditions that defines such things as who will sit next to whom at official dinners, and how many guns will be fired in a salute to a visiting envoy. For networkers, a protocol won't tell you which fork to use, but it is similar in that it's a set of rules that govern behavior—in this sense, the procedures to follow when transmitting and receiving information over the network. Specifically, a *networking protocol* sets the format, sequence, and error checking of data sent out on the network.

If you've used your computer's modem to transmit and receive files, you may have used—or remember using in the pre-Internet days—communications protocols like Zmodem, Xmodem, and Kermit. There are a number of different network protocols, as well. Each has its own advantages and disadvantages, but only a few are suitable for home networks. In this section, we'll take a quick look at some of the ones you'll most likely be using in your network.

NetBEUI

NetBEUI is a simple protocol that is commonly used on small networks. It stands for *NetBIOS Extended User Interface* and is pronounced "net-booey." Microsoft includes NetBEUI in its networking products, including Windows 95/98.

NetBEUI is not used much on big networks, because it can't be used to route information between networks, offers little support for anything but Windows PCs, and doesn't offer much in the way of network analyzing tools. But NetBEUI is a very fast protocol and is a very popular choice for small networks. If you use only Windows computers, NetBEUI is the most likely choice for your home network.

Transmission Control Protocol/Internet Protocol (TCP/IP)

TCP/IP is the world's most popular networking protocol. More properly, TCP/IP is a collection of protocols that work together, and is referred to as a *protocol suite*, or *protocol stack*. By any name, TCP/IP is the one used on the Internet and many other networks of networks. It stands for *Transmission Control Protocol/Internet Protocol* and is pronounced by saying each letter separately, disregarding the slash, as in Tee-Cee-Pee-Eye-Pee. TCP/IP was developed by the Defense Department to hook together all of its different types of networks, sometimes over very long distances. It is the standard protocol of the Unix and Linux operating systems as well. A lot of the acronyms you may have run across relating to using the Internet, including FTP, or File Transfer Protocol, and SMTP, or Simple Mail Transfer Protocol, come from the TCP/IP protocol suite.

Like most flexible and powerful things, TCP/IP is not as easy to use as it might be. However, if you have an Internet connection, you are already using TCP/IP. It's also very useful for mobile networkers who are trying to reach their networks over phone lines.

AppleTalk

AppleTalk is a set of network protocols used by Apple Macintosh computers. Unlike PCs, which generally have to be made network-capable by the addition of software and hardware, Macs are ready to network, AppleTalk-style, right out of the box. AppleTalk, like most of the major network protocol schemes, has been developed over the last 20 years. It's now a flexible and full-featured protocol that can be used successfully on very large, as well as very small, networks.

IPX/SPX

IPX/SPX, standing for *Internetwork Packet Exchange/Sequenced Packet Exchange*, is the protocol used in Novell NetWare networks. This type of network is popular in many businesses. NetWare isn't a likely choice for many home networkers, but Microsoft builds a version of IPX/SPX into its operating systems to give you that option.

Summary

Networks come in many varieties and are all around us. Lots of our daily activities involve using and participating in networks of various types. We're also exposed to networks of computers every day, in many different activities. One of the best known, the Internet, is actually a network of networks.

The distinguishing characteristic of computer networks is that they are for exchanging information. When it comes to home computer networks, that means improving your ability to swap files, share printers and other resources, and even play online games.

Networks of all kinds, including home networks, consist of hardware and software, arranged in a handful of basic designs. Once you've made the decision to network your home, you are ready to choose how you'll use your network and then what type of network you'll put in place. Those choices will drive all the others you make in designing and installing your own home computer network.

What's Next

Now that you have an idea of what a computer network is and how its various parts work with each other, we will look at some of the jobs a network can do.

CHAPTER 2

Why Networks Aren't Just for Offices

Overview

The computers at the place where you work are probably networked. But why should you network your home computers? The answer is, for the same reasons that businesses network. Namely, it makes their computers work better and provides all sorts of new ways to use them. In this chapter, you'll learn some of the most compelling reasons to network your home. Odds are, you'll find one or more will offer more than sufficient payback to justify your interest, your investment, and your effort in setting up your own network of home computers.

Motivations for Networking Your Home

If you're the kind of person who just has to have the latest, smallest cellular phone, or the newest, most responsive stereo speakers, then home networking is a natural fit for you. While the technology behind home networking has been proven for decades in the workplace, it's just now arriving in the home. Unless you live in the heart of a high-tech mecca, chances are excellent you'll be the first on your block with a home network. So, for some early adapters, the novelty of home networking alone is plenty to excite interest.

For most people, though, home networking has to offer more than the buzz of being up-to-date. And the good news is that it does so in spades. Networking your home PCs is one of the best ways to get more out of your existing investment in personal computers. You will find that the work and fun for which you are already using your home PCs will be much more effective and entertaining. Some of the major benefits of home networking include the following:

- Sharing Internet access accounts
- Sharing gear such as printers, modems, and disk drives
- Sharing files and software between computers
- Playing online, head-to-head, multiplayer games
- Communicating between PCs on the network

Computing on a network is quite different from computing on a standalone machine. A network offers advantages that you probably haven't even thought of. For instance, say you're considering buying a new disk drive for one of your computers because it's running out of storage space. With a network, you may be able to delay or even cancel that outlay, because you'll be able to share disk space on another PC with a larger drive. Similarly, if you're thinking about buying a new printer that will let you print in color, you may be able to justify purchasing a fancier, more costly model because everyone on the network will be able to share it.

NOTE *Network effect* is a term from economics that describes the situation occurring when something such as a product or technology becomes more valuable because more people are using it. Telephones, fax machines, and the Internet are good examples of products and technologies that have become more valuable thanks to the network effect. When you network your home computers, they'll also become more useful and valuable.

Share Information and Equipment

Sharing is the essence of computer networking. Connecting your computers in a network is like getting a group of people to grab onto a rope in a game of tug-of-war: Together, they're much stronger than they are alone. Networked computers accomplish this effect by sharing, as seen in Figure 2.1. You can share information, such as financial records, word processing documents, and schedules. You can also share software, such as spreadsheet programs and games. And you can share equipment, including printers, modems, and scanners.

FIGURE 2.1

A network lets computers share many different types of equipment.

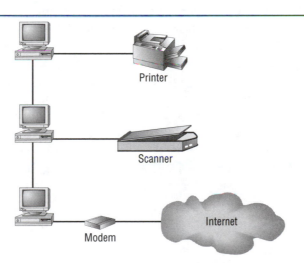

Printer

Scanner

Modem

Internet

Share Internet Access

Perhaps one of the most important motivations for networking home computers is to share Internet access. When your home computers are networked, you can share a single Internet account between all the PCs in your home. You will usually be able to let two more users log on to the Internet simultaneously, again using only one account.

No longer will you need a separate subscription to Road Runner or Earthlink for each PC and person on the network. If that sounds like a great opportunity to save money, it is. Not only will you possibly be able to get rid of one or more Internet accounts, you may also be able to get rid of an extra phone line. Those savings alone should add a significant amount to your monthly bottom line.

Shared Internet access is also a great convenience, since you'll be able to, say, check stock prices online while your spouse looks up the results of that day's European soccer league games and, at the same time, one of the kids researches a homework assignment on Africa. If you have more than one Internet user in your house, you probably have experienced the bottleneck that occurs when more than one person wants to surf the Net, especially in the high-usage evening hours. With a home network, those days will be over. The time and money people save sharing Internet access is one of the prime motivations for networking home computers.

Share Computers and Peripheral Devices

When you network your computers, you're doing more than connecting PCs. You're also giving yourself the ability to connect all the peripheral devices that those PCs use. These include modems, printers, disk drives, scanners, and other gear. Sharing lets you get more use out of expensive peripherals by making them available to more than one computer at a time. By increasing the use of one of your existing peripherals, you may be able to avoid having to buy additional equipment for another PC on the network.

 NOTE   See Chapter 17, "Setting Up Shared Resources," for more information about sharing peripheral devices.

Share PCs

You don't have to be a long-time PC owner to know that last year's high-flyer is this year's lame duck. You can call it accelerated obsolescence or simply the march of progress, but the fact is that even relatively new PCs may seem underpowered when you're trying to run the latest disk-hogging, processor-smothering software. It's one thing to buy a new PC every few years, perhaps hanging onto your old one and using it for word processing or other simple tasks. But who wants to go out and buy a whole new houseful of PCs? You've almost certainly got better uses for your money.

One solution to the lame-duck phenomenon is to network your PCs. Attaching an older PC to a network can give it a much longer lease on life. If it's strapped for disk space, it can tap into the disk space of other PCs on the network. If it's low on memory or hobbled by a slow processor, it can run application software on newer PCs, again through the network. Or it may be able to serve files, function as a firewall—thus serving as a system protector—or perform other tasks.

Having a network lets you get much more use, for a longer time, out of older PCs on the network. You may be able to obtain, for very low or even no cost, used PCs or outdated PCs your office is getting rid of, and use them effectively on your home network. Networking lowers your investment and leverages your return on every PC you connect.

Share Modems

If you go back far enough, you'll find the adjective "high-speed" has been applied to modems operating as slow as 1,200 bits per second. That's ridiculously slow by today's standards, when almost all new PCs come with modems rated able to transfer data at 56,600 bits per second. But, rest assured, those 56K modems, as they're known, will also soon be outmoded. Cable modems, Digital Subscriber Line (DSL) modems, Integrated Services Digital Network (ISDN) modems, and modems that work through orbiting satellites are all relatively recent technologies that operate far faster than 56K.

While most modems aren't terribly expensive, compared to printers and PCs, it is a nuisance to have to go out and buy a new one, as well as install it, every few years. That nuisance is multiplied if you have more than one PC. And that's where networking comes in. If you network your PCs, all PCs on the network can share a single modem. That means you only buy and install one of whatever is "high-speed" at the moment. Modem sharing is one of the most compelling reasons for networking your home PCs.

Share Printers

Chances are, if you have more than one PC in your home, you also have more than one printer. When you add them up, buying all those printers can amount to a significant sum. Plus, you're almost certainly not getting full use from each one.

Let's say you have the high-speed laser printer hooked up to the home office machine. That makes sense, since you may have to print out lengthy reports. You have the color inkjet printer, on the other hand, hooked up to the machine the children use, so they can print out colorful maps, Web pages, greeting cards, and perhaps coloring books. That also makes sense. But what if the children's PC is being used to print out a long report? It's costly to do that on a color inkjet machine.

The solution to all is, once again, to network your PCs. When everything's connected and you can share printers, you can send print jobs to the appropriate output device. You'll save money and time, providing another powerful incentive to network.

Share Drives and Other Storage Devices

When you buy a new PC or update an older one with a bigger disk drive, at first the expanse of digital storage space seems to stretch out forever. Before long, however, you'll have filled up most of those megabytes and gigabytes with new programs and data files. Not long after that, anytime you want to add something to your hard drive, you'll have to delete something else.

This is a frustrating part of computing. But until software publishers start shipping new versions that are compact instead of disk-hungry, it's going to continue. Fortunately, home networking provides some unusually neat and successful solutions to the problem of creeping disk consumption. The answer is disk sharing. You can give older PCs, or ones with smaller disk drives, space on the newer machines with larger drives. When you're reading files off a network drive, it can be nearly as fast as if the drive was right inside your machine, instead of at the other end of the house.

You can also load applications and data files onto only one machine, letting other PCs access them over the network, and freeing up scarce disk space elsewhere. Yet another solution is to purchase one of the new *file servers* designed for home networks. These black boxes contain oversize disk drives and can be connected to your network as if they were PCs. It is easier to install a home-oriented file server than to install a new disk drive into an existing PC, and cheaper than buying a whole new computer.

Regular fixed hard drives aren't the only ones you can share over your network, either. Removable drives, including Zip drives, conventional floppy drives, and removable hard drives are also amenable to sharing. You can share rewritable CD-ROM drives, DVD drives, and other kinds of drives, too. This can be really handy if you have an older computer without a CD-ROM drive, especially if it's a laptop or mini-tower case that doesn't leave room for adding a CD-ROM. If you have software that only comes on a CD-ROM, you can load it onto one of your CD-ROM-equipped PCs, then transfer it to the non-CD-ROM laptop or other PC using the network. The same goes for DVD-ROM drives. While few computers have enough drive bays to accommodate more than a few of the various kinds of drives, there's no reason why every computer in your home can't have access via a network to any kind of drive you want.

Share Scanners

Scanners are nice to have if you want to e-mail photos of the new baby to grandparents, design your own electronic greeting cards, create a digital photo album, or perform lots of other tasks. But you don't need one connected to every PC in the house. And, unlike printers, you probably wouldn't do it that way. If you do have a scanner and want to use scanned-in images on a PC other than the one the scanner is connected to, you probably save the pictures on a floppy or Zip disk and use SneakerNet to move them to the right computer. This works all right most of the time—unless, as often happens with high-resolution images, the file is too big to fit on a floppy. You can fiddle around with compression schemes to make the file floppy-size, or you can simply zap it across the network in a fraction of the time. But, again, it's not making the most of your investment in a scanner, and it may be creating a bottleneck with people trying to use the PC that the scanner is connected to.

The solution, of course, is to share the scanner among all the PCs connected to the network. You'll still have to physically be in front of the scanner to feed in your photos or other documents to be scanned (unless you can convince another family member to do it for you.) But you can shelve SneakerNet, because you'll be able to save the images to any PC connected to the network.

Share Digital Cameras

Digital cameras that store photos electronically instead of chemically are one of the most engaging new technologies to arrive in the home computer market in years. These digital images can be stored, copied, edited, and transmitted much more readily than traditional film. But there are a couple of problems with digital photography.

Cost is one limitation. For the price of a modest lunch you can buy a throwaway film camera. If you want a digital camera that will take pictures as sharp as the throwaway, it will set you back hundreds of dollars. So even if everybody wants to have their own electronic photo album on their computer, you're probably not going to want to buy one for every PC in your home. If you try to get by with one camera on a house full of non-networked PCs, you will find it is a significant hassle disconnecting and reconnecting a digital camera when you're moving it from one PC to another.

You may be thinking: I can always use the camera with only one PC, and then copy images to floppies and use SneakerNet. But photo files tend to be very large. A normal floppy's capacity of 1.44 megabytes (or 1.44 million characters) may not have enough capacity to hold even a single high-resolution photo.

Networking handily solves these problems. You can buy a single digital camera and set up a single PC to connect to it, then use your network to move pictures around to any networked PC.

Share Files

Networks are all about sharing information. You can share all kinds of data files, from personal financial records and electronic mail messages to a greeting card you're designing. You can also share application software such as games, word processors, and other programs. By allowing more than one person to access files and programs that previously were restricted to one computer, you can get more use out of your financial investment in software, as well as your time investment in creating files of useful data. Once you start sharing information over a network, you're likely to realize some completely new benefits you couldn't get any other way.

Share Financial Records

If you've ever had two people using one checkbook, you know how frustrating it can be to try to share financial records. When one person has the checkbook, the other can't use it. If one person forgets to enter a withdrawal or deposit in the register, the other may never know about it—until the rent check bounces.

But with a home network, you and your spouse or other family member will be able to view and update any financial records, including your checkbook, that you keep on any of the computers connected to the network. This means that any time you are logged on to the network, you—or your spouse or other person with check-writing privileges—can enter checks you've written, deposits you've made, or automatic payments that were scheduled. You'll have a better chance of keeping your account balanced and knowing how much money you really have.

Sharing financial records over a network can be a significant contributor to peace of mind, as well as helping you make the most of your financial resources. Given the popularity of personal finance software, sharing financial records is one of the more valuable and appealing uses of a home network.

 WARNING   Financial records are sensitive information, so you naturally won't want just anyone looking at them. When you place documents of any variety on a network, they are less secure than if they are in a locked file cabinet. Which is not to say your financial life will be an open book if you keep your checking account on a networked PC. Later, in Chapter 20, "Network Security," we'll discuss some effective ways you can control who shares and has access to your privileged data.

Share Household Documents

Just about every home has one. It might be a bulletin board in the laundry room, a scattering of magnets on the kitchen refrigerator, a table in the hall, or just a clear spot on your home office desk. It's a place where you can drop off notes, reminders, to-do lists, and other documents for family members to read, review, and act on. When you finish the annual family holiday letter to go out to relatives and friends, you may drop a copy off for other family members to critique. It may be a copy of the invitation to a child's birthday, or the annual guest list for your summer barbecue party. In any of these cases, the idea is that you're sharing the document by physically posting it where other people in your home can see it. Why not do that through a network?

Why, indeed. Businesses have long recognized that networks excel at letting groups of people share documents easily, quickly, and effectively. In many ways, network-based document sharing is much better than bulletin board–type postings. When documents are shared across a network, you can

- Restrict access to just the eyes you want to see them.
- Either allow or disallow any changes to the document.
- Do it all with a few keystrokes—no rummaging through drawers for thumbtacks.

Perhaps best of all, by posting them across the network, you can avoid losing one-of-a-kind documents in the usual household litter. It's difficult to drop a stack of newspapers headed for the recycling bin down on a network document and carry it off to oblivion, because it's always residing safely on the disk drive of one of the computers on your network.

Share Software

When a program is installed on a standalone PC, the only way anybody else can use that program is to sit down at that PC. When you're networked, things are different in several ways:

- Many programs are now networkable, meaning someone sitting down at a PC elsewhere on the network can run them, even if the software is not actually installed on that PC.
- Licensing, or paying for a program based on the number of users, rather than the number of copies, is cheaper than buying a whole new copy of a program for each user.
- If you install the shared application on one of your network's newer, faster machines, networked users are likely to get better performance.

The opportunities to save money and improve performance by sharing network applications are probably only limited by your imagination and creativity. Among other things, you don't have to store a separate copy of the application on each computer's hard drive—and that is likely to let you put off purchasing new PCs or upgrading their drives for more space. Since there's only one copy of the program, you know everybody's using the same program and the same version. This can be important if you are working on the same files, such as word processing documents or family budgets in spreadsheet format.

 WARNING   Just because a program is networkable doesn't mean you can legally let everyone on the network use it. Many networkable programs require you to purchase a license for every person or PC on the network that will be using it. Although licensing a program for an additional user is generally cheaper than buying, it's not optional. If you exceed the number of users your networkable application is licensed for, you'll need to pay for more licenses. Otherwise, your software provider isn't likely to take it well. Many vendors will not let you open the application if you exceed the number of licenses. Read the end-user licensing agreement for your software, or contact your software vendors for more information.

Improve Communications

Communication is the essence of networking. Computer networks offer many powerful tools for communicating, ranging from sending simple text messages to videoconferencing. And it's safe to say that, whatever their primary purpose, all computer networks are used greatly for communication. If you never use your computer network for anything else, you will get a great deal of value out of its ability to enhance and extend your communication with family members and others.

Send E-mail

Long before computer users played online games or surfed the Web, they sent electronic mail over networks. E-mail continues to be one of the most popular uses for networks of all varieties, including the Internet. And, when you network your home computers, you'll find all sorts of ways to get more use out of electronic mail.

- You'll be able to check and respond to your e-mail from any computer in the house, not just the one where your personal e-mail account is set up.

- You'll no longer lose track of messages that you downloaded and read on a particular machine, because you'll be able to access them from any other machine.

- By setting up a computer with an e-mail program, such as Microsoft Outlook Express, to be used by more than one user, you can free up disk space on other computers.

Electronic mail is a natural for home networks—you may even find yourself sending e-mail to a family member who's just down the hall. It's a lot easier and faster than putting a note on the refrigerator with a magnet.

Chat Online

E-mail is incomparable when it comes to swapping news with a relative across the country or a pen pal around the globe. It may seem a little impersonal for communicating with a family member who lives in the same house, though. Far more friendly is chatting, which works like a cross between e-mail and a phone conversation. In the same way that someone hears what you say as soon as you say it, chat transmits keystrokes of a typed message as you type it. It's admirably suited for brief messages or dialogues requiring a lot of back-and-forth.

 TIP Microsoft NetMeeting is a powerful program that allows you to hold meetings online through computer networks, including your home network. You can use text chat and an electronic whiteboard to communicate with people almost as if you were in the same room. If you wish, you can add video cameras and microphones to networked PCs and hold your own videoconferences using NetMeeting. To go with the communications tools, NetMeeting provides ways to transfer files and share software while you're communicating.

Schedule Family Events

In many families, schedules are somewhat like checkbooks—everybody's got one and they're hard to share. Without regular peeks at other family members' pocket planners, or perhaps having a central bulletin board where everyone is (supposed) to post their plans, you have to rely on intuition to know something as basic as who's coming for dinner. But a network can make keeping track of where everybody is much smoother.

When you can share files over your computer network, everyone can keep a text file with a list of their upcoming activities on their personal computer. When you're trying to recall if swimming lessons are tonight or tomorrow night, you can simply log on to the network, look into the file that has the swimming students' schedules, and you'll know.

If you and another family member use scheduling software such as Microsoft Outlook 2000, which comes loaded free on many computers, you can take a much more sophisticated look at each other's schedules over the network. You will be able to quickly find out when others in the family are available for a meeting to plan a vacation, take a trip to the ice cream parlor, or have a sit-down family dinner. You'll even be able to jointly schedule a meeting, trip to the mall, or other activity, selecting times when everyone who needs to be there is free. Sharing files over a home network truly can make your life easier.

Play Games with Other People

If playing games were the only justification for purchasing computers, then computers probably wouldn't be as widespread in businesses as they are today. But they would probably be almost as common in the home because, as countless fans of games from Tetris to Quake have found, computer games are simply a lot of fun. The one major problem of most computer games is that you're playing a computer, as opposed to a human. If you would like to add the element of actual human opponents to your computing gaming, then networking is an excellent way to do it.

Odds are, you have never played an online, multi-player, head-to-head computer game. Businesses understandably frown on playing games over their networks. And, while you can engage in head-to-head gaming over the Internet and on some online services, the limitations of modem communication create performance problems. In other words, the games tend to be slow, the connections are unreliable, and the overall effect is less than perfect.

Home networks can fix all that, and open up a whole world of exciting online gaming. Many popular computer games, including commercial action titles like Quake, as well as shareware or freeware card and casino-type games, now have the ability to be played by several players simultaneously, over a network. Many more games will undoubtedly be released with head-to-head features. If you've ever fretted over the limitations of a computer opponent in a single-player game, or wished you could test your skills against a human opponent, you'll find playing computer games over a network fills the bill nicely.

What Your Home Network May Control Tomorrow

Though home networking has come quite far in the last year or two, the next few years will be even more exciting. An impressive number of uses for home networks have been tried and proven successful in the real world of the marketplace. That list includes all the uses described previously. But that's not all. There are several other intriguing uses for home networks. Some may be only a year or two away from proving themselves, while others may remain unfulfilled ideas. Still, considering that until fairly recently home networking itself was considered a pie-in-the-sky concept, they bear looking into.

The Killer App of Home Networking

A *killer app* is what people in the computer industry call an application or technology that is so useful few people can resist it. The original killer app of the personal computer was the electronic spreadsheet. VisiCalc, the first electronic spreadsheet, came out in 1978, four years after the first commercially successful microcomputer was introduced. Businesspeople were enchanted by VisiCalc and its successors, including Lotus 1-2-3 and Microsoft Excel. It's safe to say that, without the killer app of VisiCalc, the personal computer might not have been nearly as successful early on. What's the killer app of home networking? The leading candidate right now is shared Internet access. Tomorrow? Nobody is quite sure.

Video Intercoms

If you live in a rambling ranch-style home, or a townhouse with several floors, you probably already appreciate the usefulness of intercoms. Audio intercoms, which use FM radio waves or wired connections to transmit sound between rooms, save steps and time when you need to talk to someone in another part of the house. Talking to disembodied voices emanating from a squawk box isn't ideal, however. Wouldn't it be nice if you could see the person you're talking to? With a video intercom, you can.

A video intercom isn't all that strange. Some advanced baby monitors already let anxious parents keep an eye as well as an ear on youngsters. Having a video intercom, however, does, require video cameras in each room on the system and, even more important, some way of getting all those bandwidth-gobbling video signals from room to room. Most video intercom systems fall down on this score, transmitting jerky, fuzzy pictures that don't appeal to many users. They work better with special wiring connecting the rooms of the house, and this is where your network comes in.

Computer networks, especially the faster, higher-bandwidth varieties, are just what the doctor ordered when it comes to video intercoms. They have the speed you need to get clear, clean moving pictures. And, you can view them right there on your computer monitor. Video intercoms probably aren't going to be the first use to which many people put their home computer networks. For those to whom this engaging technology appeals, however, having a home network is an important first step.

Networked TV

The typical home today is full of video screens. There's a TV in the family room, perhaps another in a bedroom or two. You've got PCs in the game room, home office(s), and perhaps kitchen and bedrooms as well. If you include the screen on the laptop that you, your spouse, or older student bring home, the count goes up even further. And don't forget the portable TV/VCR combo you sometimes plug into the car for long trips. One way you can get more use out of your collection of screens is to use the PCs to receive and display television programs.

If you haven't tried it, being able to check the latest news or see who's on Oprah without having to leave your PC can be a great convenience. Television tuner cards that let you surf channels from your PC are not expensive. Some PCs come with them already installed. You can set up programs to display in a corner of your computer screen, and enlarge them if something interesting catches your eye. And, like most things, having TV on a network of PCs makes it even more useful. Even if, like most of us, you've been watching TV your entire life, you'll quickly discover new ways to do it if you network TV-capable computers. For example:

- You can keep watching a show while wandering from room to room, checking it out on the screens as you pass.

- You can share an interesting program with someone at another PC in another room, by both watching it simultaneously on your own computers.

- You can use your PC as a VCR, recording and storing programs or pieces of programs for later playback.

Networked TV is a good way to get more use out of your electronic investments, and to find new ways to enjoy both computers and TVs.

TIP Don't draw the line at using your PC like a TV. WebTV is a popular Microsoft product that lets you surf the Web using your television set. It's a hardware-software combination that, for much less money than a typical PC, gives you a way to browse sites and check e-mail, just as you do with your computer, without leaving the comfort of your couch. It also allows you online access to program channel guides, making your TV viewing a lot more intelligent as well.

Security Systems

Home security systems are networks, just like home phone systems, electrical power systems, and cable television systems. Instead of PCs, printers, and modems, a security network consists of motion detectors, smoke detectors, sensors that detect glass breaking, and other sensors that tell you when a door or window is open. Security systems also have a controller that provides the intelligence to the system, handling jobs like analyzing the sensor reports, checking passwords, and dialing the fire department if there's trouble. This controller is similar in some ways to a PC, just as the wiring that connects a security system operates like the connections in a home PC network.

Unlike video networks, security systems don't have the problem of transferring enormous volumes of information. What they do have is the problem of interfacing with that control unit. Most security command centers consist of a telephone-type keypad, a handful of other buttons, some blinking lights, and perhaps a liquid crystal display screen little larger than a calculator's. Some security controllers can be interfaced with a PC, however, which adds to the mix a full-size keyboard, color screen, and vastly more powerful processing capabilities. You probably wouldn't want to devote a PC exclusively to help run your security system, but you can connect the two networks through a PC controller, thus giving yourself expanded scheduling and control features for your security system. Add it up, and security systems are good candidates for integrating into a home network.

Home Automation

Home automation is a generic term for what other people have called the *smart home* or the *intelligent home*. Basically, it just means connecting many of the simple, mechanical, standalone devices to a central control unit, which in turn lets you command and program them. It sounds great to be able to control your home's lighting, air conditioning, heating, and appliances without having to go through the whole house flipping switches. It sounds even better to be able to remotely control all those systems and appliances or even to program them to work intelligently. Think of the oven automatically firing up mid-afternoon and the A/C coming on just before you leave work so that you arrive to a cool house and a hot roast.

Despite its appeal, however, home automation has never achieved great popularity. Part of the reason is the cost and complexity of home automation. To smarten up dumb machines like lamp switches, you have to buy and install a plethora of gadgets such as lamp and appliance modules to allow them to be controlled electronically.

Another reason home automation has dragged its feet is the lack of a workable network connecting all those home devices. A home computer network is, in the opinions of many home automation experts, just what is needed to finally make home automation a popular, practical technology. Appliance makers are already designing models with built-in modules. Some can send and receive information, such as software updates and problem alerts, over the Internet. There's a thought—someday you may get an e-mail from your networked furnace telling you it's time to change the filter.

Home automation, networked TV, and networked security may not be part of your immediate plans for a computer network. But one thing you hear over and over from people who have already networked their homes is that once they did it, for whatever initial reason, they found lots more uses for the network than they ever dreamed of. It's nice to know that, while you're getting all the benefits of networking your computers now, you may be preparing yourself for a future that's even better.

Summary

You will find innumerable uses for your home network. Of course, there's the simple convenience of accessing a file from any computer in the home. But you can also share printers and other peripherals, get longer life out of an obsolescent hard drive, share applications and e-mail accounts, and manage your household calendar. No more competing with family members for Internet time; no more missing social functions or important family events; no more bouncing checks. A home network can't bring harmony to a dysfunctional family; but it can save you time and money and hassle and household spats.

What's Next

Now that you have some ideas about why you might want to network your home PCs, it's time to take a look at whom your fellow home networkers are likely to be. That's the subject of Chapter 3, "Who's Networking?"

CHAPTER 3

Who's Networking?

Overview

Home networking is projected to be one of the fastest-growing sectors in the entire computer industry over the next several years. One trend-tracker sees a growth rate of 600 percent over the four years ending 2003. When you compare that with other predictions that see little or no growth in purchases of actual home computers over the same time frame, it's clear that home networking is, indeed, a major focus of computer users.

You know all about one potential home networker—you. As you read the following descriptions of people who are networking their homes, you'll probably recognize quite a few characteristics as ones you exhibit. But who are all the rest of these people you see down at the local computer store with hands in pockets and furrowed brows, looking over the networking gadgets? This chapter will identify the people driving home networking, and provide some more insight into why they—and you—are making home networks one of the most exciting areas in computing.

Learn about Networked Homes

Despite the fact that many millions of people will become home networkers in the next few years, the members of this huge group have some very distinctive features in common. First of all, of course, most of them have more than one computer at home. They tend to have high-speed connections to the Internet. Many are telecommuters, home-based business owners, self-employed people, or regular corporate employees who spend some time working in a home office.

Networked home computers function beyond just a replacement for—or extension of—an office. A lot of people who are networking home computers are parents, their children, and students both young and old. People are networking computers in single-family residences in the suburbs, loft apartments in the inner city, rural farmhouses, penthouse condominiums, and just about every other kind of home you could imagine. Where you live doesn't seem to make a lot of difference. Other characteristics of your household make you a prime candidate for networking, however, and the first of those is, naturally, having two or more computers you want to hook together.

Multiple-PC Households

As of this writing, some 21 million American households have more than one computer. Some have several, including perhaps a PC for use in a home office, a Macintosh for the kids, and a laptop that gets carried back and forth from work. There's no magic number of computers a household has to have before home networking starts looking like a good idea. But it's safe to say that as the number of computers grows, the desire to share information among them grows as well.

Networking More Than Just Computers

Electronic devices that aren't your standard desktop PC can also be networked—and we're not talking about Macintoshes here. Communication devices such as Palm Pilots and entertainment devices such as televisions are expected to be among the faster-growing areas of home networking in the 21st century.

Already, millions of PC-free consumers are using WebTV—a hybrid of a living room television set and home PC—to surf the Web, send and receive e-mail, and play online games. Other non-PC devices that can be networked include Personal Digital Assistants, such as the Palm Pilot and the many palmtops that run Windows CE. Networkable gadgets include so-called thin servers, which are radically stripped-down PCs that can be hooked up to a home network to do, typically, a single job, such as provide security, store files, or control printers. Even more stripped-down machines, called thin clients, can be used as inexpensive network-access devices that get most of their processing power by tapping full-fledged servers on the network.

In the future, your home network may well include all kinds of household machinery, ranging from kitchen appliances and lighting to air conditioners and even your telephone system. Each of these prospective members of the home network of the future offers specific advantages, such as the portability of a palmtop computer, the cost savings of a thin client network, and the convenience and increased efficiency of home appliance controls.

In addition to households with multiple PCs, those with multitudes of peripheral equipment such as printers, scanners, and digital cameras are also highly likely to look at networking. There is little reason to go to the trouble and expense of having one of these peripherals attached to every PC in the house. With a home network, multiple-peripheral owners are finding that they can share costly, complicated, and rarely used peripherals in a highly effective fashion.

Households with High-Speed Internet Access

Perhaps the biggest group of people most likely to network home computers consists of those with high-speed Internet access. And sharing this speed is the most important reason why they're into it. Rather than needing a modem for each computer, or a high-speed connection for each computer, the network allows all of the networked computers to share one access point. High-speed Internet access, also sometimes referred to as broadband Internet access (the terms aren't identical in meaning, but the differences are mostly technical) is one of the most exciting developments in home computing in years.

High-speed is a pretty vague term when it comes to Internet access. A number of ways of connecting to the Internet are considered high-speed, although they may vary in speed by a factor of 10 or more. But, basically, high-speed is anything faster than a regular analog 56K modem. A 56K modem, as you may know, is actually limited to a transfer rate of 53 kilobytes per second, because the Federal Communications Commission restricts the amount of electrical power that can be emitted by any device hooked up to the public phone network. Table 3.1 lists the major high-speed Internet access options, with information on the providers of those servers, the kind of connection, and other important features.

High-speed Internet, like the 56K-modem standard, is not always as fast as advertised. It can be powerfully affected by a variety of factors, including the number of people using your Internet access service, the speed and memory on your own PC, and the speed of the interface you have to the high-speed service. And, as you might expect, high-speed access tends to cost quite a bit more than a regular Internet connection. However, if you're tired of waiting for Web pages to appear and files to download—and what regular Internet user isn't?—then high-speed access has a lot to offer you.

TABLE 3.1: MAJOR HIGH-SPEED INTERNET ACCESS OPTIONS

Option	Source	Connection	Features
Cable Modems	Cable-television providers.	Special digital modem and coaxial cable, similar to the one that brings you cable TV.	Very fast, up to millions of megabits per second, more than 20 times faster than a 56K modem.
DSL (Digital Subscriber Lines)	Local telephone companies.	Digital modem over regular copper phone wires.	Speed typically 10 to 20 times as fast as a regular 56K modem.
ISDN (Integrated Services Digital Network)	Local phone companies.	Regular phone lines and special digital modem.	Speeds of up to 128 kilobytes per second. Widely available.
Direct satellite	Satellite TV broadcasters and Internet Service Providers.	Dish antennas similar to the ones used for direct satellite TV receptions. Also requires phone line connection.	Speeds of up to 400 kilobytes per second retrieving information from the Internet.

It may seem like there are a lot of confusing choices when it comes to high-speed Internet access. In practice, at this writing, it's a lot simpler than it looks because there are not many areas where all these options are available. As a result, you'll likely be limited to what's available in your geographic area. Cable modems and DSL, in particular, are only offered in limited areas of the country, typically in or near major cities. However, the cable TV operators and phone companies are rolling out their high-speed Internet services as quickly as they can (of course, if you're waiting for the service to arrive in your community, it can seem like an eternity). Before long, though, it seems likely that most people who want fast connections to the Internet will be able to get them.

That's not all. A lot of energy is being expended by people trying to come up with new, faster, cheaper, more flexible, and reliable ways to connect to the Internet. One of the more creative solutions is hooking two 56K modems and two phone lines together on one PC, to deliver approximately twice-as-fast access. In addition, older but costlier technologies, such as the flexible and high-speed service, called fractional T1 and sold by phone companies, are becoming less expensive and may challenge the new high-speed connection technologies as well.

The bottom line is this: Keep your eyes open for new options for high-speed Internet connections. You probably haven't seen the last—or the fastest, cheapest, or easiest— choice for getting onto the Internet.

NOTE   You'll find more detailed information on sharing modems and high-speed Internet access in Chapter 17, "Setting Up Shared Resources."

Types of Home Networkers

In addition to multiple-PC and high-speed Internet access households, certain other types of households are also rapidly ramping up to home networks. These include people who get some sort of business edge from having networked homes, such as home-based business owners, telecommuters, self-employed professionals, and other home-based workers. People who aren't after purely economic benefits, such as students and families, are also likely networkers.

It's a little risky to try to characterize home networkers. After all, a good candidate for networking is anybody who owns a couple of computers and uses the Internet, or plays computer games, or has a budget that limits purchases of high-priced peripherals, just to name a few of the more important motivations. That description covers a lot of ground, demographically. However, there are some useful generalizations you can make about home networkers.

Many of the following generalizations are based on extensive market research of current networkers, and have considerable validity. If you see yourself on this list, odds are good you would get significant benefits from a network. If you already have one or are in the process of setting yours up, you may spot some useful applications of the network that you haven't thought of. At the very least, you'll have a good idea of why some other people are getting into networking.

Furthermore, if you are training to become a Microsoft Certified Systems Engineer, a home network will be an invaluable learning tool and a test bed for new applications and technologies.

Networking by Home Office Workers

You probably know at least one person who works part- or full-time from a home office, and you may even be a home office worker yourself. That statement can be made with confidence because, if you look at the growth trend of home offices, it's clear that what was once an oddity is now perfectly ordinary. In 1998, more than a third of the nation's 101.1 million households had home offices, according to the technology market research firm International Data Corporation. Of these, fewer than 1 million, or about 1 percent, had home networks.

That, however, is just the beginning. By 2002, according to a study by International Data Corporation, nearly 50 million U.S. households will have home offices. And, this researcher predicts, more than 8 million of those will be networked. Table 3.2 shows IDC's statistics on the number of home offices, in millions, and the number of networked home offices, also in millions.

TABLE 3.2: HOME OFFICE AND HOME OFFICE NETWORKING GROWTH

Year	1998	1999	2000	2001	2002
Home Offices	37.3	40.2	43.2	46.5	49.6
Networked	0.9	1.3	2.4	4.4	8.2

In millions. Source: International Data Corporation.

You don't have to be a statistician to see that home offices are growing amazingly rapidly. Nor do you need to be gifted with prescient insight to notice that, as fast as home offices are popping up, networking home offices are growing even more rapidly. Clearly, networking is a very attractive option for home office workers in general.

Networking by Telecommuters

More than one-third of the U.S. workforce will engage in at least part-time telecommuting by 2005, according to a projection by the Gartner Group, a technology consulting company. Many of these workers carry laptop computers back and forth between the office and home. They often have a desktop machine at work and also one at home. Naturally, this leads to having multiple sets of files, programs, and so on. You can synchronize data between a laptop and desktop pretty easily, using a program such as LapLink, but it's even easier and more effective when a telecommuter has a network set up at home.

The laptop needs to be outfitted with a network card or have a docking station that connects to the home network. Either way, the telecommuter has only to plug his or her laptop into the home network to be able to instantly synchronize files, use files and programs that are residing only on the home machine, print out using any printer attached to the network, and otherwise exploit the advantage of a network. Because of their nomadic, dual-location workstyles, telecommuters are prime candidates for home networks.

Networking by Home-Based Business Owners

Businesses and networks go together. That's just as true when the business is located at home. And, considering there are more than 24 million U.S. home-based businesses, generating in the neighborhood of $400 billion in annual revenues, this connection can be pretty significant.

Home-based business owners network for pretty much the same reasons businesses do: to share files and peripherals and to communicate between workstations. Since home-based businesses tend to be smaller than other companies, and have lower revenues and less cash to play with, they are also more likely to want to save money by parceling out a single Internet connection among several PCs. Finally, since few homes are built with big, open "cubicle farm" type rooms, the workers in a home office tend to be scattered into several smaller rooms. This can inhibit communication among employees. But a network quickly solves that problem, as well as making it easier to save money on fancy peripherals like high-speed printers and DVD drives.

Networking by Self-Employed Professionals

Self-employed professionals include consultants, freelancers, salespeople, programmers, and many types of non-traditional business people. They may operate in many different fields, including graphic design, information technology, advertising, copywriting, law, and medicine. They all tend to have a couple of things in common. Namely, that they're well educated and earn good incomes. And those two factors happen to be two of the best indicators of a household's likelihood to network.

There are a couple of reasons why self-employed people are good networking candidates. Many of them travel, so they may have a laptop in addition to one or more desktop computers. And laptop carriers, especially those who do lots of work at home, are another group of likely networkers, because of the way a network makes it easier to let laptop and desktop work together. Self-employed professionals are, almost by definition, knowledge workers, so they tend to be more interested in and literate about information technology, including networks, than the average corporate employee.

NOTE There is a grain of truth, perhaps more, in stereotypes of self-employed professionals lounging in a backyard hammock while fielding client calls and sipping mint juleps. In addition to a home office where they do the majority of their work, many self-employed professionals who work at home have other places in the house where they spend time working on their laptops or other desktops. These spots may include the bedroom, kitchen table, or living room couch, as well as the aforementioned hammock. Having a network makes it easier for a self-employed professional to work in multiple locations in the home. And some networking technologies—including wireless networking—make it even easier to have network access wherever they choose to work. A network also allows them do so without sacrificing access to the data files, applications software, communications channels, and other resources of their desktops.

Networking by Students

Computers have always been closely tied to education. Many people's first exposure to computers is in a classroom or computer lab. Today, most school computer installations are networked, if for no other reason than to simplify the maintenance and management of the computers. In addition, educational and governmental policymakers have targeted the further computerization of America's schools as an important goal, which will make networking an even more integral aspect of education in the near future.

Networks can be very helpful to learning. Networked computers allow students to have common access to useful reference materials, including CD- and DVD-ROM resources, as well as online card catalogs and the entire expanse of the Internet. Networks make it easy for pupils to communicate questions to teachers or other students. Networks also allow instructors to employ computerized testing—administering questions and capturing answers—all through the network.

Although it's not likely that mom or dad or college roomie will administer tests over the home network, many of the same resource-sharing advantages gained in the classroom are also valuable to students at home. They can share high-speed access to the Internet for doing research, share a single household printer to turn out dazzling reports and projects, and do it all without running one of their parents off of the office computer.

 NOTE Not all students study exclusively in classrooms. Some practically never set foot in any place smelling of chalk and ballpoint ink. Instead, they do all their learning online. You can actually get a bachelor's degree from legitimate online universities, without ever getting within shouting distance of an actual campus. While this idea may be anathema to college-culture aficionados, online higher education is a great idea for people who are disabled, live in remote areas, or simply can't find the time to commute to college.

You don't have to be a serious academic to be interested in taking advantage of the learning opportunities afforded by a network. There are many professional training courses available online as well. Topics range from how to write grant proposals and master business etiquette, to becoming a Microsoft Certified Professional or Microsoft Certified Systems Engineer. For pure fun, you can learn a foreign language, study astrology or—believe it or not—learn the finer points of wine appreciation, all online. Having a network makes all these learning experiences easier and more convenient for all the students in the home.

Online learning is easier and more convenient in a number of ways. For one thing, there is less competition for high-speed Internet access. You'll also be able to research assignments, print papers, or do other school work from any networked location in the home. You'll even be able to move your networked classroom around the home: kitchen during breakfast, family room in the morning and, following afternoon classes, the student's bedroom during the evening.

Families and Networking

Homes aren't just for families, of course, and there's no reason why a bunch of twenty-something roommates—or even a solitary bachelor—can't network their computers. But there is a strong and steady correlation between the presence of children in a household and that household's propensity to network. For instance, one market research study conducted by Forrester Research, Incorporated found that children under 18 were present in 46 percent of the households most likely to network their computers. That's quite a bit more than the 34 percent of all U.S. households with children.

The family ties are not really surprising because networking offers many enticing benefits for parents, kids, and other members of networked households. A network can help adults be better parents by keeping a closer eye on their offspring and, at the same time, by increasing the kids' opportunities to be exposed to new things. Children can use networks to reach more learning resources, use computer gadgets like DVD drives that they might not have been able to afford before, and, as you might expect, have more fun. All told, families and networks are a good combination.

Children and Networks

Home networks and children are tied together for one unassailable reason: Homes with children are more likely to own computers than those without children. According to Forrester Research Incorporated, half of U.S. homes have PCs, but the number rises to over 60 percent when you look only at homes with children. Another key number: Among PC-owning households with children, 56 percent have more than one PC. Again, this number is far higher for homes with children than for others. It seems clear that networks and kids are going to be spending some time together. And the good news is children can get a lot out of computer networks.

Education is the first thing most people think of when they consider the kid-computer connection. And networked computers, by making all the household's resources available to any PC on the network, can turbocharge educational opportunities for any child sitting down to a networked computer. The ability to share Internet access, for example, will mean that kids researching homework assignments can enjoy the same high-speed connections as Dad's home office. They'll be able to use any of the software and peripherals that are on the network, even if, as is common, the kids' computer happens to be an underpowered hand-me-down machine. To cite a specific example, if the home office PC has a CD-ROM player and the kids' computer doesn't, the kids can still access reference disks on that player, using the network.

Fun is probably the first thing kids think of in connection with computers, and networks can deliver that commodity in bulk. In fact, some studies say that the desire to play online head-to-head games is the second-strongest motivation for setting up home networks. Playing online games is also a great way for parents and children to spend time in friendly competition together.

Another key reason kids and networks get along is that kids are the earliest of the early adopters. Youngsters embrace things that their parents haven't even thought about. For example, you can count on teenage buyers of portable digital MP3 music players to far outnumber older consumers. And these devices, along with such kid-friendly gadgets as DVD players, cell phones, and satellite TV receivers, are eminently suitable for connecting and using over a home network. Clearly, networked households can bring many benefits to children. And parents who recognize those benefits are among the most eager networkers of all.

Networking for Parents

Parents will find that networks help them in many ways, not least, in being better parents. For instance, when computers are networked, it's very easy to see what is going on with your child's computer. You can monitor where he is going on the Web, what games are being played and for how long, and even which files are being accessed. All this you can do without having to leave your own PC because your machines are connected via the network.

Home networks aren't just for Big Brother-like surveillance, either. You can also make the resources of your own, presumably higher-powered, PC available to younger members of the household, who might otherwise have to make do with machines unequipped to run up-to-date software. (In the event that the kids have the better machine, the reverse applies as well.) If you're the kind of parent who enjoys spending time playing games with your kids, networks can provide excellent arenas for head-to-head online competition.

 NOTE In Chapter 17, " Setting Up Shared Resources," you'll learn how to configure your home network to enable playing head-to-head multi-player games.

Finally, networked computers are far more valuable as learning tools than stand-alone machines, for a variety of reasons, including the ability to share learning resources such as CD-ROM encyclopedias and high-speed Internet hookups, that will be discussed further in upcoming chapters. If you want your children to have the best in-home educational opportunities and resources, today a home network might be as important as a household set of encyclopedias was in another era.

Summary

Are you well educated? Self employed? A parent? A child? A student? A technophile? Then you are among the cohort of Americans who are at the forefront of the networking craze. If you don't just want to keep up with the Joneses, if you want to be the Joneses, then it's time to network your household.

What's Next?

Understanding who is doing home networking will help you determine how to network your home. That's because the type of home network you choose will be determined in large part by who you are and why you intend to network. The various kinds of networks will be explored in the next chapter, "Home Networking Technologies."

CHAPTER 4

Home Networking Technologies

Overview

O
ver the years, there have been many types of networks. Some have come into wide popularity and then gone away more or less completely, replaced by newer and better approaches. Today, there are four common approaches to home networking: traditional Ethernet cables, phoneline networking, powerline networking, and wireless. In this chapter, you will learn about each of these approaches and how they work. Before you decide which type of home network technology is best for you, you should understand how each type of network operates.

Your Home Networking Options

Home networking is still at a relatively early stage in its evolution compared to technologies such as, say, floppy disks. Over many years, floppies have evolved from 8" flexible envelopes created by IBM and capable of holding only 100 kilobytes of data, to today's standard 3.5-inch, 1.44 megabyte disks. In between, many disk storage media have presented themselves as the technology to beat, including 5 1/4-inch floppies and 720K low-density 3.5-inch floppies. Today, high-capacity Zi drives are making their bid to become the dominant standard.

The old days of floppies were similar to where we currently find ourselves in home networking. There are a number of competing approaches to networking, including standard Ethernet cable networking, home phoneline networking, powerline networking, and wireless networking. Each offers its own special benefits and limitations. Some, for instance, allow you to set up your network without installing any new wires. Others offer better performance, more mobility, lower cost, or other advantages. Unfortunately, each of them suffers incompatibility problems with the others—you can't freely mix and match different types of networks without encountering problems, some of them intractable.

Unlike, say, the choice between PC or Macintosh, the choice of a network type is not based primarily on personal preference. Each variant has significant differences in performance, convenience, and special features, as compared to the rest. Once you understand how you'll use the network, as well as your requirements for installation, cost, and other concerns, you should be able to make a definitive choice from among these technologies.

None of this is impossible to sort out. You simply need to understand the pluses and minuses of the various types of home networks. Then you have to decide what you want your network to do. After that, it's simply a matter of matching needs to capabilities.

Understanding Standard Ethernet Cabled Networks

Ethernet is based on ALOHA Net, a network that was invented in the 1960s at, you guessed it, the University of Hawaii. ALOHA Net was originally used in wireless networks. Researchers at Xerox's famous Palo Alto Research Center refined the technology and adapted it for use in wired networks.

The first Ethernet LAN products were introduced by Xerox in 1975. After that, Xerox, Digital Equipment Corporation, and Intel all continued to work on Ethernet, resulting eventually in the adoption of the standard known as *IEEE 802.3* that today defines Ethernet. The standard for today's most popular type of Ethernet network was first introduced in 1990, using Ethernet over twisted-pair wiring.

The Story of the IEEE

The initials IEEE—usually pronounced "Eye-triple-E"—are ones you'll see a lot as you get into networking. They stand for Institute of Electrical and Electronic Engineers. IEEE is a New York City-based organization with about 300,000 members, including engineers, students, and scientists. It was founded in 1962 and has become an important standards-setting body for the information technology industry. Often, IEEE standards become more or less synonymous with the name brands of the technologies they describe. Thus, IEEE 802.3, which is the number of the IEEE standard for Ethernet, is sometimes used to describe an Ethernet network which conforms to the IEEE standard. Not all IEEE standards have to do with networking—just the ones that start with 802. For instance, IEEE 1284 describes the Enhanced Parallel Port, or EPP standard for parallel printer ports. Other 802 standards refer to other network approaches. For instance, 802.4 describes token passing, 802.5 refers to token ring networks, and 802.11 refers to wireless networks, which you will learn about later in this chapter.

In the beginning, Ethernet could connect 100 computers at speeds of 3 megabits per second. Modern Ethernet can connect more than 1,000 PCs, or nodes, and do it at speeds of 10Mbps or, with a variant called *Fast Ethernet*, 100Mbps.

Fast Ethernet – The Second Generation of Ethernet Technology

Fast Ethernet is not the last word on high-performance Ethernet networks. Like most information technologies, networking isn't standing still, but is constantly changing and experiencing new levels of performance. What may be surprising is the magnitude of the improvements. Magnitude is just the right word, too, because the latest generation of Ethernet, called *Gigabit Ethernet*, operates 10 times as fast as 100Mbps Fast Ethernet. That's a gigabit, or 1 billion bits of information, flowing across the network every second. While some home network owners will doubtless feel constrained by 10BaseT Ethernet, and feel the urge to move up to 100BaseT to transfer their big graphics files, send digital video throughout the house, or perhaps play bandwidth-gobbling online games, it's hard to see how any home network could come close to straining the resources of the proposed next generation of Ethernet. Then again, not too long ago, the idea that millions of homes would be networked for computers at all, seemed unlikely.

Ethernet has been so successful as a networking technology that many types of networks, including some not commonly referred to as Ethernet, actually use the same underlying method for accessing the network. However, in practice, this is not as confusing as it sounds. As a general rule, when a network is described as an Ethernet network, it's a network that, in addition to using the Ethernet access method, also uses special cables to hook the computers together (as opposed to using existing phone- or powerline wiring, or wireless radio connections).

Ethernet Topology

In terms of physical typology, Ethernet generally uses the star physical topology (as shown in Figure 4.1), although it can also be used in a network with the bus physical topology. While most Ethernet networks have a star *physical* topology, they all have a bus *logical* topology. This means that whenever a computer connected to the network is sending data to another computer on the network, it broadcasts the data to the whole network. Each computer on the network checks to see whether the data is addressed to them. If so, it accepts the data. If not, it ignores the data and keeps listening.

FIGURE 4.1

Ethernet generally uses the star physical topology.

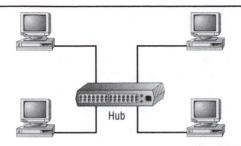

Hub

Ethernet uses an approach known as *carrier sense multiple access/collision detection*, or CSMA/CD, to make sure that only one computer is actually trying to use the network at any one time. With CSMA/CD, computers on the network that have something to send out first check the network connection to see that it's not already being used. If not, the computer sends the information. Sometimes, two computers will send their information at the same time, resulting in a collision on the network between the two messages. When data collides, both packets of data are destroyed and must be resent, as shown in Figure 4.2. If a collision occurs, each computer that sent data waits a random length of time, then resends.

FIGURE 4.2

Collisions occur when two packets of data are sent to the network at the same time.

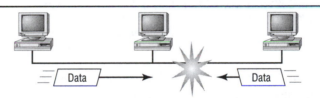

Data   Data

The fact that Ethernet uses the bus logical topology isn't likely to be highly significant in your home network. However, bus topology does carry a couple of potentially important pieces of baggage. First, the use of this topology limits the maximum distance between two points, such as between two computers on the network, or between a computer and the hub. Using coaxial cable, Ethernet has a limit of 185 meters (about 600 feet); using standard twisted pair wiring, Ethernet has a limit of 100 meters (or 328 feet). This means that the network cable can be no longer than either 100 or 185 meters, respectively, before it must be boosted by a repeater. In addition, the CSMA/CD access method used with a bus logical topology, may not perform well on busy networks, like those operating in many companies. In some cases, the computers sending information may create so many collisions that too much of the network's capacity, or bandwidth, is used up resending data.

Ethernet Cable Types

Ethernet networks require all the computers and network devices to be connected with cables, but not just any cables. The first Ethernet networks used bulky, stiff cables that were hard to handle. Over the years, Ethernet technology has been adapted to use a variety of different types of cables to ease installation and accomplish various other tasks. The four major cable types are:

10Base5 Also called *thicknet,* uses thick, stiff coaxial cable to connect workstations

10Base2 Also called *thinnet,* uses a thinner coaxial cable

10BaseT Uses unshielded twisted pair cable

10BaseFL Uses optical fiber

 NOTE Each Ethernet cabling scheme uses different signaling techniques to adapt to the characteristics of the cable. Depending on the type of cable you are implementing, then, you generally have to use different network interface cards, connectors, and other equipment. Some networks use more than one type of cable. For instance, 10BaseFL optical fiber, which can span up to 2,000 meters, might be used to connect two widely separated local area networks, each of which is using a 10Base2 thin coaxial cable connection scheme. The key is to use the right type of network equipment for your Ethernet cables.

For Ethernet home networks, 10BaseT is the most likely choice. This cable looks slightly thicker than the six-strand cable used to wire home telephone systems. The cards, hubs, and cables are inexpensive, and the flexible cabling is much easier to install than coaxial cables. This type of cabling is known as *unshielded twisted-pair*, or UTP, because it has no shielding other than a vinyl cover, and consists of pairs of wires that are twisted around one another.

 NOTE The twisting of wires in twisted-pair cabling is no accident, nor is it intended just to simplify identifying and handling wires. The twisting works to reduce interference in the signals transmitted over the wire. Varieties of unshielded twisted-pair cabling are distinguished by, among other things, the precise number of twists per foot of wire. If you're installing a network using twisted-pair cabling, don't untwist the wires more than you have to, or you may expose your network to electromagnetic interference.

Unshielded twisted pair wiring comes in five varieties or categories, each classified by the Electrical Industries Association.

Category 1   Used for voice telephone communications

Category 2   Also used for voice telephone systems

Category 3   Acceptable for Ethernet data networks

Category 4   Another data-grade cable

Category 5   Graded acceptable for Fast Ethernet networks

Fast Ethernet, also known as 100BaseT, uses Category 5 wiring, which is somewhat more expensive than the Category 3 wiring used in regular Ethernet networks. Fast Ethernet also requires special NICs and hubs, which are more expensive than the 10Mbps variety. Many NICs and hubs are dual-speed, meaning they can operate at either 10Mbps or 100Mbps. Even if you're installing a plain Ethernet network, it's a good idea to use Category 5 wiring, and possibly dual-speed hubs and NICs, in case you do want the faster speed later on.

 NOTE   Among the recent changes in the networking world is a pretty sharp reduction in the price of dual-speed NICs and hubs. As a result, the cost differential for dual-speed network cards is pretty negligible, and the cost differential of dual-speed hubs is getting closer. So don't rule out 100BaseT for a home network.

Although Category 5 cable is the hands-down choice for most home networkers, you may want to consider coaxial cable under some circumstances. The most likely set of circumstances under which coaxial makes sense is when you can get it for free. This is not as unlikely as it may sound. Many offices and businesses are upgrading from coaxial cable to easier-to-handle Cat 5 cable. If you can locate one of these business network upgraders, you may be able to lay your hands on more coaxial cable than you can use for no money at all. That kind of savings can make the added hassle of installing coaxial worthwhile.

Summing Up Ethernet

Ethernet is an old, popular, tested network media that is well-standardized and comes in many different varieties. The most likely choice for most home Ethernet networks is a regular Ethernet network, operating at 10Mbps or 100Mbps over Category 3 or Category 5 cables.

Understanding Phoneline Networks

Phoneline networks use the existing wiring of your home phone system to connect your computers into a network. For that reason, along with powerline and wireless options, it's known as one of the "no-new-wires" network technologies.

Most phoneline networks are based on technology developed by Tut Systems. Tut, based in Pleasant Hill, California, doesn't sell its products directly to consumers. Instead, it sells components to other companies that use them to create products for sale down at your local computer store. Tut came out with its first phoneline network offering in 1992. The HomeRun technology Tut introduced in 1997 has proven very popular with many phoneline networking consumer product vendors.

Worthwhile Wiring

It's hard to overstate the economic value of using already available wiring. Approximately 94 percent of U.S. homes are already wired for telephone service, even more than have VCRs, according to the U.S. Census Bureau's *Statistical Abstract of the United States.* The same report says there are more than 104 million residential telephone lines in the U.S., more than twice as many lines as businesses have.

This massive network didn't develop overnight, or without cost. In fact, the telephone companies have spent an estimated $200 billion over the last 25 years installing copper phone wiring to cover the so-called "last mile"—the distance between home telephones and the telephone company switching stations, also known as central offices. The whole local loop, including last-mile wiring and central office switches, has a book value of $296 billion.

The net effect of all this expenditure of time and money is more than dial tone. In addition to allowing you to make regular voice calls, the telephone system in your home provides the basis of an economical and effective means of home networking.

Although networking using home phonelines is a relatively new idea, the technology has come a long way in a short time. The Home Phoneline Networking Alliance, or HomePNA, is a group of large computer companies (including Intel and Compaq) that has pushed to establish standards in an effort to make home networking easy and available to almost everyone. This has helped push phoneline networking into the public's eye, and made a fairly broad array of equipment readily available through retail channels.

The Home Phoneline Networking Alliance

The Home Phoneline Networking Alliance (HomePNA) is a non-profit association of companies working together to help ensure adoption of a single, unified industry standard for phoneline networking. They also seek to rapidly bring to market a range of interoperable home networking solutions. It was founded in June 1998 by 3Com, AMD, AT&T, Wireless, Compaq, Conexant, Epigram, Hewlett-Packard Company, IBM, Intel, Lucent Technologies, and Tut Systems. Since then, more than 70 companies working in networking, telecommunications, hardware, software, and consumer electronics, have joined the alliance. This organization has made rapid strides in refining, improving, and standardizing the technology, as well as introducing home networking products based on it. For more information see `www.homepna.org`.

The main distinguishing feature about phoneline networks is that they don't require any new wiring other than the cord running from the computer's NIC to the telephone jack. Nor do they need hubs or other external hardware. This makes them exceptionally easy and convenient to install, as well as inexpensive. At the same time, they let you do all the essential network tasks, including sharing Internet connections, sharing files and peripherals, and playing online games.

On the downside, the performance of phoneline networks somewhat lags behind Ethernet. Early products on the market ran at approximately 1Mbps per second, about 10 percent of the performance of a regular Ethernet network. Phoneline networks aren't all that slow, however, when you consider that 1Mbps is almost 20 times as fast as a 56K modem. And the technology is constantly improving. By the time you read this, phoneline networks that provide speeds of up to 10Mbps, matching regular Ethernet, will be available.

How Phoneline Networks Work

Phoneline networks work by piggybacking a network signal over the same wiring used for your home's telephone system. You can still use your phone system for telephone calls, fax transmissions, and modem connections, even while your computers are communicating over the same wires. That's because the phoneline network cards use a high-frequency signal that telephones can't detect, so the signal doesn't interfere with your phone's or fax's normal operation. See Figure 4.3.

FIGURE 4.3

Phoneline networks, Digital Subscriber Lines (DSL), and Plain Old Telephone Service (POTS) can share the same lines because each uses a different set of frequencies.

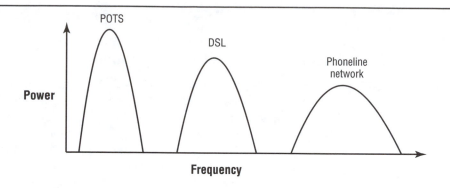

Specifically, the *Plain Old Telephone Service* uses the frequencies from 20Hz to 3.4kHz. DSL or *Digital Subscriber Line* high-speed data service occupies from 2.5kHz to MHz (million hertz). Phoneline networks take the highest road of all, working above 2.4MHz.

Phoneline networks use regular telephone cabling, both for the existing stuff inside your home's walls, and for the short length between the computer and the wall jack. The PCs are connected to the wall jack with regular RJ-11 jacks, just like the ones you use to connect telephones, answering machines, faxes, and modems. The technology developed by Tut is what makes high-speed data transfer work over what are otherwise non-data grade copper wires.

Some new PCs are sold with built-in phoneline networking capability. If you have an older PC, or a new one without built-in phoneline networking, you need to install a phoneline network interface card in each PC you want to connect. Some phoneline network devices plug into a parallel port or USB port, so you don't have to open up the PC case. Otherwise, you install the phoneline card just like an Ethernet card, modem, or other expansion card. After creating your network interface connection on each PC, you plug each one into a nearby telephone jack and install the software.

NOTE   Phoneline networks access the network using CSMA/CD or carrier sense multiple access with collision detection. This is the same type of network access method as Ethernet. In fact, phoneline networks can be considered basically as Ethernet networks running over telephone wires, with the main difference being the slower data transfer rates. This is significant, in that it allows phoneline networks to use much of the vast quantity of Ethernet-compatible software and hardware on the market.

Unlike Ethernet networks, however, which use a variety of connectors, phoneline networks generally use just the familiar modular telephone jacks known as RJ-11. These connectors hook the phoneline NIC to the phone outlet on the wall, in just the same way as you connect telephones, answering machines, and faxes.

Summing Up Phoneline Networks

Phoneline networks use the existing wiring of your home phone system to connect your computers into a network. Phoneline networks are exceptionally quick and easy to install and offer reasonably good performance. They are compatible with most Ethernet technologies as well. By the time you read this, phoneline networks that provide speeds of up 10Mbps, matching regular Ethernet, will be available.

Understanding Powerline Networks

Like phoneline networks, powerline networks operate by piggybacking a network signal over your home's existing wiring. In this case, however, the signal travels over the electrical powerlines.

How Powerline Networks Work

People have known how to transfer data over electrical powerlines for more than 20 years. The technology has been used for a number of tasks, including setting up home automation systems. But powerline networking hasn't been widely adopted for computer networking because, until recently, it has been too expensive, slow, and unreliable.

There are a number of vendors offering various types of powerline networking for the home. These technologies include:

X-10 A 20-year-old technology initially developed for simple purposes, such as turning on lights and controlling home appliances. It's very slow compared to newer approaches.

Intellon CEBus A much faster powerline network than X-10, reaching up to 10Mbps transfer rates in tests.

Echelon LonWorks A control network designed to work with a computer network such as Ethernet or phoneline, for networking lights, security systems, sprinkler systems, and other home appliances.

Intelogis A newcomer whose fast (over 10Mpbs in tests) and inexpensive approach has made it the most popular home powerline networking vendor so far.

Powerline networks use a scheme similar to phoneline networks to transmit data over electrical lines. They do so without disrupting—or being disrupted by—the ongoing use of the lines for transmitting power. As seen in Figure 4.4, the powerline network transmits over higher frequencies than those used for power transmission.

FIGURE 4.4

Powerline networks share data transmissions with power transmissions by using a different set of frequencies.

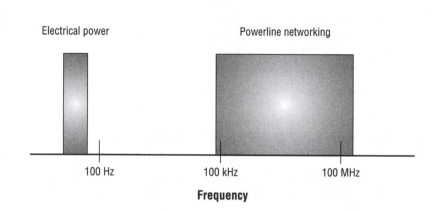

Electrical power   Powerline networking

100 Hz   100 kHz   100 MHz

Frequency

Except for the fact that they run on powerlines rather than phone or data transmission cables, powerline networks work much like other networks. Users can share files and printers, send e-mail, play games, and share high-speed Internet connections. Unlike most Ethernet networks, they don't require hubs. And some powerline networks don't even require the installation of network interface cards. They simply attach to the computer through a parallel port, then plug into a wall power outlet to hook to the network. In addition, they're designed to work with Windows 95/98 networking. So powerline networks are much the same as other networks, on the surface at least.

When it comes to performance, however, it's a different story. Although some powerline networking equipment vendors have reached Ethernet-like speeds in tests, in the real world, data-transfer rates of 350kbps or so are more typical. These speeds may be adequate for many home networkers, but they're certainly far less than what is offered by some of the other technologies.

Summing Up Powerline Networks

Powerline networks have been around for years, but are undergoing a renaissance of interest due to higher speeds and lower costs offered by new refinements. Using a different frequency lets them share wires with power transmissions.

Understanding Wireless Networks

Wireless networks are the ultimate no-new-wires approach—they don't require any wires at all. Using radio frequencies to connect computers rather than wires, they allow computers on the network to be almost anywhere.

How Wireless Networks Work

Modern wireless networks started at the same time and place as Ethernet, at the University of Hawaii as ALOHA Net. This wireless radio network was designed to tie together computers at seven campuses on four islands. Ethernet migrated to a wired environment, but ham radio operators, often using homemade black boxes called terminal node controllers, experimented with ways to turn their home personal computers into nodes on wireless Wide Area Networks.

Wireless networking got a big boost in 1985 when the Federal Communications Commission began allowing public use of the Industrial, Scientific, and Medical band of the radio spectrum. This bit of spectrum sits just above the area used by cellular phones, from 902MHz to 5.85GHz. One of the good things about this move was that it allowed networkers to send radio transmissions in this band without getting a license from the FCC.

One of the first results of the frequency allocation was the creation of wireless Wide Area Networks. Companies such as Ardis and RAM Mobile Data set up wireless networks that, in some cases, spanned the entire country. Then they began selling the ability to wirelessly communicate between PCs, printers, and other devices. Because of the high cost of the services, customers were mostly businesses. But it did get people aware of the advantages of wireless networking, which allowed them to be anywhere, anytime, unconnected by wires, yet still communicating with other resources on the network. As seen in Figure 4.5, computers connected in a wireless home network also use radio waves instead of wires to communicate.

FIGURE 4.5

Computers connected in a simple wireless home network use radio waves instead of wires to communicate with stationary desktops and roaming laptop computers. Additional nodes may be needed to interface with the telephone network or other wired network.

Another shot in the arm to wireless networking came in 1997, when the IEEE published its 802.11 standard for wireless LANs. This was what the market had been waiting for, and within a year, a large number of companies had come out with wireless networking products. These were cheaper than renting access to the private networks run by Ardis and RAM and others like them. But they were still too expensive for home networkers. It took until late 1998 and early 1999 for the first truly affordable wireless radio home networking products to hit the market.

Home RF Working Group

Like phoneline networking, wireless networking has a group of large, powerful companies that have banded together to promote the technology. The Home RF Working Group, whose members include Microsoft, Intel, and Motorola, wasn't quite as speedy as the HomePNA organization, however, in getting its specification finalized. So Home RF decided to pare back the speed requirements for its initial specification, dubbed *Shared Wireless Access Protocol*, or SWAP. Home RF originally planned to specify a speed of between 1Mbps and 2Mbps. The new specification allows speeds from 800Kbps to 1.6Mbps. The change will allow wireless networking vendors to come up with products meeting specification several months earlier, thereby providing the phoneline networking crowd with some competition. For more information see www.homerf.org.

Wireless networks require that a radio transceiver is installed in each computer or other device attached to the network. Once these adapters are installed and the necessary software is configured, you're ready to run a simple peer-to-peer network—no wires to run, new or old. (Exceptions include cables that might be run to an external antenna, or to a wireless interface to the wired network, such as a wireless modem.)

Most wireless networks today use the 2.4GHz band. At first, wireless networks used the 902MHz band, but the need for more bandwidth drove them to a higher, wider band. The 2.4GHz band means higher cost and shorter range for wireless networks, but this band is available around the world, while the 902MHz range is generally only allowed to be used for wireless networking in North America. The 2.4GHz also offers wider bandwidth. The IEEE 802.11 specification for wireless networks endorses the 2.4GHz band. See Figure 4.6 for a comparison of bandwidth frequencies.

FIGURE 4.6

Wireless networks use the 902MHz, the 2.4GHz, and eventually, the 5.725GHz bands.

Wireless network radio spectrum

Wireless networks adhering to the SWAP specification, promulgated by the Home RF Working Group, use the *carrier sense multiple access with collision avoidance* CSMA/CA method to allow data nodes to access the network. The CSMA/CA works similarly to the collision avoidance multiple access with collision detection method that Ethernet networks use. Nodes on the network check for traffic before sending data. The difference with collision detection is that collision avoidance involves waiting a random amount of time, after a node has detected traffic, before sending its own data. Since most collisions occur immediately after the network is freed up, this very short delay reduces collisions at the expense of some performance.

With wireless networking, you can realistically expect a data transfer rate of 1Mbps to 2Mbps, under good circumstances. And, while wireless can go around many obstacles that would stop a wired network, such as a historical building facade, its performance can degrade seriously in the face of such seemingly ephemeral obstacles as a poorly placed file cabinet, or a newly constructed room divider. It's possible, using a laser-powered straight-line narrowcasting link (don't worry, you don't need to learn this term) to achieve performance with a wireless network that rivals Fast Ethernet. However, that kind of performance comes at far too high a price in dollars and low practicality to be of much interest to home networkers.

In addition to speed, range is a more significant issue with wireless than with wired networks. The maximum range of most home wireless networks, at about 150 feet, is much less than the maximum distance wired networks can cover. Also, since you are untethered, you are likely to roam around the house and yard while using the network, increasing the likelihood of unintentionally moving out of range.

 WARNING The U.S. military doesn't necessarily adhere to the Federal Communication Commission decisions that opened certain bands of the spectrum up for public use. If you're going to operate a wireless network on a military base, you'll need to ask for a special permit. Otherwise, you might interfere with military radio transmissions.

Security is not as big a problem as you might think, considering that your data is being sprayed out broadcast-style by radio transmitters. That's doubly true when you reflect that wireless networks use the same frequency bands as some cordless phones. In fact, the technology that makes home wireless networks possible is basically an extension of cordless phone technology and the technology behind commercial grade wireless LANs. However, by using digital encryption and changing frequencies 50 times a second, wireless networks can, in fact, achieve levels of security comparable to some wired networks, in spite of sharing the air with cordless phones.

Summing Up Wireless Networks

Wireless networks have a unique set of features compared to all other network technologies. They've been around almost as long as any networking technology, but are only now becoming feasible for home use. Performance is going up and prices are coming down rapidly. As a result, the next few years should see many wireless home networks up and running.

Understanding Hybrid Wireless-Wired Networks

Hybrid wireless-wired networks are the go anywhere/do anything network. They offer the performance of a wired network where you need it, plus the freedom of a wireless connection where that is required.

How Hybrid Networks Work

In reality, most wireless networks are and have always been hybrid wired-wireless systems. In most cases, a transceiver-equipped PC or other device, called an *access point,* connects to a wired network such as the telephone network or a wired LAN, using standard cabling. This access point can receive and transmit data between the wireless and wired worlds.

In home use, you're most likely to mix and match wired and wireless equipment, especially when it comes to connecting to a modem. You may also want to connect the networked computers directly to a printer without going through a wireless-equipped PC. For either use, you can install a bridge that connects to both the wireless network and, through regular cabling, the printer, modem, or other device connected to a wired network.

You may also prefer to have most of your PCs on a wired network, but also connect a laptop computer, or perhaps a computer that is located an inconvenient distance away, through a second, wireless network, as shown in Figure 4.7. This is not quite so simple. You may want to set up one of your PCs to work with two network cards, one for the wireless network and one for a wired network. *Multihoming*, the term for having more than one NIC per PC, is tricky with Windows 95/98 PCs.

FIGURE 4.7

A hybrid wired-wireless network allows you to have most of your PCs on a wired network, but also connect a laptop computer to the network.

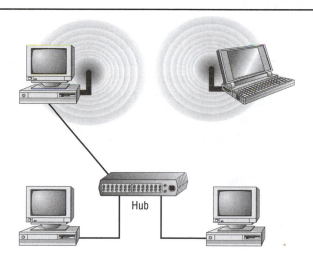

Hub

Summing Up Hybrid Networks

Hybrid networks have many uses. If you have a wireless network, odds are good that you'll go beyond a simple peer-to-peer pure wireless setup, and find some way to add a wired interface to the system. If you want to run two networks, one wired and one wireless, it may be more complicated, but the advantages of having roaming capability where you want it, coupled with performance where you need it, may outweigh the trouble.

Summary

Each of the four common types of networks used in the home—Ethernet, phoneline, powerline, and wireless—along with the hybrid wireless-wired networks, has enough history, standardization, performance, and convenience to make it viable for home networking scenarios. Though four distinct and, for the most part, incompatible approaches may seem to present an unnecessarily confusing number of choices, each of these varieties of network has its own legitimate reasons for being.

What's Next?

Now that you have been exposed to the four main types of networks used in the home, you are ready to take this information and compare it to your needs. This will help you make the important decision about which type of network to install. That process is the subject of the next chapter, "Making a Smart Choice."

CHAPTER **5**

Making a Smart Choice

Overview

Choosing the type of home network you'll install is more than a matter of picking the fastest or the cheapest or the easiest. At this point, there simply is no hands-down, best-for-everybody home networking choice. For many people, speedy Ethernet using 10BaseT or perhaps 100BaseT will be the best bet. For others, inexpensive and convenient phoneline networking is a wise choice. Users who want to roam untethered by any kind of cables will want wireless or, more likely, a hybrid wireless-wired network. This chapter specifically looks at the pros and cons of each approach, and sums them up to help you make the final choice.

Sizing Up Ethernet

Ethernet is the most widely used local area network in the world, and for good reason. Choosing to use Ethernet cabling in your home offers a number of significant advantages, including speed and reliability. It isn't the best choice for everyone, however, and installing new wires throughout your home can be troublesome. To help you evaluate your options, in this section you'll learn about the advantages and disadvantages of using this technology for your home network.

Ethernet Pros

Ethernet is time-tested, reliable, and inexpensive. It offers the best performance of any available home network. You can buy the equipment to wire a home for Ethernet at any sizable computer store, as well as many consumer electronics outlets and hobbyist shops.

Ethernet is Reliable

The technology behind Ethernet goes back more than 30 years, during which time it has proven itself in all sorts of circumstances. In addition, there are plenty of trained technicians, diagnostic gear, techniques, and informal experts you can turn to for help, if and when you need it.

Ethernet is Relatively Inexpensive

Ethernet isn't the cheapest networking alternative. However, it isn't expensive when compared to the cost of a new PC, or another printer, or scanner, or high-speed Internet connection. And Ethernet's costs are actually less per computer than wireless networks.

Ethernet Offers Good Performance

Ethernet stands above all the competition when it comes to performance. Only the latest phoneline networks can match the 10Mbps speed of regular Ethernet. None of the alternatives can come close to the 100Mbps speed of Fast Ethernet. (Not to mention Gigabit Ethernet which, although not a practical option for most home networks, is 1,000 times as fast as the first-generation phoneline networking standard.)

The 10Mbps speed of Ethernet should be more than adequate for the vast majority of home networks. If you need more speed to transfer big files, run an in-home video network, or perhaps play bandwidth-hogging head-to-head games, you may opt for Fast Ethernet. The cost differential between the two is not all that significant, compared to the speed advantages you gain. To begin with, you will probably use the same cable. The cards cost basically the same—only a few dollars difference in price. Fast Ethernet hubs, on the other hand, are somewhat more expensive. Still, a Fast Ethernet hub with ports to hook up four devices is going to run you only around $75. Those kinds of costs aren't all that significant. In fact, by the time you read this, or not long after, Fast Ethernet may cost the same as regular Ethernet.

Ethernet Cons

If Ethernet were the best choice for all home networks, there wouldn't be any need for this analysis. As it turns out, however, Ethernet does have some drawbacks and limitations that you need to consider before making the choice of a home networking approach.

Ethernet Requires Cables

Ethernet is the only one of the popular home networking schemes that requires new wiring between all the computers on the network. This is a significant obstacle in many residences, especially those with computers that are widely separated. The problem isn't the distance—computers on a 10BaseT Ethernet network can be separated by 300 feet or more. It's the problem of getting the cable through the barriers.

It's no problem, of course, just to string a cable between two or more computers in the same room. But unless you like crawling through the attic, teetering on a ladder in the basement, or stapling unsightly cable all along the exterior of your home, then installing a network of Ethernet cables is likely to be a significant obstacle. Not to mention the hassle of drilling and pulling cable through walls, floors, or ceilings.

Renting and Building

Two special cases concerning wiring for a network deserve mention. If you are renting your home or apartment, you may need to get permission from your landlord before drilling holes or performing other work to install cabling for a network. Also, if you are building a new home, consider having the wiring installed before the drywall goes up. Installing a network cable system during construction is much cheaper, easier, neater, and more convenient than even the simplest retrofit installation.

Connections Can Be Problematic

Ethernet connections are weak points in the network. Corrosion, moisture, or simple jostling can cause one of the many connections in an Ethernet network to loosen or come completely out. When that happens, the computer, hub, or other device will stop communicating with the network until the problem is fixed. For this reason, it's a good idea to make sure that all Ethernet cable connections are out where you can get at them, rather than buried in a wall or hidden in the attic.

Connecting Coaxial

In the past, connecting Ethernet cables, cards, and hubs has been a major hassle. To attach a connector to a Thicknet Ethernet cable, for instance, required an installer to drill a hole into the cable cover, attach something called a *vampire tap*, and then tighten it all down. All this had to be done at no less than 1.6 meters from the next-closest connector, or the network might not work properly. *BNC connectors*, small cable connectors resembling the ones used to hook TVs up to cable television outlets, are used for Thinnet coax networks and are only somewhat easier to use than Thicknet vampire taps. Today it's much simpler. Almost all home networkers will opt for cards, cables, and hubs that use the simple, reliable *RJ-45 connector* that looks like a fat telephone plug. You can buy premade cables in a variety of lengths, with RJ-45 connectors on each end, and simply plug them into the proper receptacles on your hubs.

Summing Up Ethernet

To sum up, Ethernet offers these significant features:

- Proven technology
- Broad compatibility with the most popular networking standard
- Excellent performance
- Higher installation costs and possible problems routing cables

Ethernet is an excellent choice if you don't mind running wires throughout the house, or if all the PCs to be networked are located very close to one another. If you live in a place that can't be wired easily, for instance, in a historical building, and high performance is not a critical concern, then one of the "no new wires" networks described below may be a better choice.

Sizing Up Phoneline

Phoneline networks have received considerable attention from computer manufacturers and others who want to push home networking. Phoneline networks can be easy to install, offer adequate performance, and are relatively inexpensive. There are a number of factors to consider regarding using a phoneline-networking technology as the basis for your home network. You will want to consider these factors when determining whether to use this home networking method.

Phoneline Pros

Phoneline has the best performance of the no new wires technologies (which include powerline and wireless) and is also low-cost and widely available. Its data transfer rate will soon match regular Ethernet's 10Mbps, and since it requires no wires, it will always be cheaper than cabled Ethernet.

Phoneline Uses Existing Wiring

There's no doubt, the big advantage to phoneline networking is that it uses existing wiring. Many homes are wired adequately for phones, so that every PC you want on the network can reach a suitable phone jack. For those devices that don't reach a jack, it's easier and cheaper to wire a room for a new phone jack than it is to install a wired network.

Phoneline is Relatively Inexpensive

You can already buy a PC with built-in phoneline networking, including software, for an extra fee of less than $50. In a year or two, phoneline networking could cost half that per station. Because it needs no new wiring, it's likely to be less costly than cabled Ethernet. And because phoneline NICs are cheaper than wireless network transceivers, it will probably also underprice wireless networks as well.

Phoneline Standards Are Relatively Stable

With big players like Compaq and Intel lining up behind phoneline, it's a safe bet that standards are going to be set and maintained. The creation and maintenance of standards protect you against having an outmoded network that can't be upgraded or work with newer, better network equipment. This has proven important in the Ethernet world, where many manufacturers have come out with dual-speed hubs and NICs to allow networkers to upgrade when and how they choose, instead of having to replace the entire network at once. Standards also encourage competition, as equipment manufacturers feel confident that whatever they make will work with the competition.

 NOTE If you recall the flap over 56K modem standards, you know how important standards can be. Two competing standards for transmitting data over phone lines at a nominal 56Kbps were offered by rival firms. Neither took off, especially when it was announced that a joint standard would be agreed upon. The result was that, for almost a year, modem sales almost completely dried up and consumers were reluctant to purchase a costly, cutting-edge modem that might prove incompatible with the new standard. In the end, most 56K modems could be upgraded to the new V.90 standard when it was released. When that happened, by the way, modem sales took off, prices dropped very low, and nearly anybody could afford a faster modem.

Phoneline Cons

Phoneline limitations include the fact that all the PCs on the network have to be connected to a phoneline that has the same number. If you have several lines in your house, not all of which are connected to each phone jack, this could be a problem.

 NOTE You can tell whether PCs are on the same phoneline by attaching a telephone to each of the phone jacks you intend to use in your network. Then dial the phone number using another phone on a different line. If all the phones ring, they're all on the same line.

Another issue is how you will use the phoneline network with high-speed Internet connections, especially cable modems. In order to connect a PC to both the phoneline network and the cable modem interface card, you will probably need two NICs in the PC. For a variety of reasons, including the fact that every PC has a limited number of expansion slots, *Interrupt Request lines* or IRQS, and other resources, this can be tricky.

 NOTE Allowing one PC to connect to more than one network is called *multihoming*. It is a moderately advanced networking trick, and most professional network managers prefer a one-PC/one-network approach as being simpler and more reliable. However, home networkers often find themselves attempting it in order to connect their PCs to both a home network and a cable modem, which operates as a connection to another network.

Phoneline Performance Lags Behind Ethernet

Recently, phoneline network vendors have introduced products that claim to offer speeds competitive with regular Ethernet, which runs at 10Mbps. It remains to be seen how well these will work in practice, however. And meanwhile, 100Mbps Fast Ethernet is becoming more widespread, inexpensive, and standardized than ever. Given the limitations of most home phone wiring, it's probably safe to say that phoneline networks are always going to have lower performance than networks set up with cabling designed for high-speed data communications.

Phoneline Requires Handy Phone Jacks

The average home has only two to four phone jacks. So although odds are that at least one of your PCs is close to a phoneline (so you can reach the Internet through a modem) it's not as likely that a phone jack will be handy to all your PCs. That's especially true if your PC is located in a bedroom, garage, work room, or anyplace besides the kitchen, living room, master bedroom, or home office. You can always run a wire to a phone jack in another room, but if you're going to do that, you might as well run Ethernet cables (unless, of course, you also need a phoneline in that room.)

Summing Up Phoneline

Phoneline has powerful forces pushing it as the home network of choice. Its main advantages include the following:

- It requires no new wires, assuming your home is well-supplied with telephone jacks.

- Standardization is progressing rapidly, with some computer makers already offering it built-in.

- Performance is second only to Ethernet.

- It's inexpensive and relatively easy to set up.

If having the utmost in performance isn't essential, or if you simply can't bring yourself to drill holes in walls and ceilings to wire a network, phoneline networking is a convenient, cost-effective approach for many home networkers.

Sizing Up Powerline

Powerline networking is nearly as old as Ethernet, but of late has been changing as rapidly as the much newer phoneline networking technology. It has important advantages when it comes to ease of set up and convenience, especially regarding the number of points where you can access the network. In this section, you will learn about some of the advantages and disadvantages to this type of networking.

Powerline Pros

Phoneline is one of the "no new wires" technologies, which makes it attractive to many home networkers off the bat. It's also unusually easy to get one up and running. And the power grid, which provides the wires used to connect computers on powerline networks, is simply the biggest, most ubiquitous network of them all. That's a powerful combination that makes this technology worth a close look.

Powerline Uses Existing Wiring

When it comes to the sheer number of outlets or ways to reach existing wires, nothing comes close to powerline. Almost all homes have far more A/C outlets than they do phone jacks. Newer homes commonly have one or more power outlets on almost every interior wall, including bathrooms, kitchens, and garages. Many have exterior power outlets as well, providing the opportunity to access your network from the back porch or patio.

Powerline Networks are Easy to Install

Powerline networks can be very simple to set up, as easy as plugging a connector into your PC's parallel port, plugging the adapter on the end of the cable into a power outlet, and running the setup program. It's hard for any other networking technology to claim to be that easy. Many phoneline networks, for instance, require you to open the back of your PC to install an adapter card. The powerline networking process is also far easier than installing an Ethernet cabled network. If ease of installation is a paramount consideration, then powerline might be the best choice for you.

Powerline Cons

Although it sounds ideal to be able to simply plug your PC into a nearby A/C outlet and start networking, in practice, powerline networking is often not that perfect. Before you settle on a powerline network, consider the issues of standardization, performance, reliability, and security.

Powerline Networking Lacks Standardization

So far, no single standard has emerged as dominant in the powerline networking arena. Most of the companies offering powerline networks use their own approach for signaling, each of which is incompatible with the others. They include the Ethernet-like *peer-to-peer CSMA/CD* approaches of Intellon and Echelon. CSMA/CD stands for Carrier Sense Multiple Access with Collision Detection, and is a means of detecting data transmission errors caused when multiple computers on a network try to transmit simultaneously. It's the network access method used by Ethernet networks. Intelogis uses a client-server approach that places the bulk of the processing load on a PC server, reducing the cost of the rest of the network gear.

This lack of interoperability means, among other things, that if you purchase a powerline networking system, you'll probably have to buy any expansion or add-on equipment from the same vendor. In addition, the lack of a dominant standard means should you later wish to switch to a new, faster powerline networking technology, you may have to scrap your whole network to do so. Other technologies, such as Ethernet, have preserved backward compatibility with older approaches by using such tools as dual-speed hubs and NICs.

Powerline Performance Lags

Powerline networking is catching up fast to the other networking technologies when it comes to speed. But, so far, the 10Mbps standard of both regular Ethernet and the newer phoneline networks, has only been demonstrated for powerline networks in lab tests. While you may not need 10Mbps now, it's a safe bet that, before long, you'll find some use for any extra bandwidth you get. Meanwhile, of course, the other networking approaches—Ethernet in particular—aren't standing still. Fast Ethernet's 100Mbps transfer rate is something powerline networkers can't even dream about at the moment.

Noise Plagues Powerline Networks

Powerlines were designed for transmitting power, of course, not data. This creates a number of problems when it comes to using those wires for computer networks. Among them are high levels of noise, distortion, and attenuation (the tendency of the signal to fade out quickly).

Noise enters powerlines from a variety of sources, including dimmer switches, intercoms (some of which also use the powerline to communicate), baby monitors, and electrical motors attached to the power grid. Networking vendors use various techniques to clean up their signals and protect them from noise, but so far, none are as clean as a wired Ethernet system.

Powerline Has Security Issues

When you're using a powerline network, you may be exposing yourself to higher security risks than with other networks. Powerline networks can't connect computers into a network if they have a power company transformer located between them. This usually is no problem for home installations, although it can be for businesses. But it does raise security issues because in many neighborhoods, more than one home shares a transformer. If one of your neighbors is on the same transformer, they may also share your network wiring and be able to easily snoop on your network. Powerline networks usually use data-encryption and other security techniques to control this risk.

Summing Up Powerline

Powerline may be for you if:

- You aren't overly concerned about high performance.
- You don't want to go to the trouble of pulling wires or opening PCs.
- You have lots of A/C outlets and few phone jacks.

Powerline is a promising technology with lots of useful advantages that may make it a viable way to network for many home users.

Sizing Up Wireless

Wireless is unique among networking technologies in that it allows true mobility. It's not the cheapest, nor the fastest, nor the easiest, but it does match up fairly well across the board, and it has that one major plus: no wires. Here you will learn about many of the factors you need to consider about wireless home networking before choosing this method.

Wireless Pros

Free roaming is the big advantage of wireless, and these untethered networks can also be very easy to install. With the advent of new low-cost home RF networks, they can be inexpensive as well.

Wireless Needs No Cables

Cables are both good and bad. They can carry data at faster rates than wireless networks, but they are also points of trouble. Cables can get worn, their connectors can disconnect or become loose, and a short or flaw in one of them can bring down the entire network. People trip on them, or roll their chairs on them, or place electrical transformers so near them that data flowing through the cable gets corrupted by electromagnetic interference. The fact that wireless isn't exposed to these particular risks is a good reason for many home networkers to consider it.

Furthermore, wireless may be the only logical choice in many situations. If you can't drill holes and don't have adequate phone or power wiring, which may be the case in some old buildings, it's either go wireless or go without. Similarly, if you only plan to be in your residence for a short while, but want to set up a network anyway, then wireless makes an excellent ad hoc, temporary, and exceptionally easy-to-relocate network.

Wireless Is Easy To Install

A simple peer-to-peer wireless PC network may be the easiest of all home networks to install. You simply install the transceiver cards in the PCs or, in the case of a laptop, insert a PC card into the PCMCIA slot on the side, power up the machines, run the software, and you're done.

Wireless Allows Untethered Roaming

When cellular phones first came out, the idea that you could easily and (relatively) cheaply make a phone call from just about anywhere was astonishing and powerful. In the same way, being able to check your e-mail, or transfer a file you need to a wirelessly networked computer, is highly empowering and engaging. Given the short range of most wireless networks, perhaps a cordless phone is a better analogy. But still, if you ever want to be able to develop a spreadsheet or shoot-em-up at Quake while relaxing in a backyard hammock, a wireless network may be your only way to achieve it.

Wireless Cons

If wireless is going to become the de facto standard in home networking—and some believe it will—it's going to have to overcome some significant limitations and risks. Chief among the problems is performance, followed by cost, interference, and range limitations.

Wireless Performance Is Lacking

You're not going to get the performance, in terms of data transfer rate, from a wireless network that you would get from a regular Ethernet based system, or from one of the new, higher-speed phoneline networks. Wireless is also more sensitive to interference. Placing a transceiver too close to a wall, or on a different floor from another PC, or just behind too many sheetrock walls, can cause signals to drop out. The signal can also fail if you place a transceiver too close to a transformer used by another electrical device. As a result of the signal dropping out, the workstation will fall off the network.

You can fix some of these problems by using external antennas, but that defeats some of the purpose of using easy-to-install wireless, and won't help roaming workstations. Unfortunately, there's almost no way to tell in advance whether wireless will work in your home without just trying.

Wireless Is Costly

Until recently, wireless has been prohibitively expensive for home networking. Now, however, the prices have been more than halved, and you can set up a simple two-PC network for around twice what a wired network would cost. Given the advantages of wired, this isn't much of a premium. However, if you're on a budget, or if you take into consideration the performance limits of wireless as well as the premium price, wireless may be too costly for many home networks.

Wireless Has Range Limitations

The typical home wireless network has a rated diameter of approximately 150 feet within which network transmissions can be reliably sent and received. This is going to be adequate for many non-billionaire homes, certainly, but conditions such as obstructions or sources of electromagnetic interference can reduce that range significantly.

Wireless Standards Are Still Evolving

The IEEE 802.11 standard provides a good base for wireless networking, especially for business LANs. Efforts by the Home RF Working Group to come up with a standard more suitable for home networking, have had trouble meeting expectations so far. Its initial SWAP specification for home wireless networks runs at only 800Kbps to 1.6Mbps, about half of what was expected. While this decision will allow home networking products to reach the market sooner and cost less, it's clear that SWAP is going to have to be improved before long. Meanwhile, any SWAP home wireless networks you purchase will have to be upgraded to meet the new standard when it appears.

Summing Up Wireless

To sum up, wireless offers these significant features:

- No new wires needed
- Excellent portability
- Higher equipment costs
- Higher potential for interference

Sizing Up Hybrid Wireless-Wired Networks

Hybrid wireless-wired networks offer unique advantages to people in certain situations. Matching two different technologies can be challenging, however, so you'll want to carefully consider whether a single type of network may be able to solve your particular problems. For instance, if simply adding a few more ports to your network would do the trick, you could choose to go with an all-powerline or all-phoneline network, instead of trying to mix and match a wired network with wireless.

Hybrid Wireless-Wired Pros

The fact is, the advantages of having a wired-wireless hybrid network are such that you're unlikely to have a pure wireless network for long. Eventually, you're going to want to hook up to a cable or DSL modem, or attach a printer without using a PC as a print server. When that happens you'll need some kind of bridge between the two systems, and suddenly you've gone hybrid. A more advanced two-network hybrid setup offers additional advantages, chiefly the fact that you retain the option of roaming or reaching out to otherwise inaccessible areas with the wireless portion of the network, but you can save money or improve performance by going wired on the rest.

Hybrid Wireless-Wired Cons

There's no free lunch, and the all-things-to-all-people promise of hybrid wireless-wired networks does come with a price tag. To begin with, when you connect wireless and wired networks, traffic between them will occur at the speed of the slower network, in this case most likely the wireless. In other words, the computers will not talk to each other at the faster network's speed. So you'll be unable to capture any performance advantage from the network on your workstations. In addition, any wireless network suffers from interference and cost compared to a wired-only network.

Summing Up Hybrid Wireless-Wired

A hybrid network is not for everyone, but its unique mix of access to a wired network and untethered freedom make it a solid choice for certain users. Its major features are as follows:

- Ability to roam with laptops, while using desktops in a wired network
- Ability to interconnect with modems, printers, and other non-PC devices
- Sometimes challenging technical difficulties of interfacing two networks

Making a Smart Choice

There's nothing irreversible about choosing the kind of the network you will install in your home. You can always remove the NICs, yank the wires out of your walls if necessary, and try something else if you decide you've made a mistake. Then again, it would be better to do it right the first time. Making a good decision involves a simple six-step process:

1. First, decide what your needs are. For instance, is performance paramount for that bandwidth-gobbling game you love to play online?

2. Next, match your needs against the features of the various home network approaches. For instance, if you want to network to a PC that's in the workshop across a cement driveway, wireless is a good match.

3. Consider carefully the most appropriate locations for network nodes. You wouldn't want to choose a phoneline network only to find out that a key location, such as a child's bedroom, doesn't have a phone outlet.

4. Think about what type of devices you will want to attach to your network. You may be pretty disappointed if you plan to hook your video camera up to a powerline network, because this technology's low-end performance is poorly suited to the bandwidth needs of transmitting video over a network.

5. Before you make your decision, look into the future. Will your network be adequate in a few year's time? What is the likely upgrade path?

6. Finally, shop around—a topic covered in detail in Chapter 11, "Shopping for Network Equipment,"—to make sure you're getting the best service, support, and price available.

Summary

Even though there is a profile of the typical home networker, the needs of those networkers, the physical layout of the spaces in which they're networking, and their budgets are varied. Fortunately, one of the four networking methods, Ethernet, Phoneline, Powerline, Wireless, and Hybrid Wireless-Wired will meet your networking needs.

What's Next

The next chapter delves specifically and deeply into Ethernet networks, from selecting and installing network interface cards, to pulling cable and configuring software.

PART

I

Networking Now

PART II

Networking Nuts and Bolts

LEARN TO:

- **Install Ethernet Networks**

- **Install Phoneline Networks**

- **Install Powerline Networks**

- **Install Wireless Networks**

- **Install Hybrid Wireless-Wired Networks**

- **Install Cross-Platform Networks**

- **Shop for Network Equipment**

CHAPTER <u>6</u>

Ethernet Networks

Overview

thernet is the most popular kind of network, for business and home networkers alike. Ethernet networks can give home networkers advantages over other types of networks in several areas. These include:

Performance   Fast Ethernet at 100 megabits per second is far and away the fastest option for home networkers.

Standardization   Ethernet has been a popular computer networking technology for more than 20 years. Therefore, it's easy to find Ethernet components such as network adapters and hubs that work together.

Upgradability   You can grow an Ethernet network without much difficulty, from two to 100 or more computers.

Reliability   As a result of Ethernet's advanced age, the bugs have mostly been worked out of it, so your Ethernet network is likely to be up and running more than some other types.

Cost   Despite the cost of running cable, Ethernet is considerably less expensive than some other types of networks, especially wireless, and comparable to the others, especially when you consider the price-performance ratio.

In this chapter you will learn how to plan, select equipment for, and install an Ethernet network in your home.

Selecting Your Equipment

One result of the fact that Ethernet has been around a long time is that there are lots of choices to make when it comes to selecting equipment for your home Ethernet network. Many options exist for products made by various vendors, using different types of connectors and cables, and offering various speeds. You also must choose what type of adapter card you will use—generally either PCI or ISA—as well as the type of hub or concentrator you will use.

What Speed of Ethernet? 10BaseT or 100BaseT?

One of the first decisions you'll have to make in choosing your Ethernet setup is the speed at which you want your home network to run. This will dictate whether you go with 10BaseT (Ethernet) or 100BaseT (Fast Ethernet). Fortunately, it's actually an easy decision, almost no decision at all.

The difference is performance and, to a much less significant extent, price. 10BaseT Ethernet network equipment operates at 10Mbps. That will be enough for many home users, but if you move or copy a lot of big graphics files, play bandwidth-intensive games, or perhaps even videoconference, more speed would come in handy. That speed is ordered up in orders of magnitude. 100BaseT operates at a sizzling 100Mbps.

It used to be that Fast Ethernet gear was a lot more expensive than regular Ethernet. But today, the difference in cost is minimal. Best of all, the most recently manufactured Ethernet equipment is, in fact, dual-speed 10/100, set up to operate in either networking environment. Dual-speed network interface cards cost just a few dollars more, though there will be a slightly bigger price difference in the network hub you use.

The only time you want to go with the slower, older Ethernet standard is if you have access to some used networking equipment, perhaps rendered obsolete by an upgrade to your employer's network. Otherwise, it's Fast Ethernet all the way.

PART

II

Networking
Nuts and Bolts

There's a good chance that selecting Ethernet gear will seem more complicated than it is, however. While there truly is an amazing plethora of technologies and options in Ethernet, few of them are suitable for home networks. For instance, business network planners may agonize over whether to use thicknet coaxial cable, thinnet coaxial, shielded twisted pair, unshielded twisted pair or fiber optics. That decision is practically made for you, as a home networker, without you needing to think it over all that much. Twisted-pair cabling, specifically the type known as Category 5 unshielded twisted-pair, is far and away the most likely cable solution for a home networker, with thin coax coming in second.

As you look over the choices for home networking using Ethernet technology, try to keep in mind that you should generally choose the simplest, cheapest, easiest networking solution available. That way, you'll spend less time worrying about what you're going to do, and more time enjoying your network.

Home Networking Kits

Several manufacturers produce kits with all the hardware and software you need to create your home Ethernet network. These are just what they sound like: one-box solutions to home networking needs. Typically, they contain a pair of network adapters, a small hub, and a pair of cables to hook it all together, plus any special drivers or other software that's required. You can generally rely on the promise that this is all you will need to get your network up and running. When you examine the components list—and the small box they come in—it is likely to seem that Ethernet networking isn't so complicated after all.

Ethernet kits are very popular among home networkers. But not quite as ubiquitous as you'll find in other types of networks, such as powerline or wireless. One reason is because there are many manufacturers of virtually every type of Ethernet hardware. You'll have no problem finding nearly any kind of Ethernet gadget you need, up to and including *brouters* that cost hundreds of thousands of dollars (if you can imagine ever needing or wanting such a thing for your home network).

 WARNING If there's one area where kits fall down, it tends to be on the cabling. Kits typically come with a pair of 25-foot cables. There's not likely to be anything wrong with these cables as far as their quality. But it is often a stretch—perhaps literally—to connect two computers that may be in far corners of even a modest-sized house with a measly 25 feet of cable. This is especially true if you're running cables up through the attic and down to the PCs. Check your installation plan before buying a kit, to make sure the cables will fit. If you can't find a kit that comes with a long enough cable, add a price for buying a longer cable into your networking budget.

Pros

When businesses are creating networks, they rarely know exactly how many PCs they're trying to tie together, or even exactly where those PCs will be. In any event, the numbers are usually so large and fluctuating that equipment procurers for business networks buy their networking in bulk and a la carte. The situation is completely different when you're networking your home.

Instead of hundreds or thousands of PCs, you've mostly likely got two or perhaps three. Instead of a vague notion of where in a large building or campus these PCs and other devices will be, you probably have pretty well-designated locations for your computers—one in the family room and one in the home office, for example. In these circumstances, a home networking kit makes good sense.

Convenience

One-stop shopping is the hallmark appeal of a kit. You don't have to go driving all over town to find the network adapter cards, hub, and cables to make your Ethernet network, only to find out that some key item is unavailable. If you've ever gone shopping for the ingredients for, say, a cake and chased all over a grocery store assembling everything in your basket except for one thing, which the store was out of, then you know how frustrating it can be. (You also know why cake mixes are so popular.) That won't happen with a kit. They contain everything you need to get your network up and running.

WARNING   Almost all kits will provide you with enough equipment to set up a workable network. But don't think that, just because you bought a kit, you have everything your network will ever need. Phoneline kits, for instance, are likely to come without a duplex telephone jack. You'll need one of these gadgets if you plan to hook more than one device into the phoneline you're using for networking. Fortunately, duplex phone jacks, which are also used for connecting answering machines, faxes, and other devices to the phone system, are inexpensive and easy to come by.

Compatibility

When you buy a kit, you greatly reduce the odds of winding up with two pieces of networking equipment that don't work together. Because Ethernet has been around for many years and is a very widely adopted standard, compatibility isn't as big an issue with Ethernet as with some of the other networking technologies, especially wireless. At this writing, the wireless networking vendors' products are pretty much incompatible with everyone else's. Standardization will likely improve that. However, the current situation makes a wireless networking kit an easy choice, compared to trying to assemble all that you'll need a la carte.

Cost

A typical Ethernet kit to connect two PCs, like the one in Figure 6.1, can be had for under $100.00 at this writing. That includes two 10/100 NICs, a pair of 25-foot cables, and a four-port, 10/100 hub, along with the required drivers, and some accessory software such as games and Internet sharing programs. This is less than the price you will pay to buy all those items separately, but not a great deal less. Unlike, say, office suite software, where the savings when you buy the whole kit and caboodle is enormous compared to individually purchasing them, network kits are primarily about convenience, not cost savings.

FIGURE 6.1

Contents of a typical Ethernet home networking kit include two network adapter cards, a four-port hub and power supply, two Category 5 connecting cables and a diskette of software.

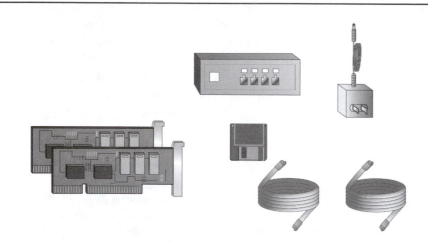

Cost might be an issue if you want to connect a number of computers that is different from what the kit-maker had in mind. For instance, most kits are set up to connect two computers, with one hub, two cables, and two NICs. If you have three computers, you probably will be better off not buying two kits, obviously. In this case, you might want to buy one kit and an extra NIC and cable. Or, perhaps you'd do better buying everything separately. With the current costs of NICs hovering around $20.00, it's not an earthshaking issue, but it is something to consider. (These are low cost NICs and they usually work fine for home networks. Expensive NICs used in servers can exceed $350.00 in cost.)

Cons

With all the advantages of kits, you still see pieces of networking equipment offered a la carte by network gear manufacturers. So clearly, there must be at least some reason why not everybody goes with a kit. And, in fact, kits are not perfect—at least they may not be for you. The big question about a kit is whether it fits your precise needs. If it does, great. If not, you may be better off buying a la carte.

In the end, the decision about whether or not to go with a kit may come down to numbers. If you have just two PCs to connect, and they're not more than 25 feet apart, you may do very well with a kit. If you have three or more computers, or you have a long run of cable between one or more of them, you aren't likely to be able to find a kit that will do just what you want. If you buy a kit in such a situation, you're likely to buy stuff you don't want. This is similar to purchasing a new computer that has a hard disk loaded with a lot of software you aren't going to use. Unless you have an alternative place to use, or enough closet space to store, the extra cables and NICs left over from a kit that didn't fit your network, you're better off buying the network equipment individually.

Networking on the Road

You may still miss your familiar mattress when you're having to travel on business, but you could have access to a network compatible with your home network, thanks to a new trend toward *visitor-based networks* or VBNs. According to a study by International Data Corporation, VBNs are popping up at hotels, airports, convention centers, and other places frequented by mobile PC users. One of the main benefits they offer traveling networkers is the chance to use high-speed shared Internet access instead of the analog dial-up connection through one of the office telephone systems known as a PBX, or *private branch exchange*. Right now, PBXs are typically the only option for mobile users looking to connect from hotels and other public locations. Dial-up is slow, and, due to PBX firewalls or other security measures, may be unworkable for tasks such as surfing the Internet or even handling e-mail. A visitor-based network gives you the same fast, familiar way of reaching cyberspace that you're used to at home.

If there's no VBN where you travel, or if you have already tried a visitor-based network with unimpressive results, be patient. Analysts foresee rapid growth in the concept and eventually near-ubiquitous VBNs offering inexpensive, simple, high-performance speed networking. VBNs may someday be offered on sites as disparate as college campuses, corporate branch offices, and even office and apartment complexes. Meanwhile, look for a VBN coming soon to a hotel or airport near you.

Summary of Networking Kits

Networking kits offer a strong combination of convenience, compatibility, and cost advantages over networks assembled from individual pieces. And a kit is probably a good choice for many home networks. Exceptions include networks that will connect odd or large numbers of computers, as well as networks that span large distances, since kits are set up to handle the typical network that is smaller and connects fewer computers.

Selecting Cable Types

If you ever crack a professional networker's manual, you'll probably be struck by the charts and tables and extensive discussions of all the cable choices that can be made for an Ethernet network. There's little sense, however, in a home networker spending much time learning about fiber-optic or thicknet coaxial cable. That's not because you're not smart enough to understand the choices, nor is it because the experts are trying to keep all the good stuff for themselves. It's just that you're not likely to be hooking up a couple of hundred workstations to a mainframe computer, nor connecting several LANs into an internetwork hundreds of miles across.

For what home networkers are doing, the overwhelming majority of times the choice will be the cable known as *unshielded twisted pair* or UTP, as shown in Figure 6.2. To most people, this looks like fat telephone wire. And, in essence, it is the same technology that is used to transmit telephone conversations. However, computer data is less tolerant of things like static and interference, and a network is operating at a far higher speed than a home telephone system. So UTP network cable has to be rated data-quality. The best quality suitable for home networks is Category 5, which will allow you to go all the way up to 100Mbps Fast Ethernet. There is also Category 3 cable, which is used in many telephone networks and older Ethernet networks. Cat 3 is rated at speeds of up to 16Mbps.

FIGURE 6.2

An example of unshielded twisted-pair cable

 NOTE For this book's own, somewhat abbreviated, table of Ethernet cable options, see Chapter 4, "Home Networking Technologies."

Cat 5, as it's known, isn't the only possible choice for a home network. Coaxial cable, or thinnet, in the jargon of the networking community, may be a winner for you if you can get it cheaply.

10/100BaseT Cable

One of the problems with networking, as with so many other fields, both technical and non-technical, is not so much that it's loaded with jargon. It's partly that the jargon so often has meanings that are counter-intuitive. Remember learning in Chapter 1 that Ethernet networks have a logical bus topology even though many have a star physical topology? Another problem, which is the one at hand, is that a lot of times the jargon has two meanings, or one item may be referred to by two different names in the professional argot. That's the case with what we've been referring to as Cat 5 UTP cable.

In many catalogs and stores, Cat 5 cable is referred to as 10/100BaseT cable. It's the same cable in either case, it just has a different name. Whether you're an old pro or a nervous newbie, and whether you call it Cat 5 or 10/100BaseT, this cable is used in Ethernet networks based on the star physical topology.

 NOTE   See Chapter 1, "Understanding Computer Networks," for more on network topologies.

The first part of the name refers to the fact that it can operate at up to the 100Mbps speed of Fast Ethernet, as well as, naturally, the slower 10Mbps of regular Ethernet. The second part, BaseT, shows that this is this is unshielded twisted pair cable. You may occasionally run across cable referred to as 802.3 or 802.3u cable. These names are derived from the specifications set by the IEEE standards-setting organization. They refer to, respectively, 10BaseT cable and 100BaseT cable.

 NOTE   See Chapter 4, "Home Networking Technologies," for a deeper discussion of both the IEEE standards and the various types of cables available for home networking.

Pros

One of the most attractive features of Category 5 10/100BaseT cable is that is easy to handle. It is much thinner than coaxial cable, especially the bulky variety known as thicknet, which you will rarely run across outside of an older network, or one tying workstations to a mainframe. It is even thinner than so-called thinnet, or 10Base2 coaxial cable. Being thin is important when you're trying to snake a cable through tiny drill holes, or between building studs.

Because Cat 5 is *unshielded* twisted pair cable, it lacks the layer of foil insulation found in most *shielded twisted pair* or STP cable. This foil insulation makes STP much stiffer than UTP cable, again easing installation. And Cat 5 is far more flexible compared to coaxial cables of any variety.

Cost   Category 5 cables are not particularly expensive. You can buy a 25-foot *patch cable*, complete with connectors and suitable for connecting two PCs or a PC and a hub, for about what it costs to take yourself and a friend out to a fast food restaurant for lunch. That is, around $7. You can pay more for cables that are certified reliable and, of course, for longer pre-made cables. These costs can add up if you envision lots of long cable runs, or if you are connecting a large number of workstations, as many businesses do. But as a general rule, Cat 5 cable cost is not a major concern for home networks.

Availability   Cat 5 cable is about as widely available as any networking equipment. You can buy it in just about any good-sized computer store, as well as from online retailers, some electronics superstores, and even building supply centers (because an increasing number of new homes are being wired with Category 5 cables).

Much Cat 5 cable is sold in the form of so-called patch cables, which are relatively short (usually 25 feet or shorter) networking cables that already have connectors on both ends. If you need a longer cable run, you may have to buy a special crimping tool to attach the RJ-45 cables to the ends of the cable. The advantage of this is that you can cut the cable to the exact length you require, eliminating wasteful purchases, as well as the nuisance of finding somewhere to store coils of unused cable.

Cons

If you use Cat 5 cable, you must use a star physical network, which means you must have a hub. For many home networkers, this is the indicated configuration anyway. However, sometimes you might prefer to use a bus physical topology without a hub. This won't be an option with Cat 5 cabling.

WARNING   Category 5 cable lets you create a generally superior network than Category 3, but the conditions have to be right for it to work right. In particular, that means the whole network has to use Category 5, including the cables, connectors, NICs, hubs, and other equipment, or performance will suffer. In addition, you must use a star physical network with a hub.

Summing Up 10/100BaseT

There are some good reasons why the dominant network cable today is 10/100BaseT. If you are concerned about performance, cost, availability, reliability, and ease of construction in your Ethernet network, odds are you will go with Cat 5, and be glad you did.

Coaxial Cable

Coaxial cable for computer networking is the same stuff used to connect cable television boxes to television sets. It has been used for computer networking for many years but is now being shoved aside by twisted-pair wiring, especially as performance of UTP wiring improves. That's because performance is not coaxial cable's strong suit.

If you're not familiar with it, coaxial cable is about a thick as a pencil and is covered with a jacket of insulation on the outside, as shown in Figure 6.3. Just beneath that is a layer of foil or braided aluminum that works as a shield. Another layer of insulation is next. Finally, you have the conductor wire, which is where all the action takes place. The rest of the coaxial cable is for insulation and protection for the inner conductor and the signals that travel over it.

FIGURE 6.3

An example of coaxial cable showing, outside to inside, the outer insulating layer, the braided aluminum conductor, the inner insulation and, last but not least, the inner conductor

Pros

One of the major advantages of coaxial cable for networking is that you can create a simple Ethernet network to connect computers without having a hub. You simply add network adapters to the computers, plug them together with the coaxial, and you have a simple computer network admirably suited to joining two computers in the same room.

TIP Another nice thing about coax is that, unlike any other type of cable, you may have a chance of getting it for free. Many businesses are ripping out their coax networks to replace them with higher-performance UTP cabling. This coaxial cable then becomes essentially scrap. If your company upgrades, ask about whether you can obtain some of this cabling. The cost savings may be worth a performance hit.

Although it's rarely an issue in a home network, a signal on a coaxial cable doesn't degrade as rapidly as it does on UTP. This allows for a greater distance between workstations—about 185 meters or 600 feet, compared to 100 meters or somewhat more than 300 feet with UTP.

 TIP If you are running Windows 98 on both computers, you can set up a *hubless network* of sorts without even using network adapters. You simply install on both computers the Direct Cable Connection software that comes with Windows 98 and connect the PCs through their printer or serial ports using a cross-over cable. This network won't be nearly as fast or flexible as one with network adapters, but it will work for file transfer.

Cons

If speed is your main concern, then coaxial is probably not your cable. That's because the design of coaxial cable limits its top data transmission speed to 10Mbps. That's as fast as regular Ethernet, of course, but is much slower than the 100Mbps speed of 100BaseT Fast Ethernet network cable.

Installation is another problem with coaxial. Because the cable is thicker and stiffer, it's harder to manage. You'll have more trouble getting it around sharp corners and through holes. Another concern that is especially relevant for the home is that coaxial is more unsightly. If you've ever had a repairman from your local cable TV company out to install, move, or add an outlet, you may have wound up with black or white coaxial cable snaking around the corner between ceiling and wall all over your house. Unless you like this look, or you've grown so accustomed to it that it doesn't matter, be forewarned that coaxial cable doesn't go with many decorating schemes.

Coaxial cable connectors are another issue. While you'll need only RJ-45 connectors for a typical Cat 5 cable installation, coax often requires three types. The basic coax connector is called a BNC. This is a round metal fastener that is crimped on to the end of the cable, and connected to another cable or device with a twist. It is used to tie coaxial cables together via a barrel connector, as well as to connect to T-connectors, as shown in Figure 6.4. T-connectors are, naturally, shaped like a T. The BNC at the end of the downstroke of the T is plugged into a computer's network adapter card. The BNCs on the ends of the coaxial cable are plugged into the T's arms.

FIGURE 6.4

The BNC connector and T connectors are commonly used to connect coaxial cables to each other and to computers.

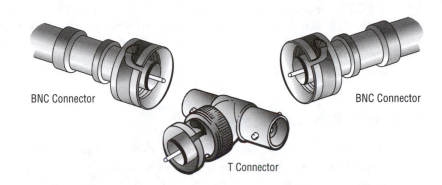

BNC Connector

T Connector

BNC Connector

As a final, moderate disadvantage, coaxial cables also require special caps, called terminators, on the ends of the cables to prevent signals from reflecting off the ends of the cable and bouncing around the network, thereby creating unnecessary traffic and data collisions. While these terminators are neither expensive nor difficult to install, you do have to be careful to match the terminator's electrical resistance to that of the cable. (Thinnet uses RG-58 A/U cable and requires a 50 ohm terminator.) Terminators also create another opportunity for problems to develop, if they fail to function properly due to becoming loose or getting knocked off.

Summing Up Coaxial

Although it comes with significant performance limitations and installation hassles, the opportunity to create a hubless network will keep coaxial as a viable cable choice for some cash-strapped home networkers.

Network Adapter Cards

Your *network adapter cards*, also known as network interface cards or NICs, are your PCs' gateways to the network. There are many considerations to mull over when it comes to selecting the network adapter cards for your home network. The decisions you make here will affect your network's future performance and convenience, as well as the selections you make for cable, hubs, and other components of your network.

PART

II

Networking
Nuts and Bolts

The reverse is also true, as the cable and hubs you go with will, in some cases, virtually dictate what NIC you use, sometimes down to the manufacturer and model number. And you'll frequently also have to address the type of expansion slots or, in some cases, input-output ports, you have available in your PC.

 NOTE If you're planning a network other than cabled Ethernet, such as wireless, phoneline, or powerline, you'll find information on equipment selection and installation in Chapter 7, "Phoneline Networks," Chapter 8, "Powerline Networks," and Chapter 9, "Wireless Networks."

Selecting Ethernet Cards

NIC selection is a bigger issue for Ethernet networks than for other types, because Ethernet cards come in a plethora of varieties. Indeed, some adapters are not cards at all, but expansion boxes that plug into your computer's parallel or USB ports. The main considerations you have to take into account when selecting cards for an Ethernet network are your network's intended speed of operation, the type of cable you'll use, the type of connectors you'll use, and the kind of open expansion slots and input-output ports available on your PC.

Your network's intended speed of operation comes down to either 10Mbps or 100Mbps Fast Ethernet, or both. Your best choice of a NIC for Ethernet today is most likely a card supporting Fast Ethernet. These cards aren't much more expensive than regular Ethernet cards, certainly not when you consider they offer 10 times the performance of regular Ethernet.

As previously mentioned, most of the Ethernet cards being sold for networking today are dual-speed 10/100 NICs. These don't cost much, if any, more than single-speed cards designed for either 10Mbps or 100Mbps Ethernet networks. Their primary market is for people building new networks with wiring that doesn't support the faster speed, or for people who are adding new computers or upgrading their network in a stepwise fashion and don't want to commit to moving everything up to the Fast Ethernet standard.

Most likely, the 100Mbps standard will take over the market before long, especially for new installations, and the slower regular Ethernet cards will become even less widely available. If you have a network cabled with coaxial cable or the slower Category 3 unshielded twisted pair wiring, there's no sense in paying more to purchase 100Mbps cards, of course, since these cables won't support that kind of speed. So, unless 100Mbps cards continue to come with support for slower regular Ethernet, there may still be a market for 10Mbps regular NICs in the future. For now, however, even if you are willing to have a slower network, it's a good idea to go with the slightly more expensive 10/100BaseT network cards, to preserve flexibility and an upgrade path for the future.

The type of cable you'll use, probably either Cat 5 UTP or coaxial cable, will also influence your choice of cards. To begin with, a coaxial cable network will run at a maximum of 10Mbps per second. So if you have a coax cable network, there's no need to obtain Fast Ethernet cards, unless, of course, you are considering upgrading at a later date to faster Cat 5 UTP cabling. This might be the case, for instance, if you are only interested in connecting two computers, both located in the same room, but may later want to hook up additional machines located some distance apart.

 TIP If you're running Windows 98 on your network, try to get a card that has a driver conforming to the *Network Driver Interface Specification* version 4.1. NDIS 4.1 lets you run in faster 32-bit protected mode, allows you to install and remove network driver software without rebooting your computer, and provides other advantages.

The type of connectors you'll use are another issue. Your options here include RJ-45 for Cat 5 or BNC for coaxial or, again, both. Many Ethernet cards come in dual-port configurations. These cards have two or, sometimes, more types of ports on them. Typically, this includes an RJ-45 port, a coaxial cable port for a coaxial cable T-connector, and perhaps an *Attachment Unit Interface* or AUI (pronounced "owie") port, as shown in Figure 6.5. These cards provide you with a networker's best friend, flexibility, because they don't lock you into one networking scheme. Rather, they allow for easy, inexpensive upgrades when the need arises.

FIGURE 6.5

Dual-port network adapter cards usually have RJ-45 jacks for Cat 5 UTP cables, BNC ports for coaxial cable, and an AUI port, as shown on the back of this typical dual-port card.

RJ-45 port   AUI port   BNC/coaxial port

The type of open expansion slots you have in your PCs, usually either ISA (*Industry Standard Architecture*) or PCI (*Peripheral Component Interconnect*), is another crucial concern. As a general rule, you'll want cards for PCI slots. For one thing, PCI slots are faster than ISA slots. The ISA card moves data back and forth across your PC's motherboard at a speed of 8MHz. PCI operates at 33 or 66MHz. PCI cards are also easier to install, because they often take advantage of the "plug and play" auto-setup features of modern operating systems, including Windows 95 and Windows 98. That's not a trivial concern.

Also, as noted, some adapters do not use an expansion slot, connecting instead to your PC by a Universal Serial Bus (USB) port, as shown in Figure 6.6. You may want to go this way if you have no or few expansion slots available, if you want to have the option to easily remove the network adapter—perhaps to transfer it to another computer—or if you simply don't want to go to the trouble of opening your computer's case to install an adapter card into an internal expansion slot.

FIGURE 6.6

Some network adapters plug into the USB ports on newer computers.

USB Interface

NIC with RJ-45 adapter

In addition to these issues, you may also get into other concerns, such as whether you already have access to some network cards, or hubs of a particular variety. While Ethernet technology is particularly well standardized and reliable compared to other types of networks, networking equipment in general can be cranky. Sometimes it's best to try to build a network that doesn't use a broad range of different cards of various ages and from diverse manufacturers. When your network uses only one kind of card, it may simplify troubleshooting network problems, not to mention avoiding them.

Summing Up Network Adapter Cards

The selection of a network adapter card is an important decision, integrally related to your entire approach to networking. In large part, the NICs you pick will be preselected by your choice of a networking technology, by your performance needs, and by the way you plan to expand or refine your network in the future. For the most part, however, dual-speed 10/100BaseT PCI network adapter cards will be the most popular choice for most home Ethernet networkers.

Selecting Hubs and Concentrators

Hubs are placed more or less in the middle of all star networks, but hubs don't necessarily play as dominant a role as their location suggests. Home networks can be built around so-called *passive hubs*, which are basic-level devices that simply provide electrical connections for cables between personal computers, modems, and other devices on the network. Passive hubs are easy to spot; they have no power supply. An *active hub*—one of its distinguishing features is an A/C adapter and a place to plug in a power cord—is a better bet for your home network. You can get one for under $100, or even as part of a kit with NICs, cables, and software, that sells for around that price, and active hubs add a lot in the way of functionality.

As shown in Figure 6.7, a typical active hub will have four RJ-45 ports, an array of LED indicator lights that show such things as the status of the ports, and a power input. There may also be an uplink port, in which you can plug another hub, thereby increasing the number of ports available.

PART

II

Networking
Nuts and Bolts

FIGURE 6.7

A typical active hub suitable for home networks with ports for four RJ-45 connectors, indicator lights, and a power input

The LED status lights on an active hub can be helpful for diagnosing network problems. For instance, if a PC is plugged in but the status light over its port is not lit, you can assume there's a problem there. But there is more to an active hub than power and lights. An active hub can repeat and regenerate the signal it receives from the workstations on the network, improving the effective performance of your network. All in all, it's a small price to pay for a significant advantage.

NOTE Many companies build their networks around *managed hubs*, which are more intelligent (and costly) than active hubs. Managed hubs, also called *intelligent hubs*, have network management features that can help you monitor your network for performance and problems, and troubleshoot solutions when they arise.

Multihub Networks

One question that may occur to you while you're selecting a hub for your network is: What happens if my network grows and I run out of ports? Or, what if I want to have two terminals farther apart than the 300 feet that a Cat 5 Ethernet network permits? Those are both good questions, but the answer to both is: Not to worry. By plugging additional hubs into the uplink port on a hub, as shown in Figure 6.8, you can create a network that is very much larger than the one you started with. In fact, the upper limit for an Ethernet network is a total of 1,024 workstations or other types of nodes.

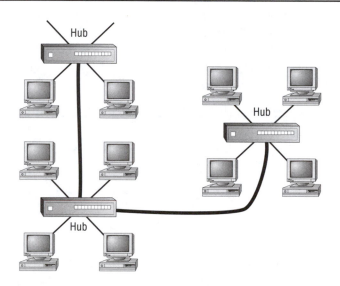

FIGURE 6.8

By plugging additional hubs into the uplink port on a hub, you can create a network much larger than the one you started with.

 TIP The expandability of hubbed Ethernet networks gives you a chance to save some money while preserving your options. Hubs with 8 or 16 or more ports are commonly quite a bit more expensive than the 4- or 5-port models used in most home networks. That's because the larger hubs often have more intelligence and management capability to go with their greater capacity. If you don't need network management features, you may find it cheaper to purchase two small hubs and link them together. So there's little sense in spending the extra money to buy a bigger hub until you actually need it.

Hubless Networks

As you'll recall from the discussion of coaxial cable's advantages earlier in this chapter, you can create a simple computer network, with a bus physical topology, using coaxial cable without a hub. Assuming both computers have NICs (with coaxial connectors), all you'll need is a short piece of coaxial cable, a couple of T-connectors and BNCs, and a pair of suitable terminators.

FIGURE 6.9

It doesn't get much simpler than this. A hub-less bus network created by connecting two NIC-equipped PCs with coaxial cable and T-connectors.

Terminator   Terminator

Hubless networks, as shown in Figure 6.9, are efficient at using cable, since you don't have to run a cable from each workstation back to the hub. However, bus networks in general suffer from vulnerability to going down completely any time there is a problem with the network connection of any terminal on the network. These problems can range from a loose T-connector to a chair rolling over a cable to an ill-timed attempt to logoff by an unwary user. Troubleshooting bus networks can be a significant headache.

 TIP   Although hubless bus networks are generally associated with coaxial cable, you can get unshielded twisted pair cables configured to do the same job. These are called *crossover cables*, and are essentially cables wired to perform the work of a hub in simple networks.

Thin Clients: PCs on a Diet

According to a famous saying, you can never be too rich or too thin. An emerging trend toward so-called *thin clients* in networking equipment may help to keep home networkers richer. A thin client is another name for a stripped-down PC consisting of no more than a monitor, keyboard, CPU, video processor, and an Ethernet network interface.

Continued ▯▶

PART

II

Networking
Nuts and Bolts

CONTINUED

There's no hard drive and only minimal memory. Software to access the network is stored on read-only memory.

Software applications, such as games, word processors, or other programs in a thin-client scenario, run on a central PC server. No processing is done by the thin client, other than passing on keystrokes and decoding graphics from the network. However, the programs look and feel like applications running locally.

Thin client computers cost about half as much as comparable PCs. But the real savings is in ongoing maintenance and support. According to one study, thin clients cost about half as much as PCs to operate each and every year, including all costs of technical support and training.

Why doesn't everybody already have a thin client? For one thing, thin clients only work on client-server networks; most home networks are peer-to-peer networks. Also, thin clients are designed for Windows NT networks; most home networks run on the bundled networking capability in Windows 98 or Windows 95. But with their advantages, thin clients may soon be more popular among home networkers than their fat, PC predecessors.

Selecting Network Software

Just as a computer is useless without software to make it run, you are not going to do much networking until you have network software up and running. In years past, this has meant significant trouble and expense. Today, however, networking software is extremely common and can be installed, configured, and used by a moderately experienced and determined computer user.

 NOTE For more information on how to use network software, see Part 3, "Network Software."

Windows 95/98

For most of us, selecting networking software is a breeze. We already have perfectly suitable software installed on our machines; we just haven't been using it. Microsoft has included peer-to-peer networking capability on all Windows machines since Windows 95 came out. Even before that, Windows for Workgroups, a more business-oriented edition of the operating system, had networking capabilities.

 NOTE For more information on using Windows 95/98's peer-to-peer networking capabilities, see Chapter 12, "Windows 95/98."

While Windows networking may be free, it's far from without value. For instance, the Windows Network Neighborhood tool provides an easy and intuitive way for Windows users to access other computers and devices on their network. You may have even seen the Windows Network Neighborhood as an icon on your own computer's desktop screen, without realizing what it was for. Look for the icon on your computer screen, and take a look at the ease with which you can access devices on your network from this software, as seen in Figure 6.10.

PART

II

Networking
Nuts and Bolts

FIGURE 6.10

Windows Network Neighborhood provides friendly and easy access to other computers on your network.

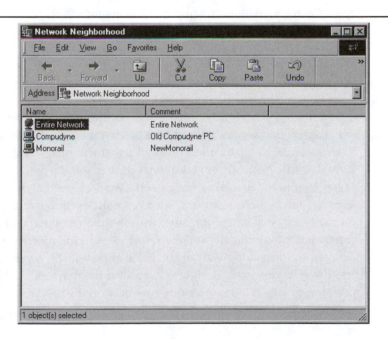

TIP Windows 98 added some important new networking features to the world's most popular operating system. Some of the most important advances came in the second edition of Windows 98, which added software for sharing high-speed Internet connections.

Windows 2000

Windows 2000 is more than the next edition of Windows, following up on Windows 95 and Windows 98. It's actually a completely different operating system modeled on Windows NT. In fact, Windows 2000 was originally called Windows NT 5.0. It's been in beta release for a year or so now, as Microsoft ironed out all the bugs. However, it's still far from certain how Windows 2000 will work as a networking operating system and otherwise. One of the reasons is that Microsoft plans to market different versions of Windows 2000 to individuals and giant corporations. It remains to be seen how well consumers will take to what has been a business-oriented program.

Some people may not like certain things about Windows 2000, including its lack of support for old DOS-based programs and the fact that it is a very large, complex program. For instance, the minimum system requirement for Windows 2000 Professional is a Pentium 166 with 32MB RAM (64MB is recommended), and up to 4GB of disk space, with a 650MB minimum disk space required.

However, Windows 2000 should offer some significant advantages over Windows 98. Windows NT is more network-oriented, offering additional network tools and management features that Windows 98 just doesn't have. Also, Windows NT and, by extension, Windows 2000, is a more reliable and stable operating system than Windows 98 has been.

Windows 2000 gets rid of the separate locations for Dial-Up Networking and Ethernet adapters that confused Windows 98 networkers. Both are placed together in a Network and Dial-Up Connections folder that will make it easy to add a modem, a Virtual Private Network, or an Ethernet connection.

Another new networking feature is the Active Directory, which acts as a database of users, resources such as printers, and even policies for operating the network. While primarily aimed at large companies with thousands of users, Active Directory will be a convenience for home networkers. Other networking niceties include built-in Internet connection sharing—already included as part of the Windows 98 second edition—and the ability to wake sleeping systems over the network. All in all, Windows 2000 promises to take Windows' already-easy networking to a new, simpler, and more rewarding level.

NOTE For more information on Windows 2000, see Chapter 14, "Other Network Operating Systems."

Macintosh NOS

Apple Macintoshes have shipped with Apple's proprietary AppleTalk network software ever since the first Mac came out in 1984. Connecting an Apple Macintosh to most types of networks, including those using Windows PCs running on Ethernet, is possible using third-party software such as PC MACLAN from Miramar Systems. You can learn more about that at `www.miramarsys.com`.

Today, reflecting the advances in networking in recent years, Apple's latest Mac OS version 8.6 offers some significant advances in the speed of copying large files over the network, moving data to removable disks, and using high-bandwidth network and Internet access more efficiently. Apple's Sherlock technology, which is part of the OS, lets you query multiple Internet search engines simultaneously, again reflecting the increasing importance of networking and the Internet in computing today.

The Apple OS lets you navigate your network easily and seamlessly by using folders to reach out to information and resources stored anywhere on the network. Macs using the latest operating system can also use the high-speed IEEE 1394 Firewire interface, an Apple invention that offers data transfer rates of up to 400Mbps, as well as more conventional USB ports, without requiring any additional software.

If you're a dedicated Apple user, then selecting the Apple networking software to run your home network is an easy decision. Even if you are a PC fan, the ease of use, long track record of reliability, and tight integration of networking features with the Apple operating system, make it a plausible choice. You can learn more about networking with the Apple operating system at `www.apple.com`.

 NOTE For more information about using Macintosh NOS, see Chapter 13, "Networking with Macintosh Computers."

Apple AirPort Wireless Networking

Apple teamed with Lucent Technologies to design a wireless radio frequency networking approach called AirPort. It offers Apple users the ability to share resources, including high-speed Internet access, with the characteristic Apple ease of operation and reliablity, but without wires and at a spritely data rate of 11Mbps. Also unlike the proprietary—and slow—AppleTalk network, AirPort is based on the IEEE 802.11, so several other companies can make products that fit into, and enhance, an AirPort network. Pricing is somewhat steeper than low-end wireless, at $99 for a card and $299 for the AirPort Base Station, but Apple's foray into wireless, standardized networking still looks promising.

Linux

A few years ago, the idea that a public domain operating system would lure users from the commercially packaged operating systems like Windows was laughable. Today, however, the Linux operating system is winning fans at a rapid clip, based in part on its powerful networking features. Many businesses, for instance, elect to run their Web sites with Apache, another free public domain program for managing Web servers, that runs in the Linux environment.

The Linux Story

The basic Linux operating system was written by Linus Torvalds, then a student at the University of Helsinki in Finland. Torvalds was interested in compact versions of the venerable, academically oriented Unix operating system, and decided to develop his own system that was better than anything he could find. In 1994, Torvalds finished the first complete release of Linux as version 1.0. Then in January 1999, he released version 2.2. This version (and the others since) reflected the efforts of the many developers around the world who contributed ideas and code to the finished product.

The Linux source code is available to anyone for free, and anyone is welcome to modify it in any way they see fit, although Torvalds oversees which features make it into the official Linux releases. That makes Linux a strong contrast to the approach taken by commercial operating software vendors, who guard their source code jealously and forbid

Continued ▶

CONTINUED

anyone to tamper with it. The ability of countless software developers to tinker with the program has, moreover, allowed Linux to add new features at a rapid pace. Linux runs on more types of hardware than Windows NT, for instance. In addition, Linux is so forgiving of hardware limitations, that it will operate well even on older machines, such as 486-based computers that the average Windows user would have scrapped years ago.

Not all Linux distributions are free, however. There are many editions of Linux, such as Red Hat and Caldera, for which their individual developers charge a fee. At present, there are an estimated 8 million users of Linux worldwide, and a large number of software applications for business and pleasure that work in the Linux environment. You can learn more about Linux at many sites, including Red Hat's at `www.redhat.com` and Caldera's at `www.caldera.com`.

PART

II

Unix is a popular operating system for very large networks, such as in the university world where it has long had a stronghold. At home, however, Unix and Linux are currently largely confined to the computer hobbyist world. Will that change? Unix and Linux have some powerful advantages when it comes to managing files over networks, which is a large part of their appeal. However, the fragmented nature of the Unix/Linux world, without a single leader such as Microsoft Corporation with its vision of Windows, probably means that Linux will never take over the computing world, as much as its devoted fans would wish it to.

 TIP The Unix operating system is famously tricky to install and configure, and the same can be said of Linux. This is especially true of the versions available for free over the Internet. A big advantage of purchasing one of the packaged editions of Linux is that the software comes on a CD-ROM, often with manuals and various utilities that make the installation and setup much easier. If you want to try networking with Linux, it's a good idea to lay out the modest investment for one of the packaged distributions.

 NOTE For more information on Linux, see Chapter 14, "Other Networking Operating Systems."

Networking Nuts and Bolts

Novell NetWare

The Novell NetWare network operating system was for years a standard for business networks. However, the popularity of this networking stalwart has declined in recent years, as the various flavors of Windows networking, including Windows NT, have increased their own user base among networkers. Also affecting NetWare has been the growth in popularity of Linux and Unix networking.

Will NetWare go away eventually? With its huge installed base, that's not likely to happen any time soon. However, NetWare isn't going to make much of a dent in the burgeoning home networking market. The software is expensive and complicated and offers home users few advantages over the more readily available networking software out there.

 NOTE For more information on NetWare, see Chapter 14, "Other Network Operating Systems."

Installing Your Network

Networking your home might be described as the triathlon, or perhaps the pentathlon, among computing endeavors. First, you have to fire up your intellectual engines to select and design your network. Next, you exert your financial muscles to purchase the gear. Finally, you'll need to limber up your actual body muscles to pull the cable where it needs to be and get everything hooked up and working.

Just think about that image of the computer geek couch potato as you're squirming through a crawl space to deliver a cable to a waiting PC, or leaping as high as you can to snatch at an RJ-45 connector dangling from a hole punched in the ceiling. Nobody's saying computer networking is a great weight loss activity, but neither is it always an ideal avocation for the truly indolent. With that in mind, here is what it will take to install all the equipment you have just selected.

Routing Cables

The shortest route between two points is, in computer networking as elsewhere, a straight line. Unfortunately, you don't often get to choose that option when you're routing cables for a network. Instead, as shown in Figure 6.11, you're likely to find yourself snaking cables through such rarely visited and unlikely locales as the crawl space beneath your house, far corners of the attic, and high on outside walls. Effectively and efficiently installing a cable setup for a network requires some planning, a moderate amount of sweat, and determination to see it through. When you're finished, it will likely provide you with one of the best networks you could hope for. But there's no denying it: The cabling portion of a cabled Ethernet network is at once one of the most critical and challenging parts of the entire project.

FIGURE 6.11

There are many options to route your network cables, including runs through attics, basements, across inside walls, and over exterior walls.

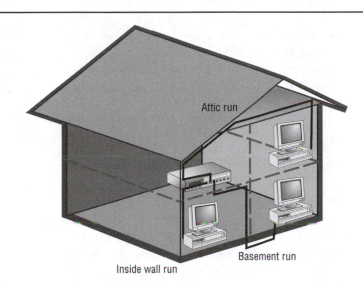

Planning Your Cabling Scheme

Cabling a home for a network is a little like painting one; some of the most important work gets done before you ever swing a brush. You need to prepare a surface for painting carefully by filling and sanding. Similarly, you need to plan a network cable system by studying your home's architecture and cable routing possibilities. Before you start poking holes in any walls, you also need to take into account special considerations, such as the historical status of your building and the proximity of neighbors.

 NOTE   A careful cable scheme starts with a look at the blueprints for your home. You will want to check for ventilation ducts, plumbing pipes, and electrical and telephone wiring. Also, keep your eye open for opportunities afforded by gaps between wall studs, ceiling rafters, and floor joists to make long, easy runs of cable between different parts of the house.

Architectural Concerns   When you install cables for a network, it's going to become part of your house. So you need to think a little bit about architectural issues before you decide where to put all those wires. For instance, if you have a beautiful Spanish stucco home, it's going to look a little odd to have all those black or blue or white cables crawling all over the exterior. Thinking a little bit about how you'll route your cables can provide you with ideas about how to hide cables and preserve your home's architectural integrity.

 WARNING   Many communities prohibit wire showing on exterior walls, much as others don't allow television aerials, satellite dishes, and boats parked in the front yard. It's not a bad idea to check your deed and your homeowner's association regulations for restrictive covenants that might nix any wires running outside of your home. If you live in such a community (and if the rules are enforced) you may want to consider an interior wiring plan, using some sort of wall-colored or otherwise camouflaged cables, or perhaps asking for a special dispensation to wire up your network.

Historical Buildings   If you are fortunate enough to live in a home with historical value, you'll have to take extra care when installing a network. In fact, if your home is a recognized landmark or is in an official historical district, odds are you will be required to observe some restrictions when it comes to stringing wires. For instance, you may be prohibited from exposing wires where they can be seen from the street. You will certainly wish to take care about drilling into a building that may be quite elderly. Building standards many years ago were not quite what they are today, and homes, while not necessarily any weaker, may not be as amenable as modern dwellings to being poked full of holes.

Basements   Few homes have the drop ceilings of commercial buildings that ease the task of cabling networks in businesses. However, in a pinch, a basement can go a long way toward simplifying the job of stringing wires. Frequently, if you are wiring up two computers that are on the ground floor, you can simply punch a small hole in the floor near each one, and run the wire over the ceiling of the basement in between. If the basement below is a finished one, there is likely to be space between the basement ceiling and the ground floor where you can fit the wires. The cable will also be easier to reach, in the event the network goes down and you suspect a problem in the cable. About the only thing a basement won't help you with, in fact, is wiring a computer on a second floor.

Attics   Attics can serve a similar function to basements as conduits for network cables. One caveat here: If your home's heating and air-conditioning ducts run through this space, you may want to use a special *plenum-rated* grade of cable. The plenum is the space above the drop ceilings in business environments, and plenum-rated cable is designed not to produce any of the toxic gas that polyvinyl chloride-coated cable can emit in the event of a fire. Local building codes may require plenum-rated cable in spaces where smoke from a burning cable could enter the ventilation system.

New Homes under Construction   The ideal situation for a network cabling crew is a home under construction. With no drywall or plaster to obstruct the cable runs, you can easily and unobtrusively put in as many outlets for networked computers as you wish. A house pre-wired for networking isn't as unusual as you may think. Four thousand homes near Houston were constructed with IBM's Home Director network hubs built into their closets or garages. At an 8,000-home development outside of Scottsdale, Arizona, houses come pre-wired for networks with cables and outlets in the walls. In this Arizona subdivision, a fiber-optic network links together the homes, providing data services, digital television, and digital phone service. An even bigger project near Las Vegas, totaling some 50,000 homes, will also include networks as a standard feature. Computer networks, according to some experts, will be as common in 21st century new construction as telephone and electrical wiring became in the nineteenth and twentieth centuries.

Multidwelling Buildings   Apartment complexes, condominiums, and co-ops present special issues for networkers. The dwellings, especially the older ones, are likely to have the same sturdy concrete-and-steel structure that bedevils people retrofitting older office buildings for networks, but without the drop ceilings to serve as ad hoc cable conduits. In addition, the proximity and number of neighbors means that you are more likely to run into interference problems, both of the electromagnetic variety, from electrical appliances and the like, and the personal variety, from nosy neighbors who want to know what all the drilling and pounding is about.

Rental tenants must take care to inspect their leases before installing cables. While most landlords don't mind a few picture hanger holes, an extensive network wiring scheme might involve ventilating a few more walls than even the most tolerant landlord will allow. For this reason, many rental tenants install what are in effect temporary networks, with wires laid loosely on the floor or tacked up near the ceiling, hidden behind bookcases, and covered with carpets. Although this is a little more unsightly— and prone to producing damaged cables from people stepping on them—it's also a lot easier to remove and pack up than a more permanent cable installation.

Maximum Cable Lengths   Rarely will you run up against the maximum allowable cable runs when installing an Ethernet home network. Unless your house is several thousand square feet in size, has many different floor levels, is located in widely separated buildings, or requires tracing cable through some truly Byzantine routes, it's unlikely you'll use even a significant majority of the 300 feet you have between workstations and hubs.

Having said that, the distance limitation on Ethernet is a real one. A data signal degrades pretty rapidly on a UTP cable and, if you get the workstations too far from the hub, they won't be able to detect the other workstations' messages. Because Ethernet uses a collision detection access scheme, workstations will too frequently try to send data over the network at the same time. This will lead too an excessive number of data collisions, an overburdened network, and poor performance.

If your network looks like it's going to be over the limit for UTP, you may want to consider going with coaxial, which provides for longer runs between workstations, or use linked hubs to expand your UTP network's reach.

Drilling Holes   It's pretty hard to design an effective multi-room network cable setup without breaking a few eggs or, in this case, poking a few holes. All those cables have to go somewhere and, all to frequently, there's a wall standing between where they are and where you want them to go.

You don't need a lot of fancy equipment to drill holes for a network; remember what you're after are holes, not big bills from the tool store. However, what you will need, you'll definitely need. The tools required to create the pathway for a network cable include:

- A drill—a real, electric drill, not a battery-powered screwdriver. The corded drills are generally more powerful and less expensive than their battery-powered cousins, at the expense of some loss of mobility.

- At least one drill bit that is larger than the largest connector you'll be passing through the holes.

 WARNING   Be sure you don't force connectors through holes that are too small for them to pass through easily. These connectors are the weakest links in the cable and prime spots for trouble even without being manhandled. A special concern with RJ-45 connectors is that you don't fit them through an even slightly tight hole if there's a possibility you might want to pull them back out. Those little plastic clips on there can make removal well-nigh impossible without completely wrecking the connector and/or cable.

- A drill bit extender, which is simply a long piece of steel that lets you drill much deeper holes than with an ordinary bit. This can be very useful if you have to go through any unusually thick walls, pierce holes in hard-to-reach places, or drill at a sharp angle.
- A cable fish, which is a long piece of metal tape that you can use to reach through holes, attach the cable to, and pull it through. Without a fish, many cable jobs would be practically undoable.

Along with some other common household tools such as a ladder, hammer, some tape, cable ties, and u-shaped tacks for securing the cable, that should do you.

 TIP You might not have to budget these tools into your networking allowance. Some local libraries have tool-lending branches, where you can check out everything you will need for the low cost of a library card.

You'll also have to apply a moderate number of rules for installing cable, such as:
- Never crimp the cable around sharp curves. This can damage the conductor or insulation and produce poor performance or outright network failure.
- Be careful not to pound staples or u-shaped tacks into the cladding on the cable. Obtain staples large enough to fit the cable without damaging it.

Connecting Cables   Connections are weak points. If you are hiring someone to do your cable job for you, they are also expensive points, since many contractors charge by the number of connections as well as by feet of cable installed. Either way, you don't want to have more connections than you need.

One way to avoid having excessive connections is to buy more cable than you'll need. Pulling cable too tight places the conductors as well as the connectors under tension, and a connector under tension is a connector that will fail early and often. Also consider that, sometime in the future, you may well decide that a few feet to the left is really where you wanted that terminal in the family room. Coil a few loops of cable here and there in out-of-the-way places along your cable runs, just to provide yourself with some flexibility. If you don't have the extra cable available, you'll have to splice on another piece, which is more trouble and prone to lead to still more trouble.

PART

II

Networking
Nuts and Bolts

TIP It's a good idea to place labels on cables to identify what they're connecting. Do this as you install them. You may recall perfectly well, just after finishing the installation, that the cable jacked into Port 1 goes to the home office PC, while Port 2 connects the kids' computer. But after a year or so, that knowledge may have evaporated. Typically, this happens about the time this information becomes critical, when you're attempting to trouble-shoot a network problem. This is truly one of those cases where the faintest ink is better than the best memory.

Connecting 10BaseT Ideally, you'll purchase 10BaseT cable that is of the proper length and already equipped with RJ-45 connectors. It's a good idea to do this even if you have to special-order it. If you don't do this, you can connect two lengths of Category 5 cable using couplers that look like larger versions of the connectors used to join two phone cords into one longer one. A cable spliced together in this manner is generally not as reliable as one with connectors only on the ends. Moreover, even though you can buy RJ-45 connectors loose in bags, and cable in economy-sized spools of 1,000 feet, you will still need a special crimping tool. The savings is generally not enough, in a small network installation, to make all of this cable splicing worth your while.

Connecting Coax Connecting coaxial to make longer cables is no big deal. A coaxial cable is really just a bunch of shorter cables attached to each other by T-connectors anyway. You can use T-connectors for joining two short cables, just as you do to connect the cables to a PC; or you can use barrel connectors designed for just that purpose.

 TIP While you're minimizing the number of connections in your network cable, think about trying to place the connections you do make in places that are convenient to get to in case of trouble. The worst case scenario has a problem popping up in a connector that is buried in a wall with no way to reach it.

Installing and Configuring Cards

Installing and configuring networking cards used to be considered the part of networking where they separated the goats from the sheep, men from the boys, and the geeks from the cool dudes. Nowadays, with the prevalence of plug-and-play computer systems out there, setting up network cards is no longer quite so harrowing. However, plug and play doesn't always work. And if you're installing cards on an older system, you may still wind up going to the mat with your network card in an old-fashioned struggle to parse out your PC's resources in a manner that will allow your expansion devices to coexist amicably. Step one is to identify your expansion slots and make sure you get the proper cards.

Identifying Your Expansion Slots   It's essential that you properly identify the type of expansion slots you have available in your PC so that you'll get a card that will work. For most computers, there are two choices: either PCI or ISA slots. Figure 6.12 shows the difference between the two.

FIGURE 6.12

You can tell whether you have available PCI or ISA slots by looking for distinguishing features such as the color and length of the slot, and placement of the divider.

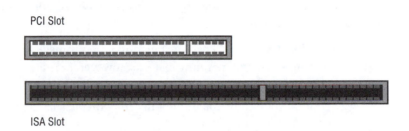

PCI Slot

ISA Slot

PART

II

Networking
Nuts and Bolts

PCI, or *Peripheral Component Interconnect*, cards can be used in most new PCs. PCI slots are shorter than ISA slots and have the divider closer to the end. They are usually white plastic. ISA, or *Industry Standard Architecture*, cards can be used in expansion slots in almost any PC, including older machines. You can spot an ISA card slot by its color, usually black, and by the plastic divider that splits the slot about a third of the way from one end.

PCMCIA   *PCMCIA* cards, or PC cards as they're often referred to, use the expansion slots on portable computers or on some desktop computers. These cards are easy to identify. They fit in the slot on the side of a notebook computer and no where else. They are also usually easy to install. You simply push the card into the slot, and the machine should recognize and install drivers for the card, or prompt you to insert a diskette containing the appropriate driver. You can even do this while the computer is running. Have your Windows CD or set of diskettes handy when you do this, since you may be asked to insert the Windows disk to load the card driver.

Built-in NICs   More and more PCs are coming with networking capability built in. This is similar to what has happened in the past with video cards and I/O adapters: What once required an add-on card in an expansion slot is now allotted space right on the motherboard. At first, this sounds like an unbeatable idea. No installation needed, and you're practically guaranteed that the NIC will work in your computer, since it was designed precisely for that system. However, if you look at the evolution of the video adapter market, you'll see that motherboard-mounted video adapters have never come to totally dominate the field. Why?

There are a number of reasons why built-in NICs, like built-in video adapters, aren't for everybody. One reason is that the network adapter may not work properly with the other networking gear you've installed for a variety of reasons. If that happens, you may have to go out and buy and install an add-on NIC anyway. Another reason is that as standards evolve and performance improves, you may want to upgrade your network adapter. Again, you'll be going back to the add-on route.

If you're buying a new PC and there is an option to have a built-in NIC onboard, consider the possible outcomes before making your decision. It's not always the best idea to go with a built-in NIC.

Installing PCI Cards PCI card installation varies somewhat by the card manufacturer and the system you're running it on. However, here are the basics:

1. Turn off the computer and unplug its electrical cord from the wall.

2. Ground yourself by touching something metal, such as a file cabinet or the steel chassis of the computer.

3. Open the computer case. Depending on your computer model and maker, this may require you to remove screws at the back of the computer and slide the whole case open, open any catches at the sides and flip up the top, or perform various other maneuvers.

4. Locate the slot where you intend to install the NIC.

5. Adjacent to the NIC slot is a metal plate that covers a hole in the back of the computer. Remove the screw that attaches this metal end plate.

6. Pull out the end plate.

7. Handling the NIC only by the edges, insert it into the slot and press it down firmly until it seats completely.

8. Insert the screw that you removed from the end plate covering the hole (from step 5) into the end plate and tighten it.

9. Carefully close the case, making sure not to pinch or tangle any loose wires.

Configuring PCI Cards Most PCI cards should work with Plug and Play, meaning the computer operating system will do the heavy lifting on the installation. This means when you startup Windows, you'll get a message saying a new device has been found and the Add New Hardware Wizard will start. Follow the instructions to add your network card.

TIP Before you install a card that will have to be manually configured, print out a System Summary Report by clicking the Print button when viewing your Device Manager. You reach Device Manager by clicking My Computer ➢ Control Panel ➢ System ➢ Device Manager tab. This summary lists all the IRQs, DMA channels, port I/O addresses, and upper memory your system is using, and will be a help when choosing resources for your new card.

Installing ISA Cards Follow the same procedure for installing ISA cards as was given for PCI hardware above. One difference, of course, will be that you'll install the card in an ISA slot, usually black, instead of the distinctive white plastic PCI slots.

Setting IRQs Setting interrupt requests using jumper switches on the card used to be the bugaboo of installing network cards, as well as a variety of other add-ons. Few cards today require setting jumpers manually, as this job is handled with software. If you wind up with one of these tricky installations, you'll need to carefully check the card's manual to determine the jumper switches' proper settings. It's important to take a lot of notes while doing this. Write down the current jumper switch settings before you start, as well as any settings you make during the process. These notes will help you retrace your steps in case you need to undo anything later.

Once you get your network adapter installed, check to make sure it's working properly. Click the Start button ➢ Settings ➢ Control Panel ➢ System. Now click the Device Manager tab and click Network Adapters on the list in the window. You want any devices listed to be free of any question marks or exclamation points, as in Figure 6.13. No marks means the card is working properly.

PART

II

Networking
Nuts and Bolts

FIGURE 6.13

When a network adapter card shows free of exclamation points and question marks in Device Manager, that means it's working properly.

USB Network Interfaces   *Universal Serial Bus interfaces* have been standard on most new PCs for the last couple of years. You can also install a USB interface as an add-on. However, you'll need the Windows 98 USB driver to use it. Installing a USB network interface is simple. USB is set up to allow hot-swapping of devices, meaning you can plug and unplug them while the machine is running. Your USB NIC should ship with a diskette with drivers. Insert the driver when requested and let the operating system copy and install the drivers.

Connecting NICs to Cables   If you've ever plugged a phone into an answering machine, you already know how to connect a Cat 5 cable to an Ethernet NIC using the RJ-45. As shown in Figure 6.14, you simply align the RJ-45 connector with the port and push it in until you hear the click that means it's connected. That's all there is to it. To remove, push down on the plastic spring and pull it out.

FIGURE 6.14

Connecting a Cat 5 cable to an Ethernet card using an RJ-45 jack is a snap.

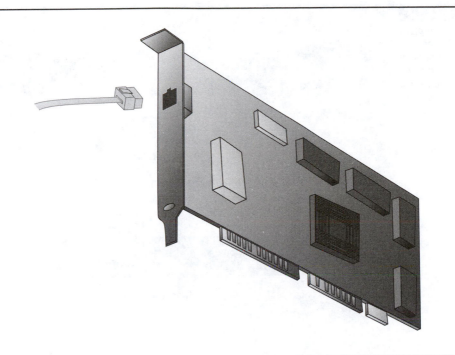

 WARNING While the RJ-45 may look like a fat RJ-11 used in phone systems, don't get them confused. Plugging an RJ-11 into a network card isn't going to work. Period.

BNC Connectors   Connecting coaxial cable to an Ethernet NIC is somewhat more complicated than using an RJ-45, but not terribly. You push the T-connector into the port on the back of the NIC and turn it gently to engage the locking pins. Then you do the same to connect the cable to both ends of the crosspiece of the T-connector. Don't forget to terminate the end of the cable with an appropriate terminator if this is the last bit of your cable. Figure 6.15 depicts these connections.

FIGURE 6.15

The T-connector plugs into the BNC connector on the back of an Ethernet card and then connects to the coaxial cable on both ends of the crosspiece.

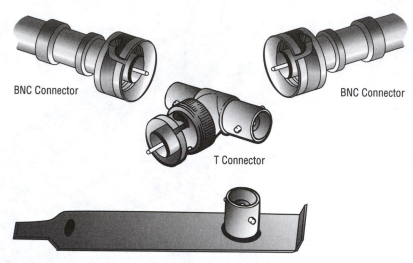

BNC Connector

BNC Connector

T Connector

Network Interface Card

Concentrators

Ethernet *concentrators*, more commonly and concisely referred to as hubs, are very little trouble to install. If you're used to the manifold hassles of setting up modems, scanners, and other personal computer peripherals, then getting a hub ready to go may come as an almost unbelievably pleasant surprise. About all you have to do is make sure you pick a location that isn't too far away from each of your devices, has access to a good power source, and allows for adequate ventilation. Otherwise, installing a concentrator is almost a no-brainer.

 NOTE   Easy installation isn't the only good news about hubs. They are the networking world's equivalent to the fire-and-forget laser-guided missiles used by jet fighters. You basically just plug them in and, other than an occasional dusting, never think about them again. The exception, of course, is if there's a problem with the network hardware. Then you'll want to look at the cables and connectors in your hub, as well as the hub itself, and other cables and connectors in the network, as part of troubleshooting your setup. For more on network troubleshooting, see Chapter 20, "Troubleshooting."

Your network doesn't have to look like the neatly balanced star diagrams in this book in order for it to work. It can have one or more arms much longer than the others and, as long as you don't exceed the maximum allowed distance between hub and workstation, you should have no problem. However, at the same time, there's no reason to place the hub too far from the nominal center of your network. A central location is good, if for no other reason than that it's the most efficient use of cable.

It can be handy to have the hub where you can see it, in case you need to check the status of any nodes by looking at the LED indicator lights. However, there's no reason why you can't place the hub in a room by itself. Most business networks do just that with their network management servers. Hubs, too, can function just fine without any oversight.

Power Needs   Most hubs are powered, meaning they require an A/C adapter and access to a power outlet. Passive hubs don't need even this, and can be placed in just about any location that is dry and protected from pets, children, and other inquisitive creatures. A small hand unplugging a critical network connection toward the end of a long file transfer or heated online game can be highly frustrating and also, should the plug be reinserted quickly and without comment, a puzzle for a network troubleshooter trying to find the problem. So put your hub where you can get to it, but where no one else is likely to tamper with it. On top of or behind your computer is fine; so is an out-of-the-way shelf.

Hubs do put out some heat, and heat, of course, is bad for electronic components. That doesn't mean you need to locate your hub in the refrigerator, but you should be sure that it has a minimal level of ventilation. It's fine to place it in a closet that rarely gets opened, in other words, but don't toss all your winter coats in a pile on top of the hub and then close the door for the summer.

Connecting a Concentrator   Connecting concentrators to the cable is exactly the same as connecting NICs to the cable. The connectors on both ends should be the same. Simply make sure you hook the right cable into the right port on the connector and see that all connections are secure.

Connecting two or more concentrators is only slightly more complicated. To connect two hubs, you have to use a special uplink port on the hubs. This port will be designated by a label on the back of the hub. It may be a dual-purpose port operating as a regular port, unless a switch is pushed to engage its uplink properties, as shown in Figure 6.16.

PART

II

Networking
Nuts and Bolts

FIGURE 6.16

The uplink port on the back of a typical home networking hub will have a label designating its special status as well as possibly a switch to engage it as an uplink port.

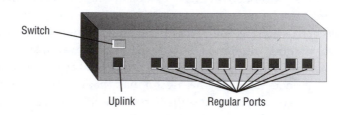

Summary

Ethernet is a solid choice for many home networks, offering unbeatable speed and reliability, and comparable costs to the other options. If you've got the time, and the place to put the cables, Ethernet should be high on your list of choices.

What's Next

Now that you've taken a look at the most popular and well-established kind of home network, it's time to examine some of the newer approaches. Chapter 7 covers phone-line networks.

CHAPTER <u>7</u>

Phoneline Networks

Overview

Phoneline networks are growing rapidly in popularity among home networkers, primarily because they are remarkably easy to install. That ease of installation is due to the fact that they use your home's existing phone system to connect devices on the network. Phoneline networks also have won many proponents among large computer and networking equipment manufacturers and vendors, who see phoneline networks as the first logical step into networking for most home computer users.

 NOTE Although we distinguish between Ethernet and phoneline networks, actually, phoneline networks use the same basic technology as Ethernet. In technical terms, phoneline networks conform to the HomePNA specification and so use IEEE 802.3 CSMA/CD (carrier sense multiple access/collision detect) for accessing the network. That's the same as Ethernet. You could describe phoneline networking as Ethernet over telephone wiring, with the main downside being lower speed, at least with the first generation phoneline networks. On the upside, with phoneline networking you don't have to install new wiring.

Understanding Phoneline Networks

Phoneline networks offer many home networkers a good compromise between performance and ease of installation. The latest releases of phoneline network equipment provide speeds that equal standard Ethernet. Theoretically, it may even be possible to achieve the 100 megabit per second data transfer rates of Fast Ethernet. Home phoneline network vendors, represented by an industry group called the Home Phoneline Networking Alliance, are committed to maintaining backward compatibility with new versions of phoneline networks. That means that if you start with a 1 megabit per second phoneline network today, you will be able to easily upgrade to the new 10 megabit per second standard. Someday, you may be able to move up to a 100 megabit per second phoneline network, all without sacrificing your existing investment.

Given comparable or nearly comparable performance, the advantage of avoiding running wires is significant. There is one caveat however: You must have a modular phone jack handy to the computers you want to network before you can take advantage of the no-new-wires convenience. If you don't have many phone jacks in your house, or if you are one of the few who don't have the modular-type RJ-11 phone jacks on your walls, you are going to have to do some wiring or jack upgrading anyway.

WARNING Before you buy a phoneline network setup, check to make sure your home phone system is wired in accordance with your network plan. It's not enough that each computer have a phone jack handy. The phone jacks must be connected to the same line. This may be an issue if, like many homeowners these days, you have more than one phoneline running into your home. It's easy to check: Just plug a phone into the outlets you want to connect to, then dial the number. If all of them ring, they're all hooked up to the same set of wires.

Selecting Your Equipment

You have less equipment to buy when you're doing phoneline networking than if you're running Category 5 cable for an Ethernet network. The list includes only:

- Network interface cards (or a PC that comes equipped with a phoneline NIC or phoneline networking built into the motherboard).
- Telephone cords to connect the NICs to the phone wall jack. (Your phoneline may come with a cord and, in any event, it should be no problem because phoneline networks run on plain telephone cables like those you can buy almost anywhere.)

The software to run your network will come with the NIC. Often, you can buy all the components, including cards and cables for connecting two or more PCs, in a kit. In the case of a new PC with built-in phoneline networking, the computer will come with cables and software.

Selecting Phoneline Networking Kits

Buying a phoneline networking kit makes sense if you're planning to connect two or more PCs that don't have built-in phoneline networking. Most kits come with cards for two PCs. You can buy individual cards for any additional PCs beyond the two that you want to connect. If you're buying a kit, look for these features:

- Network interface cards that match the slots available on your PCs. Some phoneline kits come with two PCI cards, some with two ISA cards, still others with one PCI and one ISA card.
- Sufficient phone cords, in number and length, for connecting you to the wall jack. (These aren't particularly expensive but there's no sense in buying them if you don't have to.)

- A bundle of additional software to help you make the most of the network, such as shared Internet access utilities, games, and so forth.

- A symbol or notation on the package that says the product is certified by the Home Phoneline Network. This ensures compatibility with other products and upgradability to future standards.

- A product that will work with a minimum computer system configuration that is no less powerful than the computer you plan to use.

- 24-hour, 7-day support by phone or via the Internet.

WARNING   Don't assume that a vendor offers good support just because it claims to. Support quality varies widely. It's not a bad idea to call the support number or surf the support Web site of any product you are considering buying. Look for short phone hold times, agreeable and expert technical support staff, and a broad array of searchable help files on the Web site.

Selecting Phoneline Networking Cards

Choosing phoneline networking cards is an important part of your equipment selecting process. If you do this step right, setting up your phoneline network can be remarkably easy. Done wrong, it can turn a simple task into a real knotty problem. The first big issue here is whether you choose ISA bus cards or PCI bus cards. As a general rule, you should choose PCI cards for two reasons. First, PCI cards offer superior performance. Second, but no less important, they tend to be much easier to install than their ISA cousins. Most of the time, when you install a PCI card, your computer will automatically detect and configure the card.

NOTE   For more detailed information about ISA and PCI cards, see Chapter 6, "Ethernet Networks."

If all your PCI bus slots are full, or if you have no PCI slots in a PC you want to network, you'll have to use ISA bus cards. The important thing is to decide what type of bus card you are going to use before you buy it.

Installing Your Phoneline Network

The ease of installation of a phoneline network is one of the cardinal attractions of this type of network. If you have done almost any kind of upgrade that involves opening the case of your computer, you should have little or no trouble installing a phoneline network. With luck, it's merely a matter of installing the network interface card, plugging the card into the wall phone jack, and installing the software. In general, only if you have conflicts with other system resources is it much more difficult.

 NOTE You can skip the next section, "Installing Phoneline Cards," if you're using a new PC that comes with built-in phoneline networking. You'll still want to look at the section after that, "Connecting to the Phoneline," as well as "Installing Phoneline Software."

PART

II

**Networking
Nuts and Bolts**

Installing Phoneline Cards

There's nothing necessarily difficult about installing phoneline adapter cards. If you've ever put in a new internal modem, video adapter, or other card, you know the drill. Here are the basics:

1. Turn off the computer.

2. Ground yourself by touching something metal, such as a file cabinet or the steel chassis of the computer.

3. Unplug the computer's electrical cord from the wall and open the computer case. Depending on your computer model and manufacturer, this may require you to remove screws at the back of the computer and slide the whole case open, open catches at the sides and flip up the top, or perform various other maneuvers.

4. Locate the slot in which you intend to install the NIC.

5. Adjacent to the NIC slot is a metal plate that covers a hole in the back of the computer. Remove the screw that attaches this metal end plate.

6. Pull out the end plate.

7. Handling the NIC only by the edges, insert it into the slot and press it down firmly until it seats completely.

8. Insert the screw that you removed from the end plate covering the hole (from step 5) into the end plate and tighten it.

9. Carefully close the case, making sure not to pinch or tangle any loose wires.

NOTE For more detailed information about installing network adapter cards, see Chapter 6, "Ethernet Networks."

FIGURE 7.1

A typical phoneline network interface card

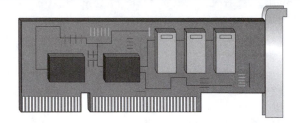

Not all phoneline networking cards are alike, although they generally look similar to Figure 7.1. Your card may, for instance, require that it be installed in a PCI Bus Mastering slot, as opposed to a PCI Bus Slave slot. You'll need to refer to your computer's documentation to determine which type of slot you have.

 NOTE In addition to network adapters you install inside the PC, Intel's AnyPoint home networking lets you opt for phoneline adapters that simply plug into the parallel port on the back of your computer. This saves you the trouble of opening the computer. More options are probably coming. At this writing, you can already buy Ethernet adapters that plug into the Universal Serial Bus connectors on the back of a PC, although no one yet has come up with a similar USB adapter for phoneline networking.

Connecting to the Phoneline

Phoneline network adapter cards connect to the network wiring by plugging regular phone jacks into the phone outlet on the wall, as in Figure 7.2. That's really about all there is to it. You can use phone cable of any length, provided it has the standard RJ-11 connector on both ends.

PART

II

Networking
Nuts and Bolts

FIGURE 7.2

Connecting a PC to a phoneline network is as simple as plugging in a telephone or answering machine.

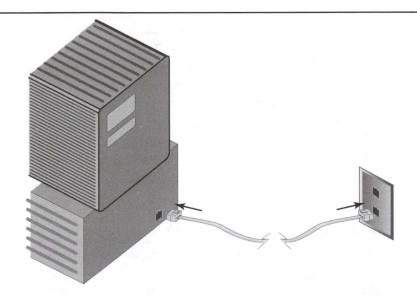

Phoneline networks are different in several ways from networks that are specifically wired for computers. For one thing, they use different wires, which, until recently, were not considered of sufficient quality to meet the more rigorous requirements of transmitting data. For another, they are likely to have all kinds of things hooked up to them, in addition to computers and computer peripherals. The wiring diagram for a typical phoneline network is called a random tree diagram, as shown in Figure 7.3.

FIGURE 7.3

A phoneline network is structured as a random tree.

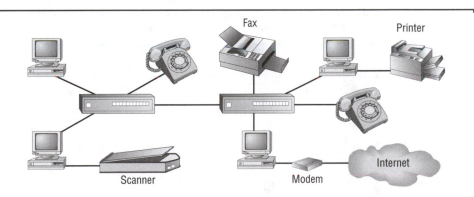

The random tree network structure posed a lot of difficulties for phoneline network equipment designers. In addition to coping with all these devices, they had to deal with other complications as well. For example, voltages on the line tend to change every time someone picks up a phone; the Federal Communications Commission restricts signals sent out on the phone system; and signals fade as they ricochet around this chaotic wiring scheme. More recently, improvements in the quality of signal-processing semiconductors, coupled with reductions in semiconductor costs, have made phoneline networking possible. In combination with these advances, the clever use of data coding techniques developed by a company called Tut Systems now makes phoneline networking not only possible, but desirable. Tut Systems' HomeRun technology underlies the popular phoneline networking technologies on the market today.

Installing Phoneline Software

Although Windows 95 and 98 come with software for peer-to-peer networking, these operating systems don't have a clue about what to do with a phoneline network. So the software you need for your phoneline network adapter will come with the NIC. This will consist of *drivers*, which are software instructions the PC needs to be able to operate the adapter. Most likely, this software will come on a CD-ROM or, possibly, a floppy disk.

 TIP After you get your driver installed, check out the Web site of the company that made the phoneline card you're using. Frequently, during the several months that typically elapse between the time they shipped the card from the factory and the time you install it, an updated driver has been released. This new driver may fix a bug, improve performance, or reduce conflicts with other resources. As a general rule, you should always try to download and use the latest release of the driver for your card.

After you have installed the NIC and loaded the driver, you will want to install your software. Although Windows can't yet run the phoneline network on its own, it should prompt you to insert your disk and install the software. Not all drivers install alike, but here's the usual routine:

1. After installing your card and closing the system case, plug your system back in and turn it on.

2. Windows should notice the card and, during the bootup process, display a screen notifying you that it has found new hardware and ask you if you want to install the driver for it.

At this point, your options diverge. If Windows finds the card, you will be instructed to install the drivers as follows:

1. Follow the instructions of the Windows driver installation wizard until you get to the screen displaying a list of manufacturers.

2. Since Windows won't have a driver for the phoneline card, click the Have Disk button, as shown in Figure 7.4.

FIGURE 7.4

When Windows asks you to select the phoneline card manufacturer, click the Have Disk button.

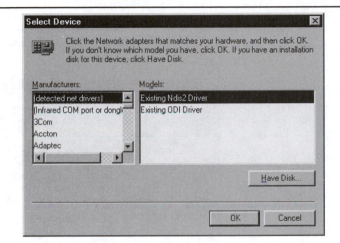

3. Insert the CD-ROM or floppy that came with the card into the appropriate drive.

4. Select the appropriate drive letter from the drop-down list shown by the installation wizard. For instance, you would select A: if you were installing a driver from a floppy disk inserted in your floppy drive A:.

5. Click OK.

6. It will take a few moments for the files to copy, then you'll be asked to restart your computer. Click Yes.

7. After Windows restarts, your adapters will be installed. You'll now need to repeat this process on the other computers you want to network.

 NOTE Some operating systems, such as Windows NT, aren't compatible with Plug and Play, so they won't recognize the card and set it up automatically. If your PC doesn't recognize and configure the card on its own, you may have to manually configure your PC's BIOS in order to resolve a conflict with IRQs or other resources. For tips about how to ease the task of manually configuring cards, see Chapter 6, "Ethernet Networks."

Plug and Play as implemented in Windows 95/98 is a big improvement over the old days of always having to manually install add-on cards. However, it doesn't always work. If Windows 95/98 doesn't notice that the new network card is there, you'll have to do it the old-fashioned way.

1. First, make sure you have the CD-ROM or diskette containing the drivers handy.

2. Choose Control Panel ➤ Network and click the Configuration tab.

3. Click the Add button, as shown in Figure 7.5, to add your new adapter.

FIGURE 7.5

Click the Add button in the Network Configuration window to begin adding your adapter.

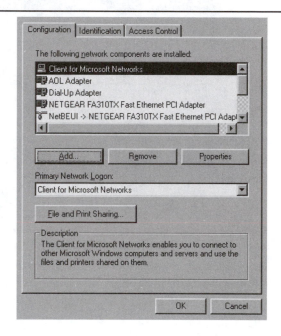

4. From the Select Network Component list, highlight Adapter and click Add.

5. At the Select Network Adapters screen, click Have Disk.

6. Insert your driver diskette, select the appropriate drive from the drop-down list in the Install from Disk window, and click OK. If Windows doesn't find the driver, click Browse and try to locate it on the driver disk yourself.

7. After the files are copied, click Yes to restart your computer.

8. After Windows restarts, your adapters should be installed. You'll now need to repeat this process on the other computers you want to network.

Using Laptops on A Phoneline Network

You can use PC card adapters to connect laptop computers to phoneline networks. But what if, like many laptop users, you carry your portable back and forth from work? Odds are excellent that your business network is a cabled Ethernet network that is incompatible with your phoneline network. You could get two PC cards, one with a phoneline adapter and one for Ethernet. But a better answer is to get one of the PC card adapters that has an RJ-45 Ethernet jack as well as two RJ-11 phoneline connectors. Then you can network at home on a phoneline network and take the notebook to the office and connect to an Ethernet LAN with the same PC card.

Upgrading from Phoneline to Ethernet

The special technology required to use existing telephone lines for computer networking means that your phoneline network-equipped PC cannot, unfortunately, also be part of another type of network, such as an Ethernet network, at the same time. However, you may be able to easily upgrade your phoneline network to a cabled Ethernet network at some future date.

Some phoneline NICs come with an Ethernet port on the back in addition to one or more RJ-11 phoneline networking jacks. This means that all you have to do to move up to 10 megabit per second Ethernet is to run the Ethernet cables, remove the phoneline jacks, and plug in the Ethernet RJ-45 jacks, and then set up the software.

 WARNING At this writing, you can't simultaneously use both the Ethernet RJ-45 and the phoneline RJ-11 on the dual-port cards available from the company that pioneered them, a firm called LinkSys. This may be an issue if you have a cable modem that requires a NIC with an Ethernet RJ-45 jack. In order to use both the cable modem and the phoneline network, you'll need to have two NICs in your machine, one for the RJ-45 going to the modem and one for the RJ-11 connection to the phoneline.

Summary

Phoneline is the most popular and fast-growing type of no-new-wires networking for the home. It's easy to install and offers good performance for the cost and trouble of setting one up. Plus, the future looks good for phoneline networking, with well-supported standards and upgrade paths promising to keep your phoneline home network up, and up to speed, for a long time to come.

What's Next

Phoneline isn't the only no-new-wires networking technology. The next chapter, "Powerline Networks," also explains how to network your home without new wires. In this case, using the existing powerline wiring in your home.

CHAPTER **8**

Powerline Networks

Overview

Networking using your home's existing electrical power wiring has some nifty advantages. Since you very likely have more power outlets than phone or Ethernet connections, a powerline network offers greater flexibility in locating your networked PCs than any option other than custom cabling. Frequently, you'll have multiple outlets in every room of the house. This means you'll have the choice not only of which rooms to put your networked PCs in, but also which wall they'll be adjacent to, all without running additional network cables.

Since powerline networks use existing wiring, of course, they are much less trouble than running new cables. Add in the fact that you don't have to open your PC's case to use popular versions of powerline networks, and overall you have a very easy installation.

 WARNING Powerline networking is usually both flexible and fault-tolerant. However, problems might occur when you move the networked PCs to different rooms. The network works fine when all the devices are in the same room, but sometimes falls apart when you relocate one of the machines. The recommended solution: Try a different power outlet in the room where you want to locate your networked PC. This seems to work in the majority of cases.

Powerline networks are also reasonably priced. At around $100 per PC, they're comparable to wireless, although more expensive than phoneline networks. When you consider the savings in cable costs, especially if you're trying to network widely separated PCs, they can be considerably less expensive than Ethernet solutions.

The only place powerline networks really fall down is in performance. It's a serious problem—much worse that it is with powerline networks. With rated data transfer rates of only 350 kilobits per second, currently available powerline networks offer marginal performance for such tasks as transferring files and sharing printers, and are really not suitable for sharing high-speed Internet access or many head-to-head multiplayer games.

 NOTE Recently, powerline networking vendors have demonstrated up to 10Mbps of reliable data transfer over ordinary residential powerlines. These designs look good: They reportedly meet Federal Communications Commission regulations and have been successfully tested in numerous real-world residential environments. The only problem with these fast powerline networks is that you can't buy them—yet. Vendors hope to have the chipsets they need ready to go in months, not years, however. And 10Mbps isn't the end. In the future, researchers envision 20Mbps and even 30Mbps powerline networking systems in the home.

Selecting Your Powerline Network Equipment

At the moment, selecting powerline networking equipment is easy: There's really only one supplier of gear designed specifically for networking personal computers via home powerlines. That company is Intelogis, of Draper, Utah, and its product is called the PassPort Plug-In Network.

 NOTE   Intelogis probably won't be the only powerline computer network gear vendor for long. There are a number of other well-established makers of powerline networking equipment. These companies, however, are oriented toward the home automation market and their approach is somewhat different. For instance, data rates that are fine for home automation are way too slow for a workable computer network. Given the size and growth of home computer networking, however, these companies can be expected to make a play to join Intelogis before long.

Selecting Powerline Kits

It's probably fortunate, given that it's the only player in the market, that Intelogis' products are generally user-friendly, work well, and are convenient. PassPort Plug-In Network comes with two PassPort plug-in adapters that go into your PC's parallel port. These are hefty, palm-sized gadgets that plug into the wall power socket. There are also the parallel cables that connect the adapters with the parallel ports for two PCs. You also get a printer adapter, a pair of powerline conditioners to plug your computers' and peripherals' power cords into, an installation guide and some Internet sharing software, and demonstration games, in addition to the networking software.

If you have more than two PCs and one printer to network, you can buy individual PassPort PC and Printer adapters as well. They're priced comparably, on a per-workstation basis, to the kits. According to Intelogis, there's no hard-and-fast restriction on the total number of PCs and printers you network, so you should have plenty of expansion capacity available.

Installing Powerline Networks

Installing an Intelogis PassPort network is not only a no-new-wires process; it's also no-screwdriver-needed. About all it involves in the way of hardware installation is plugging parallel port connectors together. You do have to perform this process in a certain order, however. Intelogis recommends you start with your printer, then connect the PCs and, finally, install the software and configure the network for printing and networking.

Connecting Your Printer

If you can plug your printer into your PC and connect its power cord, you can install a PassPort network printer adapter. Really. Here's the drill:

1. Turn the printer off. If the printer is hooked up to your PC, shut the PC down as well and disconnect it from the printer.

2. Plug the end of the printer's parallel cable that has 25 pins into the PassPort printer adapter. (This is the same end of the printer cable that you plug into your PC.)

3. Plug the PassPort Printer adapter—not the PC adapter—into any 110-volt AC electrical power outlet. (If you're not sure about the voltage of the nearest wall jack, assume it's okay. Alternating current 110-volt power is the universal standard in the U.S., with very few exceptions.)

 WARNING   Make sure you don't plug a PassPort adapter into a surge suppressor, a power strip, or the line conditioner that comes with the kit. The adapter has to go straight into a wall power plug. This goes for the printer adapter as well as the PC adapters. The adapters have built-in surge suppression in them.

4. Plug the Centronix end of your parallel cable—the end you don't plug into the PC—into your printer.

 WARNING   You must connect the PassPort PC device to your PC's parallel port last, after you have connected a Zip drive, scanner, or other parallel port device. If you have anything besides the printer connected to your PC's parallel port, the network will not work properly unless you connect the PassPort PC device last. Most parallel port devices have a pass-through port that allows other devices to have access to the parallel port, while still remaining attached to the computer. The PassPort PC device is not a pass-through device. So it should be attached to the pass-through port on these devices if you want them to work properly.

5. Turn the printer on.

FIGURE 8.1

Connecting a printer to a powerline network is pretty straightforward.

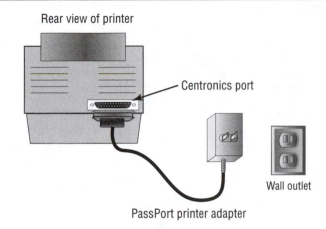

Rear view of printer

Centronics port

Wall outlet

PassPort printer adapter

Connecting Your PCs

After you've connected your printer to the powerline adapter, as shown in Figure 8.1, it's time to get started on your PCs. Here's the routine:

1. Exit Windows and turn off the PC.

2. Connect either end of the parallel cable to the PC Plug-In Adapter. Again, be careful to use the PC adapter, not the Printer adapter (they look almost exactly alike except for a small difference in the label) and also be sure you use the parallel cable included with the kit.

3. Plug the PassPort adapter into any 110-volt AC outlet. (See above warning from the "Connecting Your Printer" section about not plugging the adapter into a surge suppressor.)

4. Plug the other end of the parallel cable into the PC's parallel port, as shown in Figure 8.2.

5. Repeat steps 1 through 4 for your second PC and any additional PCs.

PART

II

Networking
Nuts and Bolts

FIGURE 8.2

Connecting a PC to a
powerline network is
straightforward.

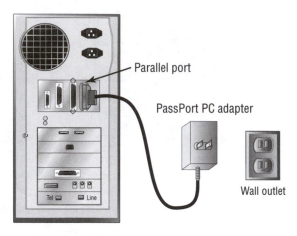

Parallel port

PassPort PC adapter

Wall outlet

Rear view of PC

 TIP To reduce noise in a phoneline network, plug your PC's power cord into the line conditioner Intelogis provides with the kit. After that, of course, plug the line conditioner into the wall power outlet. Remember not to plug the Intelogis PassPort device into a line conditioner or power strip. It has to go directly into the wall outlet.

Installing Powerline Software

PassPort uses Windows' built-in networking capabilities to create a peer-to-peer network, as well as to arrange file and printer sharing. However, since Windows doesn't recognize the powerline hardware, you'll need to install special software and drivers from the PassPort installation disk before operating your network. Here's how:

1. Turn on your PC. If it's a Windows 95 or 98 PC, at some point during the startup process it will show a message box that says Update Device Driver, New Hardware Found, or Add New Hardware Wizard.

2. Click Cancel. Because Windows doesn't have drivers for PassPort networks, you don't want let Windows try to set up your new hardware on its own.

3. Now insert the CD containing the PassPort software into your CD-ROM drive. If the PassPort Setup screen appears, skip the next step and go directly to step 5.

TIP If you don't have a CD-ROM drive, you can request diskettes containing the Pass-Port software from the company. If you have a CD-ROM drive on at least one computer but want to create diskettes yourself—for instance, to install the software on another PC without a CD-ROM drive—there is a batch file called `Makedisk.bat` on the PassPort CD-ROM that will help you create the diskettes you need.

4. Now click on the Windows Start button and select Run. Type the drive letter of your CD-ROM drive in the box and follow it with **:/autorun.exe**. Click OK.

5. When you see the PassPort Setup screen, as shown in Figure 8.3, click Install PassPort Drivers and Software.

FIGURE 8.3

At the PassPort Setup screen, click the Install PassPort Drivers and Software option.

PART

II

Networking
Nuts and Bolts

 WARNING At this point, you may get a message box instructing you to insert the original Microsoft Windows system CD that came with your computer. If you have the CD, insert it. Type the letter of your CD-ROM drive and the path where your Windows system files are located, most likely `:\win98` or `:\win95`. If you don't have a CD, which sometimes is the case if your PC came with Windows pre-installed, look for the Windows files in `:\windows\win95\cabs`. The Windows system files may be stored in compressed cabinet files at this location on your hard drive. You can look for the cabinet files by doing a file-search for files with the .CAB suffix. If you have to stop, look at the following section, "Uninstalling PassPort Software" for what to do next.

6. If you've gotten this far, follow the on-screen instructions given by the installation program. When the message box appears telling you that Windows has to be restarted to finish the installation, click OK.

7. When Windows restarts, you'll get more on-screen instructions. Follow them until you see the Setup Complete box.

8. Mark the box labeled Yes, I want to restart my computer now and click Finish.

Uninstalling PassPort Software

If you don't have the CD and can't find the cabinet files on your hard drive, don't try to continue installing PassPort software. Halt the process and find the CD before you continue.

If you can't find the CD at all, cancel the installation and remove the PassPort software from your system. You can do this by clicking Start ➢ Run and entering the letter of the drive containing your PassPort software CD followed by **:\Win9X\PassPort\Ppremove.exe**.

Or, you can use Windows Explorer to browse the PassPort CD, where you'll find the Ppremove.exe file in the Win9x/\assPort subdirectory, as shown in Figure 8.4. Double-click the file to run it and follow instructions to remove the PassPort software and drivers. You'll need to restart your system to finish uninstalling the software. If you don't remove the software, you will get error messages and have trouble reinstalling at a later date.

FIGURE 8.4

You can find the uninstallation routine for PassPort software on the PassPort software installation disk.

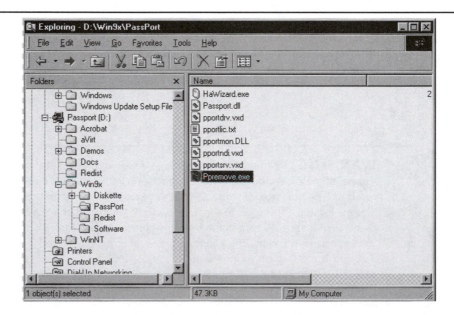

NOTE After your computer restarts, you may get a Microsoft Networking or Enter Windows Password box asking you to enter a Username and Password. If you've previously set up passwords or networking on this machine, enter your usual username and password. If you haven't, enter a username and click OK. You don't have to enter a password. If you do, be sure to remember it, because you'll need it every time you start Windows.

9. When your computer restarts, you'll get a screen informing you that the Pass-Port network software has successfully installed.

Securing Your Powerline Network

Because your powerline network shares wiring with your neighbors, security is an especially sensitive issue with powerline networks. If you don't take any steps to secure your network, anyone with a neighboring powerline network could, for instance, access your networked PCs—or even use one of your networked printers.

Imagine seeing one of your neighbor's latest financial statements appearing on your printer. Or even worse, imagine your neighbor printing out your love letters on his printer. You don't have to imagine many scenarios like this to realize that, when it comes to powerline networks, good fences make good neighbors.

Fortunately, securing your powerline is not a complicated matter. Here's how to do it:

1. Click Start ➢ Programs ➢ PassPort ➢ PassPort Administrator.

2. The first time you run PassPort Administrator, a Secure Network wizard starts and asks you if you want to create a secure network. Click Yes ➢ Next.

3. The next screen will prompt you to enter a name for the secure network. Type in a name of up to 10 letters and numbers and select Next.

4. You will next be shown a dialog box with all the network's PCs and printers. The computer you are using at the moment won't show up on this list, however. Mark the boxes for all the devices you want to belong to the secure network. Click Next; then click Finish.

 WARNING Don't set up Secure Networking on more than one computer. If you do, your powerline networked PCs won't be able to communicate with one another.

PART

II

Networking
Nuts and Bolts

It's a technology truism that what one user considers a bug, another considers a feature. That's the case with the fact that separate powerline networks hooked up to the power system are, in a sense, on the same network. For instance, if you wanted to network with your neighbor for some reason, such as you were starting a home-based business together, setting up powerline networks in both homes would let you access each other's PCs and printers just like you were in the same house.

The PassPort network from Intelogis has an effective range of about a quarter mile and will easily go between houses or even across streets. It is limited, however, by whether you share the same electrical secondary on the transformer as your neighbor. If you and your neighbor share the same secondary, you'll be able to share a powerline network, as in Figure 8.5. If, on the other hand, the transformer acts as an isolator, as in Figure 8.6, you won't be able to communicate over the network.

FIGURE 8.5

If you and your neighbor share the same electrical secondary transformer, you'll be able to share a powerline network.

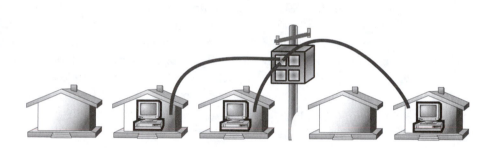

FIGURE 8.6

If you don't share the same secondary, you won't be able to share the network.

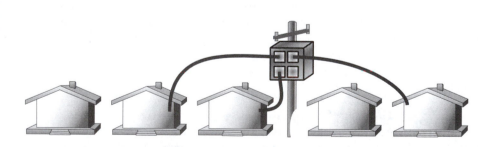

> **NOTE** See Chapter 20, "Network Security," for more about how to protect your network.

Summary

Powerline networks are easy to install and configure, but they do have a few tricks involved, and the performance with current technology is not all that could be desired. However, if convenience and ease are more important than speed, a powerline network is a solid choice.

What's Next

After looking at Ethernet, phoneline, and powerline networks, you are now about to examine networks that don't use wires at all. Wireless networking is the subject of Chapter 9, "Wireless Networks."

PART

II

Networking
Nuts and Bolts

CHAPTER <u>9</u>

Wireless Networks

Overview

ireless networking offers the unique advantage of networking without the use of any wires whatsoever, existing or new. Wireless computer networking using radio transmissions has been around for more than a decade. However, popular acceptance for home use has been blocked by high prices, tricky installation, and incompatible standards. Lately, though, prices have fallen steeply, technology has eased installation, and a new standard is taking hold. Under these developments, wireless—long considered the sleeping giant of networking—may be about ready to emerge from hibernation.

WARNING The currently prevailing wireless networks for home users all claim data transfer rates of 1Mbps to 2Mbps. Most independent tests, however, have shown considerably slower speeds due probably to interference or other common wireless problems. If you think you'll need every bit of 1Mbps speed for your wireless network, be forewarned that you may not get everything you bargain for in the real world.

Selecting Your Equipment

There are quite a few vendors of radio-based wireless networking gear, but so far, one of them has made a much larger impact on the home market than all the rest. That company is Diamond Multimedia, with its HomeFree Wireless product.

HomeFree is a simple product compared to its competitors, most of which are low-end business network systems, or are scaled-down from commercial-quality systems. In addition to being wireless, it's also hubless. All you have to do to set it up is install a wireless network adapter into the PCs you want to network, and then install the software.

You can buy HomeFree Wireless adapters both singly and in kits. This makes it easy and economical for you to purchase the right number of adapters for the exact number of devices you want to network, without the headache of spending money for equipment you don't need, and then needing to find a place to store the extras. HomeFree adapters are available for ISA or PCI bus slots, as well as in a PC card variety for laptops or PC card-equipped desktops.

If you want, though, you can do the kit thing with wireless, using kits called HomeFree Pacs. The Desktop Pac comes with one PCI and one ISA card for networking two desktop PCs. The HomeFree Wireless Combo Pac has an ISA card for a desktop machine and a PC card adapter for a wireless.

NOTE The USA isn't the only technology community working on wireless. The European Telecommunications Standards Institute is looking into a high-speed wireless LAN standard that would operate at 23Mbps. At this writing, however, that standard is still a ways from completion.

Selecting Wireless Network Adapter Cards

A wireless network adapter card is actually a radio transceiver. This transceiver is equipped to send and receive data-carrying radio transmissions to and from the PC and other devices on the network. As you'll notice in Figure 9.1, there are no connector jacks since the wireless card doesn't have to physically attach to anything. Later in this chapter, we'll discuss how to combine a wireless with a wired system.

The adapter cards on a wireless network are, in many cases, all you have to buy since wireless networks for home use are generally hubless as well as wireless. In absence of decisions to make about cables, connectors, and concentrators, your choice of a network adapter card is doubly important on a wireless network.

FIGURE 9.1

A typical wireless network adapter card, this one for an ISA bus slot

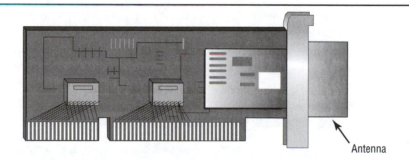

Antenna

When you're selecting network adapters for a wireless network, you have several factors to consider:

- Range
- Cost
- Slot type
- Desktop or portable

When it comes to range, the choices for most home networkers are fairly limited. While wireless networks with effective ranges of several miles or more have been developed, most of the home-suitable wireless networking products available today have an effective range of 150 feet between workstations. This should be plenty big enough to cover a network extending over the average home.

 TIP You may need more range if you are trying to network computers in two or more buildings, if interference from some source is limiting your range, or if you just have an unusually large home. If so, you may be able to use a repeater, which repeats and amplifies the wireless signal to extend the range of a wireless network.

Cost is a significant variable with wireless networks, much more so than with the other types of networks. That's because wireless hasn't been nearly as popular among the biggest networking market, namely, businesses. Those businesses that have opted to go wireless have been willing to pay a lot more than you will want to. However, in the last year or so, some quite affordable wireless networking products have become available. The ones aimed expressly at home networkers cost only around $100 per PC, while higher-performance networks suitable for businesses cost about $400 per workstation.

Wireless network cards come in three form factors: PCI, ISA and, for laptops, PC or PCMCIA. Your choice of one of these three will depend on what type of slot you have available in your computer. As a general rule, however, you should try to use PCI slots on desktops, since they are easier to configure. For portables, of course, you'll generally use a PC card-type adapter, unless you're working from a docking station that provides desktop-type card slots. Again, you'll be better off here if you can use a PCI card.

Selecting Access Points

Most home wireless networks will be hubless or ad hoc networks. These consist only of PCs and, perhaps, other devices such as printers that are equipped with wireless network interfaces. This kind of network offers basic peer-to-peer networking and is suitable for most home networkers who are doing only data communications. However, you may want the network to provide other services, such as allowing you to route voice telephone calls over the network, connect to a wired network or modem, or share a high-speed Internet access modem. For these jobs, you'll need something more than PC network adapters.

For those more complicated tasks, you'll need *Connection Points*. Connection Points—essentially black boxes—provide additional services such as routing voice telephone calls over the network. There are quite a few other accessories you can attach to a wireless network to let you perform all kinds of other tasks as well. Various vendors sell access points or bridges for hooking up your wireless network to wired networks or to cable modems, DSL modems, or other Internet connections. In addition, repeaters can extend the range of your wireless network by repeating and amplifying the signal transmissions.

SWAP for Increased Interoperability

An alliance of industries specializing in wireless networking, the Home Radio Frequency Working Group or Home RF, has devised a specification called the Shared Wireless Access Protocol. SWAP, as it's known, addresses one of the biggest obstacles to widespread adoption of wireless networking for the home. That obstacle is lack of interoperability. In other words, everybody uses different technologies for accomplishing wireless networking, with the result being that the manufacturers' products won't talk to each other. SWAP sets a standard that allows wireless network gear makers to produce equipment that works together. The first SWAP-compliant products came out in 1999, to a moderately enthusiastic reception in the market. SWAP 1.1, the first revision of the standard, is an unusual standards revision. It specifies a product line that actually runs slower than the first one. By moving the standard data transmission rate from 1Mbps down to 800Kbps, Home RF intends to let its members produce SWAP-compliant products more quickly and cheaply, at what they hope will prove to be an acceptable cost in performance.

These added devices can be expensive, costing three or more times as much as a simple network adapter card. But if you're looking for a way to connect your wireless network to the wired world, a bridge can be a helpful addition. And let's face it, with the importance of Internet access these days, you're going to want your network to be connected to the Internet. You'll need to make sure the access device you choose has appropriate connectors—usually a basic Ethernet RJ-45—to connect to the cable modem or other wired device you have in mind, as in Figure 9.2.

FIGURE 9.2

A bridge can connect PCs on a wireless network to wired devices such as modems.

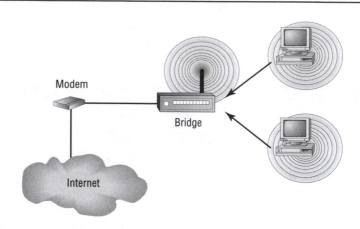

Selecting External Antennas

Wireless networks, more so than other networks, are subject to interference. You can block your signal by merely moving a metal file cabinet between two networked PCs. Sometimes, rather than jockeying heavy file cabinets around, the best way to extend the range and improve the reception of your network is to use external antennas, as shown in Figure 9.3. These are available in a variety of configurations, for indoor or outdoor use. Since you're going to be installing yours in a home, pick one that is not too obtrusive, but that will mount securely in a handy location.

FIGURE 9.3

You may need to install an external antenna to your wireless workstation, either because of an interference or range problem, or simply because the adapter you chose doesn't have an integrated antenna.

Selecting Cordless Modems

Some wireless manufacturers offer modems that connect directly to the wireless network. This gets around the problem of hooking up the wireless network to a wired modem, and allows all the PCs on the network to share access through the modem. At the moment, most wireless modems are 56K analog models. So if you need lots of speed in your Internet connection—and who doesn't?—think twice before opting for a wireless modem, at least unless and until wireless cable and DSL modems become more readily available.

Waitless Wireless

While most wireless networks offer substantially less performance than wired Ethernet, you can get Ethernet-like performance in a wireless network—for a price. RadioLAN Incorporated of Sunnyvale, California, offers a family of wireless networking products that provide the same 10Mbps speed as regular Ethernet. RadioLAN's product line includes adapter cards for ISA and PCI card slots and various bridges used for connecting wired and wireless LANs.

RadioLAN's network uses a proprietary Ethernet-compatible protocol it calls 10BaseRadio. It also uses a different radio frequency, the 5.8GHz band, compared to the 2.4GHz band used by other wireless networking products. The 5.8GHz band is less subject to interference from the likes of microwave ovens and cordless phones. RadioLAN's products have somewhat limited range compared to other competitors, only about 120 feet indoors. But the main thing is the price. Its Model 101 ISA CardLink adapter sells for $349. The Model 140 PC card adapter for a notebook lists at $499, and the Backbone Link 208 access point for connecting to a wired Ethernet network is $999.

PART

II

Networking
Nuts and Bolts

Installing Your Network

The distinguishing feature of a wireless network is ease of installation. The simplicity and speed of getting a wireless network up and running makes it a candidate for you if:

- You live in a historical building you don't want to deface with wires.

- Your home's walls are too thick, strong, or tough to drill through.

- You have an older home with few power or phone outlets.

- You don't plan to stay in your residence long.

- You plan to move your networked computers around frequently.

- You want a backup network in case your wired network fails.

- You want to network with a PC in an outlying building.

Even if none of these apply to you, you may want to look into wireless if you simply aren't sure you'll use your network much and want to try networking with minimal hassle. Wireless is perhaps the easiest of all networks to uninstall.

The Five-Minute Network?

You can literally get a wireless network up and running in five minutes. It takes little more time than it does to plug the interface into your PC and install the software. Expanding the network is similarly easy. You generally just install the card and software on the new machine, then boot up and let the other network stations find it. No rewiring, no connectors, and no crawling around under desks with snarled cables.

Installing Network Adapter Cards

Installing a wireless adapter card is like installing any other adapter card. Here are the basics:

1. Turn off the computer and ground yourself by touching something metal, such as a file cabinet or the steel chassis of the computer.

2. Unplug the computer's electrical power cord from the wall.

3. Open the computer case.

4. Locate the slot where you intend to install the wireless adapter.

5. Adjacent to this slot is a metal end plate covering a hole in the back of the computer. Remove the screw holding this metal end plate in place.

6. Pull out the end plate.

7. Handling the adapter only by the edges, insert it into the slot and press it down firmly until it seats completely.

TIP   Wireless adapters may have antennas or antenna cables hanging out the back of the card. Thread these cables through the back of the machine when inserting the card. Be sure they're clear before tightening down. Antennas are easier. You simply have to slip the card in at the proper angle for the antenna to poke out the back of the case. Then press the card into the slot and proceed with the installation.

8. Insert the screw that you removed from the end plate into the end plate on the adapter and tighten it.

9. Carefully close the case, making sure not to pinch or tangle any loose wires.

 WARNING   Although it's easy to install the cards, wireless networks are persnickety. You have to be careful about how you position your PC if it is to communicate effectively with other computers on the network. A number of things can interfere with radio waves carrying network traffic, including walls, furniture, and various electrical devices such as video monitors. Try to position your PC so that no large metallic objects block the route to the network. Also, make sure it's not right up against any walls, as this too can interfere with the transceiver's operation.

PART

II

Networking
Nuts and Bolts

Installing Wireless Network Software

As in the case of most of the networking products at this writing (with the exception of the old reliable Ethernet) neither Windows 95 nor Windows 98 comes with the device drivers needed to automatically install and operate the wireless network cards. So odds are that you'll have to do at least part of it manually. Here is the normal routine:

 NOTE   For Windows 2000, you need to get a driver from the adapter manufacturer to use any wireless networking adapter.

1. After installing your card and closing the case, plug your computer in and turn it on.

2. Windows should notice the card on startup and display a screen notifying you that it has found new hardware. Windows will ask you to install the driver for it.

(If Windows finds the card, continue to step 3. If it doesn't find the card, go to the set of instructions in the next section.)

3. Follow the instructions of the Windows driver installation wizard until you get to the screen displaying a list of manufacturers.

4. Windows won't have a driver for the wireless card, so click the Have Disk button.

5. Insert the disk, CD-ROM, or floppy, that came with your card into the appropriate drive.

6. Select the appropriate drive letter from the drop-down list shown by the installation wizard. For instance, select A: if you are installing from a floppy disk in drive A:.

7. Click OK.

8. After the files copy, you'll be asked to restart your computer. Click Yes.

9. After Windows restarts, your adapters will be installed. Repeat this process on the other computers you want to network.

 NOTE For more detailed information about installing network adapter cards, drivers, and software, see Chapter 6, "Ethernet Networks."

If Windows 98 doesn't notice that the new network card is there, you'll have to do it the old-fashioned way, like so:

1. First, make sure you have the CD-ROM or disk containing the drivers handy.

2. Choose Control Panel ➤ Network and click on the Configuration tab.

3. Click the Add button to add your new adapter.

4. From the Select Network Component list, shown in Figure 9.4, highlight Adapter and click Add.

FIGURE 9.4

The Select Network Component list lets you select the type of network component you want to add.

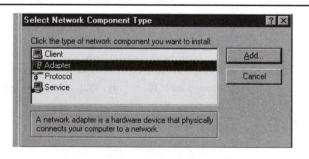

5. At the Select Network Adapters screen, shown in Figure 9.5, click on Have Disk.

FIGURE 9.5

The Select Network adapters list lets you choose from a list of Adapter manufacturers, or click Have Disk to use a disk supplied by your equipment vendor.

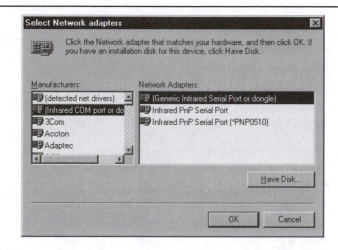

6. Insert your driver disk, select the appropriate drive from the drop-down list in the Install from Disk window, and click OK. If Windows doesn't find the driver, click Browse and try to locate it on the driver disk yourself.

7. After the files are copied, click Yes to restart your computer.

8. After Windows restarts, your adapters should be installed. You'll now need to repeat this process on the other computers you want to network.

WARNING You need to network your computers in a certain order if you're installing a Diamond Multimedia HomeFree Wireless network and plan to use Internet sharing. Start your network installation on the PC you plan to use to access the Internet. Normally, this will be the PC with the fastest modem.

Summary

Wireless networking carries a somewhat higher cost and offers only modest performance compared to its wired brethren. However, the appealing mix of flexibility, convenience, and exceptionally simple installation makes it a good solution for many types of home networkers. Although wireless has been around as long as almost any networking technology, it's also evolving rapidly. Expect better performance and pricing to make it a choice for more home networkers in the near future.

 NOTE The IEEE committee that set up the 802.11 standard for wireless networks has taken a so-called agnostic policy when it comes to the technology. That means it won't endorse any particular transmission method, whether infrared, radio, or other. Nor will the IEEE bless any of the competing radio technologies. That means you shouldn't hold your breath waiting for wireless networks to interoperate with each other over the airwaves. Still, they should work with each other when bridged to wired networks. The only hope is that some really good technology will eventually become a de facto standard, and thus convince everybody else to jump on the bandwagon.

What's Next

Ethernet, phoneline, powerline, and wireless networks are the main networking options, but not the only ones. The next chapter will examine the hybrid, cross-platform, hubless coaxial, and infrared types of networks.

CHAPTER <u>10</u>

Other Networks

Overview

While the majority of home networkers will be happy with one of the network varieties discussed in the previous four chapters—cabled Ethernet, phoneline, powerline and wireless—those aren't the only kinds of networks around. The other types of networks that you may want to use include:

- Hybrid wireless-wired networks
- Wireless networks incorporating handheld computers and PDAs
- Cross-platform networks
- Coaxial hubless bus networks
- Infrared networks

The above list is really only the beginning of the types of networks you may envision. Almost any combination of wired and wireless, portable and desktop devices, and computer operating systems from Unix to Windows, can be incorporated successfully into a home network. Although you may never want to use one of these other types of networks, it's comforting to know that home networking is as flexible as your needs.

Hybrid Wireless-Wired Networks

Most wireless networks are not completely wireless. Rather, they are networks that have some components that are wireless, and others that are conventionally connected with cables. In a business network, for instance, a wireless link might connect a portable computer rolling around on a forklift in the warehouse with the Ethernet-cabled network that the rest of the business runs on. Generally, price and performance considerations have kept wireless to a secondary or backup role in most networks to date.

 NOTE One of the times wireless networks can really star in the business world is when a disaster such as a fire, flood, or lightning strike destroys a company's cabled network. A wireless network can be set up start to finish in a matter of days, saving a company far more, in terms of production, than the cost of the wireless installation. While you may not be able to justify the expense of an emergency wireless network installation in the event of a domestic disaster, the example confirms the point that wireless will work when other solutions can't do the job.

Home networks are perhaps more likely than business networks to be entirely wireless because the convenience of wireless is a big attraction, and the performance and security issues aren't likely to be as great. However, home networks, too, can get benefits from hybrid wired-wireless networks. At home, the basic premise is the same as in business, although the details may vary.

In hybrid wireless-wired networks, the wireless part of the network is typically used to extend or expand the wired networks' reach. This allows the network to go places or to connect to workstations that wires just can't reach. One common—and extremely handy—example occurs when a networker wants to connect a computer in an outlying building, such as a garage apartment, workshop, or detached garage, as in Figure 10.1. The alternative of a hybrid wireless-wired network sure beats a long and expensive cable run.

FIGURE 10.1

A hybrid wireless-wired network can be used to connect a computer that is in a detached garage, workshop, or garage apartment to the wired network in the house.

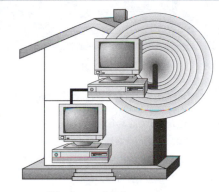

Wired network in home

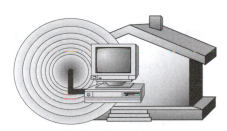

Wireless node in detached workshop

A hybrid wired-wireless network may also make sense when you have a couple of computers clustered close together in one small area, and another one further away. For example, you might have several devices in a home office, family room, or group of bedrooms along a hall, and want to also include a computer that is located on the other side of the house. If you have a computer in a secluded master suite, a dining room converted into a study, or an out-of-the-way upstairs room, as shown in Figure 10.2, you may be a candidate for a hybrid wired-wireless network.

FIGURE 10.2

Mixing wired and wireless networks can let you easily and economically connect a computer in an isolated, hard-to-wire part of the house to a group of computers in a wired network.

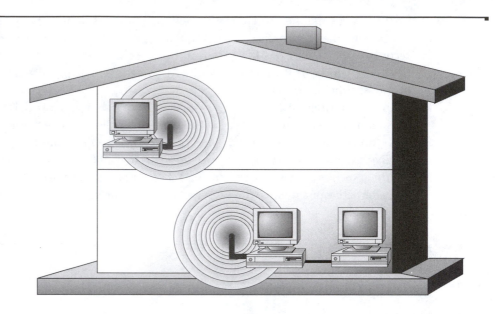

Using Laptops in Hybrid Wireless-Wired Networks

One common use is tying a mobile laptop into a wired network so the laptop can be used all over the house. As shown in Figure 10.3, when you have a laptop connected to your wired network through a wireless link, you can work or play using your computer practically anywhere you want.

FIGURE 10.3

With a laptop connected wirelessly to a wired network, you can extend your network virtually anywhere in or out of your home.

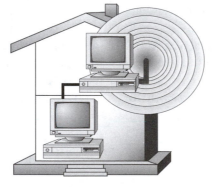

Wired network in the home

Laptop on backyard picnic table is connected wirelessly

As online connections become more and more important for work and play, it's easy to see the benefits of being able to, say, check your e-mail using a laptop in bed or in a hammock in the backyard. For some home networkers, especially those who work at home as telecommuters or self-employed professionals, a network that doesn't allow mobile access from a laptop on the go isn't of nearly as much use as one that does.

WARNING Selecting equipment in a hybrid wireless-wired network involves some extra considerations, especially when it comes to the workstations or terminal devices you'll use. Specifically, a laptop computer that is too heavy or bulky, or that has a case that is too slippery or poorly constructed to protect against falls, is only nominally portable. Such a laptop isn't likely to work well as a mobile wireless network node. Before deciding to employ a wireless network so you can move around with your laptop, be sure you can—and will—do so. Many laptops are essentially used as stationary desktops, and could just as easily be hard-wired into a network.

Laptop computers aren't the only nodes that can be connected to a wired network wirelessly. Some other types of workstations and devices that could be wirelessly connected to a wired network include:

- Desktop computers
- Palmtop computers
- Handheld PCs
- Personal digital assistants
- Handheld scanners
- Digital cameras
- Digital video cameras
- Handheld printers

Not all of these gadgets can directly connect to a wired network. Some, such as the digital camera, have to be hooked to a laptop that is equipped with a wireless NIC, as shown in Figure 10.4.

FIGURE 10.4

A wide variety of computer peripherals can be part of a hybrid wired-wireless network when interfaced through a laptop equipped with a wireless NIC.

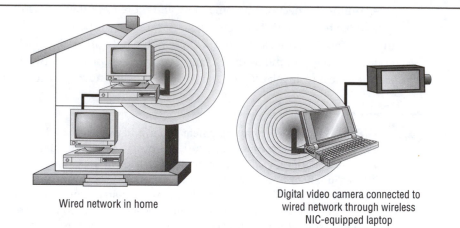

Wired network in home

Digital video camera connected to wired network through wireless NIC-equipped laptop

Using Handheld PCs in Wireless Networks

Handheld PCs are already practically weightless, at least compared to their desk-bound PC cousins. When you add wireless networking to the extreme portability of a handheld, you've really got something. A wirelessly networked HPC is perfect, for instance, for checking electronic mail arriving at your home network, even though you may be in a location far from a wired network node.

And the good news is that home networks and handheld PCs work well together, as shown in Figure 10.5. Any HPC with a Type II slot, which includes popular models such as the Hewlett-Packard Jornada, can use an inexpensive HomeFree wireless PC card adapter from Diamond Multimedia. See Figure 10.5 and learn more at www. diamondmm.com.

FIGURE 10.5

Handheld PCs are simple to add to a wireless network with the help of an inexpensive wireless PC card NIC.

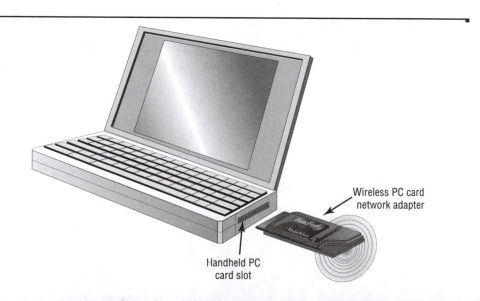

Wireless PC card network adapter

Handheld PC card slot

PDA Problems

Personal digital assistant users are (pretty much) out of luck when it comes to connecting their personal digital assistants directly to their home networks. That's because nobody, so far, has come up with a popular, proven LAN adapter for PDAs. There are some qualifications to that statement, however. 3Com's Palm VII organizer, which comes with built-in ability to connect to the Internet wirelessly, is available at this writing in the New York Metropolitan area for $599. You can get wireless modems that snap into the Palm and Windows CE PDAs and, over a dialup connection to your network PC, let you read and respond to e-mail messages on your Palm. That's all very nice, but PDA users are still waiting for a way to wirelessly turn their digital assistants into full-fledged network devices.

Networkability takes on another dimension when talking about networking with handheld PCs in wireless networks. Just because you can physically attach the hardware you need to the HPC doesn't mean it will create a workable network device. The added bulk of a wireless modem may make an HPC too large to fit in even a good-sized pocket, rendering what was a highly mobile computing device much less portable. In addition, the power requirements of operating a radio transceiver can drain batteries much faster than you're probably used to.

You should also consider the way you use, and plan to use, the HPC. Handhelds are easiest to use when you are seated or stationary; they are less so when you're standing or walking. Try a dry run using your portable (unconnected) in the way you intend to use it when it's part of the network. If you don't care for the experience, the trial might save you the time and trouble of incorporating it into a wireless network that doesn't give you what you hoped for.

Bluetooth

Bluetooth is the odd-sounding name for a promising technology for sending voice and data over a low-cost short-range radio link. Bluetooth devices operating in the 2.4GHz band will transfer data between themselves at 1Mbps at distances of up to 30 feet. Range can be extended to around 100 meters with an optional amplifier. Bluetooth is ideally suited to ad hoc networking, since any device equipped with a Bluetooth radio NIC establishes contact with another Bluetooth device as soon as it comes within range. These small, personal-sized networks are referred to as *piconets.* Quite a few companies have signed up with the Bluetooth interest group since the organization announced its 1.0 specification in July 1999. But so far, no actual products have appeared on the marketplace. Learn more at www.bluetooth.com.

Cross-Platform Networks

While it's no secret that the vast majority of personal computers today run some variant of Windows, it's also true that not all computers run on Windows. Apple Macintosh, after stumbling and losing much of its market share during the 1990s, has rebounded and reclaimed its place as a viable rival to the Windows world. Linux, the freeware Unix-compatible operating system, has only been around since 1994 or so, but is gaining significant numbers of adherents in the corporate and hobbyist markets. (It doesn't hurt any that Macs and Linux boxes have excellent, built-in networking capabilities, including some features that are superior to what Windows can offer.)

When it comes to choosing an operating system for home PCs, households, like the unionization of companies, tend to go pretty much all one way or another. As a rule, you're either a Mac shop or a PC shop. But, just as companies sometimes have a renegade department that refuses to go along, whether out of an independent spirit or perhaps just an existing base of incompatible machines, some PC households will certainly host a teenager who insists on a brightly colored iMac, or a dyed-in-the-wool gadgeteer who won't use anything but Linux.

What does that mean for your network? A little added complexity, to be sure. But with the right set of tools, there's no reason why you can't add almost any kind of computer to your home network and have them working smoothly together, like in Figure 10.6.

FIGURE 10.6

With the proper equipment, you can link computers running a wide variety of operating systems into a smoothly operating network.

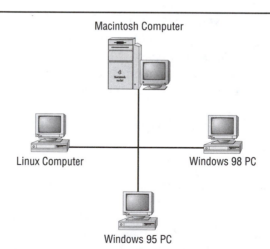

Macs in PC Networks

Although all Macs come network-ready from the factory, until recently, few home Windows PCs have been able to make the same claim. The network-ready version of Windows was reserved for corporations. Curiously, although Windows PCs far out-sell Macintoshes in numbers, the most popular way to connect a Mac to a PC network is by installing special software on the PCs, not the Mac. As a result, even if you have only one Mac and the rest of your devices are PCs and compatible devices, you will be running your network through the Macintosh, with the Mac as your primary machine and the rest of your devices as your peripherals.

In other methods of networking, including Ethernet, Powerline, or Phoneline, consumers can choose from a plethora of more-or-less comparable software options. When it comes to making mixed networks of Macs and PCs possible, however, PC MACLAN for Windows 95/98, from Miramar Systems, is pretty much the standard software package, although not the only one. PC MACLAN connects a Windows 95/98 PC with a mixed network, allowing Macs and PCs to share files, drives, and printers. After installing PC MACLAN on a Windows PC and connecting it to the Mac network, you use Windows Network Neighborhood to access resources on the Mac-PC network. In turn, Macs view PC drives with Chooser. Moreover, by using a print services tool, PC MACLAN lets a Windows PC print to AppleTalk printers.

Although you don't really have a choice of software when it comes to running a mixed network of Macs and PCs, you do have a choice of cables. The network can be wired with 10BaseT twisted-pair or coaxial cable. It's not a difficult choice. If you are installing a new network today, twisted-pair cable is almost certainly the way to go. It offers higher speed, is easier to handle, and, perhaps most important of all, is clearly the way the industry is headed.

You can learn more about PC MACLAN, including downloading a demo version of the software, at `www.miramarsys.com`. Follow Miramar's instructions for installing the software, then set up your PC to work with the Macs on the network in the following manner:

1. Select Start ➤ Settings ➤ Control Panel ➤ Network.

2. In the Select Network Component Type window, shown in Figure 10.7, click Add ➤ Client ➤ Add.

PART

II

Networking
Nuts and Bolts

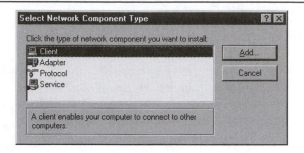

3. In the Select Network Client window, click Have Disk.

4. Insert the disk with the PC MACLAN drivers on it. In the Install From Disk window, shown in Figure 10.8, type the letter of the drive into which you have inserted the driver disk, and click OK.

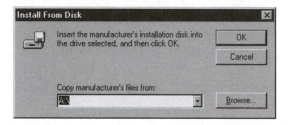

5. Select AppleTalk Protocol for NDIS 3 and then AppleTalk Client and click OK.

NOTE It's a good idea, while you're installing the PC MACLAN drivers, to check to make sure the AppleTalk protocol is bound to the correct adapter. To do this, double click on the AppleTalk Protocol for NDIS 3.*x* and click the Settings tab. Make sure your adapter is listed under Adapter. If not click the down arrow and select it.

6. Re-boot your system by clicking Start ➢ Shut Down ➢ Restart ➢ OK.

7. When the system has rebooted, double click on Network Neighborhood and then Entire Network. You should now be able to see your Apple servers and printers.

Coaxial Hubless Bus Networks

You can create a simple computer network without a hub, built in a bus physical topology, using coaxial cable. Assuming both computers have NICs (with coaxial connectors) all you'll need is a short piece of coaxial cable, a couple of T-connectors, BNCs, and a pair of suitable terminators.

FIGURE 10.9

It doesn't get much simpler than this. A hubless bus network created by connecting two NIC-equipped PCs with coaxial cable and T-connectors.

Terminator   Terminator

Hubless networks are efficient at using cable since, as shown in Figure 10.9, you don't have to run a cable from each workstation back to the hub. However, bus networks in general suffer from vulnerability to going down completely any time there is a problem with the network connection at any terminal on the network. These problems can range from a loose T-connector to a chair rolling over a cable to an ill-timed attempt to logoff by an unwary user. Troubleshooting bus networks can be a significant headache.

 TIP   Although hubless bus networks are generally associated with coaxial cable, you can get unshielded twisted pair cables configured to do the same job. These are called crossover cables, and are essentially cables wired to perform the work of a hub in simple networks.

Infrared Networks

The majority of wireless networks rely on radio signals to carry data between workstations. Infrared, the spectrum of light just below the visible range, is also used for networking. There's nothing at all exotic about these technologies. Infrared signaling, for example, has probably already made your life just a little bit better. Like when you use your remote control to signal your television that you want to mute an annoying commercial.

One kind of infrared transmission is referred to as IrDA, which is short for Infrared Data Association. The IrDA is an association of companies that provides standards to ensure interoperability of infrared technology. You can learn more about the IrDA at www.irda.org.

The IrDA has set a group of standards for transmitting computer data over short distances of less than about a yard. Unlike radio waves, however, infrared is blocked by objects between the infrared transceivers. As a result, the IR ports must be in direct line-of-sight contact.

Data transfer rates are also low, ranging from a high end of 115Kbps for regular IrDA to up to 4Mbps for Fast IR. One of the good things about IR is that most laptop computers and many PDAs have IrDA ports. In addition, some printers and digital cameras also include ports.

 WARNING Not all IR-equipped devices, including Palm Pilot III PDAs and Apple PowerBook 1400s, conform to the IrDA standard. However, a number of innovative tools have been developed to help even non-IrDA compliant systems use wireless networking. The BeamLink from JP Systems allows you to get wireless e-mail on a Palm III using an IR-enabled 2-way pager from Glenayre, over the SkyTel paging network. You can learn more at www.jpsystems.com.

IrDa's standard is not really a full-strength networking technology because it is mainly concerned with communication between just a pair of IR-equipped devices, such as a computer and a printer. The IEEE 802.11 standard for wireless networking, including infrared networks, covers communication between multiple IR-equipped devices. That sounds great, but the reality is that only a few devices use the 802.11 IR standard.

Despite its limitations, infrared networking technology can be used to extend either wired networks or RF wireless networks. You can even use more than two technologies. For instance, Figure 10.10 shows how a laptop computer can connect to an infrared-to-RF transceiver that communicates through radio signals to another link. The second transceiver turns the radio transmission into a signal which is sent through a 10BaseT cable to a computer on an Ethernet cabled network.

FIGURE 10.10

You can use infrared to connect a laptop to a device on an RF network, which in turn connects to a wired Ethernet network.

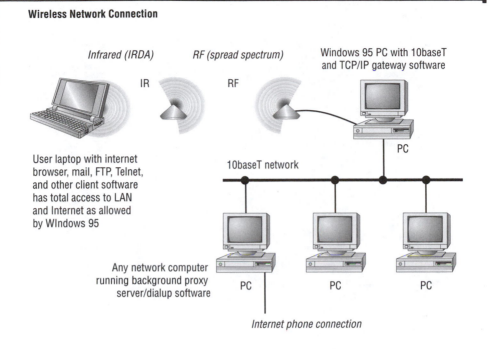

Wireless Network Connection

Infrared (IRDA)   RF (spread spectrum)   Windows 95 PC with 10baseT and TCP/IP gateway software

IR   RF

PC

User laptop with internet browser, mail, FTP, Telnet, and other client software has total access to LAN and Internet as allowed by WIndows 95

10baseT network

Any network computer running background proxy server/dialup software   PC   PC   PC

Internet phone connection

PART

II

Networking
Nuts and Bolts

Summary

There is a networking technology, or combination of networking technologies, available to meet the needs of almost any type of home network you could dream of. Whether you are trying to connect a laptop or handheld to a hybrid wireless-wired network, combine PCs and Macs into a cross-platform network, or extend a hybrid RF-wired network using infrared beams, you can be nearly certain somebody has had the same urge before you, and somebody has figured out a way to do it.

What's Next

No matter what type of network you're planning, you'll need to shop for hardware, software, and other gear to make it all work. "Shopping for Network Equipment" is the subject of the next chapter.

CHAPTER 11

Shopping for Network Equipment

Overview

You can (and should) plan your network carefully. Think long and deep about technology, performance, and upgradability issues related to your home network. But sooner or later you're going to have to leave the slow lane of planning and accelerate into actually building your network. Shopping for your equipment is where the rubber meets the road—your first stop on the route to realizing your networking plans.

In the days of the pioneers who settled America, shopping opportunities were so scarce that people had to buy a month's worth of supplies every time they visited town, or risk going hungry for lack of anyplace else to shop. Today, with all the catalogs and superstores and online retailers clamoring for our attention out there, the consumer's problem is more about how to avoid shopping constantly than how to make the most of a rare opportunity to stock up. Although you may not have noticed it in the course of a typical trip to the mall, there is a plethora of shopping opportunities for home networking equipment. In fact, the ways you can buy networking equipment pretty much mirror the ways you might buy a pair of jeans or the newest hit CD. They include:

- Retail computer stores
- Mail-order catalogs
- Online shopping
- Manufacturer's outlet stores
- Used-equipment retailers

And don't forget flea markets, yard sales, and swap meets either. These are viable options for the more knowledgeable and daring network shopper, one willing to invest some time and take a moderate risk looking for just the right piece of equipment, at just the right price.

While online retailers share some of the same distribution channels, shopping for network equipment is not quite the same as stocking up on back-to-school clothes. There are some critical issues you need to keep in mind when looking for network gear from any potential source, including:

- Compatibility with your network design
- Upgradability (or expandability or scalability)
- After-sale support, including technical support and warranties
- Price

You'll notice that price is not first on this list. It's last for a reason: Price should not be the overriding concern when shopping for network gear. Rather than focusing on paying the least, it's a better idea to try to get as much as you can for what you pay. That means thinking about other issues, such as after-sale support and compatibility, before you worry about price. It's nice to get a good low price, but it's absolutely essential that your network equipment works and works well together. So of these four issues, compatibility is probably the most important.

Computer Stores

When you're first getting started in networking, there's nothing like actually going to the store and holding the boxes and blister packs in your hands. The network equipment vendors often print informative lists of features as well as diagrams of possible network installations on their cartons. You have to look for useful information between all the usual hype, though. And the stores, too, are likely to have brochures, posters, and, if you're lucky, knowledgeable and helpful salespeople there to assist you.

Most sizable computer stores these days have significant amounts of floor space devoted to networking equipment. Having said that, you may have to look around a little bit for the networking gadgets. One place the computer retailers like to hide the network goodies is back in the section for business computing. You may have to poke through a few 1,000-foot reels of 100BaseT cable and 16-port Fast Ethernet hubs, but odds are you'll probably find lots of home networking equipment in just about any good-sized computer store.

When you shop for networking equipment in computer stores, look for the following:

- A large and varied inventory with fresh products. You deserve more than just a shelf or two of dusty packages containing two-year-old technology.

- Knowledgeable salespeople who can answer a range of questions.

- An in-store repair service.

- Technical support from the retailer in addition to the manufacturer's offering.

PART

II

Networking
Nuts and Bolts

WARNING Watch out for low prices based on rebates. Advertisements should say that a low price reflects a manufacturer's rebate. Rebates are acceptable if you don't mind waiting a couple of months to receive a check for the amount of the rebate. However, you usually have to use an official rebate form. Make sure the store has forms for you to use before you make a purchase based on a rebate. If you can't find a form, try calling the manufacturer. You may be able to receive a rebate form by mail, fax, or by printing one out from a manufacturer Web site. When you mail off a rebate, be sure to include all the requested information. That's typically a copy of the receipt, the completed rebate form and the Universal Product Code from the product carton. And keep a record of rebate requests. If more than a couple of months go by with no response, call the manufacturer or rebate service to inquire about the delay.

Ideally, of course, you'll also find excellent prices and even good financing. Computer superstores like CompUSA are following consumer electronics stores such as Best Buy and Circuit City by beginning to offer six months or more of financing with no interest charges. However, price isn't always the most important consideration. If you look first for inventory, sales help, and service, you'll probably be happy with the result, even if you don't pay the absolute lowest price.

Shopping Computer Store Sales

Like any other retailer, computer stores occasionally get overstocked on some items and need to clear 'em out. To do this, they'll offer goods at very low prices, sometimes even below cost. The products they're trying to sell are likely to be last year's, but they should carry a full manufacturer's warranty and, if you don't have to have the latest and greatest, shopping sales can be a great way to cut your home networking costs. A warning, however: If you see something you want at a price that you can't resist, don't delay. Home networking is a hot product category and if you don't move quickly to snag a bargain for yourself, chances are somebody else will, and the store may be out of stock very quickly.

Warranties

You'd have to be living under a rock not to have noticed the persistent and steep decline in computer prices in the last few years. This is not the usual discounting of last year's models, while this year's faster machines carry the same pricetags as before.

No matter how you slice it, computers are simply a lot cheaper now than they've ever been. What this means to computer retailers is that their profits are under pressure as never before, and they've got to make it up some way.

These computer industry trends affect you, the network equipment consumer. Both retailers and manufacturers have been making up for lost profits by cutting back on after-sale support and warranties. As a result, telephone support that was once commonly available 24/7, and for free (at least as long as the product was being manufactured and, in some cases, considerably beyond), is now often limited to a period of a month or two. After that, you may have to pay by the hour, or call a 900 telephone number that will place a fee on your next telephone bill.

Warranties are also not as common as they once were. Some network equipment manufacturers offer no explicit warranty, although established firms will usually stand behind their products if there is a problem. Those who do offer written warranties, mainly stick to limited warranties of one to three years. Those are reasonable terms on a device as reliable as a network adapter or hub.

The Service Contract Shuffle

Extended service contracts are like warranties in that they promise to provide repair services usually for a limited time. But unlike warranties, which are included in the price of the product, you pay extra for service contracts. Service contracts aren't all bad, nor all good. To decide whether you need a service contract take a look at the following:

- Does the service contract cover repairs during the same time period as the warranty? Or does the service contract extend the length of time during which you would not have to pay for repairs?

- Is this product likely to need repairs and what might they cost? As a general rule, anything with moving parts is going to break down sooner than anything without moving parts. For instance, a disk drive will crater long before a monitor. Anything that is able to be dropped or sat on, such as a laptop computer, is much more vulnerable than something that never leaves your desktop. Costs, of course, will vary all the way from nothing up to more than the product is worth. To get an idea, check the minimum and hourly rates at your retailer's service department. Often, shops will post standard rates for various problems, such as installing a new hard drive. Use these figures as a guide.

Continued

CONTINUED

- How long is the service contract good for? A month isn't much for networking gear, but 10 years is probably too long. Most service contracts are for from one to three years. This sounds good, but as a general rule, any electronic device that works when you turn it on is going to work for more than three years. A basic seven-day money-back return policy should cover you here.

- Who is selling you this contract? A one-man shop operating out of the owner's spare bedroom may not be there tomorrow, while a major retailer will usually stand behind its service contracts.

One thing hasn't changed: While there's no federal law that requires manufacturers to offer warranties, by law, any warranty that's offered must be written, and you must be able to get a look at it before you buy. If you're looking at a warranty, scan these details:

- How long does the warranty last?

- Who provides warranty service, the seller or the manufacturer?

- Will the company repair the item, replace it, or refund your money if the product fails?

- Precisely which parts and repair problems does the warranty cover? Labor charges and shipping charges, both significant items, are commonly excluded.

- What conditions or limitations apply? Make sure the warranty will meet your needs.

 WARNING Treat spoken warranties cautiously. If a salesperson orally assures you that the company will provide free repairs or otherwise offers a warranty, get it in writing. Otherwise, you may find you can't get the service if you need it.

Catalog Retailers

Despite the proliferation of computer superstores and the growing appeal of Internet shopping (covered in the next section) catalog retailers of computer products still enjoy robust sales. And why not? Printed catalogs are handy and highly portable shopping tools. On the downside, you can't handle the merchandise or talk to a salesperson like you can in a store. Nor is it as simple to return a defective or unsatisfactory product to a catalog retailer, and technical support may be limited or even nonexistent. To make up for it, however, mail-order retailers usually sell for less than companies with a physical storefront. And with rapid overnight shipping, you won't have to wait weeks for your new gadgets to arrive.

There are a few computer equipment catalogs that specialize in communications and networking equipment, and just about any general computer mail-order catalog, such as PC Connections or Computer Discount Warehouse, will have a section on networking gear. This section is usually listed in the product category index under "Networking." When you turn to it, you'll find primarily business-oriented networking equipment, with a sprinkling of home-suitable products mixed in.

Sometimes you'll have to go the fine print to find what you need. In a specific catalog advertisement for network hubs, the picture is likely to be of the most expensive product, such as a 24-port Fast Ethernet hub. You'll be forced to look through a list of hubs to find the 4-port model you're interested in. And, without a picture, you may have to just imagine what it looks like.

Your Rights as a Catalog Shopper

It can be a little unnerving to give your credit card number to a telephone operator to order a couple of hundred dollars worth of sophisticated electronic equipment. But you're not out there all alone. You have definite rights as a catalog shopper, whether you ordered your product by mail, phone, fax, or even computer. By federal law, these include:

- Unless otherwise agreed, the cataloger must ship the product within 30 days of your order or let you cancel your order and get a refund.
- If there is a billing error, you can dispute the charge and refuse to pay until the mix-up is straightened out.
- You can also dispute the charge and legally withhold payment if you get an unsatisfactory or defective product—as long as the vendor is located in your home state or within 100 miles, and you've tried to resolve the dispute first.

You may have other rights depending on your state and local laws. You can find out more about federal protections by visiting the Federal Trade Commission, the government agency in charge of protecting consumer rights, at www.ftc.gov.

An increasing number of catalog retailers are becoming hybrid online/paper vendors, with their Web sites prominently displayed on their printed catalogs. There's nothing really new about this. Much the same transition occurred as one-time mail-order retailers began to rely on telephone orders and began including their toll-free numbers in their brochures. You can also frequently order from catalogs by fax. With the one exception of the security of purchase information (discussed in the following section) the method of communication you use with your catalog retailer is irrelevant. Pick the one that feels right, and mail, phone, fax, or click away.

Fixing Mail-Order Problems

If you have any problems with mail or phone orders, such as overbilling or missing or damaged merchandise, there are four avenues you can travel to try to get satisfaction:

1. First, try the company that sold the merchandise to you. Write a letter to the home office describing the problem and asking for resolution.

2. If the company doesn't help you, try your state or local consumer protection office. You can look this office up in the phone book's blue pages government section.

3. If you ordered or had the product delivered by mail, bring the problem to the attention of your postal inspector. Call your local post office and ask for the Inspector-in-Charge.

4. Another avenue is the Direct Marketing Association, a trade group that operates a hotline for handling complaints about the industry. Write to CONSUMERLINE, Direct Marketing Association, 1101 17th St. NW, Washington, DC, 20036. Include the name and address of the company involved in the complaint, photocopies of your complaint letter to the company, canceled checks, order forms, other relevant documents, and a description of the problem.

Online Shopping

In a recent survey of holiday purchasing plans, the Internet research company Harris Interactive found that more than three out of four Internet users now use the Internet to shop in some way. In particular, consumers either gather information or actually buy products over the Internet. Odds are pretty good that you'll at least consider shopping with an online merchant for some of the networking equipment you require. Online shopping is a little different from catalog or storefront shopping, however, and you'll need a few new techniques to enjoy and prosper in the world of Internet consumption.

You'll be exposed to a number of new terms, such as *shopping agent*, which is a Web site or service that searches a number of online stores to find what you want. You'll have to get used to receiving electronic invoices that arrive as e-mail instead of printed bills in envelopes. On the other hand, like your neighborhood grocery store, online stores have *shopping baskets,* or electronic lists of goods you have selected to purchase on a particular outing. Despite some familiar terminology, however, shopping works very differently online.

WARNING Don't give your credit card number to Internet merchants without checking them out first. If you're concerned about an online merchant, contact the Better Business Bureau at www.bbb.org. You can also check with Internet Fraud Watch at www.fraud.org for tips on avoiding fraudulent online offers.

FIGURE 11.1

The National Fraud Information Center's Internet Fraud Watch provides information about how to avoid getting taken for a ride by an unscrupulous online merchant.

At present, Internet shoppers are more concerned with avoiding ripoffs than are consumers who browse in physical storefronts. It remains to be seen whether or not this is a valid concern, and the Internet proves, over the long-term, to be a more fertile field for scoundrels than other arenas of commerce. For the moment, at least, fraud is rising sharply. According to Internet Fraud Watch, an organization operated by the National Consumers League, complaints about Internet fraud have increased 600 percent since 1997, with online auctions proving the largest source of complaints (see Figure 11.1). Keep in mind, however, that the absolute numbers are still very small, with fewer than 8,000 total complaints registered by millions of online shoppers.

Online Auctions

Auctions on the Internet are becoming very popular ways to buy and sell merchandise. They operate much the same as any auction; bidders set the price on available merchandise. Typically when you visit an online auction, you'll see a list of open items in the category you've picked. Before bidding, click on the item you're interested in to learn details. When you see something you want to bid on, you can usually click a button reading "place bid"—or something similar—on the item's catalog page. Then you enter the amount you want to bid and, when appropriate, the quantity you want to buy. You'll also need to put in billing and shipping addresses and credit card information. If your bid is accepted, you'll be notified by the online auctioneer.

Comparison Shopping on the Web

One of the most beautiful things about shopping online is the way you can very quickly compare prices on identical items from a number of vendors. If you've ever spent a morning driving all over town trying to get the best deal on something, you can appreciate how handy it would be to do the same thing, in a couple of minutes, without leaving your desk. And you can compare a much greater number of vendors online than you could hope to do in even a whole day of driving around town. Here are a few of the online price comparison sites, also known as shopping agents or *shopping bots* (bot is short for robot):

- BottomDollar at `www.bottomdollar.com` compares prices for all kinds of products, including a wide variety of computer hardware. See Figure 11.2.

- Computer Shopper at `www.zdnet.com/computershopper` is well organized and covers more than 100 computer equipment purveyors.

- As seen in Figure 11.3, the Consumer World price comparison shopper at `www.consumerworld.org/pages/price.htm` compares prices without inserting ads on its screens.

FIGURE 11.2

You can check scores of prices in a few minutes using online comparison shopping sites, like this one called bottomdollar.com.

FIGURE 11.3

Ad-free price comparisons can be found at Consumer World's price check site.

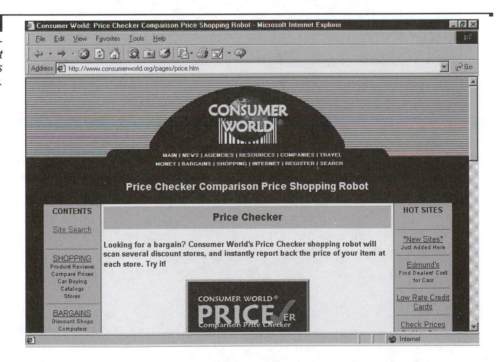

Networking
Nuts and Bolts

- eSmarts, an online shopping assistance site, provides a number of useful tips and links to price comparison shoppers at www.esmarts.com/agents.

- Excite's Jango product finder at www.jango.com catalogs a large number of guides to online shopping, as shown in Figure 11.4.

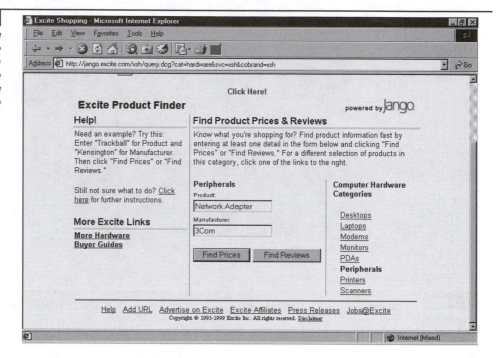

- Fido: The Shopping Doggie at www.shopfido.com lets you compare vendors for a wide variety of products, including networking hardware, by searching within a specific price range.

- HotBot's Shopping Directory at www.hotbot.com/shop lists online stores by category and lets you shop for products within price ranges.

- Shopfind at www.shopfind.com is Yahoo!'s automated shopping service.

- WebMarket at www.webmarket.com lets you search online stores based on traits such as on-time delivery and ease of ordering, in addition to the lowest price.

WARNING   Don't fall into the trap of thinking that an Internet shopping comparison site is infallible. Nobody catalogs the entire Internet; it's just too big. And some sites are better than others at pointing you toward the truly lowest price, while avoiding irrelevant results. Try a few sites until you find one that does what you want.

Online comparison shopping is much easier than trying to find a shady parking space outside a typical mall. All you do is type a description of the product you're looking for into a search box, and click Go or the equivalent.

 TIP   Pricing isn't the only information available through online comparison shopping services. You can also find links to product reviews, news stories, and vendor sites, all targeted at the product you're researching, and all available with a mouse click or two.

Ordering from Online Vendors

Ordering from an online vendor takes more than a few clicks, but it's usually fairly simple to accomplish. It's also almost always a lot faster than trundling down to your local retail storefront. In most cases, you can find and purchase what you want in not much more time than it would take many people to find their car keys. Here's a typical routine:

1. You enter the store's URL in your browser, or click on a link from a price comparison agent or other site.

2. Once at the store's site, you type your product's name in a search box and click Find, or Go, or another similar button, to look for your product. (Some sites work better if you browse by product category to narrow the search field somewhat first.)

3. When you find the product you think you want, you can click a button or link to retrieve additional details.

4. Once you've made up your mind, you will be able to click a button labeled Add to Shopping Cart or the like. You can now shop for more items to add to your cart, or proceed to the checkout screen to pay.

5. At the checkout screen, you'll enter your shipping and billing addresses, select a shipping method such as UPS or US Postal Service, and enter your credit card information.

WARNING Always pay with a credit card when shopping online, as the card issuer's protection policies will provide you with added security from possible fraud. According to the Internet Fraud Watch, the vast majority of fraud complaints about online merchants involve offline payments by check or money order sent to the company.

6. You'll get a chance to cancel or submit your order and will receive an e-mail confirmation telling you when your order was shipped.

 WARNING Look for sites with a key icon in the corner, or that have a URL beginning with https://www instead of http://www. This means the site is secure, and therefore safe to order from. Paying with a credit card is crucial since it will give you a written record of the transaction. If you can't order over a secure site, you may prefer faxing your order in. It works just as well and is more secure.

Here are a few tips for online ordering:

- In the beginning, try online ordering with retailers you know from other methods of shopping. Knowing with whom you're dealing will improve the experience.
- Check fees carefully, as shipping and handling charges can add up quickly even on small items.
- Check the vendors' return policy. Look for an offer of a full refund if you are dissatisfied for any reason.
- Stick close to home. Sure you can order from Tibet if you want, but long distances increase shipping charges and delays.
- Write down the name, address, phone number, and contact information for the store before you make your order. If you stick to this rule, you will never order from a store that doesn't provide contact information online.
- Be sparing about providing personal information on order forms. Required questions are usually marked with asterisks. Skip the rest.

 WARNING Remember, you never have to give your Social Security Number to make a purchase.

- Check privacy policies. Information about you and what you buy is valuable and many companies will try to sell it. Reputable sites post their privacy policies. Look for those that promise to never share your information without your permission.

 WARNING   TRUSTe is a non-profit group with a wide variety of information about privacy issues on the Internet. Learn more at www.truste.org.

Used Equipment

Secondhand computer equipment may never be as popular as "pre-owned" cars and "recycled" clothing. That's because the reality of obsolescence means that even if a used computer works as well as when it was new, it's likely to be scarcely usable when running up-to-date software. The same isn't entirely true for network gear, however. The standard for regular 10Mbps Ethernet has been essentially unchanged for years, and odds are that a network adapter or hub that is several years old would operate quite well enough for a home network's purposes. And when it comes to PCs, which are discussed in the next section, a network can actually extend the useful life of a machine that would otherwise be suitable only as a doorstop.

Used equipment also isn't as well distributed or serviced as new, so you may have to look hard to find what you want. However, the benefits of a lower price may outweigh all that. And if the right deal presents itself, there is often no reason why used equipment can't help you build your network as effectively as the newest gadgets on the market.

Office Hand-Me-Downs

The average business computer has a useful life of only a few years before the requirements of upgraded software or higher benchmarks for performance relegate it to obsolescence. What happens to these old machines? A few are handed over to charity, some are scrapped for their valuable innards, and many more are given or sold cheaply to employees for use as home machines.

One of the great things about getting a used machine from your office, besides the fact that you're liable to get a great deal, is that odds are good it already has some kind of network adapter in it. Unless it's an archaic network technology or is otherwise unsuitable to your network plans, you may be able to save the time and trouble, as well as the added expense, of purchasing a network card for any ex-office machines you obtain for your network.

You're somewhat less likely to obtain networking equipment per se, as opposed to old computers, from your work. That's because while businesses may upgrade their PCs every few years, they tend to leave their networks largely in place for much longer, only upgrading and adding to them as they are forced to. However, if your company decides to scrap its old coaxial cable system or replace all its regular Ethernet NICs with Fast Ethernet models, you could be in the way of an excellent opportunity. Of course, a lot of other employees are likely to have the same idea. To make sure you can get in on the action, pay attention to your company's announced plans for its network, and even try to get some inside information. Your network administrator is a good place to start.

Older Family Machines

Personal computers that are several years old are perfect for use in home networks. In fact, installing one of these old dinosaurs in a home network may be the only way you can get any more use out of it. When connected to a network that also has more powerful computers on it, the obsolescent PC can:

- Tap into the newer machines' disk drives and other peripherals
- Take advantage of software it might not otherwise be able to use, by running network-capable applications on later-model machines with more memory and faster processors
- Act as network workhorses to take the load off of other machines, handling tasks such as backing up files from the network

Of course, PCs need to have a minimum system configuration before they are likely to be of much use on a network. An original IBM PC from 1981 sporting an 8086 processor and no hard drive won't be able to run much, if any, modern software. However, just about any five-year-old 486 with several megabytes of memory and a spare industry-standard expansion slot can probably fill in on the network.

Keep in mind: This is a network, not a magic act. No amount of cable and network adapters is going to make a laptop computer with a 486Mhz CPU and 2MB of memory run like a 700MHz Pentium III with 128MB of RAM. For instance, your display is a limitation that is impossible to get around. A game on that dazzling 19-inch monitor on the new Dell OptiPlex in the home office is going to look better than it does on a 14-inch VGA monitor dating from 1992, no matter how you slice it. However, the point is that you can greatly augment and extend the useful life of older machines by using them as networked companions to more powerful PCs—much as Palm Pilots and other PDAs act as companions to desktop PCs.

Flea Market Bargains

A flea market might seem like a strange place for a home networker to be looking for high-tech networking equipment. And, to be sure, most flea market merchandise is far more likely to consist of quasi-antique furniture than the latest technology. But some flea markets could easily fill the bill for almost any conceivable home network shopping list. For instance, the First Saturday Sidewalk Sale is a huge monthly outdoor electronics sale that has been held in the same part of downtown Dallas for more than 30 years. After beginning as a ham radio swap meet in the 1960s, First Saturday has evolved into a computer smorgasbord where you can find anything from the latest Intel processors to antiques like a Commodore 64.

 TIP   One of the nicest things about flea markets is that they carry goods, many of them scavenged out of closets and garages, that other stores simply don't keep in stock. If you've been craving some such rarity as an Atari 2600 game cartridge or a good old box of 5.25-inch floppies for some purpose, a flea market may be your only hope. A flea market is a good place to look for computer parts to get an old, otherwise useless machine up and running, and ready to be a part of your network.

Not everybody likes flea market shopping. The sight of a rickety card table piled high with old disk drives, monitors, and modems makes some people slightly queasy. And there's a lot to be said for shopping at an established merchant with warranties and a service center, as opposed to someone whose store consists of the trunk of a car, and whose mode of business is openly of the fly-by-night variety. It's reasonable to ask a flea market vendor to show you that a network hub lights up before you buy, but don't expect to be able to return it a month later if it quits. Spirited haggling, another flea market standard practice, is also a turn-off for many low-key shoppers. But if you love bargains and don't mind a little dust and drama, flea market shopping for network equipment can be a great way to pick up a bargain or two.

Flea markets don't exactly buy commercial time during the Super Bowl to advertise their presence, and they're often located in out-of-the-way parking lots and former cow pastures. You can find one easily, however, by using the Flea Market Guide of U.S. Flea Markets. This directory, available online at www.fleamarketguide.com, provides information such as hours of operation, types of merchandise, number of dealers, and directions for flea markets in all 50 states.

TIP If you really like life on the edge, you can buy used computer equipment from classified ads in newspapers, want-ad magazines, and online message boards. Caveat emptor is trebly emphasized here. While you can make these transactions and never get burned—and many do—the risk involved in buying used computer gear from strangers is obviously significant. Never hand over your credit card number to a stranger selling used computer equipment. Instead, pay a little extra to have UPS deliver the item COD. That way, at least you'll have a return address in case there's nothing in the box.

Computer Factory Outlet Shopping

Factory outlets are stores set up by manufacturers to sell surplus, returned, or discontinued merchandise directly to consumers. The traditional retailers who have to compete with these low-price, no-frills operations aren't too crazy about them. But consumers have embraced them enthusiastically. As a result, they've sprung up nearly everywhere, selling name-brand clothing, housewares, and other goods in big outlet malls, generally located on the outskirts of cities. Computer equipment factory outlets aren't quite as popular yet, but they do exist.

Dell Computer Corporation has a big Dell Factory Outlet in Austin near its headquarters in Round Rock, Texas. Compaq Computer Corporation also operates an outlet in Houston. These stores are likely to stock anything and everything that their companies manufacture, including varying amounts and types of home networking gear. The equipment generally falls into one of the following four categories:

Excess new equipment   Gear that the manufacturer hasn't been able to sell for one reason or another, and has marked down and placed in its outlet store to move it out.

Discontinued equipment   Items that have been replaced by newer models.

As-is merchandise   Older machines that haven't been refurbished, or floor models that have some shop wear. The key is: You take it as-is, along with the risk that it won't work properly.

Refurbished equipment   Discussed in detail in the next section.

If you live near one of these outlets, you're in luck. Despite the necessary warnings about buying refurbished or discontinued equipment, outlets represent good deals on name-brand networking gear. You are generally safe buying from a manufacturer's outlet, despite the fact that the equipment generally won't carry as good a warranty as one purchased from a traditional retailer. The selection is, on the other hand, typically pretty limited. You never really know what they're going to have on any given day, since manufacturers don't stock the stores the way a regular retailer would. Frequently, the best thing to do is just drop by every couple of days until you see what you want at the price you can afford.

Refurbished Networking Gear

Refurbished network equipment is usually sold by a computer or equipment manufacturer. Refurbished merchandise may be used equipment coming off a lease, or new equipment that was returned by the buyer. It's been tested and repaired as necessary, and is likely to carry a 30- to 90-day warranty. Electronic components that work out of the box are likely to work for a long time, whether they're refurbished or straight from the factory. And the repair and testing work in refurbishing is generally done by the same (or at least similarly trained) technicians as the ones that assemble and test new equipment.

The main reason to buy refurbished gear is the price. You can easily save 30 percent off the price of a new version of what you're buying, whether it's a complete networking kit, or a handful of components such as network adapters. The downside of buying refurbished equipment is that it's usually older technology. For example, computer leases typically run anywhere from two to four years. So what you save in price you'll give back in performance. In a young, fast-changing field like home networking, that can be a significant disadvantage. Still, many people are happy with refurbished machines from PCs to printers.

Summary

You made the hard choice and decided upon what kind of home network you want to install. Now you find you have a dazzling number of options for purchasing network equipment. Shopping options include reliable sources, like computer stores, catalog retailers, and online; and less reliable sources, like flea markets and hand-me-downs from friends and neighbors. To make your decision, weigh the factors of available technical support, warranties, and your own mechanical know-how.

What's Next

Now that you've learned how to shop for network equipment, we'll delve into the software side of things. In the next chapter, we'll look at networking with Windows 95/98.

PART III

Network Software

LEARN TO:

- *Network with Windows 95/98*

- *Network with Macintosh NOS*

- *Network with Other Network Operating Systems*

- *Use and Configure Other Network Software*

CHAPTER 12

Windows 95/98

Overview

Since nearly nine out of 10 personal computers worldwide are running some version of Microsoft's Windows operating system, it's a good thing that the later editions of Windows, at least, come with built-in networking capabilities. Specifically, Windows 95/98 are well equipped to network out of the box, while the older Windows For Workgroups is also network-capable after some modifications. Being able isn't the same thing as being easy, of course, and networking home computers using the Windows operating system does have its share of tricks and traps for the inexperienced or the unwary.

 NOTE See Part 4, "Using Your Network," for details on how to set up new users, share resources, and perform other essential housekeeping chores on networks using Windows PCs.

Two of the networking issues you're likely to run across while networking with Windows computers are Dial-Up Networking and NetBEUI. *Dial-Up Networking* is a networking feature you can use for several purposes, including the following:

- When connecting to Internet Service Providers or other outside networks over phone lines.

- When accessing your own network from remote locations.

- When connecting two PCs using the direct-connect feature in Windows.

An important part of using Dial-Up Networking is creating your Connection Profiles. *Connection profiles* control and specify the number you dial to reach online services—and other parameters—and make networking via dial-up connection simpler and smoother than if you had to re-enter this information each time you tried to go online.

The Windows Internet Connection Wizard is a tool that leads you through the job of setting up your link to the Internet. Internet Connection Wizard is another way Windows has of making online connections easier. However, both Connection Profiles and Internet Connection Wizard take some explanation. This chapter will help you feel comfortable with both.

Dial-Up Networking

One of the most common ways of networking Windows computers, and the one you'll very likely be using in your own network, is Dial-Up Networking. Dial-Up Networking is a subset of *Dial-Up Connection*. The generic term Dial-Up Connection refers to making computer-to-computer connections over regular telephone lines. Specifically in a networking context, the term Dial-Up Connection refers to connections made using specially leased phone lines that are faster and more reliable than the lines used by the typical home consumer. When it comes to networking in Windows, the term Dial-Up Networking refers to a specific set of capabilities in Windows, which are, again, used to make computer-to-computer connections using standard phone lines.

Improvements to Windows 98 Dial-Up Networking

Windows 98 offers some significant improvements in Dial-Up Networking compared to Windows 95 and past versions of Windows. The improvements include:

Dial-up Scripting   This new feature lets you automate tasks such as connecting to online services and computer bulletin boards.

Modem Multilinking   This new feature, officially called *Multilink Channel Aggregation*, lets you install two modems in one PC and use both, at the same time, to access the Internet at up to double the speed. For instance, if you install a pair of 56K modems and use two phone lines, you could, in theory, connect at 112Kbps, although your effective throughput is likely to be less, for a variety of reasons. One reason is that the Federal Communications Commission limits the amount of electrical power that can be emitted by a device attached to the phone network. So the actual maximum performance of a so-called 56Kbps modem is no more than 53Kbps. Also, unless your Internet Service Provider supports dual-modem service, you will be limited to no faster throughput than a 56Kbps modem can provide. Finally, the quality of your phone lines may not be up to supporting the maximum practical speed.

Before you can set up Dial-Up Networking on your computer, you'll obviously need to have the Dial-Up Networking software installed, and it may not be on your particular computer. Here's how to check:

1. On the Windows Desktop, double-click the My Computer icon.

2. You should see Dial-Up Networking as an icon or entry on the list, as shown in Figure 12.1.

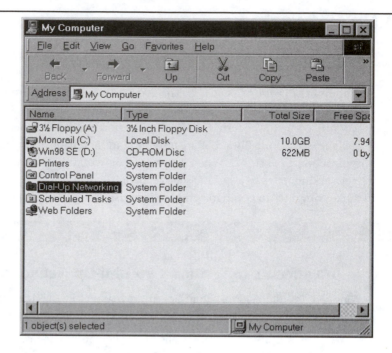

If you have Dial-Up Networking loaded, then you will want to skip ahead to the next section, "Running Windows Internet Connection Wizard." You will not have to go through the manual process outlined in the following steps. And, of course, you don't want to take the time to manually configure something if you don't have to do so.

 NOTE   If you have Dial-Up Networking loaded, skip to the next section, "Running Windows Internet Connection Wizard."

If you don't have Dial-Up Networking loaded, on the other hand, the first thing you'll need to do is install the software. Before you get started, make sure you have your Windows setup CD-ROM handy. Next:

1. Click Start ➢ Settings ➢ Control Panel.

2. Highlight the Add/Remove Programs icon, as shown in Figure 12.2, and double-click the icon or press Enter.

3. Click the tab for Windows Setup and wait while Setup searches for installed components.

4. Highlight Communications on the list, as shown in Figure 12.3, and click the Details button.

FIGURE 12.2

Begin installing Dial-Up Networking by opening Add/Remove Programs in Control Panel.

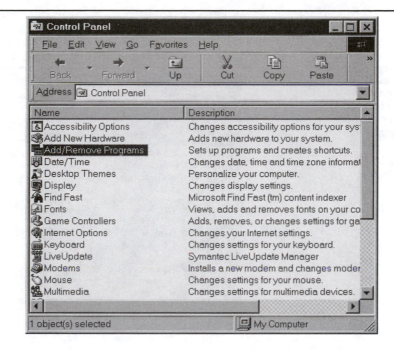

FIGURE 12.3

Select Communications in the Windows setup list and click Details to display the components you have installed.

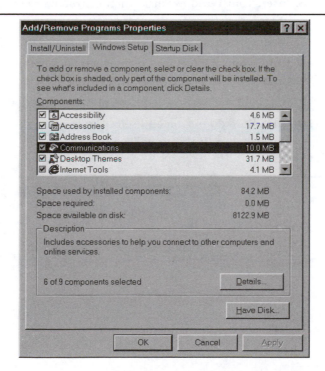

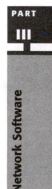

PART

III

Network Software

5. Place a checkmark next to the Dial-Up Networking component, as shown in Figure 12.4, and click OK.

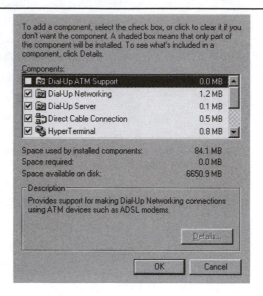

6. Insert your Windows disk when instructed to by the program and follow the other instructions that appear on-screen.

7. When the software has been installed, restart your computer.

8. If the Control Panel isn't open when your computer restarts, click Start ➤ Settings ➤ Control Panel, as in Step 1.

9. Highlight the Network icon and press Enter or double-click.

10. Click the Add button and select Protocol in the Select Network Component Type window, as shown in Figure 12.5.

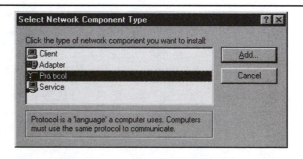

11. Click the Add button and select Microsoft in the Manufacturers window.

12. Select TCP/IP in the Protocols window and click OK.

13. The Network Configuration list should be displayed. Make sure that TCP/IP appears and click OK.

In the previous section, you installed support for the TCP/IP networking protocol suite. Now it's time to create a connection profile.

 WARNING Before you get started setting up your connection profile, make sure you have handy the phone number and other information necessary for connecting to your Internet Service Provider's PPP access. The ISP should provide you with all the connection details necessary for establishing the profile.

How to Find a Local ISP

You can use the Internet Connection Wizard to select from a directory of national Internet Service Providers, as described later in this chapter, or you can select your own. A given Internet Service Provider will generally support only a limited number of connection types; that is, dial-up telephone, digital subscriber line (DSL), cable modem, and so forth. Many, in fact, support only dial-up telephone connections. So your search for an ISP is likely to be narrowed down quite a bit once you've chosen a connection method. If you know you're going to use a cable modem, for instance, you'll have to choose an ISP that works with your local cable company.

You can find a listing of ISPs in the *Computers On-Line Services* section of your local Yellow Pages. Any sizable metropolitan area should have a good selection. These ISPs come in all varieties, some offering good service and support, and others characterized by frequent busy signals, unreliable connections, and unanswered phone lines. Call a few in the phone book and ask about these characteristics:

Additional e-mail boxes Look for two or more e-mail boxes included with your subscription.

Web page disk space You should get several megabytes of disk space on the ISP's server if you plan to have your own Web page.

Continued

PART

III

Network Software

CONTINUED

Software   You should be able to download Web browsers, e-mail, and other useful Internet software from the ISP for your use.

Support   Toll-free telephone support seven days a week and 24 hours a day is the gold standard here. Also look for adequate customer-support staffing levels, online Frequently Asked Question (FAQ) files, and searchable help files.

Special features   Other features you may want to look for include *spam filters*, which help to filter out or block unwanted commercial e-mail messages, access to Usenet newsgroups, and Web-hosting services.

Call the ISP, ask questions, and request a faxed or e-mailed description of the service offerings. Another very helpful conduit for information is found in personal referrals from people who have used the service. You can also use various specialized Web search engines to find information about an ISP. For instance, check out ISPs.com at www.isps.com.

Creating Your Connection Profile

If you have all the information you need from your ISP and you have Dial-Up Networking installed, you're ready to create your *Connection Profile*. Your Connection Profile contains information such as the phone number used to contact your ISP and the type of modem you will be using.

 TIP   A Connection Profile makes it easy to connect to the Internet. All you have to do is click on the icon for the Connection Profile, and you'll automatically begin the connection process. It's especially helpful to have Connection Profiles when you have one or more ISPs, or you use different numbers to connect to your service while traveling. You can create a different Connection Profile for each ISP or telephone number to ease the task of connection.

Here's how to set up your Connection Profile using Windows 98:

1. On the Windows Desktop, double-click the My Computer icon.

2. Select the Dial-Up Networking icon or entry on the list and double-click or press Enter.

3. You will see the Make New Connection wizard start, as shown in Figure 12.6.

The Make New Connection wizard allows you to enter a name for your computer and select the device you'll use to connect to the Internet.

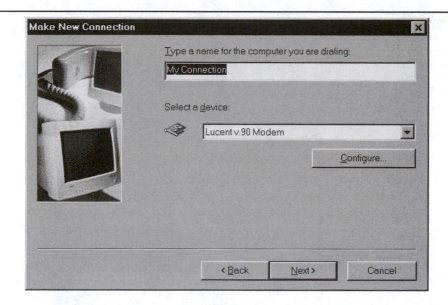

4. At the top of the screen, enter a name in the box for the name of the computer you are dialing.

 TIP If you are setting up Dial-Up Networking to access an Internet Service Provider, it's a good idea to enter the name of the provider in this box. That way, the icon for this profile in the Dial-Up Networking folder will have the name of your ISP on it, helping you to identify the proper icon.

5. Click Next and, in the next screen, enter the area code and phone number for your Internet Service Provider.

6. Click Next and go to the Finish screen. Click Finish.

7. You should return to the Dial-Up Networking window, and see an icon or folder for your new connection, as shown in Figure 12.7.

PART

III

Network Software

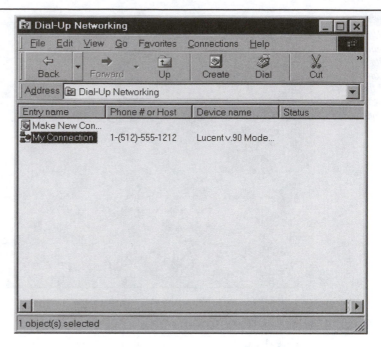

8. Right-click on the icon for your new connection and select Properties.

9. You'll see a Connections Properties dialog box for your new connection, as shown in Figure 12.8.

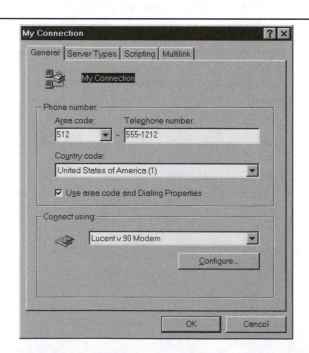

10. Click on the tab for Server Type. The Server Types dialog box will appear, as shown in Figure 12.9.

FIGURE 12.9

The Server Types dialog box lets you select the type of dial-up server you will be using.

11. Select PPP Type of Dial-Up Server from the drop-down list. To access the Internet, place checkmarks next to the options for Log On to Network, Enable Software Compression and select TCP/IP in Allowed Network Protocols.

 TIP While you need only the TCP/IP protocol suite to access the Internet, you should also check NetBEUI in the Server Types dialog box, if, as is likely, you are using Microsoft networking protocols on your network. Check IPX/SPX if you plan to use Novell NetWare protocols.

12. Click the button labeled TCP/IP. Now you'll need the information from your ISP about whether and how to fill in the radio buttons for assigning and specifying IP addresses. Be careful to answer these exactly as your ISP tells you to.

13. Click OK until all dialog boxes have closed.

Running Windows Internet Connection Wizard

If you already have the Dial-Up Networking installed on your PC, you can run the Internet Connection Wizard to perform the task of setting up your connection automatically, as shown in Figure 12.10.

 NOTE   If you don't have Dial-Up Networking installed on your PC, you will need to install and configure the software manually. See the previous section, "Installing Dial-Up Networking."

Here's how:

1. Select the Connect to the Internet Wizard on your desktop and press Enter or double-click.

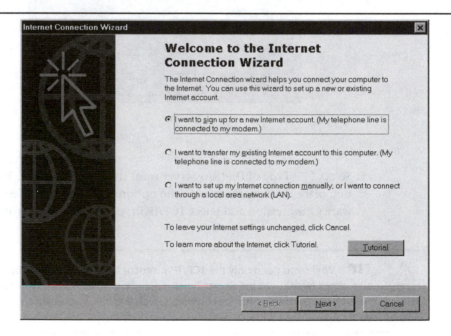

2. Select the option that describes what you're doing: setting up a new account, switching an existing account, or setting up a connection through a network. Let's say you're signing up for a new account through a phone line connected to a modem. Select the first radio button and click Next.

FIGURE 12.11

The Internet Connection Wizard automatically dials a toll-free number to connect to the Microsoft Internet Referral Service and presents you with a list of Internet Service Providers.

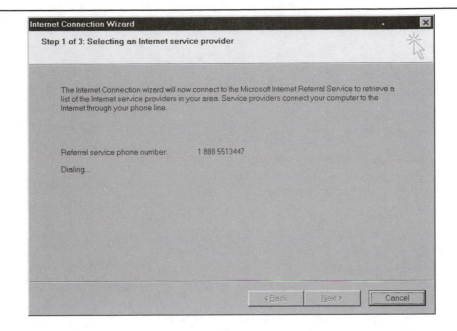

3. The Internet Connection Wizard will connect you to the Microsoft Internet Referral Service and show you a list of Internet service providers, as shown in Figure 12.11. This list and the instructions for signing up with one of the ISPs changes, so you'll have to click on the ISP you want and follow the directions.

Summary

Just because you've got a home network doesn't mean your networking has to be limited to your home. You can set up Windows Dial-Up Networking to let you reach other networks, as well as dial into your own network to access files or home network resources. And with the help of the Windows Internet Connection Wizard, you can access the entire Internet from your home network.

What's Next

Now that you've learned a little more about networking with Windows PCs, the next chapter covers home networking with Apple Macintosh computers.

PART

III

Network Software

CHAPTER 13

Networking with Macintosh Computers

Overview

t's pretty well known that Apple Macintoshes come ready to network out-of-the-box. That's quite different from Windows PCs, which generally require a good bit of extra equipment and, sometimes, software, before they can effectively network. However, being ready to network isn't the same as actually networking. Before you can share files, printers, and other resources between Macs on a network, you'll have a fair amount of setup. Plus, you'll very likely need to purchase some cables and, possibly adapters, before you can physically connect your Macs.

NOTE iMac users get all the same advantages as PC owners from home networking, such as Internet access sharing and head-to-head gaming, plus one more very important benefit, access to a floppy disk drive. That's because the colorful iMacs come without the floppy drives that have been standard equipment on personal computers for 20 years. If you have one of these, as well as one of the blue-and-white Power Mac G3s—and aren't networked—you have to buy a floppy drive that will connect to the USB port if you want to share files using floppies. But who wants to go back to SneakerNet? Lack of a floppy drive is a powerful inducement to build a home network for many Mac users.

Connecting Your Macintoshes

The network software Apple has shipped with all its computers for many years is called AppleTalk and it uses the proprietary LocalTalk protocol. To connect two Macs using AppleTalk, all you need is a special LocalTalk cable that fits into the printer port, as shown in Figure 13.1.

FIGURE 13.1

Macintoshes use the printer port on the back for connecting LocalTalk cables. The modem/printer port can also be used for networking and looks the same, except that along with the printer icon above the port is a telephone icon.

Connecting your Macs via LocalTalk is easy. Here's all you do:

1. Click the Special menu and choose Shut Down.

2. Plug your LocalTalk cable into the printer port on the back of your Mac.

You can also network Macintoshes using Ethernet or Fast Ethernet, both of which offer substantially faster speeds than AppleTalk. Newer Macintoshes, including Power-Mac G4s, PowerBook G3s, iMacs, and iBooks, all come with built-in Fast Ethernet ports. You can use the same Cat 5 cables with RJ-45 connectors you would on any Ethernet network. Other Macintoshes can be equipped with Ethernet ports using plug-in adapter cards. These Ethernet networks are the best-performing network option for Macintosh users.

 TIP You can also connect a non-Ethernet-equipped Macintosh to an Ethernet network by using a transceiver. This is a small adapter that fits into the AUI port on the back of the Mac. It has a socket that accepts an Ethernet RJ-45 jack. Transceivers come in both 10BaseT regular Ethernet and 100BaseT Fast Ethernet varieties.

Phoneline Networking with Macs

You can set up a Macintosh network using existing telephone wiring with Farallon Computing's HomeLINE phoneline networking kit. HomeLINE uses the same Home Phoneline Networking Alliance technology as PC phoneline networking kits, but adapted for Macs. That means HomeLINE suffers the same 1Mbps limitation as HPNA-compliant phoneline networks for PCs. HPNA is an acronym standing for the standard for network equipment set by the Home Phoneline Networking Alliance, an industry association of network equipment vendors.

There is one nice addition to the HomeLINE technology: You can connect both PCs and Macs on the same network as shown in Figure 13.2. Each networked Mac (or PC) must, however, have an unused PCI slot to install the required adapter. That's going to rule out directly connecting an iMac, portable PowerBook, and iBook to a HomeLine network, although you can still network Macs to other Macs, even if one of them is connected to a HomeLine network.

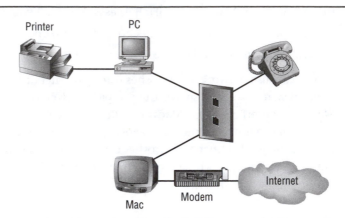

FIGURE 13.2

A phoneline network can connect Macs and PCs into the same network.

HomeLINE is fairly inexpensive, at around $150 for a two-computer setup. Add additional computers for $80 each. The package includes Internet sharing software for Macs. If one of the networked PCs is set up as the Internet gateway, you can also use Windows 98 Internet Connection Sharing software. Learn more at www.farallon.com.

Wireless Networking with Macs

While Apple's proprietary AppleTalk networking software considerably underperforms wired Ethernet networks, the tables turn when it comes to wireless. The AirPort wireless networking technology Apple pioneered with its iBook portables operates at 11Mbps, about 10 percent faster than regular Ethernet. You don't have to forget about AirPort if you don't have an iBook, either. Farallon Computing sells a SkyLine PC card that allows older Powerbooks to connect to AirPort wireless networks as well. Learn more at www.farallon.com.

Activating AppleTalk Networking

Creating your Mac network isn't over once you physically connect the computers. You also need to activate the software. The first time you turn on your Mac after physically connecting it to another Mac or peripheral, you also need to turn on AppleTalk before you can do any networking. This is somewhat more involved than plugging in the network cable. However, it's still pretty straightforward. Here's how:

1. Choose Control Panel from the Apple menu.

2. Click the Options... button.

 NOTE If you don't see the Options... button in Control Panel, go to the Edit menu and choose User Mode.... Click Advanced ➤ OK. Now go back to the first step.

3. Click Active ➤ OK.

 NOTE If the Active button isn't on when you open Options..., you may have a printer that does not support PostScript. If so, you may have to turn AppleTalk off when printing.

4. In the AppleTalk control panel, see that the connection is set properly to Ethernet, Modem Port, or Printer Port, depending on what type of connection you are using.

5. Click the Close box, then click Save.

Just as in PC networking, you have to assign a unique name to your Macintosh to distinguish it from others on the network. Here's how:

1. Choose Control Panel from the Apple menu.

2. Open the File Sharing icon.

3. Enter your name into the Owner Name box.

4. Press Tab to go to the Owner Password and enter the password you've selected into the Owner Password box.

 TIP Select up to eight characters for your password. Avoid using actual words and, ideally, mix up letters and numerals to create a password that has meaning to you but no one else. For instance, you might use your mother's maiden name, replacing all instances of the letter "S" with the numeral "5". The characters you type will be replaced by bullets, so be sure you can remember your password before moving on.

5. Press Tab again to move to the Computer Name box and type in a name for your computer.

TIP Choosing a computer name is like choosing a password in that the name must be unique, at least on your network. There can only be one computer per name on a network. However, a computer name shouldn't be kept secret like a password. Other computer users on the network will have to know your computer's name in order to access it to share files and other resources. So it should be brief, distinctive, and memorable.

Setting Up Sharing

Before you can share files, you have to turn File Sharing on. To do this, go back to the File Sharing panel just as you did in the first two steps in the previous section. This time, however, you'll skip over the naming part, since you've already done that job. Here's how:

1. Choose Control Panel from the Apple menu.

2. Open the File Sharing icon.

3. Now click the Start button in the File Sharing box to turn file sharing on.

 TIP Your Macintosh may already have File Sharing turned on. If so, instead of a Start button, you'll have a Stop button in the File Sharing box. If you want File Sharing to remain on, don't click this button. Instead, skip this step and move onto the next step.

4. Click the close square or press Command+W to close this panel.

Now that you've set up File Sharing, you have to select which folders you will share.

 TIP You can set up programs to be shared by clicking the Program Linking button in the File Sharing dialog box. Many applications will require additional setup to be sharable—consult your application manual on this one—and some can't be shared at all. In addition, sometimes you must pay the sofware publisher an extra fee to allow more than one network user to share the application.

You can either make a new folder, and designate that one for sharing with other users on the network, or you can select existing folders for sharing. When you elect to share a folder, that means other users on the network can see the files in that folder.

Users on the network can also add their own files to the folder's contents. Here's how to set it up:

1. Select a folder or group of folders by clicking it.

 TIP You can set up your Macintosh's entire hard disk for sharing by choosing the icon for your hard disk instead of an individual folder or group of folders.

2. Choose the File menu ➤ Get Info ➤ Sharing....

3. In the To Share Info control panel, place a check mark in the box labeled Share This Item and Its Contents.

4. Close the panel.

 NOTE You can quickly tell if a folder is set up for sharing by examining its icon. If you see wires poking out of the image of the folder on your Mac's screen, that means your computer's set up for sharing.

Setting Up Guest Access

Once you're set up for file sharing, other users on the network can access your files, but only as long as they know the name and password required to connect to your machine. That provides a measure of security, at the cost of some convenience. You can make sharing files easier by setting up Guest Access. This will allow people to log in to your machine as guests even if they don't know the password.

In order to let a guest access your computer, you need to set up both your computer and the guest's machine. Here's how to set up access for guests on your machine:

1. Choose Control Panel from the Apple menu.

2. Open the Users & Groups panel.

3. One of the names listed in the Users & Groups panel will be Guest. Double-click this name.

4. Click the Show menu in the Guest dialog box and select Sharing.

5. Click the box marked Allow Guests to Connect to This Computer to place a check mark in it.

6. Click the close box twice to close the Guest dialog box and Users & Groups control panel.

You can repeat this procedure to give more guests access to your machine.

Now you need to get your guests' machines set up to connect to your Mac. Guests can access your machine as follows:

1. Select Chooser from the Apple Menu.

 WARNING   Remember, now you're working at the guest's machine to set it up for guest access to your files. You also need to make sure that the guest Mac has file sharing turned on.

2. Click the AppleShare icon to display the list of available file servers.

3. Select the name of the Mac that this computer is going to be accessing as a guest. (It will likely be the only file server.)

4. Click the OK button.

5. In the dialog box that pops up next, click Connect.

6. You'll get a window showing the folders set up for Guest Access sharing.

7. Highlight the disk or folder to be accessed and click OK.

 NOTE   You can actually set up your Macintosh to automatically share information every time you start it up, as long as both your computer and the guest computer are turned on. Just click the box next to a folder or disk in the dialog box for Guest Access sharing. This capability is limited, however, to when you turn on the Macintosh especially designated to grant Guest Access, not just by starting up any computer on the network.

8. Click the Close dialog box in Chooser. You should now be able to see an icon representing the shared folder on your Macintosh desktop. Double-clicking this icon opens the shared resource.

Now that you're set up for file sharing, it's a snap to copy or move files from the file server computer to the guest's Macintosh. To add more guests, go back to the section creating Guest Access and repeat the procedure. You can also change the files or disks you'll be sharing. In step 5 of the previous section, instead of choosing the box Allow Guests to Connect to This Computer, select Different Resources for Sharing.

Summary

Overall, it's easier to network Macintoshes than PCs, in terms of the software and hardware you will need to buy, install, and configure. This is a real plus, because iMac users have a strong inducement to network, given the lack of an internal disk drive. In addition, you can network your Macintoshes to your PCs in a cross-platform network. With HomeLINE, a mixed marriage of Macs and PCs provides you access to the best each operating system has to offer.

What's Next

While networks of Macintosh and PCs make up by far the bulk of the home networks you're likely to encounter, they're not the only ones. That's why we'll look at other network operating systems, including Windows 2000 and Linux, in the next chapter.

CHAPTER **14**

Other Network Operating Systems

Overview

Y ou don't have to be nearing retirement age to recall a time when there were no Windows PCs, nor even any Macintosh computers. Even some Generation Xers remember how the whole industry only began in 1977, when Apple, Radio Shack, and Commodore introduced the first computers suitable for consumers. The Apple II, TRS-80 Model 1, and Commodore PET have since faded into history. Perhaps there will come a time when Windows based PCs and Macs will seem just as antiquated and odd. And yet, from about 1985 to 1990, it seemed that Windows was never going to come, and everyone but Mac users would be stuck with MS-DOS and the character-based interface forever. Nowadays, it sometimes seems that Windows and Macs will always be here and that, quite possibly, everything before long will be Windows or Macintosh.

But there are some excellent operating systems out there besides the ones from Microsoft and Apple, including the freeware Linux OS and the longtime networking giant NetWare from Novell. In addition, there's Windows 2000, the all-new Microsoft operating system that is expected to eventually become the operating system of choice for the majority of the world's computers. While the existing versions of the Windows and Macintosh operating systems are fine for home networking, there are some good reasons why you might choose Windows 2000, Linux, or NetWare for your home network.

Windows 2000, NetWare, and Linux are all suited for client-server networks, as shown in Figure. 14.1. In client-server networks, a central computer called a server provides file storage and access to peripherals such as printers. Client-server networks offer excellent security features and are good for managing very large networks with hundreds of workstations. That makes them popular among business networkers.

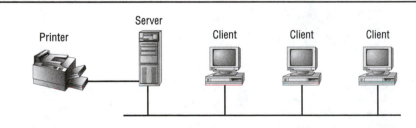

FIGURE 14.1.

Client-server networks have a central server computer that provides file space and runs printers and other peripherals for the other client computers on the network.

Windows 98 and Macintosh AppleTalk home networks are, on the other hand, peer-to-peer networks as shown in Figure 14.2. In these networks, also called peer networks, every computer can communicate with every other computer, and all share in the task of overseeing the network, providing file storage, and managing peripherals.

Peer network architectures become unwieldy in larger networks, such as those many businesses operate, but are well suited for networks with fewer than 10 workstations. That makes them excellent choices for home networking.

FIGURE 14.2.

In a peer-to-peer network, all computers share in the work of providing file storage space and access to peripherals.

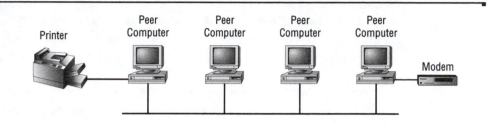

 NOTE   For more on client-server networks and peer-to-peer networks, see Chapter 1, "Understanding Computer Networks."

Networking with Windows 2000

The Microsoft operating system known as Windows 2000 is actually the next edition of the NT operating system, and was formerly known as Windows NT 4.0. It comes in four versions:

Windows 2000 Professional   This is the Microsoft operating system designed to replace Windows 98 as the desktop computer standard. It was formerly called Microsoft NT Workstation.

Windows 2000 Server   This operating system, formerly called Microsoft NT Server 4.0, is intended for computers working as file, print, application, and Web servers in office environments.

Windows 2000 Advanced Server   The Advanced Server is a heavy-duty operating system intended to help run large, company-wide networks. It used to be called Windows NT Server 5.0 Enterprise Edition.

Windows 2000 Datacenter Server   Here's an OS new to the Microsoft line, aimed at big commercial data warehouses.

The versions of Windows 2000 covered in this book are Professional and Server, since these are the ones you're likely to run at home.

PART

III

Network Software

The pedigree of every version of regular Windows (not NT, that is) goes all the way back to DOS, the original IBM PC operating system introduced in 1981. The previous editions of Windows, even including the major upgrade Windows 95, were all built on the platform of Windows 3.0, the first commercially successful version of Windows. In stark contrast, Windows 2000, which runs on the NT operating system, leaves DOS behind—in more ways than one. For the first time ever, Microsoft's plan is for its front-line consumer operating system to be unable to run MS-DOS programs. NT is also a more complex program to install and maintain than DOS ever was.

 NOTE For more on NT, see Mark Minasi, *Mastering Windows NT Server 4*, 7th edition. ISBN 0-7821-2693-6.

Microsoft at one point announced that Windows 2000 would be the next upgrade for Windows 98, and that NT technology would henceforth be the standard for home and business users. Now, however, there is supposed to be another major upgrade for Windows 98, code-named Millennium. It's due to arrive sometime in 2000 and will be based on the existing consumer version of Windows, rather than Windows NT. For the average consumer this means that if you buy a new computer, it won't necessarily come loaded with Windows 2000. Instead, it's likely to have Windows 98 until Millennium becomes available.

Meanwhile, Windows 2000 will be sold primarily to business networkers, just as NT is today. But you still can't ignore Windows 2000. Microsoft says the Windows operating system is going to go the way of Windows 2000 over the long haul. So you may still wind up running Windows 2000, or some later evolution, even on your home network. The good news is that Windows 2000 adds significant networking functionality that Windows 98 doesn't have. And it's generally more stable and less subject to crashes than the consumer versions of Windows.

Here are some of the advantages of networking with Windows 2000:

Better security A computer running Windows 2000 requires you to log on before you can do anything with the computer, and the signon process can't be gotten around as easily as the weak security features of Windows 98.

Network Identification Wizard This automatic guide helps you connect a machine to an existing network, even if you aren't an expert networker.

Network Connection Wizard This Wizard aims to make setting up private dial-up networks easier. Private dial-up networks are used for connecting to the Internet and remotely connecting to your network from another location.

Default Transmission Control Protocol/Internet Protocol   Windows 2000 leaves behind the NetBEUI protocol that was the default transport protocol in older versions of Windows, in favor of the superior TCP/IP protocol suite, which is now the default protocol.

Windows 2000 Workgroups and Domains

There are two kinds of networks from the viewpoint of Windows 2000. The first, which is the one you're most likely to be using, is a workgroup. A *workgroup* is any collection of networked computers that share files, printers, and other resources. They are set up as peer-to-peer networks, meaning that each computer connected to the network can share resources with the rest, and also that there is no centralized server computer to run the security and resource allocation tasks. In contrast to a peer network using Windows 98 computers, with Windows 2000, each computer in the workgroup maintains a database of security information, consisting of the user names, passwords, and access rights of other people using the network, as shown in Figure 14.3.

FIGURE 14.3.

Each computer in a Windows 2000 workgroup shares resources with the rest, and maintains its own local security database.

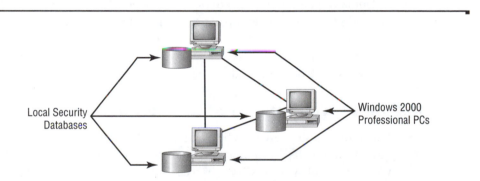

Local Security
Databases

Windows 2000
Professional PCs

The other type of Windows 2000 network is a domain. A *domain* is a group of computers that have a central directory database residing on a computer called the *domain controller*. To be a domain controller, a PC has to be running Windows 2000 Server. Figure 14.4 shows how in a Windows 2000 domain, a computer running Windows 2000 Server acts as a domain controller. The rest of the PCs can run the workstation edition, Windows 2000 Professional. This setup provides better security, since the security and administration are centralized on a single machine. It can also be more convenient, since users only need to log on to the network one time in order to gain access to all network resources. In a workgroup where all workstations have their own security databases, users have to log on to their PC and use share permissions to grant access to their resources.

FIGURE 14.4.

In a Windows 2000 domain, a computer running Windows 2000 Server acts as a domain controller.

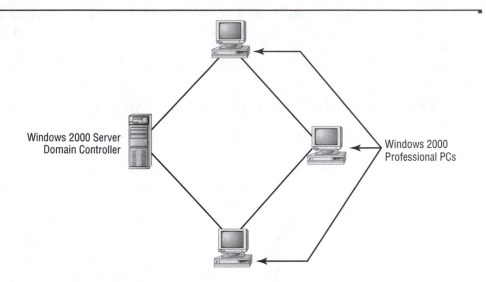

Windows 2000 Server
Domain Controller

Windows 2000
Professional PCs

Domains don't offer much to home users, but they are better suited to very large networks than the workgroup design. By grouping domains into clusters called *trees*, you can create quite large networks that are accessible to sizable numbers of users. And by grouping domains into what Microsoft calls *forests*, you can create very large Windows 2000 networks indeed.

Installing Windows 2000 Networking Features

The following steps are for a beta version of Windows 2000 Server. These steps may differ from the steps you must take to install your networking features, depending on your version of Windows 2000, as well as the features Microsoft decides to include with the final product:

1. Insert the Windows 2000 Setup CD-ROM in your CD-ROM drive. The Setup program should start automatically. If not, change to the i386 directory (for Intel computers) on the CD and start `Winnt.exe` (or `Winnt32.exe` if Windows is already loaded). Select the partition on which you want to install Windows 2000.

2. Go to the Network Settings page, select Typical Settings, then click Next.

TIP If you're changing your network properties after Windows 2000 is installed, right-click My Network Places and select Properties. Then right-click Local Area Connection and select Properties. Finally, select Internet Protocol and click Properties. To change the network ID for the computer, including domain or workgroup information, right-click My Computer and select Properties. Select the Network Identification folder and then click the Advanced button.

3. At the Domain Membership page, select the workgroup option.

4. Select the option for This Computer Is on a Network without a Domain.

5. Give the workgroup a name, such as WORKGROUP.

 NOTE When you first install Windows 2000, you will be prompted to assign a name to your computer. Be sure that this name is unique on your network, as it is the name the network will use to identify your computer.

6. Click Next. Setup will install the typical networking components, including TCP/IP configured to automatically obtain an Internet Protocol (IP) address from a special server called a *Dynamic Host Configuration Protocol* (DHCP) server. A DHCP server allocates IP addresses using the network adapter's built-in, unique Ethernet identification number. This process may take a few minutes.

7. After the Completing Setup page displays and all files are copied, configuration changes are made, and temporary files deleted. Setup then restarts the computer and starts the Setup Wizard. You can then continue with Setup, if you are installing Windows 2000 for the first time, or exit.

PART

III

NOTE You can also install Windows 2000 over the network, using a *distribution server*. To create a distribution server, copy all of the files (including hidden files) from the Windows 2000 CD's i386 folder onto your hard drive, into a folder called i386. You also need to set up the folder for others to share it. Do this by right-clicking the folder then clicking the Properties tab. Now configure the options the way you want them. For instance, you may want to enter a share name for the folder, a comment to help you identify the folder, and a limit to the number of users who can share the folder simultaneously. Click OK to accept the settings you have configured. The Windows 2000 software now resides on the distribution server. To load Windows 2000, the client has to attach to the i386 and run either Winnt.exe or Winnt32.exe.

Network Software

Installing Network Adapters in Windows 2000

Windows 2000 comes with drivers for nearly 400 Ethernet network adapters, so odds are good you'll be able to find a working driver for your adapter. At best, after you've physically installed the card, you'll be able to have Windows 2000 automatically install your network hardware. To install the card:

1. In Control Panel, double-click the Add/Remove Wizard to initiate automatic hardware installation.

 NOTE   For more on physically installing network adapter cards, see Chapter 6, "Ethernet Networks."

2. Windows 2000 will query the adapter you've installed to find out what hardware resources (such as Interrupt Request lines or IRQ) it requires. It will then install and configure them. Windows 2000 should also be able to automatically resolve any resource conflicts it finds.

With any luck, that should do it. To make sure all went well, after Windows 2000 has installed and configured the adapter drivers, verify the installation in Device Manager as follows:

1. Double-click the System icon in Control Panel.

2. Click the Hardware tab.

3. Click Device Manager.

4. Check the icons to the left of each device to see the status of the adapter you just installed. If you don't see your network adapter, expand the Network adapter tree by clicking on the plus sign for that tree.

 TIP   Device Manager shows the status of devices, such as network adapter cards, by using symbols placed on the device's icon on the Device Manager list. A stop sign on the icon means Windows 2000 has disabled the adapter because of a conflict. An exclamation point means the adapter isn't installed properly or its driver is missing. A normal icon means everything is fine.

Sometimes Windows 2000 won't be able to automatically detect or install the adapter. If this happens, after the Add/Remove Hardware Wizard runs, you'll see a window labeled Choose a Hardware Device. Selecting the appropriate device, in this case a network adapter, will start a troubleshooting Wizard to help you get the adapter installed.

Networking with Linux

If you don't want to spend the money for a commercial industrial-strength operating system, you don't have to. Linux is a freeware operating system that rivals the commercial operating systems, such as Windows, UNIX, and Mac OS, in its features. A typical *distribution* of Linux—it comes in many flavors or versions, which are known as distributions in the Linux world—comes with a very wide array of networking features, including:

- Support for Ethernet, the world's most popular local area network.
- Support for Token Ring, a networking technology used in many businesses.
- Support for the TCP/IP protocol suite used on the Internet and many local area networks.
- X.25, the network access method used in packet switching networks.
- Support for the IPX protocol used by Novell NetWare.
- Support for the AppleTalk protocol used by Apple Macintoshes.
- Support for Arcnet, a little-used networking technology today.
- Support for Server Message Block protocol, the protocol Windows networks use for file and printer sharing.
- Ability to work as a print server on a network.
- Ability to work as a file server on a network.
- Ability to work as a mail server on a network.
- Ability to work as a Domain Name Server on a network, parceling out and managing Internet domain names.
- Ability to work as a Web server, including transferring files, displaying pages, and performing other Web host work.
- Ability to work as a firewall, a computer devoted to providing security for a local area network connected to the Internet.
- Ability to route network traffic between networks.
- Ability to share Internet access with other computers on the local area network.
- Provides many other features, such as support for high-speed *Integrated Services Digital Network* (ISDN) Internet access.
- Provides support for almost any network adapter.

PART

III

Network Software

One thing Linux doesn't feature is the cost of commercial programs. While it might cost you $1,000.00, including add-on software, to get all these features using Windows-based software, Linux is available free for the downloading from many sites on the Internet. Or you can purchase nicely packaged CD-ROMs, with easy-to-use installation routines, for well under $100.00.

WARNING While Linux has a lot, it doesn't have everything. The major gap is in commercial software for Linux. For instance, you can't get a version of Microsoft's Office applications suite for Linux, although the well-regarded Star Office suite, which is similar to Microsoft Office, is available for Linux free for personal use. Learn more at www.sun .com/staroffice.

In addition to the operating system being inexpensive or even free, there are many shareware or freeware add-on programs that you can use with your Linux network. For example, Apache is a free program for running *Web servers*—computers that host Web sites—and has become the Internet's most popular software for corporate Web servers.

NOTE For more information on the origins of Linux, see Chapter 6, "Ethernet Networks."

If you select Linux for a network operating system, you can still use other operating systems on other computers attached to the home network. Linux works with many operating systems, including:

- Windows 95/98
- Windows NT
- MS-DOS
- Windows for Workgroups
- Mac OS
- OS/2
- Amiga

You can download detailed steps to set up support for these operating systems in how-to documents available, again at no charge, through the Internet.

Source Code Secrets

One of the highly touted benefits of Linux is the fact that the operating system's *source code*—the original program as written by the programmer—is freely available. Most commercial software publishers guard their source code fiercely, to protect against rivals copying or improving on their programming. In theory, making source code available makes it possible for anyone to modify the Linux *kernel*. That's the basic part of the operating system that provides its fundamental features. You might want to do this, for instance, to fix a bug or provide a new feature.

At least, you might. The catch is that you need to be a highly skilled programmer before you attempt to modify the Linux kernel. A botched attempt to program the kernel is likely to render your system inoperable. If you find a bug or miss a feature that you think you need, it's best to wait until another programmer, hopefully with the requisite skills, provides a fix or adds the feature to the source code.

Installing Linux Networking

If you've heard anything about Linux, you've probably heard that installing and configuring the operating system can be a real chore. It's no snap—few OS installations are—and the trick of downloading and installing a no-cost version of Linux is especially tricky. But the commercial distributions of Linux, such as the popular Red Hat and Caldera Linux versions, are still relatively low in cost.

They also come on CD-ROMs and are increasingly easy to install. Using one of these streamlined versions, once you've created a boot floppy and inserted the CD-ROM of Linux, about the hardest thing you'll have to do is decide how to partition your disk drive. The latest versions of Linux typically come with an easy-to-use utility, such as PartitionMagic, to help with this task.

Caldera's OpenLinux 2.3, which is recognized as an especially easy-to-install Linux distribution, uses a Linux Wizard (LIZARD) installation program with a point-and-click graphical interface. LIZARD is better at detecting and configuring add-on cards than previous installation routines. In addition the latest versions of LIZARD can run after the installation to help fix configuration problems. Learn more at `www.openlinux.org` or `www.caldera.com`.

PART

III

Network Software

TIP The Linux users and developers community is very large and vocal, which means there is a lot of free help available. You can get nearly any question related to networking with Linux answered. Just post to one of the Usenet newsgroups and discussions dedicated to Linux networking and related matters. One good one, which you can reach through the Deja newsgroup portal at www.deja.com, is called comp.os.linux.networking.

When installing most distributions of Linux, you will get the option of deciding which of the available software packages you want to install. The standard selection will be fine for most home networkers. Linux normally includes such networking packages as *Pine*, an e-mail editor; Linux network applications such as *FTP*, used for transferring files over the network; and tools like *Traceroute*, which can be used to examine the network path taken by a message from a local computer to a remote destination. If you are selecting packages individually, you will probably want to choose at least the typical or minimum selection from the *network* group of software packages.

Now it's time to configure your home Linux network. Depending on how many software packages you elect to install (and the speed of your CD-ROM drive, if that's what you are installing from) you will have to wait a few or many minutes while the installation program copies and configures the applications. The following steps are based on the Linux Installation Setup and Administration (LISA) utility provided with Caldera OpenLinux:

1. Your installation program will ask for your computer's name. Provide one, using the Internet naming conventions, such as home.com.

2. The installation program will now ask for your network card's Internet Protocol parameters. These will include the card's IP address, a typical value for which is 192.168.255.1; the network mask, typically something such as 255.255.255.0; and broadcast address, a common value being 192.168.1.255.

 NOTE Internet Protocol addresses are made up of four bytes, each written as a decimal number from zero to 255, and separated by a period. Leading zeros are dropped, unless the number is zero. The IP address is used to route network traffic to the proper destination. IP addresses beginning with 192.168 are not used on the Internet. These addresses are reserved for internal networks, such as the home network you are building. Learn more about Internet Protocol parameters in Part 4, "Using Your Network."

3. If your installation program asks whether you have a router installed, you should answer "no" (unless, of course, in the unlikely event that you do).

4. The installation program will also ask for the address of your *Domain Name System* (DNS) server. Often, you will be configuring your Linux system to serve as the DNS server for your network. In this case, provide 127.0.0.1 for your DNS server address. That IP address is known as the *loopback address* and is sort of a stand in for "this machine's address." If you are connecting the network to an Internet Service Provider, enter the address of the ISPs primary DNS server.

5. If your installation program asks whether you are planning to use the Network Information System, answer no.

Setting Up Linux User Accounts

You'll also have to setup user accounts in order to use your Linux network. There is a *root* or *superuser* account which is reserved for the system administrator, in this case, you. There is only one root account per Linux system. Root account users have complete control over the operating system and network. They can change anything they want to (whether they intend to or not).

 WARNING   Root or superuser accounts are so powerful that you should not use the root account to log on, unless you specifically need its god-like powers. Instead, create a regular user account to use when, for instance, you check your e-mail. When you log on as root, you run the risk of accidentally deleting or altering an important file, thereby rendering the system inoperable. As a regular user, you aren't allowed to make such a mistake.

During the process of creating new accounts, you should pick a good password for the root account; you don't want anyone else gaining access to this powerful account. Use a maximum of eight characters, and mix up letters and numbers. Remember that, in Linux systems, case counts, meaning you have to remember whether you typed a capital letter or lower-case letter in your password. Linux tradition calls for you to select a username consisting of your last name and initials, for instance, jqcitizen.

Installing Network Cards under Linux

When a computer running Linux boots using the standard Linux boot loader, LILO, it will look for newly installed hardware. The Linux term for this process is *probe* or *autoprobe*. If it finds a card from the long list of cards supported by Linux, you're in luck, as the drivers will automatically be loaded. You can find a list of Linux-supported network adapters at `www.ssc.com/mirrors/LDP/HOWTO/Ethernet-HOWTO.html`.

If Linux doesn't successfully autoprobe your card, your luck isn't running very well, although you're probably not quite out of luck yet. Unless you are using a one-of-a-kind network adapter you cobbled together in your garage workshop, odds are good that some Linux programmer somewhere has tried using the same card, and written a driver for it. If you search the Internet diligently, you can probably obtain a free copy of the device driver and instructions for installing it. A good place to start is the network adapter file whose address is given in the previous paragraph.

Linux has made great strides in making the installation and configuration easier, but it's still likely to be a moderately difficult project. The good news is, after you've installed and configured Linux for networking, you'll be rewarded with what is probably the most stable operating system in wide use. Because Linux's source code is freely available, any programmer who detects a bug in the operating system can attempt to create a fix for the bug. More than 10,000 programmers have contributed fixes, with the result that Linux network servers commonly rack up hundreds of days of continuous operation without a breakdown. That's a record few of Linux's commercial competitors can hope to match.

Networking with NetWare

Novell's NetWare was the dominant client-server network operating system during the 1980s, when networking first became popular in businesses. In recent years, however, a lot of NetWare networks have switched to Windows NT. Still, many commercial network managers continue to prize NetWare for its stability, its standard-setting directory services, and its lower purchase and support costs, especially compared to Microsoft Windows NT. Novell's latest, NetWare 5.0, promises to regain some of the networking ground lost to NT in the last few years.

The latest release of NetWare, version 5.0, offers some significant improvements over the previous release, NetWare 4.11. The improvements include the following:

- Full-fledged support for TCP/IP protocol.

- A graphical user interface for performing server management tasks, including remote management.

- A graphical user interface for the installation procedure.

- Built-in Netscape Web server software.

Despite these improvements, NetWare primarily remains a networking operating system for businesses. One reason is its cost. Novell NetWare 5.0, with a license for five users, will set you back in the neighborhood of $500.00. Another reason home networkers tend to avoid NetWare is the feature set and complexity of the product.

As a result of this complexity, however, NetWare is loaded with powerful, flexible capabilities. One of these is *NetWare Directory Services* or NDS. NDS is a database that holds and manages data about users and resources, such as printers, on your network.

Along with NDS, NetWare comes with powerful tools for administering users and resources, including the following:

- Security features that let you apply state-of-the-art protection to your network.

- Easy retrieval of information from the NDS database.

- Bindery services that allow older versions of NetWare, all the way back to version 2.0, to use the latest-model NDS.

- Scalability, meaning you can start small with NDS and grow to networks of nearly any size.

- Built-in replication of information, reducing the chances you'll be unable to use NDS because of a network failure.

- Flexibility, allowing you to redefine or invent key structures in NDS.

- Easy administration, so that all resources show the same identity through the network, and all system administrators see the same views.

The problem with these features is that they aren't much good for home users. As a home user, you don't have to manage hundreds of users, nor monitor scores of printers of all varieties scattered throughout an office building. So, while NDS is a selling point for commercial networkers, it's almost a negative for potential home NetWare users.

NetWare File System

While NetWare runs on MS-DOS-running PCs, when it comes to file servers it replaces rather than runs under Microsoft Windows. This is generally an improvement over regular MS-DOS, because NetWare 5.0 is a more advanced operating system than Windows, and is set up for multitasking, among other things.

Another difference between Windows and NetWare is in the file system. Windows uses network file servers. NetWare uses a technique called *redirection* to allow workstations to make hard drives on the server appear as if they were local drives to Windows-based machines. Also, NetWare lets you organize data by what it calls *volumes*, which are similar to the partitions, directories, and folders familiar in Windows.

PART

III

Network Software

When you install a server version of the software on a computer, NetWare installs a standard set of directories, each devoted to a particular type of data or function such as MAIL, SYSTEM, or LOGIN. You can create other directories, such as GAMES or EXCEL, to hold data and files for specific purposes. Many NetWare administrators create SHARED directories to which anyone on the network can have access. Otherwise, users are restricted to accessing only their own directories.

NOTE The two most important NetWare commands are LOGIN and LOGOUT. You have to LOGIN if you want to use the network, and you have to be able to LOGOUT to stop. When you type LOGIN at the user prompt, you'll be connected to the network and can access any files or other resources to which you are entitled. If you LOGIN as the administrator—a high-powered account like the root user in Linux—you'll be able to set up new users and perform other supervisory chores. When you're ready to leave, type LOGOUT and you'll be cut off from the network, able to use only what's on your local computer.

NetWare comes with a slew of commands for navigating, managing, and using directories. Here are a few of the more important:

CD command   Lets you change directories, just as the familiar DOS command does. The new version is CX, a command introduced in recent editions of NetWare. It does the job of the CD command in NetWare versions 4 and 5.

FLAG command   Lets you see and alter the attributes of directories and files. For instance, if you type FLAG with the /D switch, all the details about that file are revealed, such as who created it. If you type FLAG followed by /OWNER=username, where username is the name of a specific network user, you will be shown all the files that user owns.

MAP   Lets you define—either ad hoc in the middle of a network session, or semi-permanently as part of your login procedure—where programs and files reside on the network. For instance, without MAP, if your spreadsheet program was located on another computer on the network, you would have to type in the long path and file name to open the file. MAP provides a convenient shortcut. You use MAP to tell NetWare in which drive and directory to look for the program file. On subsequent occasions, when you type in the command to start up a program, you can use the program's name instead of the entire pathway. MAP is a great timesaver, as it keeps you from having to type in long network path names each time you open a file that exists on another computer.

NETUSER   Lets you do all kinds of jobs, such as changing your password, printing documents, and sending messages to other users.

NOTE One major difference you'll notice with NetWare is the lack of a GUI, or *graphical user interface*. Most of the Novell commands being discussed here are typed in at the command line, rather than being activated by clicking a button with a mouse. This can be a little odd for people who have grown up computing with Windows or Macintosh. However, the use of the command line instructions lets you play with the *syntax* of the command, by adding switches and the like, to make some pretty complicated things happen.

Installing NetWare

Installing NetWare is somewhere between Linux, a fairly challenging exercise, and Windows 98, the sort of task you can handle while eating lunch. Each of the currently common versions of NetWare, NetWare 3.12, 4.11, and 5.0, come with significantly different installation routines. The easiest by far is NetWare 5.0, which generally does a good job of automatically detecting and configuring hardware, and requires much less user intervention during the installation than the older editions.

Another major advantage of NetWare 5.0 is that, for the first time, Novell included a graphical installation routine. This means that you'll be able to point and click your way through the installation, rather than having to deal with a DOS-like command prompt.

 NOTE Installing NICs on a NetWare network is a lot like installing them in a Windows network. In fact, it's usually identical. That's because NetWare's client software runs under Windows. In terms of client-server networks, *client software* is the software that runs on the computers. In turn, these computers use the resources provided by servers. For more on installing network adapters, see Chapter 6, "Ethernet Networks."

Creating New Users with NetWare

As with installation, so with creating new users. The exact routine you'll follow depends on the version of NetWare you'll be using. In NetWare 5.0, you get a graphical user interface after using the NWADMIN command when you have logged in as the administrator. Here's the routine:

1. Choose Create Objects in the Directory tree.
2. Enter the username or usernames you plan to create.

PART

III

Network Software

3. Decide where in the directory tree you want to create the new user—for instance, KIDSTUFF—and click on that object.

4. Click Object menu ➢ Create.

5. Click User Class.

6. Type at least the user's login name, last name, and home directory into the dialog box that appears. You can put information in the other fields, but this is the minimum information required.

7. Click OK.

 NOTE While creating new users you can assign them all sorts of traits. For instance, you can give the user a mail address, assign various login rights and restrictions, and provide for the user to automatically run various login scripts when logging on to the network.

Summary

Networking isn't just for Windows and Macs. If you use the alternative operating systems of NetWare, Windows NT, or Linux, you can still benefit from a home network. Whether for personal or home business use, these systems give you some flexibility—and some added hassles—that you just won't get with a traditional Windows or Mac home network.

What's Next

There's more to networking software than the network operating system you select. You are also likely to use software for electronic mail, faxing, word processing, tracking finances, backing up your data, playing games, and much more. Those programs are the subjects of the next chapter, "Other Network Software."

CHAPTER 15

Other Network Software

Overview

A network doesn't really come to life until after you've got it running and have added some software applications to your operating system. Some of the most useful are e-mail programs and backup programs. There are also productivity applications, likely including networkable versions of your favorite word processor and spreadsheet programs. And don't forget the games, perhaps the most exciting of all software to employ over a network.

Understanding E-mail

E-mail is the most popular service on the Internet. In fact, it's the first thing that most people do on the Internet and, even for dedicated Net surfers, remains the favorite use of the Internet. How do we love our electronic mail? EMarketer, an online commerce research firm, counted the ways:

- Some 3.4 trillion e-mail messages were delivered in the U.S. in 1998.
- U.S. Internet users send 2.1 billion e-mail messages a day.
- Another 7.3 billion commercial e-mail messages are sent daily.
- More than 80 million Americans use e-mail at least occasionally.
- High-tech workers get more than 200 messages per day.
- On average, people receive twice as many e-mails as they send.

Clearly, e-mail is an extremely popular use for computers. And, once you have your home network going, you're likely to add your share to those trillions of electronic mail messages going back and forth.

 NOTE One of the stats from eMarketer's report on electronic mail is somewhat sobering: More than 96 percent of the 7.3 billion daily commercial e-mail messages are *spam*, or unsolicited commercial mail.

Electronic mail is like regular mail in some ways, and different in others. In terms of similarities:

- You can send a letter to anyone whose address you know.
- You write letters just as you do with regular mail.

- You can include other items, such as photographs, audio recordings, or interesting articles, along with your letters.

- You can send letters and packages anonymously as a secret admirer.

It's also different in the following ways:

- In the case of e-mail, of course, you need to know the person's e-mail address rather than street address.

- You'll be typing your messages on a computer keyboard rather than scribbling on a post card.

- You can't include physical objects, such as a lock of hair, in an e-mail message.

- E-mail is a lot faster than regular mail. In rare cases, it might take a day to deliver an e-mail. On the other hand, it's not unusual for e-mail to be delivered in seconds, even when it's going halfway around the world.

- E-mail is free, or nearly so, no matter how long your message or how far it's going.

How E-mail Works

When you mail a regular letter, it first goes into the mailbox, then into the letter carrier's pouch. Next comes a bin down at the post office, followed by a series of trucks, trains, planes, and perhaps even boats. Eventually, it arrives at another post office and performs the same routine in reverse. E-mail does the same thing, only it passes from one computer to another instead of from one box or bag to another.

When you send an Internet e-mail message from your computer or home network, it goes first to a *mail server,* which is a computer set up to store and forward e-mail messages. This mail server is probably located at your Internet Service Provider. The ISP's mail server, following the address information that you've included, sends it to another server, which sends it either to the addressee's electronic mailbox or to another server. Eventually, the message makes its way to your intended recipient, where it's stored in an electronic mailbox until it's retrieved and read.

One of the best things about e-mail is that it's very easy to use. You simply type your letter, address it, and hit the send key. The addresses are even simpler. Instead of having to remember all this...

Jane Doe
1600 Pennsylvania Avenue
Washington DC 20001

PART

III

Network Software

...you simply have to recall this:
`janed@whitehouse.gov`

 WARNING   There is one catch with e-mail compared to regular snail mail. You have to type e-mail addresses exactly right. If one letter or "@" sign is out of place, or a comma or period or dash is inserted where it doesn't belong, your mail won't be delivered to the right person, if at all. You will usually get a notice, however, if your mail is not delivered.

The "@" is pronounced "at," and the period is said as "dot." So Jane's address would be said: "Jane-at-white-house-dot-gov." As with regular mail, e-mail addresses are read backwards. The last part, after the @, is the *domain name,* identifying the country and computer to which the mail is addressed. For instance, domain.com identifies the computer named "domain" in the U.S. The ".com" part of the address is the *country code* and is one of the codes identifying a computer in the United States. Three-digit codes, such as the ones in the following list, are generally reserved for computers located in the United States.

- COM, a commercial entity
- EDU, an educational institution
- GOV, a government agency
- MIL, a military entity
- NET, a network-related organization
- ORG, a non-profit organization

Two-digit codes at the end of an e-mail address identify the originating country. Examples include UK for United Kingdom, NL for the Netherlands, and HK for Hong Kong. You can view a list of all the country codes from Andorra (AD) to Zimbabwe (ZW) at: `www.ics.uci.edu/pub/websoft/wwwstat/country-codes.txt`.

After identifying the country and computer, the mail delivery system looks at the username, which is the part of the address to the left of the @ sign. Your username must be unique on that domain to make sure that nobody but you receives your mail, gets the credit for mail you've sent, or sends mail for which you get the blame.

Little Privacy for E-mail

One other difference between e-mail and regular mail is that e-mail, at least Internet e-mail, is not as secure from prying eyes as regular mail. That's because a letter, once you've sealed and sent it, is protected by law from being opened and looked at by anyone other than the addressee.

Internet e-mail, on the other hand, is likely to go through numerous computers, starting with your Internet Service Provider, then through a major mail provider, and then perhaps through several other Internet-connected computers, before winding up on the computer of your addressee. At any one of these steps, your letter could be seen and read.

That lack of security is one reason for the popularity of personal encryption software. These programs scramble e-mail messages so that they can't be read by anyone who doesn't have the key to the code. Learn more about e-mail encryption software at `http://www.mcafee.com/products/#PGP Personal Privacy`.

E-mail Software

E-mail software, at a minimum, allows you to compose, edit, address, and send electronic messages. Other features you should expect from e-mail software include the following:

- The ability to easily print, forward, and reply to e-mail messages, including those you are receiving as well as those you are sending
- The ability to manage your mail using inboxes, outboxes, and folders
- An address book to help you manage and use the e-mail addresses of your correspondents
- The ability to attach files such as word processing documents, spreadsheets, and pictures to e-mail messages
- The ability to encode and decode attached files

Other features of many e-mail programs include spell-checkers, formatting tools, filters, distribution lists, and the ability to include signature files containing your personal address or other information. Most popular e-mail programs, including shareware and freeware packages, can do all these and more. The following sections take a look at three of the most popular e-mail programs.

PART

III

Network Software

Eudora

One of the best and most widely used electronic mail programs is Eudora, a program published by Qualcomm of San Diego, California. Eudora comes in several different versions, including commercial and freeware version for Windows PCs. Eudora Light is the freeware version of Eudora available for Windows, Macintosh, and the Apple Newton personal digital assistant. Eudora Pro is the commercial version for computers running Windows 95/98/NT and Mac OS. By any standard, Eudora is a full-featured e-mail program. Some of the features of Eudora Pro include the following:

- A background mail feature that sends and receives e-mail in the background, so you can do other tasks at the same time, such as look up addresses or compose messages
- The direct importing of settings, e-mail, and address books from other e-mail programs, including Microsoft Outlook, Outlook Express, or Netscape Mail programs
- A message preview pane that lets you view the contents of a message without opening it
- A display tool that shows graphics within the body of the message, without the need to start a separate application to view them
- Drag-and-drop, so that you can easily attach files and work with mailboxes, folders, and messages
- A built-in spelling checker
- A Setup Account Wizard that walks you through setup and configuration and helps import your configuration information from other e-mail programs
- Multiple signatures that let you personalize messages
- Mail filters that will automatically identify and file messages, including forwarding, transferring to designated mailboxes, and replying to them with automated responses
- A customizable address book that tracks contacts in a subset of multiple, more specific address books
- HTML support that lets you view and compose messages with fancy graphics and stylized text
- Support for MIME, BinHex, and UUencode encoding

There are also many add-ons for Eudora, including Qualcomm's PureVoice plug-in that lets you exchange voice messages. Third-party vendors handle foreign language translation, multimedia video e-mail, and more. Learn more about Eudora, or download a free version of Eudora Lite, at `www.eudora.com`.

A Smiley Primer

Soon after you use e-mail for the first time, you will see your first *smiley*. Smileys are punctuation marks that, viewed sideways, appear to be faces. For example, :-). Smileys are used to express emotions that may not come across accurately through the medium of mere words. They are especially helpful if you are using humor, irony, or some other mode of expression that carries a high risk of misunderstanding. For instance, if you ask, "Are you ever going to answer my question?" you will reduce the risk of someone getting the wrong idea about your e-mail message if you add ":-)" after the question mark.

Smileys, also called *emoticons*, were first used, according to Internet lore, in 1981, and the typographical glyphs proved very popular among e-mail users who wanted to make sure that their messages were being understood. There are many different smileys, communicating a wide range of emotions. These include:

:-(for sadness or disappointment

:-D for a really big smile

:-O for shouting

<:-O for surprise

And many more

You can find an enjoyable and informative survey of the history, uses, and definitions of smileys at `www.newbie.net/JumpStations/SmileyFAQ`.

Outlook Express

Outlook Express is the e-mail program that comes with Microsoft's Internet Explorer Web browser software. Outlook Express comes in versions for UNIX and Macintosh computers, as well as, of course, for Windows from version 3.1 on. Outlook Express was a trendsetting mail program when it first came out, introducing triple-pane window views of messages and folders, support for HTML-formatted mail, the use of fancy stationery, and the ability to receive mail from several e-mail accounts in one inbox. The latest version, Outlook Express 5, which comes with Internet Explorer 5, has basic e-mail functionality plus these significant features:

- Identity management is handy if several people in your home share a single computer for e-mail. You can set up as many individual and group accounts as you like for yourself and others, each with its own mail and address books.

PART

III

Network Software

- Mail sorting and filtering with a rules editor will automatically move, delete, color-code, flag, or perform any combination of these actions on messages, based on the sender, content, size, and other features.

- Connection management tracks your dial-up connection to the Internet, automatically redials if you are disconnected, and automatically hangs up when you are finished sending or receiving mail.

- Online/offline synchronization helps manage e-mail messages offline by letting you download all or part of your e-mail to your computer for later reading and responding. You can elect to download all messages, only new messages, or only messages with a selected subject, author, or date.

- An integrated contact book with management features lets you share selected contacts and access address information with others, and allows others to share with you as well.

- Multiple customized signature files let you add text or HTML files to outgoing messages. You can designate different signatures for each individual piece of e-mail, or preselect a signature based on the addressee or the e-mail account you're using.

- Stationery lets you send e-mail with fancy background colors, images, fonts, sizes, and text colors, by using included templates or custom ones created with a wizard.

- Hotmail support lets you use Outlook Express 5 to read and send mail through the popular anonymous Web-based e-mail service, as well as save time by synchronizing Hotmail and Outlook Express mail folders and address books.

You can download Outlook Express as part of Internet Explorer from Microsoft's Internet Explore download site at: www.microsoft.com/windows/ie/download/ie5all.htm. Learn more about Outlook Express features at www.microsoft.com/windows/oe/.

Pegasus Mail

Pegasus Mail is an electronic mail program written by David Harris, and anyone can use it without charge. There is no shareware or commercial version, however. The Pegasus Mail is a full-featured e-mail application that comes in versions for Windows PCs and Macintoshes, and also works on Novell NetWare and TCP/IP networks. Pegasus Mail is conspicuously easy to install and maintain, and is a rugged, stable product. Furthermore, it is in near-constant development. Pegaus Mail comes with the following standard features:

- Mail folders that help you keep and manage copies of all your outgoing and incoming messages

- The ability to attach up to 64 attachments per message
- Extensive mail filtering tools that help you organize incoming messages
- A spell checker
- Support for the popular mail encoding schemes Mime, UUencode, and BinHex
- The ability to request confirmation of delivery and reading of your messages, so you know when they arrived, were received, and even opened by the recipient
- Easy installation, with little ongoing maintenance
- A full-featured address book, including provisions for creating distribution lists for sending messages to large groups of people
- Context-sensitive online help
- A slew of sorting and searching options for your mail, including the ability to automatically respond to messages with prepared messages, and to add or delete addresses from a distribution list
- A mail merge capability that lets you merge form letters with prepared lists of e-mail addresses

There are also many extensions or plug-in modules that provide additional enhancements to Pegasus Mail. These include versions of Pegasus Mail for speakers of languages from Czech to Catalan, converters to translate a variety of address book formats into Pegasus Mail format, and many other helpful utilities. Unlike the program itself, most of these plug-ins are available as freeware or shareware.

Pegasus Mail is available free for the downloading at www.pegasus.usa.com. You can also obtain a variety of help files and other information at this Web site. Installing Pegasus Mail is very simple and fully explained in the program's help files.

No Pegasus Mail for Linux Users

To the dismay of many, you can't get a version of Pegasus Mail that will run on Linux computers. The creator of Pegasus Mail, David Harris, reports getting about five requests a day for a Linux version. However, Harris says there are no plans to create one, both because he lacks experience with Linux and because he's already keeping busy supporting Mac and Windows versions.

Nor, adds Harris, will he make available the Pegasus Mail *source code.* The source code is the program in its original form as written by the programmer, before it is *compiled* into a form that the computer can use. Pegasus Mail isn't going the *open source* route, says Harris, because, while he is happy to develop and give away the ready-to-run software, he has no interest in letting go of the source code.

Installing E-mail Programs

The e-mail programs described in the preceding sections are available in freeware versions downloadable from their providers' Web sites. You can also obtain a variety of help files and other information at the sites. For the most part, installing them is very simple and fully explained in their `readme` and `help` files.

However, before you get started installing any of them, you'll need a few items of information. You should be able to obtain this information from your Internet Service Provider's Web site, online manual, help files, or other documentation, or, if all else fails, by calling the ISP help desk and asking them for:

- The address of your POP3 server

- The username you should use to check your e-mail

- Your password for checking mail

- The address of the ISP's SMTP server

Write all these bits of information down as you receive them. Once you do, you're ready to install your e-mail software following the program's instructions.

Networked Applications

There is a theory in economics about network effects. It says, among other things, that the value of a network increases as the number of devices connected to it increases. It's pretty obvious that one fax machine by itself, for instance, isn't much good. Whom would you fax to? But when millions of them are everywhere—including those with whom you do business—a fax machine is golden. That's a network effect. Network effects operate in computer networks, telephone networks and, really, any kind of network. In the same way, the more software applications you include in your network, the more uses your household will get out of it, the more your family or roommates will connect to it, and the more valuable it will become. In addition to networking peripheral devices, such as printers and scanners, and sharing e-mail accounts, you can benefit greatly from networking applications software, such as backup software, games, Microsoft Office programs, and much more.

Using Backup Software

One of the best examples of a network effect in home networking is in the area of backing up files. Backing up files is a nuisance. Even with the latest backup software that runs unattended, you have to remember to leave your computer running. It will probably have to run overnight if you're backing up a lot of data on a slow tape drive. Then you have to remember to insert a new tape every now and then. And then, as often as not, there's been some problem with a power outage or a plain old computer glitch. As a result, the backup has a problem, so you have to do it over. Or, worse, it's not there when you need it, either because you didn't do it right or because you never took the trouble to begin with. If you're using some lower-capacity media such as Zip drives or even floppies, the trouble is only compounded. When you have several computers in your house, it quickly gets to be entirely too much trouble. Unless, that is, you do *network backups*.

 WARNING Home users, including home-based business owners, are among the people most at risk for losing significant information stored on their computers, according to *Managing Office Technology* magazine. It's a truly significant risk. The magazine quoted an International Data Corporation study that found that the cost of losing and having to re-create 100MB of data can reach $500,000.00. Multiply that times the multigigabyte storage capability you're likely to have on each of the computers in your home, and you can see that it gets ridiculously expensive very quickly. So take care to back up important financial records and other data.

With a network backup, you can back up all the computers on your network to one machine. This has some nice advantages:

- Since you're only buying one backup device, you can afford to get something really fast and good, such as a removable hard drive, like a Jaz gigabyte-sized removable media drive, or a huge tape drive system.

- Since you only have one backup system, you only have to remember to swap backup media on that machine.

- Likewise, you only have to run or schedule the backup on one machine. The other computers only have to be left running and connected to the network to enable the backup to proceed. You can use your computer while it is backing up files from another machine, or while its own files are being backed up. However, be warned that if the backup software attempts to copy a file that is being used, it will likely fail to copy the file and return an error message.

 NOTE For more on network backup techniques and tricks, see Chapter 19, "Disaster Prevention."

Using backup software over a network is easy. When you're selecting the drives or files to back up, select data on the network, rather than just on your local machine. For instance, in Figure 15.1, the backup software has selected Drive C on another computer for backup.

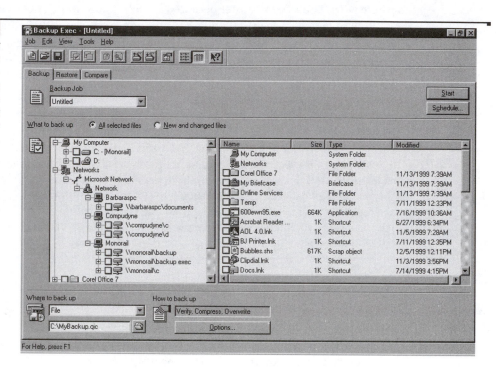

> **WARNING**   There's one major caveat about network backups, namely, that not all backup software is network-ready. To find out whether a given piece of backup software is network-ready, check the documentation.

Networking Games

You can also see the network effect in computer games. No longer do you have to play games on an isolated machine, against the computer. Nearly 500 computer games can be played over a network, according to a count maintained by one network gaming fan, known simply as Leon. There's one good reason for that high number: Playing computer games against human opponents over a home network is great fun.

 NOTE For a seemingly inexhaustible list of games for Local Area Networks, check out Leon's Web site at `http://www.si.hhs.nl/~95102479/list.html`.

You can, of course, play games over the Internet against human opponents, as well. However, a home network offers some serious advantages over playing multiplayer head-to-head games over the Internet, including:

- Speed. At 100Mbps, a Fast Ethernet home network is many times faster than even the fastest Internet connection.
- Monetary savings. You don't have to pay for online time, or even have an online or Internet Service Provider account, in order to play games over your own home network.
- Personal interaction. You can talk to your opponent when you're in the same room, rather than being limited to chat windows, or no communication at all, when playing over the Internet. In fact, playing network games is a good excuse to get family or friends together.

Installing Network Games

Installing network games is not a big deal. There are many games, each with its own installation routine. However, there are a couple of consistent requirements for playing games over a network:

- Everyone playing the game must have Client for Microsoft Networks enabled.
- Most games require you to have both the NetBEUI and the IPX/SPX protocols installed.

Here's how to make sure that Client for Microsoft Networks is activated on the computers connected to the network:

1. Click Start ➢ Settings ➢ Control Panel ➢ Network.
2. In the Configuration tab, as shown in Figure 15.2, click the button labeled File and Print Sharing.

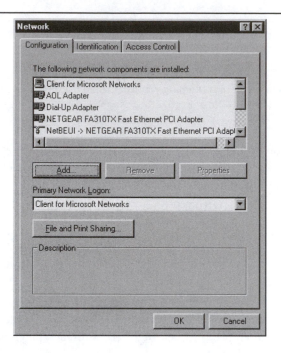

3. In the File and Print Sharing dialog window, as shown in Figure 15.3, click the boxes for I Want to Be Able to Give Others Access to My Files and I Want to Be Able to Allow Others to Print to My Printer(s).

4. Click OK twice to finish.

5. Go to the next computer on which you want to play network games, and check to see that File and Printer Sharing for Microsoft Networks is installed on it as well. Repeat this process until you've checked all the network computers you want to play on.

WARNING Bear in mind that when you grant others the right to access your files, you are exposing yourself to a risk that someone else might accidentally or intentionally delete or damage files you want to protect. If you want to protect certain files or directories, start Explorer and right click on the folder or file you have in mind. Select Sharing… then Shared As:, and then Read Only. This will still allow others to see the files you have selected, but the files will be safe from loss or corruption. You may not be able to run programs, however, if you restrict others to read-only access to the folders containing them.

Network Patches

Does your favorite computer game lack networking capability? Never fear, network patches and add-ons are available for many popular computer games, including Destruction Derby 2, from Psygnosis, and Mechwarrior 2, from Activision. You can find a listing of network patches at www.si.hhs.nl/~95102479/patches.html.

If you want to network a game that's not on the list, check your game publisher's site for a network patch. Many game publishers maintain a patches page or section on their sites. With luck, you'll be able to locate an add-on that will add network capability to your favorite game.

Most network games require you to install the IPX/SPX protocol, which is the protocol used on Novell Networks. If you're running a Windows peer-to-peer network, you may not have IPX/SPX installed. Here's how to set it up:

1. Click Start ➢ Settings ➢ Control Panel ➢ Network.
2. In the Configuration tab, as shown in Figure 15.4, click the Add button.

PART

III

Network Software

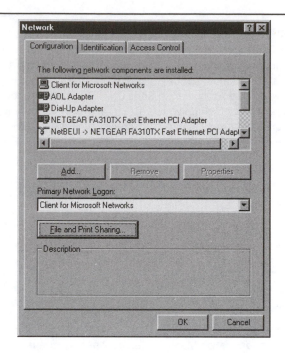

3. Highlight the Protocol entry in the Select Network Component Type dialog box, as shown in Figure 15.5, and click Add.

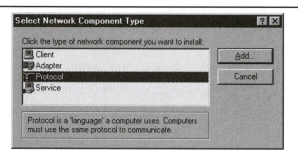

4. The Select Network Protocol box will appear, with a right- and left-hand window, as shown in Figure 15.6. In the left-hand window of this box, select Microsoft. Then, in the right-hand window, select IPX/SPX-compatible Protocol. Then click Add.

FIGURE 15.6

Choose Microsoft and IPX/SPX-compatible Protocol, then Add, in the Select Network Protocol box.

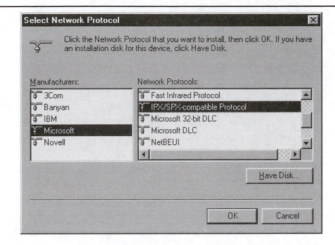

5. Click OK. If the program prompts you for the Operating System disk, supply the disk and drive letter as required.

You should now see IPX/SPX-compatible Protocol in the Network Configuration tab. To begin a networked game, start your game as usual. In the game selection menu, select Multiplayer. Next, select Local Area Network (IPX). At this point, you are normally asked for a player's name, or given a selection of players. Type a name for your player, ensuring that everyone on the network is using a different name. At this point, start the game. Some games require the first player to begin the game prior to anyone else. Happy gaming!

Networking Application Software

When you network your computers, you can share more than just data files, hardware resources like printers, and services like high-speed Internet access. One of the greatest network effects is that you can also share application programs. In other words, you can load and run programs on one computer that are stored on another machine on the network. Such network-ready applications don't have to exist on your machine's hard drive. You can even store the files you've created, such as word processing documents or spreadsheets, on the hard drive of the other machine. It's almost as if you're having that other machine do your PC's work for it. But there's more to using networkable application software than feeling like you're getting away with something. Network-ready applications software has the following benefits and characteristics:

• If you have a small hard drive on a particular machine, you can run an application, like Word or PowerPoint, from another computer on the network. That way, you take up valuable disk space for the application on only one computer.

PART

III

Network Software

- Ditto with the files you create, saving even more disk space.

- With a speedy network, such as Fast Ethernet, you will notice little relative loss of performance—especially if the application program is something that, due to disk space limitations, you might not be able to run at all on your local computer.

- If you prefer, you can install the application on your local machine by running an install program from the machine containing the original program. This saves an incredible amount of time and floppy-disk copying when you're installing a large program on a machine with no CD-ROM drive.

WARNING Be sure you are not violating the terms of your software license agreement by using the application program on multiple computers (even though the program remains loaded on only one computer on the network). You may need to purchase additional licenses, or purchase a *site license*. Site licenses cover the number of computers on which you plan to use the program. You need to determine how many computers the standard license permits you to run a particular program on without breaking the agreement, and, perhaps, the law. Some software publishers are strict about this, while others will allow home users to share applications pretty freely. Read your software license and follow its restrictions.

Sharing Microsoft Office over A Network

Even Microsoft's massive Office 97 suite can be set up so that the full set of files— approximately 200 megabytes for a full install—can be left on one computer while still allowing the other computers on the network to use Word, Excel, PowerPoint, and the rest. (This is assuming that you have a license allowing you to use the program on more than one machine. See warning above.) Here's how to do it:

WARNING Oddly enough, you can't run Setup.exe directly on the computer you're setting up as the application server. You need to run Setup.exe from another workstation on the network. This other computer needs to have write access (not just read-only access). And beware: Don't try to establish a computer as an administrator by clicking Setup.exe. This will perform a regular client installation, not the administrator installation you're after.

1. On a client computer, run the Office Setup program from the CD-ROM, using an administrative switch by clicking Start ➢ Run and typing **d:\ setup.exe /a**, where d: is your CD-ROM drive.

2. From the client computer, install all the CD's Office files onto the administrator's computer.

 NOTE The computer onto which you're installing the actual files must have at least 320MB of free disk space. You, as the administrator, need permission to read, write, delete, and create files on this computer. (Users only need read access.)

3. Follow the instructions on the screen. When the setup program requests the server and path for the shared Office programs, type in the name the way that users will specify it when installing Office. If you use a drive letter, such as E:, users will have to map the drive.

4. When Setup asks where to put the shared files, you can select either Server or User's Choice. If you select Server, this will store files on the server. At the same time, it will allow the files to be run remotely from other computers on the network. If you select User's Choice, users at other computers pick whether to keep the files on the administrator PC or load them on their own local hard drives. Be sure to select Server, so that applications files are not accidentally deleted, or moved and thus lost to other users on the network.

 NOTE Remember, we are talking here about Office application files, like PowerPoint and Word, not individual files created in these programs. Users will still be able to determine on which computer to store a document that they have created.

5. After Setup copies all the files, be sure to share the \Msoffice and \Msapps folders so that other users on the network can access them.

Now that you've set up the administrator computer, the client computer no longer needs the ability to write. You should now switch to read-only access on the client computer.

NOTE See Chapter 17, "Setting Up Shared Resources," for more on how to set up sharing for file folders.

After you've gotten Office installed on your administrative computer, it's time to set up the client machines. Here's how:

1. From the client computer, use Explorer or Network Neighborhood to connect to the main Office folder on the administrative PC.

2. When you find `Setup.exe` in Office folder on the administrative PC, double-click it to start setup.

3. When you see the Run From Network Server option, select it to keep the main Office application files on the administrator PC, with the ability to run them remotely.

 WARNING Microsoft sensibly suggests that you have a read-only connection to the administrator PC's Office folder when you're running Setup on a client computer. Likewise, use read-only sharing when running the applications remotely. This will keep you from fouling up the main Office files in the event something goes wrong during installation or use.

Now you are ready to share applications programs over the network. Starting shared applications is easy. All you do is start the program as you would a non-shared version, by clicking Start and then the program's icon.

Personal Information Managers

It might seem surprising, but sharing your personal information is one of the most powerful things you can do with a network. A network-ready personal information manager, such as Microsoft Outlook 2000, lets you save loads of time and effort by letting you do the following:

• Share resources such as contact databases, phone books, and lists of e-mail addresses among other people in the house. This way, you don't have to enter everything twice.

• Set up an electronic honey-do list, bulletin board, or household blackboard, so that you can share to-do items.

- Share notices of upcoming events. You can eliminate missed birthdays, anniversaries, and the like (although some users may prefer to keep their excuses intact).

- Use the ability to check out network-based schedules of other members of your household, and thereby pick a time when everyone is available for a meeting, a meal, or a party.

Setting Up A Personal Information Manager (PIM) for Networking   The best way to share personal information is through a *Personal Information Manager* program. There are many networkable programs that fall into the category of personal information managers, as well as many, including Microsoft Outlook and Symantec ACT!, that do much more. Time & Chaos is a well-designed shareware product produced by iSBiS-TER International, Incorporated, for Windows 95/98 and Windows NT 4.0 that boasts some powerful networking features. You can download it for evaluation and try it before you buy. Like almost all the networkable PIMs, it works well for non-networked use as well. Learn more at www.isbister.com.

Here's how you set up Time & Chaos for networking:

1. Decide where on your hard drive you want to keep your database files. This can be on any computer on the network.

2. Create a Nodemanager file in Time & Chaos by clicking on File ➢ Preferences, then the Network tab.

3. Select the Build A Brand New Workgroup option and click Next.

4. In the next window, select a folder where you want to place your Node file. Please note: This folder has to be shared.

5. Now you'll get the option to create an Administrative Password. It's a good idea to use a password to protect the privacy and integrity of your data.

6. Now connect each database to the Node files by returning to the Network tab, choosing the Connect to an Existing Network option, and clicking Next.

7. Click the File Cabinet button and use the browser function to reach where you have stored the Nodemanager folder on the network. Select that folder and click Okay.

8. The window labeled Step #2 should fill in automatically. Now you can pick an icon from the scrolling list to identify your data. Finish the process by clicking OK. You'll be able to exchange information with databases connected to the same Node files.

Summary

Of course, after you network your home computers, you could enjoy spending all your free time playing multiplayer games with your roommates, kids, or friends from around the world. But your home network will also provide you with benefits that will save you time and money. Networking provides you with greater options for backing up your precious documents, which a standalone computer just cannot offer. Just as important, you can share e-mail accounts, files, and applications, providing you with a convenience and savings that, after a little while, you'll wonder how you ever lived without.

What's Next

Once you've got your network installed, configured, and loaded with some applications, it's time to put yourself on the network. Setting up new users is the subject of the next chapter.

PART IV

Using Your Network

LEARN TO:

- *Set Up New Users*

- *Set Up Shared Resources*

- *Access Your Network Remotely*

- *Set Up Personal Web Servers*

CHAPTER 16

Setting Up New Users

Overview

I f this were a company's network, then the network administrator would set up the user profiles and choose the way users would log on to the network. Since the network is at home, you are elected administrator and you will have these (fortunately easy) tasks to accomplish. While none is particularly difficult, they are important, as they will have significant effects on how easy and friendly your home network is to use. If you will have more than one user on your home network, then you will need to set up user profiles to distinguish between users, personalize settings for each user, select a logon method, and choose passwords.

Setting Up User Profiles

A user profile is a collection of settings that a particular computer user employs to customize the desktop and other features of the computer. A user profile can control each of the following:

- Shortcuts on Quick Launch bar
- History and cookies in Internet Explorer
- Address book in Outlook Express
- Program groups under Start button
- Desktop colors
- Screensaver

Each member of your household probably has their own preferences, from the pointers they use (animated hourglass versus blossoming rose) to the background colors on the inactive window (navy blue versus bubble gum pink). Each user will also see only their own Favorites links, and can set up personal folders to which no one else on the network will have access. To accommodate the range of tastes of your network users, you will first have to set up the network for multiple users.

Fortunately, setting up user profiles is straightforward. If you're using Windows 98, however, first you will likely have to set up the machine to be able to profile multiple users. That's because Windows 98 ships from the factory set up for single users. Start by going to the User section in Control Panel:

1. Click Start ➢ Settings ➢ Control Panel.

2. Highlight the Users icon, as shown in Figure 16.1, and double-click or press Enter.

FIGURE 16.1

You'll find the Users icon in Control Panel.

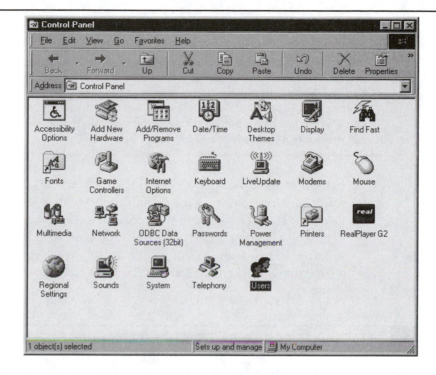

3. After double-clicking the Users icon, you'll see the Enable Multiuser Settings window. Click Next to continue.

4. At the Add User window, as shown in Figure 16.2, select a username and type it into the box labeled User Name.

FIGURE 16.2

The Add User window is where you select your username.

TIP The username you select isn't nearly as important as the password you select. It must, of course, be something that you can remember. But other than that, about all that matters is that it be a name you're comfortable with; that describes you in some way; and that isn't confusing, embarrassing, or annoying to other people who might run across it. Business network users have traditionally been asked to choose a dull, boring username such as their first and last name, first initial and last name, first name and last initial, last name, or just first name. But, since it's your network, you can let your imagination run wild. Just make sure it's something you can remember.

5. In the next window, as shown in Figure 16.3, you'll be asked to enter your password. Entering a password is optional, as the window indicates, but it's a good idea to do this. See "Selecting Passwords," later in this chapter, for tips on how to choose a password wisely and well. You have to enter the password twice so Windows will know it's got it correctly. If you get the password wrong the second time, you'll see the screen shown in Figure 16.4. Once you get it right, click Next.

FIGURE 16.3

In the Enter New Password window, you'll be asked to type in your password twice to confirm it.

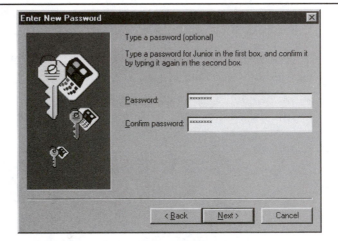

FIGURE 16.4

You'll see this window if you make a mistake typing your password in the second time to confirm it.

6. At the Personalized Items Settings window, shown in Figure 16.5, you'll be presented with several options for customizing your settings, including the following check boxes:

Desktop Folder and Documents Menu   If you select this option, you'll save your personal settings for the Desktop and the recently used documents list in the Documents menu on your Start menu. It basically gives users control over how their desktops appear, including which programs show up on the menu.

Start Menu   If you've made any changes to your Start Menu, such as adding programs or changing the order in which they appear, this will preserve the changes.

Favorites Folder   Your Favorites folder contains links to files and programs on your hard drive, as well as links to your most-used Web pages. Select this option if you want to preserve those links.

Downloaded Web Pages   Cookies, cached Web pages, and other temporary Internet files are stored in your personal folders. Selecting this option will save them in your personal profile.

My Documents Folder   If you select this box, it will have the effect of making the My Documents folder a personal folder for your use.

PART

IV

Using Your Network

FIGURE 16.5

The Personalized Items Settings window is where you select the items you want to personalize.

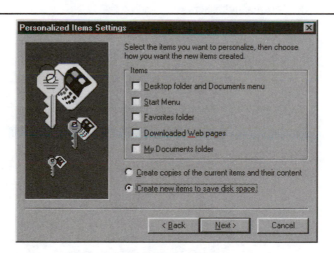

TIP You can set up your personal profile so that it retains the list of documents that already appear when you click Start ➤ Documents. To do this, select the radio button labeled Create Copies of Current Items and Their Contents. If you were to select the radio button labeled Create New Items in Order to Conserve Disk Space, on the other hand, you would get a clean, new Documents list. Selecting to create new items is a good way to set up a clean, new personalization.

7. Click the Next button in the Personalized Items Settings window to go to the Enable Multiuser Settings window and complete the process of setting up your user profile.

8. The final step in setting up your User Profile is to restart the computer—Windows should restart by itself—and log on with your new password and username. When you do this, Windows will automatically save your desktop settings for you.

Since the whole point of setting up user profiles is to make it convenient for more than one person to use a computer, you'll probably want to set up other members of your household with user profiles. To do so, follow these steps:

1. Click Start ➤ Settings ➤ Control Panel.

2. Double-click Users.

3. In the User Settings window, as shown in Figure 16.6, click New User.

FIGURE 16.6

Click New User from the list in the User Settings window to begin setting up a new user.

WARNING Be careful about using the Delete button in the User Settings window. You can't delete the user who is logged on at that moment, but you can delete other users. If you do, you may create a significant hardship for anyone whose profile has been deleted, since they will likely have to re–set up their desktop, Start button programs, and other features.

4. In the Add User window, as shown in Figure 16.7, click Next.

FIGURE 16.7

Click the Next button in the Add User window to continue creating a new user profile.

From this point on, the process is the same as steps 4 through 7 in the previous section on setting up multiple users. The one exception: You won't have to Enable Multi-user Settings, since you have already done so.

You can also alter the settings for a user. To do this, follow these steps:

1. Click Start ➢ Settings ➢ Control Panel.

2. Double-click Users.

3. In the User Settings window, as shown in Figure 16.8, select the user whose settings you want to modify and click the Change Settings button.

FIGURE 16.8

*Pick a user whose set-
tings you wish to mod-
ify, and click Change
Settings.*

4. In the Personalized Items Settings window, shown in Figure 16.9, select the items you want to change and click OK.

FIGURE 16.9

*The Personalized Items
Settings window is
where you select items
to change when alter-
ing a user profile.*

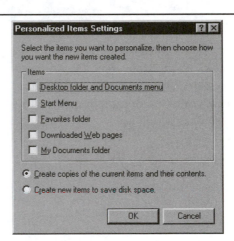

5. When you return to the User Settings window, click Close to finish.

Now multiple users can use the same computer—or network of computers—while enjoying their personalized settings. Enabling the multiusers function is a great way to avoid complaints and conflicts among the people using your network.

Selecting a Logon Method

One of the inescapable parts of life as a user of networked computers is the logon/ logoff sequence. You also have to log on and log off when you are using non-networked Windows computers on which multiple user profiles are set up.

Logon, also referred to as login, is the act of establishing a connection to an online service or network, or, in some cases, starting up an individual computer. Logoff, also called logout, takes place when you end a session using a computer, network, or online service. When you log off, your computer sends a message notifying the system that you are signing off. Logoff is not the same as turning the computer off. As you probably are aware, you can cause problems with your Windows system by just turning it off without shutting down Windows first. The same is true of the network. If you just unplug your computer from the network, or turn it off without logging off first, you can cause problems with the rest of the network.

Once you have multiple users set up, even on a non-networked computer, you'll have to log on each time you use the computer. The logon box will pop up each time you

- Turn on the computer

- Restart the computer

- Log off and log back on

- Log on after someone else has logged off

You have two basic choices of logon methods in Windows 95/98:

- Microsoft Family Logon

- Client for Microsoft Networks

The big difference between Microsoft Family Logon and Client for Microsoft Networks is that with Microsoft Family Logon, you don't get to share files or printers. Microsoft Family Logon is well suited for a single computer used by several people.

The Client for Microsoft Networks logon allows you to select different user profiles at logon, just as Microsoft Family Logon does. In addition, Client for Microsoft Networks provides you the network advantages, such as file and printer sharing. So Client for Microsoft Networks is the logon you'll be most likely to use if you are connected to a network.

While Client for Microsoft Networks is the most likely client you'll install, it's not the only one available with Windows 98. You can, in addition to or instead of, install:

- Microsoft Family Logon, which provides a simplified way of logging on to Windows 95/98 PC using profiles.

- A Banyan DOS/Windows 3.1 client, for connecting to Banyan VINES networks.

- Microsoft Client for Netware Networks, which will allow you to access a Netware server.

- Clients that allow you to use the old Novell NetWare NetX and newer VLM workstation shell software.

Setting Up Client for Microsoft Networks

Your computer has to have Client for Microsoft Networks installed and selected as the primary logon client, before you can take advantage of most of the networking features, including file and printer sharing.

 NOTE You also need Client for Microsoft Networks for playing most head-to-head multiplayer games. See Chapter 15, "Other Network Software," to learn more about this.

Here's how to install and select Client for Microsoft networks as the primary logon method:

1. Click Start ➤ Settings ➤ Control Panel.

2. Select Network, as shown in Figure 16.10, and double-click or press Enter.

FIGURE 16.10

Highlight the Network icon in Control Panel and double-click to set up Client for Microsoft Networks.

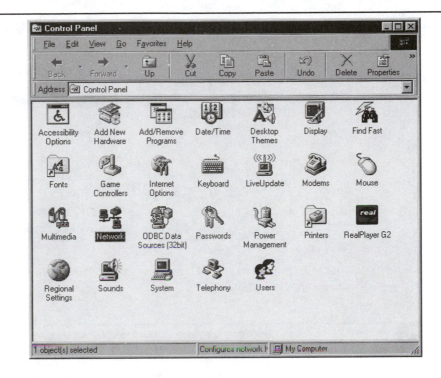

3. At the Configuration tab, click Add.

4. At the Select Network Component Type box, as shown in Figure 16.11, click Client ➢ Add. You may have to wait a moment while Windows builds a driver information database.

FIGURE 16.11

Select Client and click Add in the Select Network Component Type box.

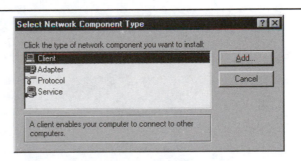

5. Select Microsoft, as shown in Figure 16.12, then click Client for Microsoft Networks ➢ OK.

FIGURE 16.12

In the Select Network Client box, choose Client for Microsoft Networks.

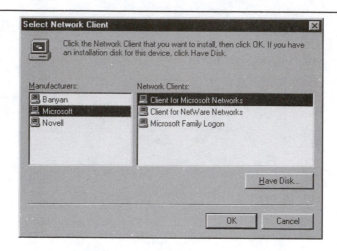

6. Under Primary Network Logon, as shown in Figure 16.13, click Client for Microsoft Networks ➤ OK.

FIGURE 16.13

The last step in setting up Client for Microsoft Networks is to select it as Primary Network Logon.

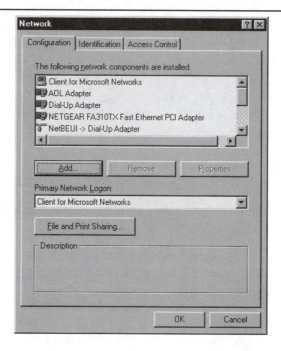

Setting Properties for Client for Microsoft Networks

After you've installed Client for Microsoft Networks, you will want to set certain logon properties. Here's how:

1. Click Start ➢ Settings ➢ Control Panel.

2. Select Network, as you saw in Figure 16.10, and double-click or press Enter.

3. Select Client for Microsoft Networks in the top window in the Network control panel (the one listing installed network components), as shown in Figure 16.14.

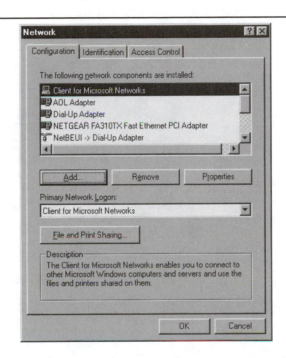

4. At the Client for Microsoft Networks Properties box, as shown in Figure 16.15, you can set properties for Logon Validation and Network Logon Options.

Logon Validation   Unless you have a Windows NT server as a domain con-troller, you should leave this check box blank. Few home networks have a Win-dows NT server acting as a domain controller. If you check this box, you will have the ability to use any of the domain's resources by merely logging on to your computer with your password. Note that if you have a domain controller you must provide the domain name and not the name of the domain controller.

Network Logon Options   You will have a choice of two Network Logon options: Quick Logon, and Logon and Restore Network Connections. The Quick logon option is faster than the other option. Both options allow you to Log on and restore network connections. Unless you specifically need to be able to access mapped network drives immediately upon logging on, you should probably choose the Quick Logon radio button. If you want to be able to access mapped network drives immediately, choose Logon and Restore Network Connections. However, this option may add significantly to the length of time required for you to log on to your network, so you should only select it if you really want to have instant access to those mapped network drives.

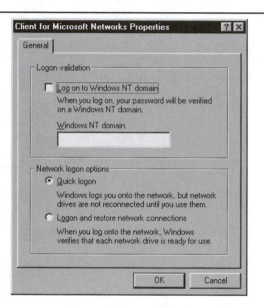

FIGURE 16.15

The Client for Microsoft Networks Properties window lets you set logon options.

5. Click OK twice to close the Client for Microsoft Networks window and the Network window and finish setting the properties for Client for Microsoft Networks.

 NOTE   There is also a set of properties for Client for Novell Networks. If you are using a Novell Networks client, you can change these properties from the Network control window in the same manner as the Microsoft Networks client.

Setting Up Microsoft Family Logon

Although you'll probably be using Client for Microsoft Networks, Microsoft Family Logon does have its uses. Microsoft Family Logon gives you a simplified way of using profiles when logging on to a computer running Windows 95/98. (Note that this is different from Client for Microsoft Networks, which gives you a way to log on to the actual network.) Microsoft Family Logon is, by the way, different from the Users tool in Control Panel. It does not let you create users or profiles, it just lets you log on to your computer using profiles. Here's how you add Microsoft Family Logon, in case it's not already installed:

1. Click Start ➢ Settings ➢ Control Panel.

2. Select Network, as you saw in Figure 16.10, and double-click or press Enter.

3. At the Configuration tab, click Add.

4. At the Select Network Component Type box, as shown in Figure 16.16, click Client ➢ Add. There may be a wait while Windows builds a driver information database.

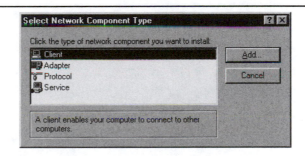

5. Select Microsoft as shown in Figure 16.17, then click Microsoft Family Logon ➢ OK.

FIGURE 16.17

In the Select Network Client box, choose Microsoft Family Logon.

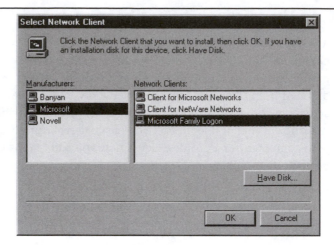

6. Under Primary Network Logon, as shown in Figure 16.18, click Microsoft Family Logon ➢ OK.

FIGURE 16.18

The last step in setting up Microsoft Family Logon is to select Microsoft Family Logon in the Primary Network Logon box.

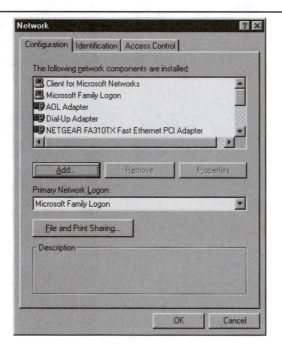

NOTE You won't see the Microsoft Family Logon dialog box when you start your computer unless you choose it as the primary network logon.

After you've installed and selected Microsoft Family Logon as your primary network logon, anytime you turn on, restart, or log off, and then log back on to the computer, you'll be presented with a logon box prompting you to select a username from a list of the users you have created. You will then enter a password. Doing this will log you on to the computer.

 NOTE For more on setting up user profiles, see the first section in this chapter.

Selecting Passwords

The proper selection and use of passwords is very important for maintaining the security of your network. There are a number of critical considerations when you are using passwords for network security. You have to make sure you don't choose a password that is easy to figure out. And you should use it properly as well, which means changing it regularly and frequently.

 NOTE For more on using passwords for security, see Chapter 20, "Network Security."

Here are some tips about the right way and the wrong way to select a user password. First, some don'ts. Don't do the following:

- Use a password shorter than six characters.
- Use all the same number or letter, as in "11111."
- Use your own name, first or last.
- Use the name of your spouse, child, parent, other family member, friend, or dog. Nor should you use your license number, birthdate, or even if they are your most closely guarded secrets, weight or age.
- Use your username or login name, no matter how carefully you think it's disguised.

- Use information about yourself that anybody could find out. That includes your phone number, Social Security number, street address, ZIP code, city of residence, or anything that is public record.
- Use an actual word from the dictionary, English or foreign language, including a spelling list or other word list.
- Use the same password all the time to log in to more than one system.
- Write your password down and stick it on a yellow note on the side of your computer.

Some of these rules are bendable, of course. If you are sure that no one but yourself is going to get a look at the PC you have in your home office, go ahead and jot down passwords on a piece of paper you can find when you need it. But don't do it if your PC is located in, say, the kitchen, where anyone passing by can copy down your passwords.

Here is the right way to pick a password:

- Use more than six characters.
- Use uppercase and lowercase alphabet letters.
- Use numbers and punctuation marks, as well as letters.
- Pick a password that is easy to remember, so you don't feel you have to write it down.

Easy-to-Remember Passwords

The subject of easy-to-remember passwords is a fun one. How can you pick a password that is both hard to figure out and impossible to forget? Password selectors have devised a number of clever, effective ways to accomplish these two seemingly incompatible goals.

- Take two words of five or more characters and join them with a punctuation mark, as in coffee!rapid, sandal#kilter, etc. Online services have assigned similar passwords to some of the consumers who took them up on offers of free online trials.
- Pick a sentence or phrase you can remember, such as the title of a book or song, a popular quotation or even a marketing slogan, and create your password by using the first letters of the words in the phrase. Thus, "If you can't beat them, join them" becomes IYCBTJT. Music students use a similar technique to recall the notes that fall on the lines of a musical staff by memorizing "Every good boy does fine," which becomes EGBDF.

Continued

CONTINUED

- Use an actual, easily remembered word and substitute numerals or punctuation marks for some of the letters. For instance, "Thomas" could become "+h0ma5" with a plus sign for the T, a zero for the O, and a numeral 5 instead of the S. The letters 0, 1, and 5 are commonly substituted for the letters O, L, and S using this technique.

- A nonsense word that is pronounceable is easier to remember than, say, xc4l%opy. So, when making up your password, alternate between one consonant and one or two vowels. These will tend to be pronounceable, as in foybow and mibizoto.

- Think visually, choosing a combination of keys that, when pecked out on a keyboard, forms a memorable pattern. For instance, the keys used to type EWQAZXC form a shape resembling a letter C on the keyboard.

If you're really going to do passwords right, you have to change them frequently. Setting up a system will help you to do this without losing easy memorability. Here are some tricks to do this:

- Pick your three favorite songs and use the first letters of the first lines of all three as your three separate passwords. You can use them in alphabetical order or reverse-alphabetical order to further mix them up.

- Pick two phrases of equal length and combine successive words from each to make three different joined passwords. Using this system, something like "might#love" and "makes%conquers" and "right&all" would be your next three passwords.

If you really want to get serious about passwords, you can use software to generate truly random passwords of any length and character content. One example is Advanced Password Generator, a shareware program from Segobit for Windows 95/98 and NT machines. As shown in Figure 16.19, it will create passwords of any length you specify (the unregistered version limits you to four- or five-character passwords) and assemble them from alphabetic, numeric, alphanumeric, or any other keyboard characters, including lowercase and mixed case. The program generates a list of two or three potential passwords, or up to 40 in the registered version. You can print the passwords or clip and paste them into other applications. Get more information or download Advanced Password Generator at http://segobit.virtualave.net/apg.htm.

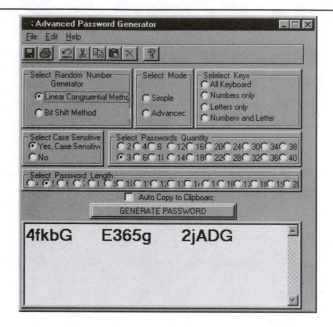

FIGURE 16.19

Advanced Password Generator is an easy-to-use shareware program for creating truly unguessable passwords.

Summary

Although some solitary users network their home computers, most home networkers will want to provide many household members access to the plethora of resources available on the network. Fortunately, the available networking software makes it possible to do this relatively easily. And best of all, the ability to customize options cuts down on the potential for family strife.

What's Next

The next chapter, on setting up shared resources, is one of the most important, interesting, and useful in this book. You'll learn how to prepare and share everything from modems to removable drives, as well as even create your own personal Web server.

CHAPTER 17

Setting Up Shared Resources

Overview

Sharing resources is what networking is all about. When you share resources over a home network, more people will use those resources more often. That means you get more value out of them. And that's a good idea. Why else do you think phone companies offer discounts when you call long distance at night and on weekends? Those are the hours when their network isn't being fully used, so they're anxious to get people to call during those times. You don't have to offer your household a discount for sharing. All you have to do is set up your network so that the valuable resources connected to it can be shared. When you do, the combination of convenience and just plain fun will prove irresistible.

What network resources can be shared? Practically speaking, they include:

- Modems, including cable and DSL modems
- Hard disk drives
- CD-ROM and DVD-ROM drives
- Removable drives, such as Zip drives and floppies
- Software, including productivity applications and games
- Data files, including everything from a text file of phone numbers to your schedule for next week

You can share these resources in endless combinations. For instance, let's say a child's birthday is approaching and you want to shop for a gift using the computer in the family room, as shown in Figure 17.1. Here's how you could do it all without stirring from your chair, using shared network resources:

1. First, you could look at the wish list the child keeps as a shared text file on the PC in the child's room.

2. Next, you'd take a look at the checkbook balance, kept on the kitchen PC in a shared Quicken database, to set your shopping budget.

3. Then, you could use the shared cable modem on the office machine to shop for the gift online using high-speed Internet access.

4. After making and ordering your selection, you could print out the receipt on the shared printer in the home office where, presumably, it will be safe from curious eyes.

That adds up to a significant savings in sneaker wear, and it's just one of an infinite array of possible ways that you can benefit by sharing the resources on your network.

FIGURE 17.1

Sharing network resources lets you use computers, peripherals, and files that are spread all over the house to shop for a birthday gift quickly, conveniently, and easily.

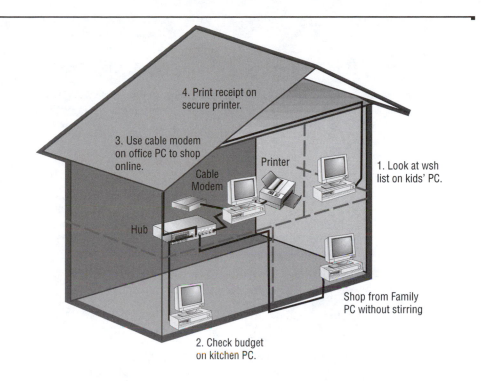

4. Print receipt on secure printer.

3. Use cable modem on office PC to shop online.

Printer

1. Look at wsh list on kids' PC.

Cable Modem

Hub

Shop from Family PC without stirring

2. Check budget on kitchen PC.

Setting Up Shared Modems

Networking became popular in the business world because people wanted to be able to share files and printers. But those attractions, on their own, weren't enough to bring networking into the home. The lure of sharing modems and high-speed Internet access is, in the minds of many observers of the home networking scene, the thing that is going to make home networking ubiquitous.

How Hot Is Home Networking—and Why?

You're going to have a lot of company as a home networker before long, because the growth in home networking over the next few years will be nothing short of explosive, according to a long-range report by the market research firm Frost & Sullivan. Here's what they found:

- After totaling less than $35 billion in 1998, manufacturers' sales of home networking equipment will top $2 billion by 2005.
- From 1998 to 2005, the annual growth rate will be a sizzling 79 percent.
- Growth in unit sales will be equally impressive, as shipments of hubs, bridges, and adapters, including PC cards and external devices, swell from under a million in 1998 to more than 73 million a year by 2005.

What's driving it? Several factors, according to the Frost & Sullivan researchers, including the following:

- Growth in multiple-PC homes
- Drastically lower prices for PCs
- New home networking products operating at 10Mbps or better
- Better interoperability of home networking products
- And, last but far from least, wider home use of broadband Internet access such as cable and DSL

Continued growth will depend on a number of factors. To further stimulate growth, networking equipment manufacturers will probably have to continue to build industry standards and come out with higher speed phoneline, powerline, and wireless technologies. And of course, companies will need to develop more consumer interest in residential gateways and appliances.

In addition to the history of industry growth, the Frost & Sullivan report also looked at trends related to the different home networking technologies. Although Ethernet owned nearly 77 percent of the market in 1997, powerline, phoneline, and wireless are expected to gain. Today, Ethernet's edges in speed and installed base are being countered by the difficulty of cabling and by the desire of PC makers to try other technologies. On the other hand, phoneline benefits from widespread adoption of the HomePNA 2.0 standard. At the same time, though, phoneline is being held back by poor-performing first-generation products and low consumer visibility. Powerline networking is hurting due to slow speeds, noise issues, and lack of open standards. Although wireless offers much in flexibility, its high costs, low performance, and standards confusion balance a boom in portable device use, helpful FCC licensing changes, and the benefits of mobile roaming. Learn more at: www.frost.com.

WARNING *Always-on* Internet connections such as cable modems and DSL modems pose an added security risk. Hackers using port-sniffing programs scan the Internet looking for PCs with always-on connections that lack adequate security. When you're using a regular telephone modem, you're unlikely to be connected long enough to let a hacker invade your machine. With an always-on connection, it's a different story. Take precautions to protect your data if you are using a cable modem or DSL Internet connection.

NOTE For more on securing always-on Internet connections, as well as other aspects of network security, see Chapter 20, "Network Security."

Sharing Cable Modems

With one or two exceptions (Hint: The initials are A-O-L), Internet Service Providers are pretty much the same. ISPs all tend to have similar policies, similar pricing, and similar technology. Just a few years ago, of course, it wasn't that way. You could choose from any number of pricing plans, ranging from pay-as-you-go to the monthly flat rate schemes that have become the standard today. Right now, the cable modem industry is about where the ISPs were a few years ago, on a somewhat reduced scale. Whereas there are hundreds if not thousands of small and large ISPs, only a half-dozen or so cable system operators provide cable modem access to the Internet. But they all have slightly different ways of operating, and those differences come front and center when you're talking about sharing cable modem access over a home network.

WARNING Many of the cable modem system operators do not allow you to access the Internet using more than one computer if you have only one subscriber connection. You may be disconnected and refused service if you try to use connection-sharing software, such as Microsoft Internet Connection Sharing, in violation of the cable operator's Terms of Service agreement. Read the Terms of Service information provided by your cable modem system to learn more.

NOTE Sharing a cable or DSL modem between computers connected with a wireless, phoneline, or powerline system is different than sharing over an Ethernet network, thanks to the fact that there is no network hub into which you can plug the modem. To share with these kinds of networks, you need to have two network adapters installed in one of the networked computers. Then, you connect the modem to the adapter that is not being used to connect to the phoneline, powerline, or wireless network.

The key question is whether you get more than one IP address with your subscription to a particular cable modem service. Some systems give you only one; others provide up to three IP addresses as part of the base rate. You can usually get more IP addresses for an additional fee ranging from $5.00 to $15.00 a month. Assuming that you have more than one IP address, here's how you set up an Ethernet network to share a cable modem on a typical system:

1. Connect the cable modem to your hub. Plug the cable modem's RJ-45 Ethernet adapter into your hub's uplink port and make sure the port's LED status indicator light, if it has one, is lit.

 NOTE If the hub lacks an uplink port, you may be able to use a *crossover cable*—a network cable specially wired to perform the work of a hub—to connect the hub and modem.

2. If you have not already done so, connect the other PCs on your network to the hub. Check to make sure the PCs see each other on the network by using Windows Network Neighborhood.

 NOTE For more on fixing network problems, see Chapter 21, "Troubleshooting."

3. Make sure that TCP/IP networking is installed on all the PCs.

 NOTE For more on installing TCP/IP networking, see the following section, "Sharing Internet Access."

5. Install the login software for your cable modem system on all the PCs you want to be able to share the cable modem.

NOTE If your cable modem system uses DHCP to assign TCP/IP addresses, you won't have to adjust Windows 95/98 networking parameters. If not, you'll have to follow the directions for your cable modem system operator to assign TCP/IP addresses.

6. Try logging on to the cable modem service from all the PCs to see if everything works.

If you have a problem, it may be that you are trying to connect more PCs to the cable modem than you have IP addresses. Connections are another common source of problems: Make sure all the computers on the network can see each other, and that the LED status light is lit on the port where the cable modem is connected.

WARNING Support is a particular problem when sharing cable modems over a home network. Cable providers are likely to blame any problems you have on your network, and refuse to help you set up sharing over a network. Your network equipment vendor, on the other hand, is not likely to be familiar with cable modems—at least not yet. Fortunately, users have set up some excellent resources to help people in this jam. Learn more at: www.cablemodemhelp.com.

Sharing DSL Modems

Digital subscriber line (DSL) modems offer high-speed Internet connections that are easy to set up for sharing. The easiest way is to obtain enough IP addresses from your DSL service provider to accommodate all the PCs you want to share the connection with. This, unfortunately, is usually going to cost you extra. In the case of a basic DSL service, offering 348Kbps download speed and 128Kbps upload speed, the extra IP addresses will cost you about $5.00 each. For instance, instead of paying $55.00 a month for one IP address, you'll pay around $75.00 for five. If you want the really fast DSL, with 1.5Mbps download and 385Kbps upload, it's probably going to cost you around $200.00 a month. The good news is that you'll probably get more than one IP address with your faster DSL account. If you have a hubbed Ethernet network and enough IP addresses to accommodate all the PCs you want to share the connection, the setup process is easy. The modems vary somewhat according to manufacturer but, typically, all you have to do is:

1. Plug the DSL modem into the phone wall jack, using the RJ-11 telephone connector and standard telephone wire.

2. Plug the DSL modem into the uplink port on your network's hub, using the RJ-45 connector and cable that came with the cable modem. The resulting configuration will look like Figure 17.2.

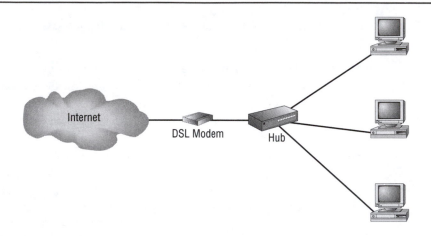

FIGURE 17.2

You can connect multiple PCs to a DSL modem by plugging the modem into your Ethernet hub.

3. Run the installation software that you got from your DSL provider.

NOTE You can also set up the DSL modem to be shared by two or more PCs using Internet sharing software. To learn more, see the "Internet Connection Sharing" section in this chapter.

Sharing ISDN Modems

Integrated Services Digital Network, or ISDN, is an older Internet access method that, while roughly twice as fast as regular 56K modems, is far slower than the new broadband connections, such as cable modems and DSL. Nor is it particularly inexpensive. Setup fees for a 128Kbps ISDN line are about $150.00. A terminal adapter—ISDN-speak for a modem—will run you $200.00 and up. And monthly service fees may be nearly that much on top.

NOTE ISDN isn't the only older technology still popular. You can get what the phone companies call a T1 connection that will allow you to connect to the Internet at 5Mbps speed. But the setup fee runs to four figures, and the monthly fee will start at around $500.00, and probably go up from there, based on how much you use it. Still not enough? Many large businesses and Internet-intensive smaller firms have T3 connections that roll along at 45Mbps. Setup fees for a T3 line will be closer to five figures, with monthly minimums well into four figures.

Still, ISDN is more widely available than cable modem or DSL service at this point. If you don't have one of the broadband technologies available where you are, ISDN, as shown in Figure 17.3, may be a good choice.

FIGURE 17.3

An ISDN LAN modem will give you a network hub, ISDN digital modem, phone connections, and connection sharing in one box.

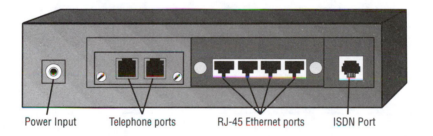

Power Input   Telephone ports   RJ-45 Ethernet ports   ISDN Port

ISDN LAN Modems

One attractive option when you're using ISDN is the choice of using a device that functions as both an ISDN modem and an Ethernet hub. In effect, it's a kind of a router that simultaneously serves as the hub for your Ethernet network, connects you to the Internet using middle-speed ISDN, and also lets all the PCs on your network share the Internet connection. For example, the 3Com OfficeConnect ISDN LAN Modem, whose back plate connections are shown in Figure 17.3, integrates in one package a 4-port Ethernet hub, a router using the Internet protocol, an ISDN terminal adapter or modem, and two analog ports.

Continued

CONTINUED

Despite their seeming complexity, ISDN LAN modems are not particularly difficult to set up, since the functions of modem, hub, and router are integrated by the manufacturer. And using one of these devices, you can put as many as 25 computers and two telephones or fax machines onto a single ISDN line. Best yet, the ISDN LAN costs from $250.00 to $400.00—only a modest premium over many ISDN modems without the networking features. Learn more at www.3com.com.

Sharing Satellite Connections

Cable modems and DSL may be fast, but right now only one high-speed Internet service is truly available nationwide, and that's the DirecPC satellite Internet service. As shown in Figure 17.4, it works by taking a surfer's command, such as a request for a URL, and sending it by modem to a regular ISP. The command carries with it a tunneling code that tells the ISP to forward the request to the DirecPC network center, instead of handling it with the ISP's own server. The DirecPC gathers the request for Web content and sends it over high-speed T3 lines to its satellite uplink. The satellite beams it down to a DirecPC satellite dish at the surfer's home and into the PC.

FIGURE 17.4

Surfing with a DirecPC satellite Internet connection requires a complex chain of technology to make it work.

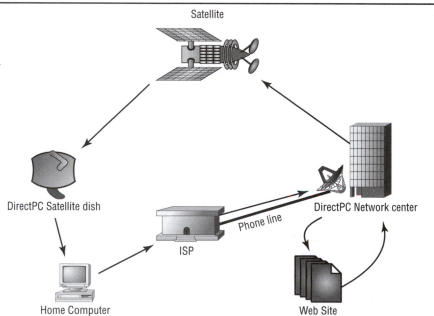

Compared to cable, satellite connection speeds are only moderate at 400Kbps. And the equipment is complex, including a satellite dish antenna (with mounting hardware), a special modem for a USB port or PCI slot, and software. Using a satellite also has its oddities. In addition to the satellite hardware, you also need a regular modem and landline telephone connection to an ISP (since you can't beam keystrokes and mouse clicks back up to the satellite, of course). At around $200.00 including installation, however, satellite Internet hardware is no more expensive than hardware for competitive technologies.

 WARNING To go with its real advantages, satellite Internet service has real drawbacks for network users. For instance, you won't get any speed benefit compared to a regular telephone modem when playing network games over a DirecPC connection. You can't use a DirecPC for video conferencing at all. DirecPC is not available on a PCMCIA card, so you can't use it with a laptop unless you connect through a USB port or docking station with a PCI slot. And, at this time, DirecPC doesn't officially run on Linux or Unix machines. However, as you might expect when it comes to Linux, there are some third-party solutions that might work for you.

The beauty of satellite is that, despite its moderate performance, complexity, and cost, its availability is superb. In addition to installation costs, satellite service costs are also moderate, ranging from $20.00 for a bare-bones 25 hours a month—yes, the limited-hours rate plans are still with us—up to $50.00 a month for 100 hours and an ISP account. As for speed, if you have an unobstructed line of sight to the southern sky and are located somewhere in the continental US, you can probably get 400Kbps Internet service.

But what about sharing it over your home network? Sharing a DirecPC connection over your home network is actually not difficult. You do have to upgrade your service plan from one of the residential offerings to the business plan. With this plan, for $110.00 a month, you get 200 hours a month of connect time, with additional hours billed at $1.00 each. For the $110.00, you also get an ISP account, various other DirecPC Internet services, four e-mail accounts, and last but far from least, four of what DirecPC call *network seats*, which are equivalent to the extra IP addresses that other broadband Internet providers sell. These will allow you to access the Internet through four networked PCs.

TIP You can also use Internet connection sharing software to allow more than one PC to simultaneously access the DirecPC network through the single connection.

Assuming that giving four PCs access to the Internet is enough for your home network needs, then:

1. Have the dish and connecting cable installed at your home or, if you're so inclined, do it yourself.

2. Make sure your network and regular analog telephone modem are connected and working.

3. Install the PCI card or USB peripheral in your PC and connect it to the dish.

4. Run the DirecPC software to configure your system and set up your ISP account.

AOL Takes Satellite Plunge

An interesting sidelight to the satellite Internet access arena is the alliance formed by America Online, the largest online service, and Hughes Electronics, owner of DirecPC, the biggest satellite data service. In the interest of providing AOL with a nationwide high-speed Internet access network and boosting the Hughes Internet and DirecTV satellite television business, the two info-behemoths have agreed to develop and market integrated digital entertainment and Internet services.

In practice, it means they'll develop a device that will sit on top of your television set and allow you to receive both DirecTV and AOL. Even before this happens, AOL's broadband AOL-Plus service is supposed to be available nationwide via the DirecPC satellite Internet network. Given that, at this writing, AOL has nearly 20 million subscribers, Hughes has seven million DirecTV customers, and the companies have pledged to invest billions of dollars into the efforts, even these ambitious plans have to be taken seriously. You can monitor their progress at www.direcpc.com and www.aol.com.

Sharing Bonded Modems

When they first appeared in mainstream products in 1997, technologies that melded two or more 56K modems together to produce, theoretically, two or three or even four times the bandwidth of a single modem seemed miraculous. They were, however, quickly branded by at least one analyst a "bubble gum and paper clips" solution to the search for faster Internet hookups. And, given the vastly greater speeds available these days from cable modems and DSL, bonded modem setups may well have had their (brief) day in the sun.

Having said that, it is interesting to note that many of these products, unlike the other high-speed Internet access options, were specifically designed to be shared in network environments. The WebRamp M3 from Ramp Networks used three lines to reach theoretical speeds of up to 168Kbps. But the product was designed to be used by three computers at once, at a maximum speed of 56K, so the net effect per user was the same as an analog modem.

WARNING   One limitation on modem bonding is that, to get the higher speeds with some products, you have to connect to an Internet Service Provider that supports modem bonding. Check product specs and make sure your ISP supports it, or that you can find an ISP that supports it, before installing it.

Modem bonding isn't dead, however. Diamond Multimedia, now a part of S3, intelligently integrates two 56K modems on one board in its SupraSonic II dual-line modem. You can learn more at www.s3.com. And software from MidCore, called MidPoint Companion, works as a combined Internet connection sharing and modem-bonding tool, as shown in Figure 17.5. It can be used to combine two connections of any type, including ISDN as well as analog, for speeds that can reach into the hundreds of kilobits per second. Learn more at www.midcore.com.

FIGURE 17.5

Modem-bonding software can let you integrate two modems together, as well as let two computers share them for Internet access.

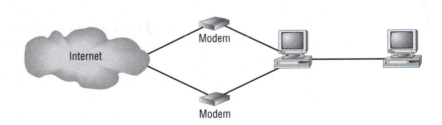

Using Internet Access Sharing Software

Sometimes, you may not be able to get extra IP addresses to allow all your networked PCs to share high-speed Internet access without a hassle. At other times, you may simply not want to. The fallback technique for sharing Internet access is by using Internet connection sharing software. Sharing software has the following advantages:

- Economical setup. You don't need to buy any additional hardware. And some of the Internet sharing programs are available as shareware or even freeware.

- Low ongoing costs. Since you're sharing a single IP address, you don't have to pay more than one monthly surcharge.

 WARNING   Your Internet access provider might not approve of Internet sharing software in all cases, especially if you have a cable modem system operator or a DSL service. Always check your Terms of Service to see if sharing Internet addresses is acceptable to your provider.

If you decide to look into Internet connection sharing software, you have two technological approaches to choose from:

Proxy Server   With this approach, not all the PCs on your network connect directly to the Internet. Instead, they connect to a PC on your network that is set up as a proxy server. The proxy server handles the job of getting and passing on data that the internal PCs request.

Network Address Translation   With this approach, a PC on your network is set up as a router. As with the proxy server, other machines send their messages and commands for the Internet to it. The NAT router swaps the network PC's Internet Protocol address with its own IP address and passes this on to the external machine. When information comes in from the Internet, the NAT gateway translates the address and sends it out to the appropriate PC on the network. NAT is easy to set up and works with most applications. One of the differences between NAT and proxy servers is that proxy servers can be set up to perform other functions, such as storing commonly accessed Web pages for faster retrieval and limiting network users' ability to access certain Web sites.

NOTE There are still other ways to share connections. Linux network servers use a technique similar to NAT called *IP masquerading*. Many home networks use a hardware NAT router. Hardware routers are easy to set up but more expensive than software-only solutions.

One of the best and most reliable means of sharing an Internet connection over a home network is through a proxy server, and so that is what we will explore in more detail here.

 NOTE If you are interested in other ways to share Internect access, such as those involving Networking Address Translation or solutions for Linux users, you can learn more at sharing expert Tim Higgins' site at www.timhiggins.com/ppd/sharing.htm.

Setting Up Proxy Servers

Sharing an Internet connection with a proxy server is appealing to many users because it offers good security–an important issue with an always-on Internet connection such as a cable modem or DSL line. On the downside, not all software applications will work with proxy servers. Still, proxy server software may be the most widely used way to share Internet connections. If you want to try the proxy approach, here's how you can set up a Windows 98 system to share a cable modem with one popular Internet connection sharing program, WinGate 3.0, which is published by Deerfield.com, an Internet software company in Gaylord, Michigan.

To use a program like WinGate with a cable modem, your host computer needs to have two network interface cards and a cable modem. One NIC connects to the cable modem and the other connects to the network. You can't use WinGate if you plug your cable modem into a hub.

1. First, make sure you can connect to the Internet using the computer on which you will install WinGate.

2. Install the TCP/IP protocol on the network adapter that connects to the internal network.

NOTE For more on installing TCP/IP, see the following section, "Setting up TCP/IP."

Now you have to set the internal network adapter up with a static IP address. This is a network address that will be used strictly on your home network and will not be seen by anyone on the Internet. Here's how:

1. Right-click the Network Neighborhood on your Windows desktop.

2. Select Properties.

3. In the Network Configuration window, select the TCP/IP protocol entry for the network adapter that you will be using to connect to your home network and click the Properties button.

4. Click the IP Address tab and click the button for Specify and IP Address.

5. Enter 192.168.0.1 in the text boxes next to IP Address.

6. Enter 255.255.255.0 in the text boxes next to Subnet Mask.

7. Click the tab for WINS Configuration and click the button for Disable WINS Resolution.

8. Click the tab for Gateway. Remove any entries under New Gateway or Installed Gateways. There should be no entries for Gateway.

9. Click the Bindings tab. Remove any checks next to Microsoft Networks and File and Printer Sharing for Microsoft Networks.

 NOTE When you try to leave the Bindings tab without any bindings checked, Windows will ask you whether you want to select any bindings. Click No.

10. Click the Advanced tab. Place a check mark next to Set This Protocol to Be the Default Protocol.

11. Click OK. Finally, configure your cable modem NIC according to your ISP's instructions.

 NOTE Check to make sure you can access the Internet from that machine. Now you are set up to share an Internet account over your home network, using a proxy server and cable modem. To learn more about Wingate, see Deerfield's Web site at `wingate .deerfield.com`.

Using Windows Internet Connection Sharing

Another proxy server is the Internet Connection Sharing software that Microsoft included with Windows 98 Second Edition update. This software hasn't blown the third-party sharing software vendors out of the water. But it's obviously very popular and does have the important plus of low cost. It's free if you already have Windows 98 SE running on the host computer, which is the only machine that connects directly to the Internet. The other PCs on the network can be running any software that is capable of using the TCP/IP protocol, including Windows 95, Windows NT, earlier versions of Windows 98, Windows 3.11, and even non-Windows machines.

ICS uses the Network Address translation approach to sharing a connection, automatically assigning unique IP addresses to computers on the network, and relaying data between those PCs and the Internet. Since the other PCs aren't directly connecting to the Internet, they need only have a TCP/IP driver and a network interface card. Microsoft ICS will work with an analog phone modem Internet connection as well as a cable modem, ISDN line, or DSL line. The home network can be phoneline, wireless, or Ethernet. If you use an Ethernet network adapter card, you'll need a hub. Here's how to set it up:

1. Click Start ➤ Settings ➤ Control Panel.

2. Double-click the icon for Add/Remove Programs, as shown in Figure 17.6.

FIGURE 17.6

Start installing Internet Connection Sharing by double-clicking Add/Remove Programs in Control Panel.

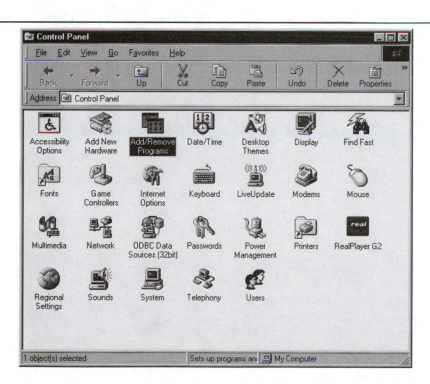

3. Click the Windows Setup tab in the Add/Remove Programs Properties dialog box, as shown in Figure 17.7. Windows will search for installed components.

FIGURE 17.7

Clicking the Windows Setup tab in the Add/Remove Programs Properties dialog box causes Windows to search for and display installed components.

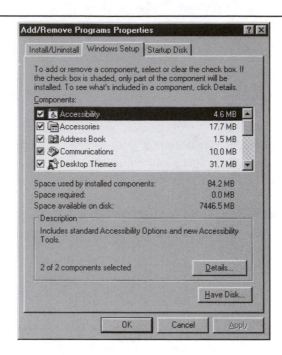

4. Select Internet Tools in the Components window, as shown in Figure 17.8, and click the Details button.

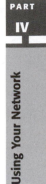

FIGURE 17.8

The Internet Tools item in the Components windows is where you'll find Internet Connection Sharing.

5. Place a check in the box next to Internet Connection Sharing, as shown in Figure 17.9, and click OK.

FIGURE 17.9

Check Internet Connection Sharing in the list of Internet Tools to select it for installation.

From here on, follow the instructions provided by the Internet Connection Sharing Wizard. It will help you pick an Internet connection, configure dialing, select the network adapter, and set up automatic IP addressing for the other computers on the network.

 TIP   You can set advanced Internet options or edit your home network's ICS settings by clicking the Internet Options icon in the Windows Control Panel and then clicking the Connection tab.

Setting Up TCP/IP

TCP/IP, or Transmission Control Protocol/Internet Protocol, is the networking protocol used on the Internet and other networks of networks. You need to install it on any machine that is connecting to the Internet, such as a proxy server. Here's how to install TCP/IP:

1. Right-click the Network Neighborhood icon on your desktop.

2. Click the Properties item on the drop-down list.

3. In the Network window, as shown in Figure 17.10, click the Add button.

FIGURE 17.10

Click the Add button in the Network window to begin installing TCP/IP.

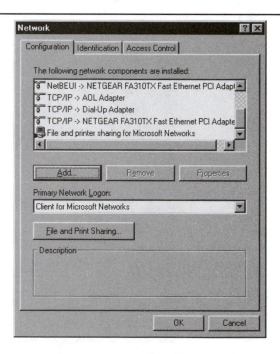

4. Highlight the Protocol entry in the list box.

5. Click Add.

6. Select Microsoft in the left window and scroll down in the right window to highlight TCP/IP, as shown in Figure 17.11.

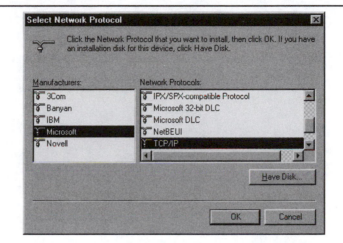

7. Click OK and then, in the Select Network Component Type window, click Cancel.

8. Click OK to reboot Windows.

After you've installed the TCP/IP protocol, you need to configure TCP/IP for the network adapter that's connected to your home network. Here's how to do so for the WinGate proxy server software:

1. Right-click the Network Neighborhood icon on your desktop.

2. Click the Properties item on the drop-down list.

3. In the Network window, highlight the TCP/IP entry for your internal network adapter, as shown in Figure 17.12.

FIGURE 17.12

Select the TCP/IP entry for the adapter that is connected to your home network to begin configuring the protocol for sharing.

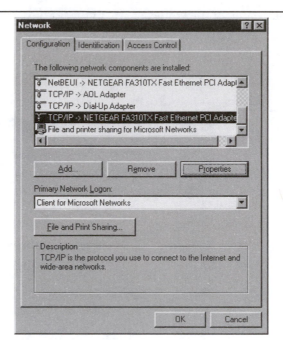

4. Click Properties.

5. Click the IP Address tab, and select the Specify IP Address radio button.

FIGURE 17.13

This is how your IP Address window should look after setting it up for proxy server software.

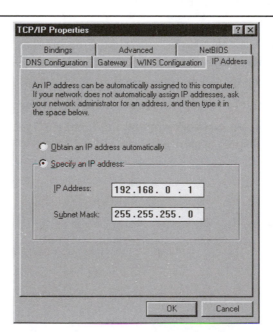

6. Type the numbers 192.168.0.1 into the IP Address field, as shown in Figure 17.13.

NOTE IP addresses beginning with 192 are part of a special group that is not used on the Internet. That means you can assign these addresses for use on your internal network, knowing that the Internet will not recognize them.

7. Type 255.255.255.0 into the Subnet Mask field, as shown in Figure 17.13.

NOTE The *subnet mask* is used to determine what subnet an IP address belongs to. The subnet in this case includes all computers and other devices whose IP addresses begin with 192.

8. Click on the DNS Configuration tab. Don't make any changes to this window, but do note for future reference whether DNS is enabled or disabled, as shown by the presence of a dot in the radio button.

9. Click OK.

10. Click OK and let the PC reboot.

NOTE After setting up TCP/IP, you'll still need to install the WinGate or other proxy software in order to share an Internet connection.

In addition to setting up TCP/IP on the server PC, you'll need to have it installed on the other computers, known as client PCs, that will be sharing the Internet connection through the proxy server. If you're running a proxy server such as WinGate, you have two choices in setting up TCP/IP Properties when it comes to how your computer will obtain an IP address.

1. You can set the machine up to use a static IP address, as shown previously.

2. You can set it up to obtain an IP address automatically using DHCP—*Dynamic Host Configuration Protocol*, a system that allocates Internet Protocol addresses based on network adapters' unique identification numbers.

Using DHCP is the generally recommended approach. Here's how to set it up on your client computers:

1. Right-click the Network Neighborhood icon on your desktop.

2. Click the Properties item on the drop-down list.

3. In the Network window, highlight the TCP/IP entry for your internal network adapter.

4. Click Properties.

5. Click the IP Address tab, and select the Obtain an IP Address Automatically option, as shown in Figure 17.14.

FIGURE 17.14

Pick the Obtain an IP Address Automatically option in the IP Address configuration tab to set up DHCP.

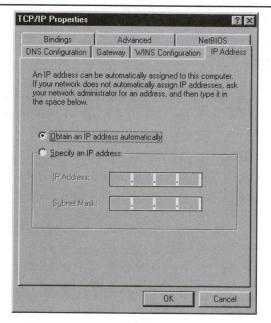

6. Now click the WINS configuration tab.

 NOTE WINS is short for *Windows Internet Naming Service*, a system that determines the IP address associated with a particular network computer's name.

7. Select the radio button for Disable WINS Resolution, as shown in Figure 17.15.

FIGURE 17.15

In the WINS configuration tab, place a mark in the radio button labeled Disable WINS Resolution.

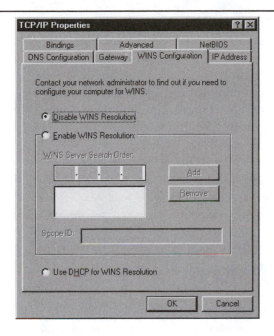

8. Click the DNS Configuration tab.
9. Select the radio button labeled Disable DNS, as shown in Figure 17.16.

FIGURE 17.16

Place a mark on the radio button labeled Disable DNS in the DNS Configuration tab.

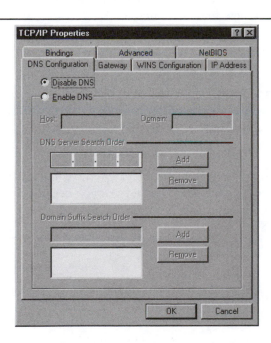

10. Click OK and let the machine reboot.

After setting up TCP/IP and installing your proxy server software and client software for sharing, you may need to make changes to any Internet applications software you are using. They'll need to be set up to connect to the Internet using a local area network and, if you are using a cable modem or DSL connection, an always-on connection. You can learn more about configuring the WinGate software and sharing in general at WinGate's corporate site, `www.deerfield.com`.

 NOTE See "Dial Up Networking" in Chapter 12, "Windows 95/98," for instructions on how to set up your computer for dial-up networking and remote access.

Sharing Printers

When laser printers first came out, they were shockingly expensive, especially those equipped with the PostScript language. So among the first killer apps for networking was sharing one or more printers among several networked computers. These days, even well-equipped laser printers are relatively inexpensive, while color-capable inkjet printers are almost afterthoughts. Indeed, low-end inkjets are practically standard items in new computer bundles.

Still, printer sharing does have value today. You may want to share printers because:

- You only have one printer and several computers.
- You have more than one printer, but still more computers than printers.
- Your printers include some combination of economical dot matrix printers, fast laser printers, and inkjet printers that do color, but are costly to operate. Printer sharing will let you parcel out printer jobs to the best machine for the task.

Sharing printers is, in reality, a powerful convenience. The first time your local printer runs out of paper and you find that you neglected to stock up on any, you'll truly appreciate being able to simply redirect the print job to another output device without having to run to the office supply store for more.

Setting Up Shared Printers

Enabling shared printers is, perhaps because of the long-standing use of networks to share printers, one of the easiest tasks in setting up and using a network. Here's how to enable printer sharing:

1. Click Start ➢ Settings ➢ Control Panel.

2. Double-click the Network icon.

3. Click the button for File and Print Sharing.

4. In the File and Print Sharing dialog window, as shown in Figure 17.17, place a check mark in the box for I Want to Be Able to Allow Others to Print to My Printer(s).

FIGURE 17.17

Click the box for I Want to Be Able to Allow Others to Print to My Printer(s) to place a check mark in it and enable printer sharing.

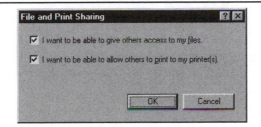

5. Click OK to return to the Network dialog box.

6. Click OK and, when the System Settings Change dialog box opens, as shown in Figure 17.18. Click Yes to restart your computer.

FIGURE 17.18

Click Yes to restart your computer when finished setting up printer sharing.

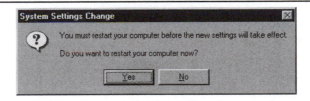

Once you've set up your networked PC for printer sharing, configure individual printers to allow other network users to print, or to restrict their printing rights. You may decide that you don't want anybody printing out any lengthy word processing documents on that color inkjet. Here's how to enable sharing:

1. Click Start ➢ Settings ➢ Printers.

2. In the Printers window, as shown in Figure 17.19, right-click the printer whose sharing properties you wish to modify.

FIGURE 17.19

Select the printer you want to share in the Printers window, and right-click.

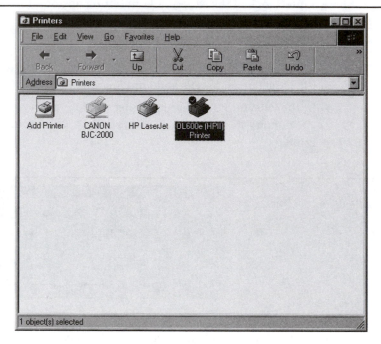

3. Now click on the Properties option in the drop-down list.

4. In the Printer Properties window, as shown in Figure 17.20, click the Sharing tab.

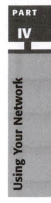

FIGURE 17.20

Click the Sharing tab in the Printer Properties window to set up a printer for sharing.

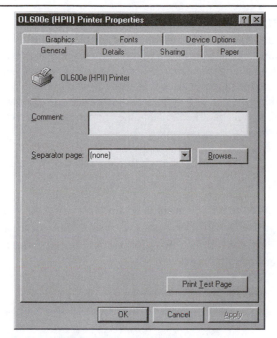

5. In the Sharing tab, as shown in Figure 17.21, click Shared As: to enable others to share the printer.

FIGURE 17.21

Click the Shared As: radio button to allow network users to share this printer.

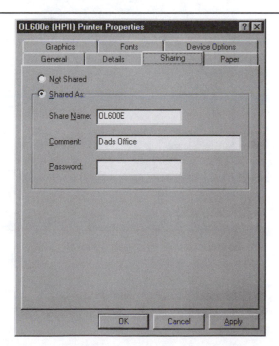

NOTE Windows will automatically generate a share name for the printer. You can enter a descriptive name such as "KidsLaser" if you wish. Just make sure the name is no more than 12 characters long and contains no spaces or characters such as ?, *, #, +, =, <, >, or %—anything that can't be used in a DOS filename. The comment could describe what room the printer is in, so that anybody who uses the printer from a network computer will know where to pick up their printout. If you use a password, anyone who wants to use this printer will be asked to fill in the correct password before the print job will be accepted.

6. Click OK and, if you entered a password, verify it by re-entering.

7. Click OK to finish setting up sharing.

Check to see if the printer is set up for sharing by looking for a cupped hand beneath the icon in the Printers window, as shown in Figure 17.22. You can make a printer not shared by performing this process and checking the Not shared button instead of the Shared As: radio button in Step 5.

FIGURE 17.22

A symbol of a hand underneath a printer's icon indicates that printer is shared.

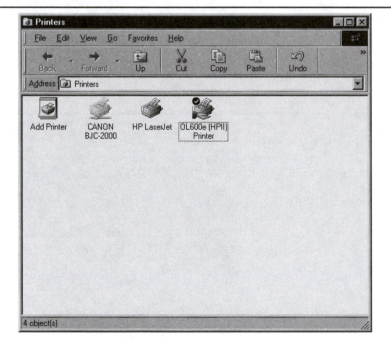

Managing Networked Printing

Now that your printers are networked, you have much greater flexibility about printing and, at the same time, greater control over how your network printers are used. You can, for instance, use passwords to:

- Limit use of all network printers by anyone who tends to overuse the printers or tie them up for long periods of time.

- Restrict overuse of certain printers that are particularly convenient to users.

- Direct users to less costly printers, such as dot matrix or laser printers, instead of color inkjet printers that have costly consumables.

You can also check on printers connected to the network by highlighting the printer in the Printers window and pressing Enter. The resulting window provides much useful information about that printer, such as how many jobs it has in its queue and whether, in the case of the printer shown in Figure 17.23, it is offline or requires user intervention.

FIGURE 17.23

You can check what's happening with any printers connected to the network by opening the printer from the Printers window and looking in the title bar and Status, Owner, and other columns of information.

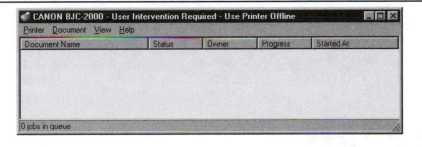

Sharing Scanners and Digital Cameras Over A Network

Most scanners can be used over a network, if only by saving scanned images to a network-accessible disk drive, where they can be viewed and edited and otherwise used by other people on the network. To really share a scanner, it has to have a network option, something that is generally reserved for more expensive models, such as the Hewlett-Packard ScanJet5 series. Other scanners can be networked only under certain circumstances. For instance, in the case of Umax, a scanner maker that rivals HP in the low-end market, the network must be a client-server network. Peer networks of the type that most home networkers use aren't supported by Umax. Umax requires three machines on the network: a dedicated server and two client machines. The clients must have the same operating systems, protocols, and the same version of those protocols.

The story is much the same with digital cameras—sharing is easily accomplished by saving image files to a shared network drive where they can be accessed from other computers on the network. One nice feature on some of the recent digital cameras is an e-mail option. This allows you to save a second, smaller copy of the image each time you take a photo. Because it is smaller, the number of pixels is reduced, the size of the image file is reduced, and the image is easier and much faster to e-mail as an attachment. The smaller image can be very helpful if you are transferring files over a slower-speed home networks such as a powerline network.

Sharing Drives

The devices you can attach to a PC have proliferated wildly in recent years. If you can find a plug for it on the back of a standalone machine—be it serial, parallel, or USB—then you can connect it to the network. Despite this wide variety of fancy devices, your plain old disk drives are among the most heavily used and critical subsystems in your computer. The more use you can make of them through sharing, the better. And the good news is, your network is ideally set up to help you make the most of that valuable magnetic square footage.

The sharing of disk drives allows you to make the most of all your disk space, using empty space on some machines to store things for other machines that have run out of room. If you add up all the disk space on all the computers on your home network, you're liable to come up with a startlingly large figure. Yet, with drive sharing through your network, that's what you've got available, almost as if it were one huge disk.

Setting up the sharing of drives, including hard disks, floppies, CD-ROM, DVD-ROM, tape and removable drives, is accomplished the same way as the sharing of folders. Here's the drill:

1. In My Computer or Explorer, right-click the drive you want to share.

2. Choose the Sharing option from the drop-down list.

3. In the Properties window, as shown in Figure 17.24, click on Shared As:

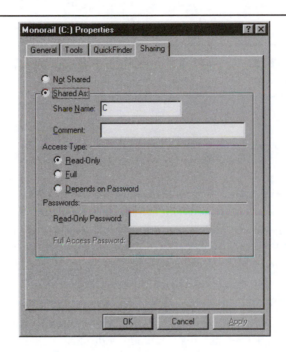

4. Click OK to allow sharing.

You can change the share name that is automatically entered to anything you want, subject to the same DOS-acceptable characters required for giving printers share names. A comment line, as shown in Figure 17.24, can be added to explain something about the drive.

Set Access Type to the Full radio button, as shown in Figure 17.24, only if you wish to give anyone on the network permission to read, move, edit, and delete files, as well as create new subdirectories. The Depends on Password option determines access to the drive by whether the person attempting to access it enters the proper password. The Read radio button allows network users to view files, copy data, run applications and document files, but not edit, delete, or move files. The Password settings are available if you select Read-Only or Full Access. Anyone who wants to use the drive will have to know the password.

 TIP You can change Share properties of a drive, including making it Not shared, by right-clicking the drive from My Computer or Explorer and selecting Sharing from the drop-down list.

 NOTE For more on the security of drives and other network resources, see Chapter 20, "Network Security."

Sharing Software

There are many ways to share hardware resources over a network, but there are far more—and more convenient—ways to share computer programs, including application programs and games. Being able to read, write, and execute files located on another computer connected to the home network offers some appealing advantages. For example:

- You can run programs you couldn't even load on many laptops and older machines, due to lack of disk space or memory.

- Even if all your machines have ample disk space and memory, you can avoid wasting disk space by having duplicate copies of commonly used programs on every computer on the network.

- You can perform all sorts of cooperative data-sharing tricks, ranging from making household members' personal schedules visible to others—a big help in planning meals and other get-togethers—to having birthday wish lists that the recipient maintains and are viewable by everyone on the network.

- You can play head-to-head games that, due to the network's (typically) greater speed than the Internet, offer a new level of enjoyment.

These are just a few of the advantages of sharing software over your home network. More are appearing all the time, as new programs become network-enabled and millions of home network users discover innovative techniques for making the most of their networked computers.

NOTE Learn more about installing and configuring networkable applications and games in Chapter 15, "Other Network Software."

Losing Latency

You can express one of the biggest reasons to get excited about playing head-to-head games over a network in one word: *latency*. Latency is the delay between the time you or one of your head-to-head gaming opponents issues a command and the time that command is executed and the result appears on your respective monitors. It's caused by a slow connection, and it is the bane of Internet gaming. Playing an online game when you have a connection speed much south of 100Kbps is like playing football in thigh-high molasses. Your mind knows where you want to go, and issues the commands to your body, but everything happens in such slow motion that the real struggle becomes one against boredom.

That's not a pretty picture, is it? Well, picture this: When you're playing a head-to-head game against opponents on your home network, you will have no latency issues, or very few compared to playing over the Internet. Even at the lower ranges of home networking speeds, including the 350Kbps data rates of powerline technology, data is still moving at several times the speed of an analog modem connection. And, at 100Mbps, an affordable and reliable Fast Ethernet home network is way over-engineered for even the most demanding of graphical games.

So, unless you're playing a head-to-head game over the Internet using a 56K analog modem, or competing against other gamers who happen to be using a slow modem, latency issues are in the past for you. Let the games begin.

Finding and Downloading Game Software

Chances are, you won't have your network up and running for long before you begin to wonder whether these head-to-head games are as much fun as you've heard. To find out, you're going to need some game software. But for that, you won't even need to leave your chair. Fortunately, locating games on the Internet is about as difficult as locating a traffic jam in New York City.

All the big game publishers and countless minor ones have Web sites devoted to promoting, explaining, marketing, selling, and providing downloads of evaluation copies and full-featured, registered versions of their games. If you're interested in finding out about a certain game—for instance, Doom, the revolutionary shoot-em-up from id Software—all you have to so is type "www.publishersname.com" into your browser, where "publishersname" is the company that sells the game. You're almost certain to be taken to a site brimming with news, tips, tricks, downloads, opponents, and other items of interest about the game.

In addition, there are many sites that review and provide links and, sometimes, downloads for a wide variety of computer games from many different publishers. A few of them are:

- Gamer's Zone at `www.worldvillage.com/wv/gamezone/html/gamerev.htm`

- GameSpot at `www.gamespot.com`

- Game Nexus at `www.gamenexus.com`

Computer games may have been primarily the province of adolescent geeks at one point, but now they are thoroughly mainstream. You can find thousands of games for the downloading at general software sites such as:

- Cnet Download.com at `www.download.com`

- Freeware Home at `freewarehome.ucpel.tche.br`

- Green Parrots Software at `www.greenparrots.com`

Finally, many excellent games have been created by people who don't work for or with big game publishers, or care about making their games available on the big download sites. You can locate these people by searching for game sites using Internet search engines, prowling Usenet news groups and simply keeping your ear to the ground. You may never find the perfect downloadable game, but you're guaranteed to have a good time trying.

Online Multiplayer Game Services

Many people who play in amateur athletic leagues for long periods don't do so for the sake of the sport. They do it for the sake of the other players. They like the conversation, friendships, long-running competitions, gossip, and other social aspects of being part of the game. In computer gaming, those benefits and more can be had from joining a multiplayer game service. These are great ways to get started in online gaming. You have only to register with one of the many services and start playing to find that you have become a member of a community of like-minded enthusiasts who are eager to chat, share reviews, point you to updates, and organize teams and tournaments and leagues. They represent the human face of computer gaming—as seen through the keyhole of a computer monitor, of course—in a way that makes it clear that computer gaming is not so far removed, after all, from the Tuesday night bowling leagues and Saturday afternoon softball games of yore.

Good multiplayer game sites will verify the version of the game you are playing to make sure you have an appropriate edition. They'll help you find opponents, schedule games, and keep track of the score. They will also usually offer downloads, updates and tips, hints and tricks. You'll generally pay for all of this, of course, since they have to make a living, too. But many people find that multiplayer online game services are well worth the expenditure.

The best way to find out whether you'd like to join one of these virtual competitive communities is to take a look at some of the better ones out there. Here are a few to get you started:

- Kali, at www.kali.net, has nearly 200,000 members playing an unusually wide array of commercial games such as Warcraft II, Descent, Duke Nukem, Red Alert, Diablo, and Hellfire. There is a one-time fee of $20.00.

- Pogo.com, at www.pogo.com, is a family-oriented site with more than 3.5 million members playing free Web-based games such as backgammon, bridge, crosswords, and video poker.

- Microsoft's Internet Gaming Zone, at www.zone.com, is the busiest online game service, with over 1.1 million members enjoying the likes of Age of Empires, Jedi Knight, Spades, Hearts, and Backgammon. You'll rarely lack opponents on IGZ, but it may cost you. While there's no charge to play classic and retail games—those requiring a store-bought CD-ROM to play online—premium games cost varying prices, with a typical charge being $1.95 for a one-day subscription, or $9.95 for a month's worth of gaming.

- GameStorm, at www.gamestorm.com, hosts games including Air Warrior, Aliens, Casino Poker, Multiplayer Battletech, and Legends of Kesmai for an appealing flat gamers' rate of $9.95 a month.

Free Multiplayer Games

Online multiplayer game service fees have been going down. Some have gone all the way to free, with game service expenses being borne by advertisers. For example, Yahoo! games at play.yahoo.com/games offers a solid selection of classic games at no charge. Many classic games are free on Microsoft's Internet Gaming Zone, including backgammon, chess, spades, and more. And, at Tournament Games, www.tournamentgames.com, you can not only play solitaire games for free, you can win cash prizes of up to $500.00. Learn more about free online game sites from TheFreeSite.com's directory at www.thefreesite.com/freegames.htm.

Sharing Files

The ability to share files is, if anything, more useful and central to the network experience than even sharing hardware peripherals such as modems and printers. In order to set up file sharing, you first have to make sure that Microsoft's file and printer sharing feature is installed. Here's how:

1. Click Start ➢ Settings ➢ Control Panel ➢ Network.

2. In the Configurations tab, as shown in Figure 17.25, click the button labeled File and Print Sharing.

FIGURE 17.25

Click File and Print Sharing in the Network Configurations tab to install Microsoft File and Print Sharing.

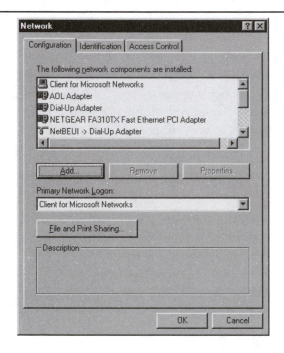

3. In the File and Print Sharing dialog window, as shown in Figure 17.26, click both boxes.

FIGURE 17.26

Place check marks in both the I Want to Be Able to Give Others Access to My Files box and the I Want to Be Able to Allow Others to Print to My Printer(s) box in the File and Print Sharing dialog window.

4. Click OK twice to finish.

 TIP You have to set up file sharing separately on every computer whose files you want to share.

Restricting Access to Files

Sharing files, including programs and data, is a good thing. But, like many good things, it's better if it's controlled or managed. With that in mind, the makers of Windows and other network operating systems have set up ways to make sure not only that you can allow people to use your files and vice versa, but also that you can prohibit them as well.

You can significantly restrict access to files (as well as other resources) by simply adding a dollar sign ($) to the end of the share name of the folder the file is in. Here's how:

1. In Explorer, select the resource—a drive, folder, etcetera–and right-click.

2. Select Sharing from the drop-down list.

3. Click the Shared As: radio button.

4. Type a dollar sign at the end of the name in the Share Name box, as shown in Figure 17.27.

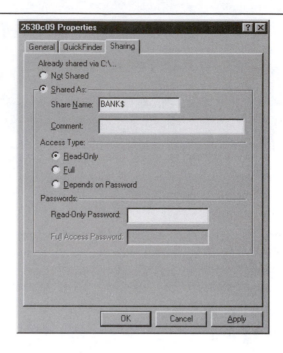

5. Click OK to finish.

The folder will become invisible on the network. Even if someone knows it's there, the folder will be inaccessible to anyone who doesn't know its user name and full file path, in this case, \\officepc\c\bank$.

You can also restrict access to your files much the same way you do with printers, by requiring passwords or, alternatively, by specifying users and groups who will have access to your files. Here's how:

1. Click Start ➤ Settings ➤ Control Panel ➤ Network.

2. In the Configurations tab, click the File and Print Sharing button.

3. Click the Access Control tab.

4. In the Access Control window, as shown in Figure 17.28, select either Share-level Access Control or User-level Access Control.

FIGURE 17.28

Select Share-level Access Control or User-level Access Control in the Access Control window.

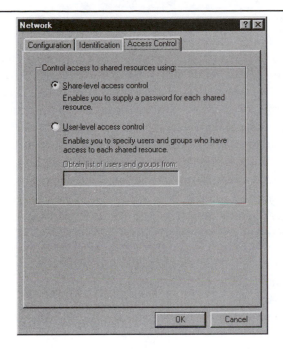

5. Click OK to finish.

 WARNING It's a good idea if you have an always-on Internet connection such as a cable or DSL modem, to disable file sharing on the computer that is directly connected to the Internet. That way, even if you don't have any added security provided by proxy server software or any other sharing software you're running (and connection-sharing programs do include significant security) you will be able to prevent your gateway computer from being damaged by most hacker attacks.

 NOTE For more on security, see Chapter 20, "Network Security."

Summary

Networking your home computers enables you to share access to software, files, the Internet, and peripheral devices such as printers. This sharing of resources is cost-effective, time saving, and extremely convenient. Even though you share access to software and printers with the members of your household, you can still retain privacy of files by limiting access to prying eyes. While you might not want to share your financial records or personal diary with your children or roommates, you can still get enjoyment out of playing head-to-head multiplayer games with the members of your household.

What's Next

When your computers are networked, you don't have to be sitting in front of one of the network resources in order to use it. Similarly, you don't have to be physically located at your network to use it. Using your network remotely, and setting up and using personal Web servers, are the main topics of the next chapter.

CHAPTER 18

Advanced Networking

Overview

Having your home computers networked allows you to share files, printers, and other resources between the computers in your home that are connected to the network. But that's not all. You're not limited to accessing these resources from a computer in your home. You can also tap into your home network from other locations, using the Windows dial-up networking component and Personal Web Server. Once you get it set up, you will be able to reach your home network while you are at work, traveling, or away from home for any reason.

Accessing Your Network Remotely

Having remote network access means you will be able to view or retrieve a shared file that is residing on one of your home computers if you find you unexpectedly need it. You'll also be able to print documents on your shared network printer at home. With the right software, you can even take control of a PC on your home network and run application software on it. Basically, you'll be able to operate away from home as if you were sitting at one of your networked PCs, except you'll be connecting through telephone lines and modems instead of network cables and adapters.

Dial-Up Networking Server

One way you can reach your network remotely is by using Dial-Up Networking Server. This is a tool that comes with Windows 98, Windows NT, or the Windows Plus! pack. After installing a DUN Server on a modem-equipped PC connected to your network, you can call in to the modem from another location and access shared files, shared printers, and other resources, as shown in Figure 18.1.

FIGURE 18.1

You can use Dial-Up Networking Server to access your files and printers remotely from a laptop or other computer.

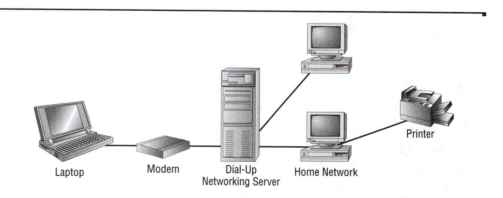

Laptop   Modem   Dial-Up Networking Server   Home Network   Printer

NOTE Dial-Up Networking Server works with Microsoft or NetWare networking protocols such as NetBEUI and IPS/SPX, but it doesn't work with TCP/IP. That means you can't use a DUN Server to reach the Internet or your Personal Web Server.

Before you can set up Dial-Up Networking Server, you have to have Dial-Up Networking installed on your computer.

 NOTE For more on installing Dial-Up Networking, see Chapter 12, "Windows 95/98."

Once you have Dial-Up Networking installed, and have configured at least one modem to work with Dial-Up Networking, follow these steps to install the Dial-Up Networking Server:

1. Insert your Windows 98 CD-ROM and, when the Windows 98 window opens, as shown in Figure 18.2, click Add/Remove Software. There will probably be a short wait while Windows searches for installed components.

FIGURE 18.2

Click the Add/Remove Software button in the window that opens when you insert the Windows 98 CD-ROM to begin installing Dial-Up Networking Server.

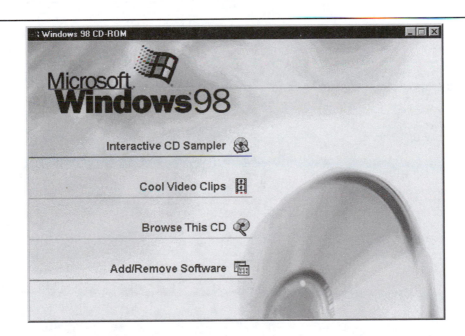

2. In the Add/Remove Programs Properties window, highlight the Communications entry in the scrolling window, as shown in Figure 18.3, and click Details.

FIGURE 18.3

Select Communications and click Details at the Add/Remove Programs Properties window to install Dial-Up Networking Server.

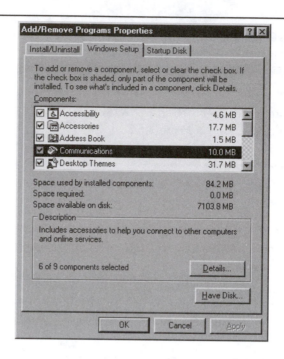

3. Place a check box in the Dial-Up Server entry in the scrolling list box in the Communications window, as shown in Figure 18.4, and click OK.

FIGURE 18.4

Click the box next to Dial-Up Server and then click OK.

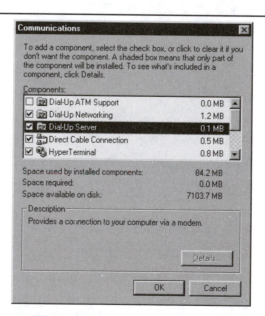

4. Click OK to finish.

Now that you have Dial-Up Networking Server installed, you need to establish a dial-up server.

1. Click Start ➤ Programs ➤ Accessories ➤ Communications ➤ Dial-Up Networking.

2. In the Dial-Up Networking window, as shown in Figure 18.5, click Connections ➤ Dial-Up Server.

FIGURE 18.5

Click Connections in the Dial-Up Networking window, and select Dial-Up Server from the drop-down list to continue establishing a dial-up server.

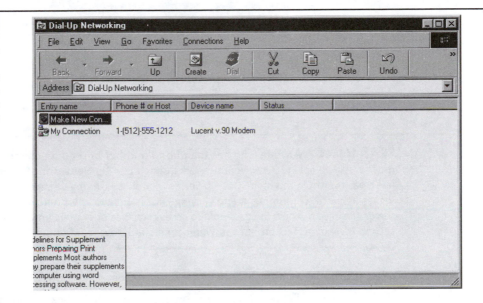

3. In the Dial-Up Server window, place a mark next to Allow Caller Access, as shown in Figure 18.6.

NOTE If your computer has more than one modem installed, the Dial-Up Server window will display a tab corresponding to each modem. To configure Dial-Up Server for the proper modem, click the tab for the modem that you want to use for the Dial-Up Networking Server.

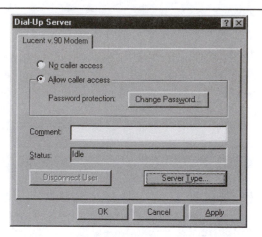

 WARNING Anyone who has the phone number of the line connected to your modem will be able to get to your network through Dial-Up Networking Server unless you use a password. Do this in the Dial-Up Server window by clicking Change Password, entering a password, confirming it, and clicking OK. Now anyone who tries to call in to this server will have to know the password to access any files or printers on your network. As a second level of protection, set passwords for shared drives and printers on the network.

4. Click the Server Type button in the Dial-Up Server window.

5. In the Server Types window, as shown in Figure 18.7, click the down arrow next to Type of Dial-Up Server to display a drop-down list with three types of servers. Here's how to make the appropriate selection:

- Select Default if you are going to be dialing in from a computer running Windows 98 or Windows NT.

- Select Windows for Workgroups and Windows NT 3.51 if you will be dialing in from a computer running either of these operating systems.

- Select PPP if you will be networking with the TCP/IP protocol or sharing files using Windows 98 or Windows NT.

 NOTE If you are dialing in with Windows 98 or Windows NT, check Require encrypted password to improve the security of your Dial-Up Server.

6. Click OK twice to finish.

FIGURE 18.7

Select from a drop-down list of three types of servers in the Server Types window.

After Windows sets up the modem to answer calls from remote computers, a small blue computer icon will show up in your System Tray modem. Double-clicking this icon will take you to the Dial-Up Server window where you can check the status of the Dial-Up Networking Sever, disable the Dial-Up Networking Server, or change your server type. To disable the Dial-Up Server:

1. Double-click the computer icon in your System Tray.

2. Click No Caller Access.

3. Click OK.

After disabling the Dial-Up Networking Server, the blue icon should disappear from your System Tray.

Once you've enabled the Dial-Up Networking Server, the computer will answer any calls that come in to the modem. To connect to the Dial-Up Networking Server and use network resources remotely, you will need:

- The modem's telephone number

- The password for the Dial-Up Networking Server

- The usernames and passwords for any shared drives or printers connected to the network

 WARNING   Dial-Up Networking Server always answers incoming calls after only one ring. You can't change this, and it may cause difficulties when you try to use fax or communications programs while Dial-Up Networking Server is set up to allow caller access. So if you want any other fax or communications programs to be able to answer incoming calls, you need to disable Dial-Up Networking Server by configuring it not to allow caller access. In addition, you will probably want at least two phone numbers in your home, one for the computer modem and one for your answering machine.

Remote Control Software

Dial-Up Networking Server allows you to access shared drives and printers on your network, but you can do much more using remote control software. Remote control software lets you dial in to a host computer from a remote machine and control the host computer as though you were sitting at the keyboard. The keystrokes and mouse movements and clicks you enter on the remote machine will actually be entered on the host machine. The host machine echoes its display to the remote machine, so any windows or dialog boxes that show up on its monitor will be displayed on the remote machine's screen. Using the remote machine, you can start and run application programs on the host machine just as though you were using that machine.

Windows does not come with built-in remote control software. However, there are a number of companies that publish remote control software for use with all versions of Windows as well as the Macintosh operating system. Here are two of the most popular commercial remote control programs:

- pcAnywhere 9 from Symantec runs on Windows versions 3.1 through 98—as well as Windows NT and even DOS computers—and offers good file-transfer and security features. Learn more at www.symantec.com.

- LapLink 2000 from LapLink lets you synchronize folders on remote and host machines, plus communicate with chat and voice messaging services. Learn more at www.travsoft.com.

Here's how to install pcAnywhere 9:

1. Insert the pcAnywhere 9 CD into your CD-ROM drive.

2. The setup program will automatically launch if Windows AutoPlay is enabled. Otherwise, click Start ➤ Run.

3. Type **D:\setup.exe** into the Open: box, where D: is the letter for your CD-ROM drive.

4. Click OK.

5. When the pcAnywhere installation screen shows, choose Install Current Software.

6. On the next screen choose pcAnywhere 9 and then follow the on-screen instructions.

You can also install pcAnywhere to the network by typing **D:\INSTALLS\ pcAnywhere\Pca32\CD\Disk1\setup/a** (again, where D: is the letter for your CD-ROM drive). You'll be prompted for a network folder into which to install the software. After the software is installed, you can install it to any workstation on the network by navigating to the folder where pcAnywhere is installed and running

Setup.exe. You can configure the workstations using pcAnywhere's administrator program by clicking Start ➢ Run and typing **winaw32 /a** into the Open box and clicking OK.

> **WARNING** Be sure you have sufficient licenses to legally run pcAnywhere on any machines to which you install from the network. The publisher, Symantec, sells additional licenses in five-node increments.

Personal Web Servers

When you click a link in a Web page, you're being taken to a Web server, a computer that publishes information to the Internet using the Hypertext Markup Language (HTML) and Hypertext Transfer Protocol (HTTP), two of the technologies underlying the World Wide Web. Using software such as Microsoft Personal Web Server, you can have your own Web server, running on a computer on your home network. PWS turns an Internet-connected Windows 98 or Windows 95 computer into a Web server, so you can publish your own Web pages to the Internet.

Web server software can become very complex. Microsoft's Internet Information Server, for instance, is an industrial-strength program used by businesses to run high-traffic Web sites for electronic commerce and other critical applications. PWS is for use with small-scale peer-to-peer networks and is simple enough for a home net-worker to install and administer, but it is powerful enough for many businesses to use for developing—and testing—Web applications.

Uses for Personal Web Servers

So if you're not running a big e-commerce Web site, what do you need a Personal Web Server for? For one thing, you can use a Personal Web Server to provide you with remote access to your network files. In fact, Personal Web Server can allow you to do most, if not quite all, the things a network can do, including sharing files. For example, because Personal Web Pages present information in some pretty complicated ways, you could use your Web server to let you look through a personal phone book or other database stored on your network from a remote location. Microsoft's Personal Web Server software, for instance, allows you to present information from databases in the form of tables or other formats on your Web page.

NOTE One limitation with Web servers is that your information is only published to the Internet while the server is connected. If you are using a dial-up connection through a modem, your Web page will only be visible from the Web while you are actually connected. With always-on connections such as cable and DSL modems, this is less of an issue. However, the agreement under which you are offered cable and DSL Internet access may restrict you from having a personal Web server on your network. Check your provider's Terms of Service to be sure.

Setting up a Personal Web Server has uses beyond remote access to your home computers. You can also use your Personal Web Page as a forum for expressing your views with surfers on the Web, sharing your photos with family and friends far away, or as a site for a modest e-business.

Software for Personal Web Servers

One of the great things about Personal Web Server is that it is relatively easy to get and set up. Plus, the price is right—free. Windows 98 comes with Microsoft Personal Web Server 4 built in. While Windows 95 does not come with PWS 1, its version of Personal Web Server, you can get a free download of the program from Microsoft at www.microsoft.com/windows/ie/pws/.

 TIP You may prefer Personal Web Server 1, the version that was introduced for Windows 95, to PWS 4. For instance, PWS 4 does not come with File Transfer Protocol while PWS 1 does. In addition, PWS 1 is faster and consumes fewer system resources than the later version.

Setting Up a Personal Web Server

Before you can set up Personal Web Server, you need to install the software from your Windows 98 CD. To do this:

1. Insert the Windows 98 CD into your CD-ROM drive.

2. Click Start ➢ Run.

3. In the Open box, type: **D:\add-ons\pws\setup.exe**, where D: is the letter of your CD-ROM drive.

4. Click OK.

5. When the Welcome screen appears, click Next.

6. If you want to install the most used components, click the Typical button in the Personal Web Server Setup window, as shown in Figure 18.8. The Typical components include the Personal Web Server; the Transaction Server, which lets you create pages for order entry and the like; and the FrontPage 98 Server Extensions, which allow the uploading of pages created with Microsoft's FrontPage Web page authoring program. Typical is a good choice for most users. You can go back and add or remove components later.

FIGURE 18.8

The Typical configuration of Personal Web Server is the best choice for most users.

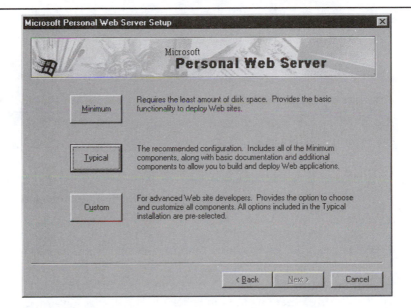

7. In the next window, click Next to accept the default folder for your Web publishing home directory.

8. When the program is finished copying files, click Finish.

When Personal Web Server is installed and running on your system, a small and rather blurry icon of a hand holding a Web page, a globe, and a red starburst will appear in your System Tray. You can open the Personal Web Manager by double-clicking this icon. Personal Web Manager, as shown in Figure 18.9, shows you that your Personal Web Server is running, and lets you perform several administrative and monitoring tasks.

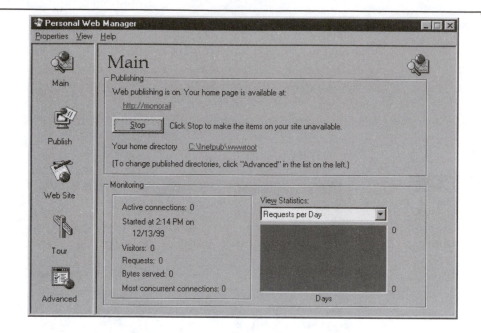

You can check your home page by clicking the link under the line reading Your Home Page Is Published At:. In a new installation, this will show the default home page, as shown in Figure 18.10.

You can turn Personal Web Server off by clicking the Stop button in Personal Web Manager. A box on the lower right provides statistics, such as how many times your site has been visited. Clicking the Publish icon on the left side of Personal Web Manager starts the Publishing Wizard, as shown in Figure 18.11. The first time you run Publishing Wizard, you should click the Home Page Wizard at the bottom to set up your home page.

FIGURE 18.10

View the default home page in a new Personal Web Server installation by clicking Link for Your Home Page in Personal Web Manager.

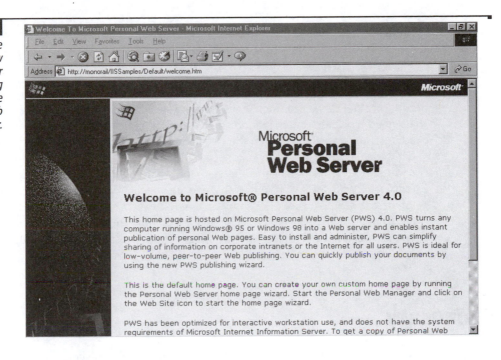

FIGURE 18.11

The Publishing Wizard walks you through the steps of publishing information to the Internet.

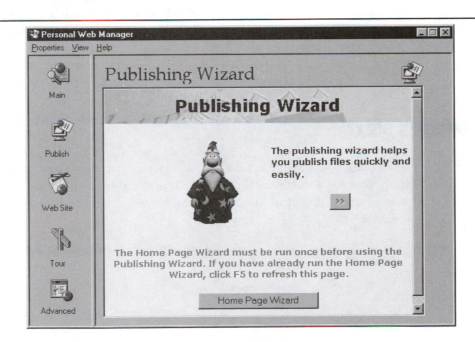

Making Your Web Server Accessible

If you are using a dial-in connection to the Internet, your Web page may be very difficult for other surfers to find. That's because each time you dial in, your computer is assigned a different Internet address. The solution is to obtain a fixed Internet Protocol address and to register it with the Domain Name Service (DNS). This is a distributed database used in TCP/IP networks such as the Internet to translate individual computer names into Internet Protocol addresses. Only after you have a fixed IP address and are registered with DNS will your Web page be practically accessible to others on the Internet. Inquire with your ISP about obtaining a fixed IP address and registering it with the Domain Name Service. A domain name costs around $70.00 for the first two years and $35 for each year thereafter. You shouldn't have to pay much more than that.

Summary

As great as sharing files, software, and hardware within the confines of your home is, networking can do so much more for you than that. You can also access any shared files remotely. So if you are self-employed and take business trips, if you are a student and forget your class assignment, or if you are just visiting with friends and get a brilliant idea, you can access your home files from just about anywhere. In addition, you can turn your personal computer into a Web server, so whenever you have something to say, you have a place where you can share your ideas with the world.

What's Next

Preserving your network against risks to its security and your privacy have been recurring concerns throughout this book. Dealing effectively with these issues, plus the related one of using parental controls to control Web surfing, is the focus of the next chapter.

PART V

Networking Housework

LEARN TO:

- *Prevent Disasters*

- *Secure Your Network*

- *Troubleshoot Network Glitches*

CHAPTER 19

Disaster Prevention

Overview

Football teams have backup quarterbacks and police officers call for backup and parents of young children like to have a roster of backup babysitters in case their main childcare provider can't make it on the night of an important social event. As a home networker, you may not have to worry about winning or criminals or even missing out on dinner and a show. But you still need backup.

Backup in a networking sense is the copying of files from the hard drive where they are kept and used most of the time to another place. It could be on another network computer's hard drive, to a floppy, tape, or removable hard drive, or even a remote backup server reached through the Internet. The basic principle is straightforward. As shown in Figure 19.1, you take an important file and make a copy of it someplace else where, if something happens to the first copy, you'll have a backup.

FIGURE 19.1

If your files are backed up to another drive on the network, a floppy, or a tape, including possibly a copy saved at your work or another off-site location, you'll have a safe copy if disaster strikes the original.

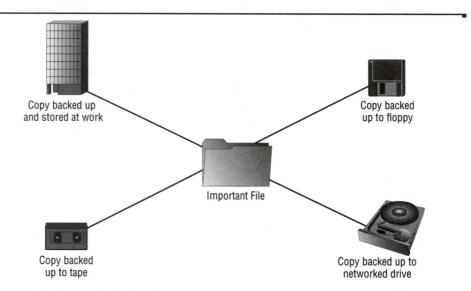

Copy backed up and stored at work

Copy backed up to floppy

Important File

Copy backed up to tape

Copy backed up to networked drive

While the basic idea behind backing up is straightforward, the entire subject of backing up is fairly complex. There are numerous decisions to make, ranging from what media to use to how often to perform backups. The first thing you need to understand is why backing up is important.

Why, What, and When You Need Backup

We know we should do it. Eat right. Exercise. Back up our computers. But the cheeseburger and fries taste yummy, the weights are heavy, and backing up our documents seems like more of a hassle than it's worth. Even though most of us have experienced the frustration of a computer malfunction, it's amazing how much faith many of us have that our data will be there when we need it.

Why You Need to Back Up

Backing up is an essential part of a professional network administrator's job. A network manager who gets caught without a backup at work had better be polishing up the old resume. Backing up files on the computers attached to a home network isn't likely to be quite as critical as it is in a business, but it's still a task worth doing. The more you use your computers—and you'll use them more when they're networked—the more valuable the information you keep on them.

How valuable is the data on your networked PCs? It may be useless to anybody else, but very valuable to you. What if you lost all the Quicken files detailing your personal finances? Or the e-mails from a big contract negotiation you were involved in for work? On a more personal level, you may have digitized photos of important events, or saved game files from computer games you've been playing for years. Recreating data files and reinstalling applications and setting them up properly can easily take hours, days, or even weeks of work. And a lot of that stuff is simply irreplaceable. That's why the value of the data on your networked PC is, when you think about it, worth more than the PC or even the entire network.

You may be thinking: The information on my computer is safe. What could go wrong? Here's a short list:

Floods   You don't have to live in a flood plain. Even a cup of coffee spilled in the right place can destroy a hard drive and all the data on it.

Fires   Here's a hypothetical question: If you were forced to flee your home due to fire, what non-living object would take with you? The most common answer, surveys have traditionally said, is a photo album. If you answered, "My backups, of course," you are becoming a true networker. Fire can happen at any time, so keep your smoke detector batteries charged and your backups fresh and handy. Better yet, store a set offsite.

Thieves   Like purse snatchers who take the cash and toss the grandkid's pictures into the trash, thieves are usually interested in computer hardware, not the irreplaceable information it contains. But that doesn't make it any less lost.

PART

V

Networking
Housework

Lightning   The electrical surge from a lightning strike can travel up power or telephone wires directly into your PC's innards, where it can destroy a hard drive or an entire machine in less time than it takes to tell.

Power outages and spikes   Fluctuations in the power supply are normal but over time, or in the event of a serious power spike or outage, can do fatal damage to sensitive electronic components, including your network disk drives.

Hard disk failure   All hard disks eventually fail. They may break if you drop them, spill something on them, poke them with a screwdriver, or simply because they're old. There's no way to know when it will happen, but eventually every hard drive fails and all the information on it, for practical purposes, becomes lost.

Human error   Anybody who has been computing long has accidentally erased or overwritten a file. A lot of people, including some who have been computing for only a very short time, have accidentally reformatted a hard disk.

Gremlins   If Windows shuts down unexpectedly, an undisciplined program alters a file it shouldn't have, or there is just a mysterious failure of data to be written properly to your drive, you can wind up with files that won't open, programs that won't run, and even a computer that won't boot. Call them gremlins if you want, but by any name these causes of data loss are widespread and frequent threats to your system's integrity.

If you're starting to get the feeling that your data is fragile and confronted by many threats, that's good. It's even better that there are plenty of things you can do about it. With a good backup strategy, reliable media, and effective backup software, there's no reason why your fragile data can't have a long and useful life.

What to Back Up

The most straightforward thing to do is just back up everything. However, if you have a very large disk on your machine, this may simply take too long. When backing up several gigabytes of data using a tape drive, it is likely to require several hours to copy and verify, a process which compares copies of backed up files with their originals to make sure no errors occurred in copying. Adding up all the disk space on all the PCs connected to your home network can result in a backup that could require overnight or even all weekend. So, while you may occasionally want to back up all your files, it makes sense to select sensitive data and back that up, while leaving other files to their fate. Here are the files you should back up:

- Any document or data files that you have personally created or modified, since these may be very difficult to replace.

- Files in the My Documents and other personal folders you have created.
- E-mail correspondence.

TIP   Microsoft Outlook users will find messages, tasks, and calendar data in a personal folder file with the .pst extension. Outlook Express users will find mail stored in their Inboxes with .mbx extensions. Index files carry the .idx extension.

- Your personal address book.
- Your favorite Internet shortcuts. Microsoft Internet Explorer will place these in a folder named Favorites, usually in the Windows folder.
- Custom templates, dictionaries, stationery, and other application options, such as those used by the Microsoft Office programs.
- System settings, including desktop backgrounds, desktop shortcuts, and folder preferences, as well as application preferences and options. Windows stores these settings in the Windows Registry. You can protect them by backing up files named User.dat, System.dat, Config.sys, Autoexec.bat, Win.ini, and System.ini.

TIP   It's a good idea to back up your CD-ROM drivers, which you will find in your Windows folder. Also save these important drivers to a floppy so you can reload Windows from the CD-ROM if necessary.

When to Back Up

You will get some shifty-sounding answers if you ask computer users how often they back up. People tend to feel guilty about backing up, even if they back up regularly. But the truth is, there is no reason to feel guilty. There is no hard-and-fast rule about how often you should back up. It is a matter of personal preference, dictated by your personal situation.

The key thing to ask yourself is: How much data can you afford to lose? Measure the answer in hours, days, weeks, months or, if you're a really infrequent backer-upper, years. That's because if you back up once a day, you're risking a day's worth of files. Wait a year, and a year's work is at stake. Balance the hassle of backing up against what you'll have to expend to re-write that novel or update all your financial records, and pick the interval that suits you.

TIP Generally, you should back up a hard drive at least once a month. You may want to back up more frequently, such as weekly, if you regularly perform time-consuming alterations to files. You probably won't need to back up every day. But it's a good idea to copy critical data to another shared drive on the network that often.

No matter how often you schedule backups, there are times when you may want to make a special copy of your system or other files. For example:

- Before upgrading your operating system software
- Before performing a major disk repair, such as defragmenting
- Before you add or remove hardware so you can go back to the original setup if you need to
- After you add or remove hardware so you will have a current copy of your configuration
- Any time your system files seem to be running particularly well, so you will have a copy of the best settings

 TIP Scheduling backups is a matter of convenience. Most people schedule their backups to run at night or on weekends. For instance, you could have a backup start at 5:30 P.M. every Friday. It's a good idea to schedule backups when you can hang around for at least the first few minutes. In case anything goes wrong, you will be on hand to keep things going.

Backup Strategies

You've got clothes for summer and winter, clothes for painting the house or attending a wedding, clothes for rainy weather and clothes for the beach. You've also got a choice of several backup strategies, the use of any of which, like your wardrobe, depends on the situation.

Backing Up to a Hard Drive

Saving your work to your local hard drive is the simplest and easiest kind of backup there is. You can save your work automatically or manually.

AutoSave

There's no reason to lose data when you can set your computer to save your work automatically. You can set many applications, such as Word and Excel in Microsoft Office 97, to automatically save backups of open files every little while. This kind of backup is especially helpful for dealing with the human-error type of data loss. If you realize you just accidentally deleted a column in a spreadsheet, it's nice to know you can get back the original document by simply opening the auto-saved backup. Here's how to set up AutoSave in Microsoft Word:

1. In Microsoft Word, click Tools ➢ Options and then the Save tab.

2. In the Save tab, as shown in Figure 19.2, place a check in the box next to Save AutoRecover Info Every:.

FIGURE 19.2

Check the Save AutoRecover Info box in Word Options to automatically save your documents at selected intervals.

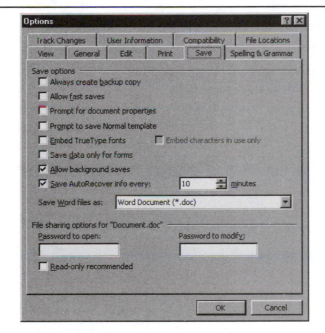

PART

V

Networking Housework

3. Enter a number in the minutes box to show how often you want to autosave your document.

4. Click OK.

TIP Even though you've got AutoSave running in Word, you still need to manually save your documents regularly by clicking File ➢ Save or pressing Ctrl-S. The reason is that when you have AutoRecover running while editing a document, your document is saved in a recovery file, which is deleted when you save or close a document. If your computer freezes up, the power goes out, or you have to restart your computer before saving or closing the document, you should still have the recovery file. When Word restarts after an unplanned exit, it automatically opens all the recovery files. You can choose to save these files, overwriting versions of the original unedited files if they exist. If you don't save it, a recovery file is automatically deleted, and all you have left is the unedited document. Note that if you want to reliably recover work after a power failure or similar problem, you have to check the Save AutoRecover Info Every: box or the "Always Create Backup Copy check box in the Save tab in the Options dialog box under the Tools menu. And you have to do this before you have trouble, not after.

To set up AutoSave in Microsoft Excel for Office 97:

1. Click Tools ➢ AutoSave. If you see the AutoSave option, go to Step 3.

2. If you don't see an AutoSave option, you need to activate it. Click Tools ➢ Add-Ins and place a check mark in the AutoSave box to activate it, as shown in Figure 19.3. Now click OK. The next time you start Excel, the Autosave Option will appear in the Tools menu.

FIGURE 19.3

Place a check next to AutoSave in the Add-Ins window to activate this feature in Excel.

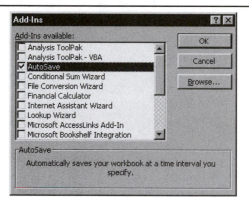

3. Click the AutoSave item on the Tools menu.

4. In the AutoSave dialog box, check Automatic Save Every and type a number, from 1 to 120, into the Minutes box, as shown in Figure 19.4.

PART

V

Networking
Housework

FIGURE 19.4

Check Automatic Save Every and enter a number into the Minutes box to autosave Excel workbooks.

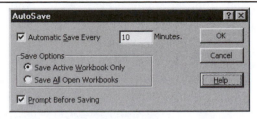

5. Select the Save Active Workbook Only option only if you want to automatically save just the workbook that is currently active.

6. Select the Save All Open Workbooks option if you want to automatically save all open workbooks.

7. Selecting the Prompt Before Saving option will let you choose whether to skip an automatic save.

8. Click OK to finish.

If you're using Office 97, you can also create backup copies of your Word and Excel files automatically each time you save them. Here's how to set this up in Word:

1. Click Tools ➤ Options ➤ Save.

2. Click the box labeled Always Create a Backup Copy, as shown in Figure 19.5.

FIGURE 19.5

Placing a check in the Always Create a Backup box in Microsoft Word Options will automatically save your work to a backup file when you close a document.

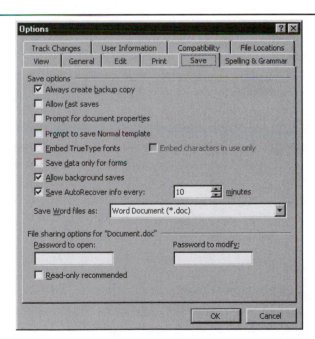

3. Click OK.

In Excel, set up automatic backup copies as follows:

1. Click File ➤ Save As ➤ Options.

2. In the Save Options dialog box, as shown in Figure 19.6, select Always Create Backup.

FIGURE 19.6

Select Always Create Backup in the Save Options dialog box to set up automatic backup in Microsoft Excel.

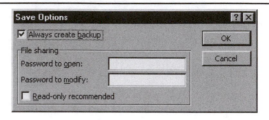

3. Click OK to finish.

TIP When you enable the autobackup option in Microsoft Word or Excel, the program makes a backup copy of a file every time you save it. This means that if you reopen the file and make a mistake when you modify it, you still have a backup of the original. The key is to remember that every time you save the file, you overwrite the old backup file with the new version. So after saving a file, you can't go back to the old one saved with auto-backup.

Application autosave and autobackup make a good—and highly convenient—first line of defense against disaster. But you should also consider making manual backups to provide more protection.

Manual Save

The simplest kind of manual backup is by copying important files to a different location on the same hard drive or a different drive. If you copy the file to a different drive, you are protecting the file in the event of a single drive failure. You can do this in Windows Explorer by creating a new folder, calling it Backups or some similar name and dragging and dropping into it files you wish to save. Although it's easy, this is a useful kind of backup. All kinds of havoc can be created when a single file becomes corrupted in some way, for instance. If this is an important device driver, a few misplaced bits can render your system all but inoperable. You can protect against this common, isolated, but potentially very troublesome problem by saving important files elsewhere on your disk.

While backing up your data to a hard drive is an essential part of any backup strategy, it only provides a first line of defense. No backup strategy is complete—and you are not prepared for disaster—unless you back up to external media.

Backing Up to External Media

The best protection, the kind of backup most people are talking about when they talk about backups, calls for saving files to a floppy drive, removable disk, or some other external media. This way, your data is insulated from local catastrophes like hard drive failure or theft. If you're using external media, there are three basic types of backup. Each is useful but, depending on your situation, one will fit your situation better than another.

Full backup   This backs up an entire hard disk or selected files.

Differential backup   This backs up selected files that have been changed since the last full backup. Use this type when you only want to save the latest version of a file.

Incremental backup   Like the differential backup, this backs up files that have been changed since the last backup. However, instead of replacing changed files, it appends them at the end of the backup.

If you don't have too much data on a drive, the easiest and best thing to do is back up the entire drive or selected files with a Full backup. Include your Windows Registry to make it easier to recreate your configuration and preferences if disaster strikes. Differential and Incremental backups take up less space on the backup media—an important consideration if you're backing up to floppies or other hard drives on your network. But Differential and Incremental backups make it more complicated and difficult to locate and restore files.

 NOTE   The flip side of backup is restore. Restoring is what you do when you copy a lost or damaged file from your backup media, such as tapes or floppies, and restore it to its rightful place on your hard drive. Depending on the backup software you are using, you can choose to restore an entire drive, selected directory, folders, or even individual files.

Types of Backup Media

For a long time, backing up meant copying files to a floppy disk. As programs and hard drives got bigger, it meant copying files to a stack of floppy disks. Nowadays, when a small drive of 1 gigabyte would require more than 700 floppies to back up completely, we are fortunate to have a plethora of other media on which to back up. They include:

Floppies   No longer suitable for a primary backup medium, the floppy disk is still very useful for backing up individual files or folders that contain less than 1.44MB of data. They're portable, pretty reliable, inexpensive, and everywhere.

Tape   High-capacity backup tapes in formats like QIC-80 offer capacities of 10 or even 20GB in an affordable device that can fit neatly inside your PC. The downside of tape is that it's slow and the tapes are not as durable as they might be. Backups that take too long tend not to get done, and unless you swap old tapes for new ones every now and then, you risk relying on a tape that itself may be unreadable when the time comes.

 TIP   All media wear out or have other problems, and there's no guarantee that a particular backup copy you have made is a good, accurate one. To minimize risk, always test a new tape or backup software program by making a backup of the files needed to run a program, then restoring them and seeing if the program runs properly. If it does, you can be much more confident that you're making good backups.

Zip and Jaz drives   These convenient, high-capacity drives with their inexpensive media are replacing the once-ubiquitous floppy on some new computers. The 1GB Jaz drives, in particular, are well-suited to network backup chores.

Removable hard drives   Hard drives that you can pull out of your machine and carry somewhere else have long been the backup medium of choice for those who demand the utmost in speed, capacity, and convenience. The downside of removable hard drives is their cost, at several hundred dollars per drive.

Rewriteable CDs   The drives and disks for recording your own compact disks are getting cheaper, so rewriteable CDs have become a viable medium for making backups.

Other network drives   The easiest and fastest backup medium is a hard drive of another computer on your home network. You can back up files to another drive as easily as clicking and dragging a file or folder to a file folder on a shared network drive.

Backing Up Your Data Online

A number of companies offer the service of *online backup*. This allows you to back up files by uploading them to an Internet server. If you lose a file, you can come back to the site and download it. Online backup is better suited to backing up one or a handful of files than to backing up many megabytes or a whole hard drive. However, it's very well-suited to backing up while you're traveling or while your other backup means, such as a tape drive, is out of order or inconvenient.

You can schedule backups to take place automatically and unattended, and you can reach your backups from anyplace, including another machine not connected to your network. Finally, since the online backup service is likely to back up its server files, including yours, one or more times a day, you've got a significant extra level of security. Some online backup services are free, others charge. Learn more at www.atbackup.com.

PART

V

Networking
Housework

Unattended Backups

One of the beauties of e-commerce, such as selling software through a Web site, is that the computer does most of the work. Running 24 hours a day, seven days a week, it can take orders and provide technical support untouched by human hands. You may be an e-commerce entrepreneur, but you can still take advantage of the superb ability of computers to perform tedious, repetitive jobs on their own by performing unattended backups.

Many third-party commercial backup programs come with the ability to perform backups unattended. That means you can set up a backup to run every Tuesday starting at midnight. Then all you have to do is leave your computer running, with a tape or other media in the appropriate drive, and know that when you wake up in the morning, your data will be secure. You can use the Task Scheduler program in Windows 98, or System Agent in Windows 95, to schedule unattended backups at any time that's convenient for you.

Protecting Your Backup Sets

Just because you have a backup, doesn't mean you're totally safe. Plenty of things can happen to backup sets that can render them partially or completely unusable. To really protect against loss of both computer and backup due to theft, fire, or flood, you should keep one copy of backup data—perhaps a full copy made monthly or weekly—someplace other than next to your computer. At the other end of the house is a pretty good choice. At a friend or relative's house on the other side of town is better. A bank safe deposit box is even better. Some people back up files from their home computer and store them at work, and back up files from their office computer and store them at home.

 TIP If for some reason you can't arrange to store a backup set off-site, consider a fireproof security box of the type sold to homeowners for storing wills, insurance policies, and other important documents. While these won't protect sensitive magnetic media such as tapes indefinitely against the destructive heat of a fire, they will improve your chances of fishing usable data out of the ashes.

Backup Software

In a pinch, you can back up any file by copying it to someplace else using no more than clicking and dragging in Windows Explorer, DOS Xcopy, or a similar command. Backup software eases this task, and makes it more effective, however. Backup software is a utility that:

- Allows you to back up data on a wide range of media, including archival tapes
- Lets you compress data to save space on backup media
- Creates and saves backup sets, which are selections of files you want to back up
- Backs up only certain types of files, such as files that have changed since the last backup

As is the case with most software, the bulk of backup programs out there are written for Microsoft Windows. However, quite a few popular backup programs are available for Macintosh computers. Retrospect Desktop Backup from Dantz Development is a well-regarded backup tool for Macs—and it comes in a network version as well. Learn more at www.dantz.com.

The most popular backup program for Linux, BRU Backup Utility from Enhanced Software Technologies, is included on several distributions of the operating system, including those from Red Hat and Caldera's OpenLinux. You can learn more, including downloading a trial version of BRU Backup Utility, at www.estinc.com.

Using Microsoft Backup

Windows comes with a backup utility that allows you to make backups of files and drives. Despite being included for free, the Windows Backup program has many of the features of third-party backup software. Best of all, you can back up to floppies or a wide variety of tapes and removeable drives including Jaz and Zip drives—although not rewriteable CD-ROMS—and you can compress files if necessary to save space. You can select the files you want to back up as well as set up groups of files for repeated backups. You can compare backed-up files with the original versions for accuracy, and restore backed-up files to their original locations, or somewhere else on your disk.

You will probably have to install Backup from your Windows CD-ROM, as it is not installed in a default installation. Here's how:

1. Click Start ➤ Settings ➤ Control Panel.
2. Select Add/Remove Programs and click the Windows Setup tab.
3. In the Windows Setup window, as shown in Figure 19.7, scroll down to highlight System Tools and click Details.

FIGURE 19.7

To install the Windows Backup utility, select System Tools in the Windows Setup window.

4. Place a check mark beside the entry for Backup, as shown in Figure 19.8, and click OK.

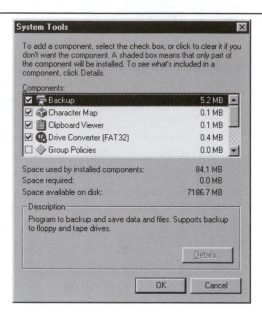

5. Click OK again and, when prompted, insert the Windows CD-ROM or enter the path for the setup files.

Backup searches for a working backup device, such as a tape drive, the first time you run it. If it doesn't find any such device, you'll get an error message like the one in Figure 19.9.

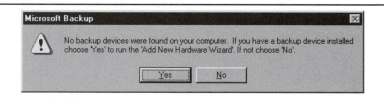

If you have a tape drive that isn't being detected, run the Add New Hardware Wizard by clicking Yes. Your system will be searched for a backup device. You can click No if you want to select manually where to save your backup. After installing Backup, here's how to start the program and perform a backup using the Wizard:

1. Click Start ➣ Programs ➣ Accessories ➣ System Tools ➣ Backup.

2. In the Microsoft Backup window, as shown in Figure 19.10, select Create a New Backup Job and click OK.

FIGURE 19.10

Backup's opening screen gives you three options for how to proceed.

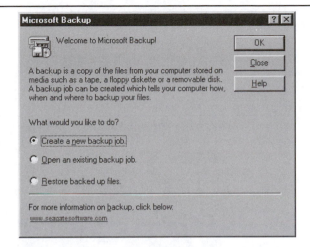

3. The Backup Wizard, as shown in Figure 19.11, will ask you what you want to back up. The first choice will copy all files on your computer. The second requires you to choose the files that will be backed up. If you choose this option, you'll be presented with a directory tree from which you select the files to be backed up.

FIGURE 19.11

In the Backup Wizard window, you'll choose whether to back up your whole hard drive, or selected files.

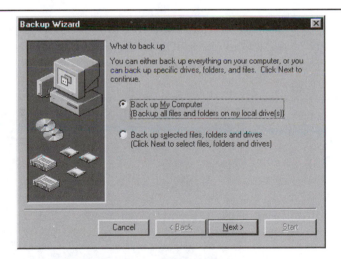

4. Assuming you want to back up your whole drive, click on the radio button for Back Up My Computer and click Next.

5. Select whether you want to back up all files, or just new or changed ones and click Next.

PART

V

Networking Housework

6. The next window, as shown in Figure 19.12, asks you where you want to save the files. This could be a network drive, a hard drive on your computer (the C: drive is shown in the illustration) or some other drive such as a tape drive or Zip drive. Click on the file folder button to navigate around your computer or the network to select a suitable location.

FIGURE 19.12

Tell Backup where to place your copies of valuable data by typing a path into the box, or navigating graphically around the system and network by clicking on the file folder icon.

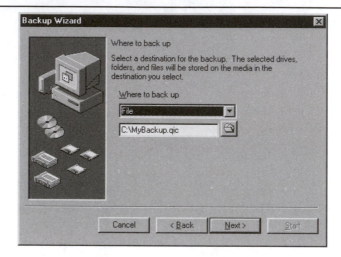

7. In the backup options screen, shown in Figure 19.13, you should generally leave both options checked, in order to save media space and ensure the reliability of your backup, and click Next.

FIGURE 19.13

Leaving both backup options checked will compress backed-up data to save space and compare backed-up files against originals to ensure accuracy.

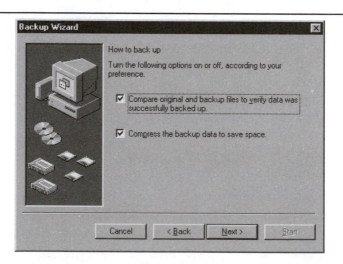

8. The next screen, as shown in Figure 19.14, recounts the details of this backup and gives you a chance to give the backup a descriptive name, which will make it easier to repeat.

FIGURE 19.14

Give your backup a descriptive name to make it easier to do repeatedly.

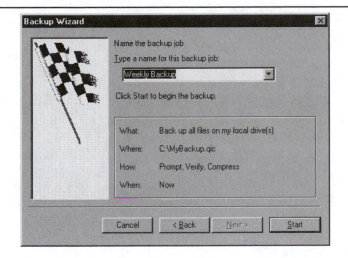

9. To start the backup, click Start in the Backup Wizard window. You'll see the progress of the backup and receive a backup report when it is finished.

TIP After you've run Backup once, your backup setup will be saved. You can choose to run the same backup again from the opening Backup Wizard window (shown in Figure 19.10) by selecting the second option, Open an Existing Backup Job.

Protecting Against Power Spikes and Outages

A sudden loss of power or fluctuation in the electric current flowing to your computer can cause the read/write head of your disk drive, which normally flies a fraction of an inch over the recording surface, to drop down and make contact with the surface. That can be bad. If it crash lands in the middle of some data or overwrites data, whatever information was there may not be recoverable. It can also permanently damage your disk drive. That's why it's important not only to back up key data, but also to protect against data loss due to power spikes and outages in the first place.

PART

V

Networking
Housework

Someday, if you don't have anything to do for a few hours, pay close attention to the lights in your home. Chances are, every now and then they'll flicker. These sudden dimmings and brightenings can be due to variations in the power supply which occur as electricity flows over the network to homes, as shown in Figure 19.15.

FIGURE 19.15

Variations in the way electricity flows over the power grid to your home cause fluctuations in the power going to your computer.

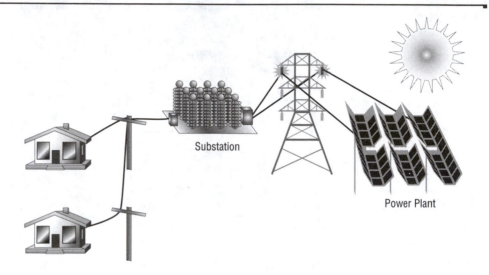

Substation

Power Plant

Lightning strikes are a serious source of danger for computer systems. When lightning hits the ground, it does so with billions of volts. This surge of electricity not uncommonly finds its way into the electrical wiring that supplies your house and then into the electrical appliances, including your computers, that are connected to your network. Given that electronic components can be destroyed with a spark of static electricity that you wouldn't even notice, a nearby lightning strike can easily do the job. It's possible for a lightning-generated electrical spike to travel throughout even a large network, knocking out all the PCs it encounters. Lightning probably isn't all that common where you live (unless you live in thunderstorm-prone South Florida, that is) but when you add up the occurrences of power fluctuations, lightning strikes, and circuit overloading, they become pretty common events. In fact, it's a rare computer networker who doesn't have to deal with pretty frequent mini-brownouts.

 WARNING The most frequent cause of power fluctuations probably originates within your own home. When your energy-hungry appliances, like refrigerators or air-conditioners, start their compressors, it's typical for your lights to flicker briefly before the load is balanced. For this reason, you should avoid connecting computers, printers, hubs, or other network gear to the same circuits to which an air-conditioner, dishwasher, or other electricity-gobbling appliance is attached.

In addition to lightning strikes, surges, and blackouts, you may also experience near blackouts, called brownouts, or line noise. Any of these can be detrimental to your computer's health. To protect against them, you can use surge suppressors, line conditioners and, the ultimate, uninterruptible power supplies.

Surge Suppressors

The most basic protection against electrical disaster is a surge suppressor, also called a surge protector. This is a device that protects a power supply and, sometimes, communications lines from electrical spikes. Your computer's power supply has a built-in surge protector that should be adequate for handling ordinary line noise, but you should get a separate device as well to protect against the more serious threats of lightning strikes and surges. You can buy power strips with some surge protection for under $10.00 at hardware stores, but to get real protection you should be prepared to visit a computer or electronics store and spend several times that for one resembling those in Figure 19.16.

 WARNING You may still be vulnerable to a surge even if you're using a surge suppressor. That's because electricity coming through a phoneline connected to a computer's modem can be just as destructive. It's recommended, therefore, that you use a surge suppressor with protected connections for both phone and electrical lines.

FIGURE 19.16

Surge suppressors such as these provide protection for both phone and electrical lines, as well as indicator lights to show you they are working.

When you go shopping, here's what to look for in a surge suppressor:

- A notice that it meets the UL 1449 surge suppressor standard
- Protection for phonelines as well as electrical lines
- Some sort of indicator light to show that it is working
- A lifetime guarantee covering not just the product, but the equipment it is protecting

Line Conditioners

Line conditioners are devices that filter and smooth the stream of electrical power, removing fluctuations and interference. Line conditioners are rated in decibels, the higher the better. People can spend a lot of money on line conditioners—and many mainframe computer owners do—but you can get the job done adequately for much less money by using surge suppressors.

Uninterruptible Power Supplies

An uninterruptible power supply, or UPS, is basically a big battery that lets your computer keep running for a short time after the power goes out. It also protects against damage from power surges. Inside the UPS is circuitry that detects a loss of power and connects the battery so that your computer doesn't go dark. You'll get a message from the UPS if you are using the computer when the power quits. That will give you time to save any open files and exit Windows properly.

UPS systems come in two varieties: standby and online. The standby UPS systems are less costly and provide a less-perfect protection than online UPS. Most UPS systems you'd consider for a home network are standby systems, and these should be adequate for your needs.

More expensive UPS systems include software that backs up data automatically when power loss occurs. If you have to do it manually, ignore the warning at your peril: UPS batteries typically only last a few minutes. If you keep working when the UPS goes dry, you'll lose any information in RAM and will be forced to exit any programs that are running.

Summary

Choosing the right backup system might be intimidating at first. But taking the time to back up your documents—and connect your computers to their power sources using surge suppressors—is not difficult, and is well worth the effort. With a minimal expenditure of time and money, you can protect your home, business, and personal files from acts of nature, the vagaries of technology, and simple human error.

What's Next

The best defense sometimes is a good offense. So, in addition to considering the defenses against disaster described in this chapter, you should consider taking action against network threats. Network security, including protecting against computer viruses and hackers, is the subject of the next chapter.

CHAPTER <u>20</u>

Network Security

Overview

The networked world of computers is a big place, growing by leaps and bounds. And, as you'll find in any large community that is experiencing explosive growth, a lot of the well-intentioned people joining the community are not well protected against a less-well-intentioned minority who are abusing it. These digital hooligans make life difficult for the rest of us by a variety of means, including:

- Releasing disruptive programs, such as computer viruses, into the networked community.
- Trying and often succeeding at penetrating the digital defenses erected by network operators, and then stealing or damaging information or misusing resources.
- Placing offensive material, including pornography, where it can be accessed by children and others for whom it is inappropriate, offensive, or both.

To continue the analogy of the Internet as frontier boomtown a little more, the local sheriff is overwhelmed by the growth of the community and the lack of familiarity with those who could compromise that community's peace of mind. The result is that, like in the Wild West, all networkers are on their own to a considerable extent. In other words, it's up to you to protect yourself against the viruses, hackers, and offensive material you may encounter via the Internet. The good news is that you don't have to tack on a gold star and unholster your trusty six-shooter to take action. With adequate antivirus software, solid security against hackers, and filters to keep out offensive material, you can keep your network and your household quite safe on the digital frontier.

Viruses

If you haven't heard about one or more of the well-publicized computer virus scares by now, you are almost certainly very new to computing (and you never watch television or read newspapers, either). But even if you have heard about the Melissa Word macro virus or another of the infamous computer bugs out there, you may not be quite sure what a virus is. The simple answer is that a virus is a piece of computer code that is hidden in another host program. When the host program is executed or activated, the virus code attaches itself to other programs, which then copy the virus to still other programs. This self-replicating action is intended, and is part of the design of the software.

In addition to copying itself, a virus usually contains a payload. This innocuous-sounding term refers to the malicious side effects of the virus. They may range from harmless messages to data corruption or destruction.

 NOTE A program need not damage, delete, or corrupt files to be considered a virus. Some definitions would even classify as viruses ordinarily benign utilities, such as the DOS Diskcopy program. However, since these programs aren't specifically intended to copy themselves, they're not viruses that you need to be concerned about.

Viruses can be highly destructive. A virus can destroy small or large chunks of data by copying over files or by replacing sections within a word processing document. In a worst case, a virus could issue a command to, say, reformat your hard drive, erasing all information on the drive. More subtle changes can be just as troublesome, however. A virus may, for instance, make random, hard-to-detect changes in numbers in a spreadsheet document. Viruses have been found that will post messages in your name—perhaps including personal documents from your hard drive—to unsavory Internet newsgroups. It's hard to put a monetary value on that kind of damage.

Many viruses are more irritating than purely destructive. They may, for instance, cause prank messages to pop up on your screen, send blank e-mails to everyone in your address book, or force you to repeatedly click a meaningless dialog box. Even the ones without any significant payload can be seriously disruptive, however. Floods of virus-generated e-mail can overload servers and cause networks to crash.

 NOTE Although having your hard drive reformatted can be truly distressing, the good news is that this is not likely to occur because of a virus. The reason is, a virus that reformats the hard disk will also tend to erase itself. That means it can't spread to other machines, including yours.

Basically, to get a virus, you have to boot your PC from an infected disk or other medium, execute an infected program, or open an infected file. Beyond that, viruses can enter your computer in several ways, including the following:

Floppy diskettes   Formerly, downloading data from floppy disks was the biggest way for viruses to get on your computer. Today, viruses are mostly spread through network connections.

Electronic mail   Today, the largest number of viruses are disseminated as attachments to electronic mail. E-mail is now the most effective, fastest way for viruses to spread themselves.

Infected files   Downloading files from the Internet represents another likely source of infection, although files from reputable freeware and shareware sites are usually scanned for viruses. You can also encounter infected files over a network.

Infected CD-ROMs   Like the floppies of yore, CD-ROMs can just as effectively spread viruses.

Malicious applets   Acquired when you view Web sites, these applets are created to spread disease.

Commercial software   Even new software in its shrink wrap has been known to ship to customers containing viruses.

It used to be said that you could not get a virus by receiving and reading electronic mail. However, viruses have evolved to the point where some can infect computers when electronic mail is merely previewed. Even more worrisome are viruses embedded in the programs used to display World Wide Web pages. These can be downloaded to your machine merely by accessing a malicious Web page.

Not all destructive programs are technically viruses. Some, such as worms and Trojan Horse programs, can do plenty of damage, however. The classification of viruses is a difficult art and gets highly technical very quickly. But, without attempting to be either comprehensive or extremely detailed, here are the different types of viruses and virus-like programs you could encounter:

Boot sector viruses   Infect the data your computer uses to start up.

File viruses   Attach themselves to executable program files, such as `.com` and `.exe` programs.

Macro viruses   Infect documents created by word processors, spreadsheets, and databases, including Word, Excel, PowerPoint, and Access files used by Microsoft Office.

Applet viruses   Are buried in Java applets and ActiveX controls. They can be downloaded when users view Web pages containing the controls.

E-mail viruses   Are viruses that spread themselves by infecting e-mail messages and e-mail programs.

Polymorphic viruses   Are complex viruses that can alter their appearance and escape detection.

Encrypted viruses Use encryption and other techniques to evade detection.

Stealth viruses Try to avoid detection and removal by the modifications they make to files or boot records.

Worms Are programs that can spread working copies of themselves to other computer systems, usually through a network. Unlike viruses, worms don't necessarily attach themselves to a host program.

Trojan horses Can be any program that purposefully does something, usually undocumented, that users don't want it to do.

NOTE Hoax viruses, as the name suggests, aren't viruses at all. They are just rumors of viruses. In some ways, these are the most popular and easily spread viruses out there, because they travel not by network connection, but by word of mouth. You can check for information about hoax viruses at virus information centers such as the Virus Bulletin home page at www.virusbtn.com.

Protecting against Viruses

Viruses can be a little unsettling. The idea that a piece of computer code that you can't see can enter your computer and destroy data is not particularly comforting. Add in the fact that there are already many thousands of distinct viruses in the wild (the lingo for viruses that have been released into the general computing world) and that many more come out all the time, and it may seem as if you are practically helpless before an onslaught of destructive code. However, it's not inevitable that you'll be harmed by a virus. By employing effective steps to protect your network, you can greatly increase the odds that your household won't get infected. And if a virus does somehow creep in, you can ensure that the resulting problems are short-lived and minor.

NOTE The first computer virus was reportedly created in the 1980s by a Pakistani programmer who was trying to keep people from pirating software. Today, there are more than 40,000 viruses of a bewildering variety of types, created by thousands of programmers all over the world, most for far less reputable reasons.

Your first line of defense against viruses is to simply be careful. The primary rules are:

- Don't accept e-mail from unknown parties, especially if files are attached. Delete them without opening them.

NOTE If you use Microsoft Outlook or Outlook Express, you should also be careful about previewing electronic mail messages. Some viruses have been found that will infect a user's machine if the preview feature in Outlook is used, even if the mail is not opened.

- Don't open e-mail from anybody, especially if files are attached, unless you are sure that the file was sent to you by someone who checked it for viruses first. This also applies to files that come in on floppies.

- Avoid Internet viruses by downloading only from safe sites, where all files are scanned by virus-detection software before they are posted for downloading. Safe sites are also called *well-known* sites, such as www.microsoft.com, www.tucows.com, and www.download.com to mention just a few.

- Make sure that you're using the latest update to your antivirus software, and buy new versions when they become available. Updates are critical with antivirus software because viruses change constantly as their creators try to come up with ways to beat antivirus defenses. Antivirus software companies post regular updates on their Web sites, and most send e-mail bulletins or automatic updates to software owners. Updates help antivirus programs recognize the signatures of new viruses.

- Make sure that everyone who uses your network knows that they have to keep their antivirus software active and running.

WARNING It's important to load antivirus software on all computers on your home network, not just a few. A single unprotected PC can infect the whole household through shared network files and the swapping of floppies.

- Authorize only one person—yourself—to issue virus alerts on the network. This will reduce downtime and confusion caused by the common virus hoaxes.

Being careful will only take you so far, however. If you want true peace of mind, you need to use antivirus software. This is utility software that recognizes the signs of infection by a particular virus—called its *signature*—and alerts you if there's a problem. Antivirus software can usually remove the virus from your system as well, although in the case of a very new or very stubborn virus, it may not work.

WARNING Your chances of getting infected with a virus may be higher than you think, and the pain may be greater. The International Computer Security Association in Carlisle, Pennsylvania, says over 99 percent of the medium-sized and larger organizations it surveyed had at least one computer virus experience. The annual infection rate is 406 of every 1,000 machines. That's very high—and a virus infection can be quite costly. The average infection of a corporate computer costs over $8,000.00, mostly for downtime and re-entering lost data. And damages from a virus infection can get worse—much worse. If you negligently forward a virus to someone else and cause their computer to be infected, you could be held legally liable for any damages that are caused.

Antivirus Software

Antivirus programs are utilities designed to sniff out, identify, report, and, when possible, destroy computer viruses on your machine. It's important to realize that not all viruses can be removed by antivirus software. Often, you will need to delete the infected files or programs and replace them with backups. This is, incidentally, why you need backups, even though you may be using antivirus software.

 NOTE See Chapter 19, "Disaster Prevention," for numerous ways to back up your documents and applications.

Antivirus software works by scanning files and memory for patterns characteristic of known viruses. Since virus-writers know how antivirus software works, they try to foil the virus-catchers by encrypting their malicious code, changing its appearance on the fly, and even intercepting internal system messages so that their presence won't be revealed. Staying on top of evolving viruses requires a significant research and development effort by the virus software companies, which is why, as a general rule, the shareware and freeware virus programs do not afford anything like the same level of protection as commercial programs. You may use a freeware word processor, e-mail program and even an operating system without missing the commercial programs, but virus software is a different story.

 NOTE Viruses can do a lot of damage, but there are limits to their destructive potency. A virus is just a software program—it doesn't have a physical being like a real germ does. It can't destroy your computer's mechanical or electronic components, such as its disk drives, network cards, and so forth. Whatever happens to your data, you'll still have a computer to rebuild it on.

PART

V

Networking
Housework

Selecting Antivirus Software

Most new computers today come bundled with antivirus software. If your new PC does, be sure to update it at the vendor's Web site before considering yourself protected. If you don't have any antivirus software, you have a lot of choices. There are many commercial publishers of antivirus software. Antivirus software is a complex product, but most products do basically the same thing: identify and remove viruses. You want a vendor that stands behind the product with vigorous research into new virus threats, frequent updates, and always-ready technical support. As far as product features, make sure that the software automatically scans floppy disks inserted into your PC, as well as downloaded files.

Here, arranged in alphabetical order, are several products that have gotten good reviews, along with Web sites where you can go to learn more:

- Aladdin eSafe Protect Desktop 2.1 from Aladdin Knowledge Systems, includes a desktop Internet firewall to stop hackers, www.ealaddin.com

- Command AntiVirus from Command Software Systems uses the well-regarded F-PROT Professional virus detection system, www.commandcom.com.

- F-Secure Anti-Virus from Finnish company F-Secure runs on a wide variety of computers and operating systems, www.datafellows.com.

- McAfee VirusScan 4.03 is the latest from long-time antivirus leader Network Associates, www.mcafee.com.

- Norton AntiVirus 2000, from Symantec, is the best-selling virus software, www.symantec.com.

- Panda Antivirus Platinum 6 from Panda Software is both powerful and exceptionally easy to use, www.pandasoftware.com.

- Sophos AntiVirus is produced by UK-based Sophos Software, which offers a free downloadable trial version, www.sophos.com.

 WARNING   No antivirus program is foolproof. Virus programmers are constantly working to find ways to beat antivirus software, and, especially in the case of very new viruses, they often succeed, at least for a time. Antivirus software programmers also make mistakes, and release buggy, ineffective products. Finally, antivirus software can be inconvenient; it has to be used to work at all.

Using Antivirus Software

The key to succeeding with antivirus software is less about buying the right kind and more about properly using whatever you do purchase. The main key is to keep it turned on. Antivirus software can be inconvenient to use. It often creates conflicts and must be turned off—temporarily—when installing other programs. Some antivirus programs give false alerts in the presence of certain types of code. Others are simply clunky to use, with unhandy user interfaces. The main thing to remember, however, is that if it's not turned on, it's not protecting you.

 WARNING Always make good backups. This is your first line of defense. Antivirus software is only your second line of defense. For more on backing up your home network, see Chapter 19, "Disaster Prevention."

Updating Antivirus Software

Of all the things you can do with antivirus software, updating it is the most important. You should regularly—say, once a month—go to the vendor's Web site and download and install the latest update. This is true even for the latest version of antivirus software that you have just brought home from the store or received in the mail. New viruses can emerge in far less time than it takes to shrink-wrap and distribute a CD-ROM of antivirus software. You need to have the latest update in order to have maximum protection.

What to Do if You Think You're Infected

Someday, you may have a sneaking suspicion that turns into a high probability and finally a certainty: A virus has infected your computer. Now what do you do?

1. Stop working immediately and completely. If you're on a network and think other machines on the network may have been infected, make sure no one is using those machines. Especially be sure that no one is sending e-mails or copying files that could be infected.

2. Using another machine if possible, download the latest antivirus update for your antivirus software from your software vendor's Web site, and update your software's database of virus signatures.

3. Run the antivirus program and follow its instructions for removing the virus. This may involve deleting any files the antivirus program identifies as infected.

TIP You can check for computer viruses even if you don't have any antivirus software installed on your computer, the stores aren't open, and you don't have the inclination to buy downloadable software. Here's how: Using the machine you suspect of being infected, go to an online virus-checking site such as www.mcafee.com and follow the instructions. Online checks let you scan for and delete harmful viruses instantly. You don't have to purchase, load, or upgrade any software—although there may be a charge for subscribing to the service long-term. You just log on after completing a form and signing up for a trial offer, and start the check. When it's done, take a look at your user report to see if any viruses have been detected.

4. See if you can determine the source of the infection. This may require some elementary detective work. For instance, if several documents you received as an e-mail attachment turn out to have been infected, the oldest document was probably the source.

5. Alert the apparent source of the infection. Do this diplomatically; viruses can be hard to detect and whoever gave it to you probably doesn't know that they are infected.

6. Finally, as with any socially transmitted disease, alert anyone you may have infected.

Reporting A New Virus

What if your computer is acting oddly, you scan for a virus, and nothing is found? In that case, chances are good that you have an ordinary system or software conflict that is causing a problem. On the other hand, it's just possible you have a virus that is so new that it hasn't been registered by the virus-detecting databases. Here's what to do if you think you've got an undetectable virus:

1. Try to make sure it's not something else by scanning your hard drive for errors, reviewing your configuration, and checking that your system is set up properly.

2. Obtain an e-mail address of a software virus lab—ideally, one provided by your antivirus software maker—to which you can send any suspicious files.

3. If you get the suspicious effect when you work on a particular document, such as a Word file, send that document to the virus lab. Failing that, send another recently used document of the same type.

Continued

CONTINUED

4. If it is a particular program that produces the odd results when you run it, or if the virus-like effect takes place when you boot the system, try to send the program file. In the worst case, if your hard disk has been erased or reformatted, check other hard drives on the network, or perhaps floppy disks for files and programs that you may have used since the infection occurred.

If you have additional questions—or even if you don't—a call to the technical support line of your antivirus software company is a good idea.

Protecting against Hackers

Once you're connected to the Internet, especially if you're using an always-on Internet connection such as a DSL line or cable modem, you become vulnerable to hackers. Hackers, of course, are computer vandals who gain unauthorized access to computer systems and networks, and there wreak mayhem by stealing or damaging information or misusing network resources. Hacking is a crime on the rise. According to Kessler & Associates, an investigative consulting company, theft of proprietary information by hackers and other unauthorized people doubled from 1997 to 1999. Misuse of network resources is another popular goal of hackers. They may, for instance, break into a mail server and use it as a place to exchange stolen commercial software.

The term *hacker* originally applied to programmers who created their software in assembly language. Assembly is the programming language just above the binary coded instructions that computers actually read. Assembly programming requires detailed knowledge of a computer's hardware architecture, and is generally the domain of only the most expert programmers. Therefore, hacker started out as a term of respect, if not admiration.

Among programmers, the people who break into computers are known as *crackers* or *computer crackers*. Over time the public has come to associate the term with people who break into computer systems. And these are the people most of us know as hackers Although they have been benignly described as people who enjoy circumventing the limitations of systems, the hacker label is generally not used as a term of respect, especially with regard to computer security. Keep in mind, however, that while many crackers are hackers, not all people who refer to themselves as hackers are out to attack computers.

Anatomy of a Hacker

The typical computer cracker is a 16-to-25-year-old male who gets interested in breaking into computers and networks to improve his cracking skill, or to preempt network resources for his own purposes. E-mail surveys of newsgroup users who claim to be hackers show that they tend to have a lot of spare time on their hands, which explains why they can be quite persistent in their attacks.

Very few hackers go so far as to pick a target in advance. Hackers are generally opportunists, running scanners to examine many thousands of network hosts for weaknesses. Interestingly, after spotting a vulnerable computer and invading it using the weakness he has identified, the hacker will often fix other vulnerabilities to prevent other hackers from gaining access to the host.

Like computer viruses, hackers pose an unfamiliar threat to most home networkers. You're probably wondering: How can you protect yourself from these Internet-borne criminals? What risk do they really pose? There aren't perfect answers to either of these questions. But there are things you can do to help you rest more easily.

 TIP You can find a wide array of anti-hacker information at AntiOnline, an electronic publication for security professionals as www.antionline.com.

Hack Attacks

The first thing to understand about hack attacks is that they come in several varieties. The most common include:

- Attempts to gain passwords or otherwise impersonate authentic users so they can gain access to network resources. This can be done using software that tricks the computers or by social engineering, which is the use of clever e-mail messages to try to trick people into revealing their passwords.

- Attempts to harm the network by overloading it with meaningless messages. Examples include pointless requests for network connections and repeated diagnostic messages such as pings. Because these attacks make the network unusable, they're termed *denial of service* attacks.

- Attempts to exploit weaknesses in the security of specific programs, such as operating systems, mail programs, and applications software. Many programs have built-in methods for allowing technicians to bypass security protections. When hackers discover these back doors, it can spell trouble.

Within these broad parameters, there are many different ways for a hacker to attack a network, and hackers are constantly thinking up new ones. Any attempt to describe how hackers attack networks would be outdated almost as soon as it was expressed. At this writing, however, here are some of the more popular and enduring types of attacks:

Back Orifice   A set of programs that can let hackers access and control computers running Windows 95/98 and NT

Changemac   A program designed to make a hacker appear to be an authenticated user

Deceit.C   A program that attempts to foil an otherwise secure network by tricking users into disclosing their passwords

Network Scanners   A type of program that scans networks looking for unprotected servers that can be easily hacked

Password Sniffers   Programs that are designed to snag passwords as they go by on the network

Ping of Death   A malicious use of a tool, normally used to test networks, that can stall or crash a computer or an entire network by tying up the system with pointless tasks

Smurfs   Attacks that can overwhelm a network by sending and requesting hordes of echoed data packets

Syn Flood   A program that floods network ports with so many bogus requests for connections that they can no longer communicate

Winhack Gold   A hacker program for Windows that scans blocks of network addresses, looking for shared files that anyone can access

What can you do about these hack attacks? One approach to network security is to arm yourself with the same Net-cracking tools as hackers, and try to compromise your own network. You can download many popular attack programs off of the Internet and use them to check for vulnerabilities. The idea is to find your own weaknesses before someone else does it for you. Learn more, and find some of the programs for downloading at `www.rootshell.com`.

PART

V

Networking
Housework

WARNING Before you obtain and use hackers' tools, be aware that these tools must be handled carefully or you could damage your own network. If you damage someone else's network, even accidentally, you could find yourself in violation of the law.

One of the basic techniques for protecting networks from Internet-borne hackers is to make sure that you do not have unnecessary services set up on your computer. The more open your network, the easier it is for hackers to gain access to it. Of utmost importance: Make sure you don't have Microsoft File and Printer Sharing set up to work with a TCP/IP connection. Finding open shares of this sort is the primary objective of many hacker scanning programs. Fortunately, it's easy to close this hole, even if you wish to retain the ability to share files and printers with other machines on your network.

 WARNING Unbinding TCP/IP file and printer sharing will mean that you can no longer share files and printers from a remote location, such as your workplace. If you need to do this, you should use a firewall, such as the personal firewall software described in "Using Firewalls" later in this chapter. At the very least, you should use long passwords composed of random characters and change them frequently, since your passwords will be your only line of defense against any hacker whose scanner sniffs out your shared files.

The same protocol that makes Windows networking so easy also makes it less secure. To smooth the configuration of Windows networking, Microsoft has elected to have adapters and services bound to each other by default. Because this mass binding is done automatically, it means you don't have to configure each adapter separately. That speeds the process of preparing your computer for the network. Unfortunately, this also creates some serious security problems.

The most serious problem is that the TCP/IP protocol is bound to Microsoft's file- and printer-sharing services. TCP/IP is the protocol for the Internet, while NetBEUI is the standard protocol for Windows local area networks. It's fine for you to share files and printers over your local area network, so it's okay to have file and printer sharing set up for NetBEUI. But do you want to share files and printers with people who can access your machine through the Internet? Unless you're accessing your network from somewhere else, and you really need to be able to share files and printers when you do, you probably should not set up file and printer sharing for use with TCP/IP. Yet that's how Windows sets up networking automatically. And it means that your computer and its files, and all the shared files on your network, are far more vulnerable to hackers than they need to be.

To fix this problem, you can unbind file and printer sharing from the TCP/IP protocol used over the Internet, but keep file and printer sharing bound to the NetBEUI protocol (used in most Windows-based LANs). The advantage to binding only to NetBEUI is that this is a *non-routable protocol*, meaning it cannot be used by anyone who is not on your local network. Here's how to do it:

1. Click Start ➤ Settings ➤ Control Panel and double-click on the Network icon.

2. In the Configuration tab of the Network window, as shown in Figure 20.1, highlight each of the adapters in the scrolling window and click the Properties button. Please note: You have to do this to each of the adapters that are present; there may be several.

FIGURE 20.1

You can identify the adapters in the Network Configuration window by their icons, which look like miniature adapter cards.

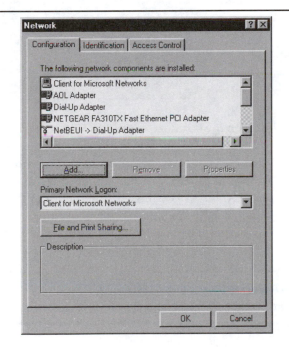

3. In the Adapter Properties window for each adapter, click the Bindings tab.

4. In the Bindings tab window, as shown in Figure 20.2, you will see listings of the protocols this adapter is set up to use. For instance, the protocols NetBEUI, TCP/IP and IPX/SPX are likely to be listed.

PART

V

Networking Housework

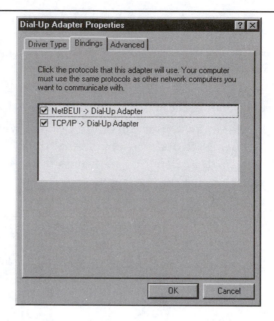

5. Click on the box next to any protocol in the Adapter Properties window in order to unbind the protocol from the selected adapter. Remember: You need NetBEUI bound to your network adapter to use your home network and its services, such as file and printer sharing. You need TCP/IP bound to your network adapter only if you are accessing the Internet from this machine. (You probably don't need IPX/SPX at all, unless you are using Netware network operating system software or playing network games that required IPX.)

 WARNING Keep the NetBEUI protocol bound to the adapter you use to reach your home network. If you don't, you won't be able to use your network.

6. Click OK.

 WARNING Be sure to repeat this procedure on every computer connected to your network. If you leave any computer out, it could compromise your network security.

In addition to setting the bindings for adapters, you should also adjust the bindings for the protocols you have installed on your machines. Here's how:

1. Click Start ➢ Settings ➢ Control Panel and double-click the Network icon.

2. In the Configuration tab of the Network window, as shown in Figure 20.3, highlight each of the protocols beginning with TCP/IP in the scrolling window and click the Properties button. Please note: You have to do this to each protocol separately.

FIGURE 20.3

Pick out the protocols in the Network Configuration window by looking for those next to an icon that looks like two wires twisted together in a "V" shape. You are interested in the TCP/IP protocol listings.

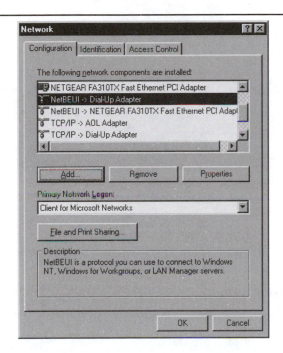

PART

V

Networking
Housework

3. In the TCP/IP Properties window, as shown in Figure 20.4, click the Bindings tab.

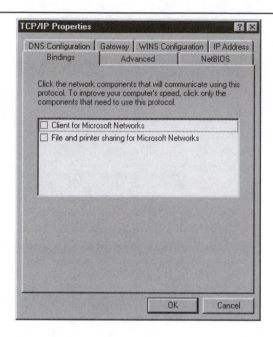

4. Unbind TCP/IP from all services listed by removing the check marks from the boxes next to the services. Please note: The services listed will vary, depending on which ones you have installed on your machine, but are likely to include: Client for Microsoft Networks, File and Printer Sharing for Microsoft Networks, and Microsoft Family Logon.

5. Click OK and, when asked if you want to select any drivers to bind to, click No.

6. Click OK again and click Yes to reboot the system.

TIP The most useful source for security related tips on how to protect yourself from hackers by eliminating unneeded services, bindings, and protocols, is Steve Gibson's Shields Up page at www.grc.com.

As a final step to deterring hackers, check to make sure your bindings are set up properly. Do this as follows:

1. Click Start ➤ Settings ➤ Control Panel and double-click the Network icon.

2. In the Configuration tab of the Network window highlight each of the protocols beginning with TCP/IP in the scrolling window and click the Properties button. Do this separately for each protocol.

3. Click the NetBIOS tab, as shown in Figure 20.5, and make sure that there is no check mark in the box next to I Want to Enable NetBIOS Over TCP/IP.

FIGURE 20.5

To make sure that NetBIOS applications are not enabled over TCP/IP, check the NetBIOS tab in TCP/IP properties for each instance of the TCP/IP protocol.

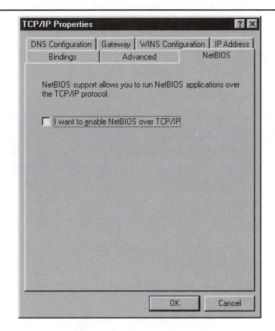

PART

V

Networking Housework

4. If the option is checked, uncheck it by clicking on the box. Be sure to do this for every instance of the TCP/IP protocol in your Configuration tab of the Network window.

5. Click OK and, if Windows asks you to reboot the system, reboot.

Removing your open invitation to hackers by disabling risky file and printer sharing over the Internet will make your network more secure. But nothing is perfect. Hackers are ingenious, and good security involves more than closing the door. To be really safe, make sure you use your locks, in the form of password protection.

Problems with Passwords

If you've read *Arabian Nights* or seen Walt Disney's animated *Aladdin* movie, you are aware than knowing a secret word or phrase like "Open Sesame!" can unlock otherwise impenetrable barriers. There are lots of other instances in which words or names are invested with near-magical powers. In some primitive cultures, for instance, each individual has a personal name that no one else may know. If it were to get out, anyone who knew it would have special powers over that person. In the networking world, knowing your password could similarly give someone special powers over you.

Signs of a Stolen Password

You may suspect that your password, or someone else's on the network, has been compromised if any of the following things occur:

- Files mysteriously appear or disappear in your personal directories.
- You receive e-mail messages that refer to a message you did not send.
- You are unable to log on to the network, despite being sure that you are typing in your username and password properly. In this case, a hacker may have stolen your password and then changed it, so you can no longer access the system.

Effective use of passwords is a primary line of defense against hackers. Ideally, if you require a user to provide an authentic password to gain entrance to your network, then nobody but authentic users will be on your network. Unfortunately, it doesn't always work that way. Here are some of the common problems with passwords:

- Hackers can easily guess many passwords, such as words from the dictionary and birth dates.

NOTE Don't stop your quest for security just by eliminating dictionary words from your password list. Also screen out names of fictional characters and proper names of family and friends. One Internet Service Provider used a program to automatically check users' passwords against the contents of their personal Web pages. It found that people frequently wanted to use as a password the names of relatives or pets. While these words might not be found in any dictionary, they could still be seen by anyone surfing their Web page.

- Passwords that are too short can be guessed by hackers using powerful and speedy password-guessing programs, even if they consist of random characters.
- Careless distribution of passwords, in such insecure media such as non-encrypted electronic mail, can place them in hackers' hands.

- Hackers can capture passwords from network traffic by using password sniffer software.

- Beware also of social engineering by hackers, such as sending you e-mail purporting to be from a system administrator or other supposedly benign individual and requesting your password.

 WARNING Cybercafes, where you can check your e-mail and surf the Internet while downing a cup of good coffee and a scone, are a great invention, to be sure. But if a hacker has installed a keystroke logging program on the machine, it could be acting as a funnel—collecting passwords for users' e-mail boxes, personal Web sites, and network logons—and saving them for the hacker to use to break into your accounts. Keystroke monitoring programs can be silent, invisible, and very hard to detect. Ask the proprietor of a cybercafe what security measures have been taken to prevent keystroke logging before using a public PC for anything more sensitive than figuring out what movie to see after you've had your coffee.

Password File Security

While Windows 95 and Windows 98 may require passwords for you to log on to your network, the truth is, these operating systems are not secure. The reason is that you can get around the password protection by simply hitting the Escape key when presented with the password dialog box, then searching for the password file, deleting it, and rebooting the computer. This will allow anyone to create their own user and have full access to your computer.

 WARNING Even more worrisome, hackers have written and distributed over the Internet programs that can decode the encyrpted Windows password files and automatically send them out in an e-mail message. While Microsoft periodically releases patches that, to varying degrees, repair these weaknesses, new ones continue to crop up from time to time.

Windows NT, which appears similar to Windows 98 on the surface but is entirely different underneath, stops this problem by refusing to operate until a user has successfully logged on. Windows 2000 also has much better password security than the versions of Windows that have descended to us from DOS. Unless you're using Windows 2000 or Windows NT—or perhaps Linux, which has even better security—it's important to remember that your Windows password protection is not truly watertight.

NOTE For more on security issues with Windows, see Microsoft's site on security at www.microsoft.com/security.

Using Passwords Effectively

Things You Should Never Do With A Password

Never is a long time, but here are things that, at the very least, you should try to never do with your password:

1. Never give your password to anyone else. This simple rule will help you control your password more than almost anything.

2. Never e-mail your password, even if it's in a letter to yourself. E-mail is insecure, and may expose your password to prying eyes.

3. Never write down your password where anyone else could find it. This especially includes a yellow sticky note on the side of your computer monitor.

4. Never use the same password twice. Instead, choose something completely different from your previous password.

There are exceptions to these rules. If the password is the one you use to log on to your Square Dancer's Joke of the Week newsletter subscription, it's probably okay to use something you've used before. But when it comes to the security of your network, don't do anything foolish.

Using Firewalls

A fireplace is one location where you definitely want to maintain separation between two areas. To keep your house from catching fire every time you want to snuggle down in front of a cheery blaze, builders use fireproof walls separating the area where combustion occurs from the area where the people are. Similarly, computer networks are protected from intruders by systems called *firewalls*. In a networking sense, a firewall is a system of hardware and software or, sometimes, software alone, that is designed to keep unauthorized users from accessing a network. They work by requiring all the messages going to or from your network to pass through the firewall. The firewall checks each message against specified security criteria, and blocks any that don't measure up. Figure 20.6 shows a dedicated PC acting as a secure server.

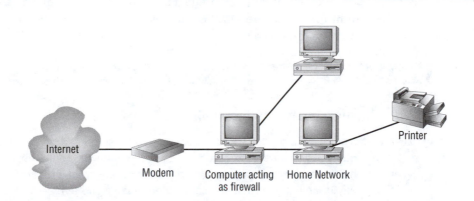

PART

V

Networking Housework

FIGURE 20.6

A firewall sits between you and the Internet, filtering incoming and outgoing messages to make sure they are from authenticated users.

 TIP Want to see if your computer is vulnerable to hackers? You can by checking it against Port Probe, a free Web-based service from Gibson Research Corporation. Learn more by going to www.grc.com and clicking the Shields Up! button.

Many networks use for a firewall a regular PC that is loaded with firewall software, or has certain security features of its operating system running. You can also purchase inexpensive hardware devices that do the same job as a PC dedicated for firewall work. Here are some firewall programs suitable for home networks:

- ConSeal Private Desktop from Signal9 in Ontario, Canada, costs only $49.95 and offers solid protection for Windows 95/98 machines. One drawback is that it can be tricky to configure properly. You can learn more, including downloading a trial version, at www.signal9.com.

- Sybergen Secure Desktop from Sybergen Networks in Fremont, California, offers truly inexpensive protection for Windows users at $29.95, at the expense of some loss of flexibility. You can learn more, including downloading a trial version, at www.sybergen.com.

- Norton Internet Security 2000 is a do-everything firewall program from the major software publisher Symantec. You can learn more, and purchase a downloadable version—but no trial—at www.symantec.com.

- BlackICE Defender from Network ICE Incoporated, of San Mateo, California, is exceptionally easy to use and runs on Windows 95/98 and Windows NT machines. For $39.95, you get the product and a year's worth of technical support, product enhancements, upgrades, bug fixes, patches, and security updates. Additional years are $19.95. There is no trial version. You can learn more at www.networkice.com.

A Simple Hardware Firewall

One effective way to protect your network is to use a simple hardware firewall that will not allow any network traffic to occur while you're connected to the outside world. This approach prevents anyone coming in on a modem connection from accessing your LAN by basically disabling your network connection while a modem session is in progress. The network connection is automatically re-established when you are finished using the modem. The Mini Firewall from Computer Peripheral Systems Incorporated, of Tucker, Georgia, accomplishes this task by using mechanical relays that are difficult for computer hackers to overcome. Although it may be inconvenient to be unable to use the modem and network at the same time, the price—$85.00—is low compared to other firewall solutions. You can learn more at `www.cpscom.com/gprod/firewall.htm`.

Privacy

Your essential data is not the only thing at risk via the Internet connection hooking your network up to the rest of the world. Most people have quite a few personal details of information that, while it may not actually be harmful to let them leak out, would be uncomfortable, inconvenient, or embarrassing. After you've used your computer for a while, you're liable to have all sorts of information in it, in the form of financial transactions, appointment schedules, personal letters and copies of e-mail messages. Once you hook your computer up to a network, this information becomes vulnerable just the same as any other data on a network computer.

Think you don't have any secrets? These potentially troublesome details may include:

- The information that an Internet user is a child or other vulnerable person.

- The results of medical tests that, if known, might result in discrimination or other harm against you.

- Your buying patterns as a consumer, which could help businesses target you for potentially unwelcome advertising.

- Your financial information, which could be used to identify you as a promising victim for criminals.

- Your peace of mind, which could be disturbed by privacy developments beyond anything we've currently run across. Who could have guessed that someday we would all commonly use a form of mail (electronic mail) in which the letters could be freely read by any number of strangers?

Clearly, there's more here to worry about than some *unsolicited commercial e-mail* or UCE. The first thing to do to address these worries is to make sure your network is secure from hackers, as described in the previous section in this chapter. But since a major source of information leakage is from data you voluntarily or unknowing supply to seemingly reputable organizations, such as the businesses you buy from online, it's also important to look at some other solutions.

The first thing to do is to make sure you do business only with reputable online firms that have publicly posted privacy policies. Be suspicious if a firm doesn't have a description of what it intends to do with the information that it gathers anywhere on its Web site. And you might be amazed at the amount of information a Web site can gather based on a simple transaction. Web site activity logs gather information about the pages you have viewed, the purchases you have made, how you are paying for them, and more. Marketers are willing to pay good money for such details because they help them identify promising prospects. Some people, such as opt-in electronic newsletter publishers, operate their sites primarily to gather and sell marketing fodder. If a Web site operator doesn't explicitly say they won't sell your information, assume they will. And, if privacy is important to you, be prepared to patronize another merchant.

You should also pay attention to what the privacy policy says. A good one will:

- State what information about you is being collected.

- Explain how that personal data is being collected.

- Describe the purpose of the collection.

- Say what use that information will be put to.

- Tell what other organizations that personal data will be shared with.

- Explain where the personal data is stored and how it is being protected.

- Describe any standards that the information-gathering effort adheres to.

- Offer you the opportunity to review that information.

- Give you the chance to opt out of any information-gathering that is going on.

It's important to check policies even if you're not aware of volunteering any information. The simple act of viewing a Web site—without even making a purchase—can reveal an astonishing amount of information about you, from your name to your e-mail address and even the name of the city and neighborhood where you live. To see an example of this, point your browser to `www.anonymizer.com` and try out the free privacy analysis of your Web browser. You may be surprised by the amount of information about yourself and your household you are giving away just by using the Web.

What can you do to protect privacy, other than check for good policies? The source for some of this information is the Internet address of your computer or the proxy through which your Internet traffic may go. There's not much you can do to conceal that. However, you can conceal a number of the more personal details, such as the user name you are using on a Windows computer, by employing the unbinding procedures described in the previous section in this chapter, "Protecting against Hackers."

Protecting Electronic Mail

One of the problems with electronic mail sent through the Internet is that it is vulnerable to being intercepted and read by other people. While you, personally, can't change the technology underlying the Internet, you can encrypt or encode your e-mail messages so that they can't be read by anyone except the person they are intended for.

Pretty Good Privacy, or PGP, is the world's most popular e-mail encryption software. It was written in 1991 by a programmer named Phil Zimmermann. PGP works by letting you send encrypted or scrambled messages that can only be descrambled by a person who has the appropriate key. *A key*, in this case, is a string of characters that can allow the possessor and only the possessor to read your message. So, if your e-mail was intercepted in transmission, or a nosy administrator tries to take a peek, it will appear to them as nothing more than a bunch of junk. To make the use of keys more convenient, people can use public key registration sites.

PGP is an effective code-making program. It's so effective, in fact, that the US government bans the use of some of its encoding possibilities. Thus, there are US-approved versions of PGP (as well as other privacy encryption programs) and others for sale to users outside the U.S. You can learn more about PGP from the Web site of the distributor of the U.S. versions, PGP Security Inc., at `www.pgp.com`.

Using Parental Controls

If you can't make your computer work, find a kid. That wisecrack—which many an adult frustrated with a PC problem has probably heard before—carries more than a little truth. Today's children are growing up with the Internet, computers, and computer networks, and they are likely to far outstrip their parents in their abilities to use these powerful technologies. But kid's mastery of network is more than a matter of opportunity. The Internet and networked computers are highly appealing to children. Children can use networks to:

- Find out what's happening in places as close as the downstairs game room and as far away as the other side of the world.

- Study distant or vanishing cultures that they might otherwise never get the opportunity to experience.

- Complete homework research assignments efficiently and effectively.

- Find new peers to associate with through chat rooms and child-centered Web portals.

- Make friends.

- Stay up on news and information of special interest to children, from sites devoted to popular television cartoons to samples of the latest song from a currently popular musical group.

- Play games of many varieties.

- Stay in touch with friends and family members by e-mail.

Clearly, network computers can be powerful forces for helping children learn and experience the world in many new and positive ways.

However, the news is not all good. There are also a lot of things on the Internet that few parents or anyone else setting up a home network would want children exposed to. These include:

- Pornographic Web sites with explicit sexual content.

- Chat rooms populated by adults frankly discussing material inappropriate for children.

- Sexual criminals who may cruise the Net searching for children to befriend.

WARNING You don't have to use the Internet for long before you are likely to stumble across highly offensive material. For instance, when searching for "fun sites for young children" you may be directed to Web pages catering to pedophiles. A search for "Bond"—as in James Bond—may produce sites devoted to bondage. Simply clicking on a harmless-looking link in an innocuous e-mail message purporting to be from an acquaintance suggesting you "Take a look at this!" may lead the unguarded surfer into a maze of X-rated sites. These sites can even directly, and without warning, download pornographic images to a hard drive. And the sites often refuse to go away, no matter many times you click the "back" button on your browser or try to close a window.

- Offensive e-mail messages.
- Marketing campaigns targeted toward minor children.

Harm might not only come to your children who use the Internet, but harm to your network can also come from your children who use the Internet. On a purely practical level, when a relatively naive juvenile is using a networked computer to access the Internet, your network may be more at risk of becoming infected with a virus.

 NOTE You could conceivably go overboard in limiting children's use of computers. It's one thing to watch and control a child's use of the network and the Internet, and quite another to choke it off altogether. Before you take too draconian a stance, keep in mind that technology skills are crucial to children's future success, that most new jobs being created in today's economy require technology skills, and that people who use computers on the job tend to earn more than workers who don't.

Software to Limit Web Access

Networked computers raise issues about protecting children, but they also provide some answers, notably in the form of software to restrict or monitor young people's access to potentially objectionable Web sites, chat rooms, newsgroups, and other online communities. There are six basic approaches to using technology to improve the appropriateness of children's use of the Web. They are:

Suggest There are many Web sites, books, directories, guides, and pamphlets that offer lists of sources of child-suitable content. One example is the Internet Kids & Family Yellow Pages, at www.netmom.com/ikyp.

Search   You can use Internet search engines to find content suitable for children. Many engines let you filter your queries to show only those matches that are appropriate for children. AltaVista, at www.altavista.com, has a Family Filter feature that you can set and control with the use of a password.

Inform   You can encourage your children to use Web site ratings, reviews, and other tools to steer them toward appropriate content.

Monitor   Some programs save a log file of surfing activities. Cyber Snoop logs all Internet activity while a child is online. You can inspect the log file later to see what the child has been up to.

Warn   Rating services such as Cyber Sitter, www.cybersitter.com, can give children advance warning about pages and sites they should avoid. Many adult-oriented sites also show a warning about their content on the first page. This approach helps kids decide on their own whether to view possibly objectionable content.

NOTE   The Recreational Software Advisory Council rating service, upon which Internet Explorer bases its ratings, is an independent, non-profit organization that rates sites by the level of sex, nudity, violence, offensive language in computer games and sites.

Block   Technology can simply keep children from getting to the stuff you think they shouldn't see. The Internet Explorer browser filter, for instance, can screen out content based on a set of criteria chosen by the parent. You can also block out all chat rooms, e-mail, newsgroups, and other content off the Web.

By mixing and matching these methods, you can find the most suitable means for protecting your children. Which methods you choose will depend largely on the age, maturity, and inquisitiveness of your children.

Software for Web Blocking

There are a number of programs you can use to block out Net content. Two of the more popular are Net Nanny and SurfWatch. Here are capsule reviews of each:

Net Nanny

Net Nanny, as shown in Figure 20.7, is an easy-to-use but powerful Internet content filtering and blocking program. It lets a parent set up a customizable screening list. You can build upon the preset list of Web sites, words and phrases, and other criteria it provides.

PART

V

Networking
Housework

As is appropriate for software of this type, Net Nanny allows for extensive customization. You can:

- Block any words, phrases, Web sites including html code, *Internet Relay Chat* (IRC) rooms, newsgroups, and personal information per values you select.

- Limit access to only sites you place on a list of acceptable sites.

- Monitor transmission of personal information, including children's names, ages, addresses, phone numbers, credit card numbers, and Social Security numbers.

- Select several actions when a surfing violation occurs, ranging from simply logging the violation to issuing a warning and refusing to access the site, as shown in Figure 20.8.

PART

V

Networking
Housework

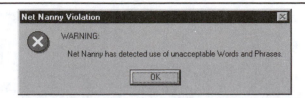

FIGURE 20.8

*Net Nanny will refuse
to allow access to sites
containing words or
phrases deemed
unsuitable.*

Net Nanny software, for Windows 95/98 and Windows 3.1 computers, costs $26.95 for a one-computer license when purchased online. You can learn more, as well as download a trial version, at www.netnanny.com.

SurfWatch

SurfWatch employs a team of professional Net surfers to rate Web sites and update filters for the sites it considers objectionable. Its software lets you use this constantly refreshed database to block unsuitable content, as shown in Figure 20.9.

FIGURE 20.9

*SurfWatch refuses
access to sites rated
unsuitable by its team
of Web analysts, based
on criteria you select.*

SurfWatch uses a basic setup starting with five categories of potentially objectionable content. As shown in Figure 20.10, you select any or all of the categories with a mouse click. You can also add your own filtering based on custom words you create.

FIGURE 20.10

SurfWatch's main screen lets you opt in or out of specific categories of Internet content with a mouse click.

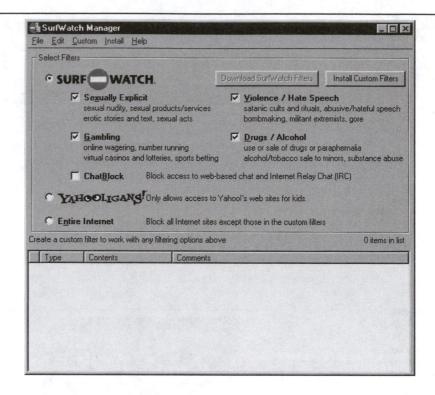

Additional features of SurfWatch include letting you:

- Block access to a list of more than 100,000 Internet sites with content in categories including pornography, violence, hate speech, gambling, and use of illegal drugs, alcohol, and tobacco.

 TIP It seems that youngsters aren't the only ones who need monitoring. The version of SurfWatch for servers running Windows NT also has Productivity filtering for 15 categories of Internet content that may not be bad for you, but can be for your work. They include astrology and mysticism, entertainment, games, general news, glamour and intimate apparel, hobbies, investments, job search, motor vehicles, personals and dating, real estate, shopping, sports, travel, and Usenet news.

- Create custom filters of your choice.
- Update filters daily from the SurfWatch database.

NOTE   While SurfWatch has a number of powerful features, it does not provide tools for logging Web activity, reflecting the company's stance that monitoring is not an appropriate tool.

- Block access to chat sites and Internet Relay Chat servers.
- Restrict access only to sites approved by the Yahooligans! Rating service.

SurfWatch is available in versions for Windows 95/98, Windows NT and Macintosh machines. Version 3.0 for Windows 98 costs $49.95. You can learn more, as well as download trial versions, at `www.surfwatch.com`.

 WARNING   It's important to remember that no filtering system is perfect. SurfWatch estimates that filtering will block no more than 95 percent of the objectionable content that may be out there.

Controlling Online Time

Since technology creates the problem of protecting children on the Internet, it's only fair that technology should provide some of the solution. But protecting children isn't all a matter of technology. There are also a number of personal practices that you can implement to make sure that children using the Internet over your home network will have the kind of experience you want them to have. To ensure this, you should also:

- Make clear rules about how your children can use the network and the Internet. These should include hours of use, places that can be visited, and activities that can be performed.
- Place children's networked computers where they can be seen, such as in a family room or kitchen.

 TIP   There's no hard and fast rule about how much time your child should spend in front of a computer screen, using your local network or the Internet. However, many experts suggest combining computer use with television viewing to create a "screen time" figure of hours or minutes per day that you are comfortable with.

- Make the Internet a family affair. Spend time surfing with your child to monitor their behavior and set standards in person.
- Know and use high-quality family-oriented Web sites, such as Yahoo's www.yahooligans.com.

 TIP You can learn more about aspects of managing children's use of the Internet and networked computers from America Links Up at www.americalinksup.org.

- Insist on knowing the e-mail passwords your child uses, and monitor the e-mail they send and receive.

 TIP With a home network, you can check kid's e-mail from another computer on the network if passwords and sharing privileges are set up to allow you access to the child's computer. To learn how to do this, see Chapter 17, "Setting Up Shared Resources."

- Look closely for unsolicited e-mail that may be from persons who intend to harm or exploit your child.
- Instruct your child never to meet alone with an acquaintance made online.
- Tell your children not to release certain personal information online. This includes phone numbers, addresses, ages, school names, and financial information.
- Be a friend, not a foe, so that your children know they can come to you with any questions, problems, or concerns.

 TIP Another reason not to place too much trust in technological solutions to parental concerns is that computers aren't just in the home anymore. Most schools and public libraries have both computers and, increasingly, Internet access. You can't be on hand to oversee your child in these venues. And free speech issues make it difficult for libraries to restrict the use of their computers to access anything a user cares to. So you should probably view home networks as an opportunity to teach good computer use practices, so children will be more likely to demonstrate good judgment when no one is around to watch.

Summary

Viruses. Hackers. Thieves. Pornographers. Marketers. It's a rough cyberspace out there. Fortunately, you can protect yourself—and your children—with antivirus software, passwords, firewalls, encrypted codes, and Web blocking.

What's Next

You've chosen your network, set up your network, configured your network, and protected it from invasions of privacy. But home networks, like any other human construction, occasionally break down. Diagnosing and fixing common network problems is the subject of the next chapter.

PART

V

Networking
Housework

CHAPTER 21

Troubleshooting

Overview

Nothing is perfect, and your network is no exception. Sooner or later, and probably the former, it will stop working properly. How soon this will happen varies widely. Businesses expect their critical networks to be up about 99.98 percent of the time. Another way to look at this is that the Mean Time Between Failure (MTBF)—a term that indicates how long a computer or computer component will last before its estimated failure of a mission-critical network is about 4,000 hours or 166.66 days. Not too many home networks are going to stay up this long, unfortunately. One reason is that consumer operating systems such as Windows 98 are not as sturdy as those that businesses rely on. A pretty decent Windows MTBF record may be a few weeks, although all that may be required to get a frozen workstation or server up is a simple reboot. Linux is one exception to this rule, however. Linux network servers not uncommonly run continuously for a year or more without requiring repairs or even rebooting.

 NOTE In addition to MTBF or Mean Time Between Failure, another stat to keep in mind is MTTR, or Mean Time To Repair. Administrators of critical business networks might set a goal of one hour to fix an average problem. Yours might take more, or less time, depending on the problem, and your skill and persistence.

Preventive Measures

Networks break for a lot of reasons. Here are a few, along with tips for preventing your computers from succumbing unnecessarily:

Heat Monitors, disk drives, and CPU chips all put out substantial volumes of heat. If a network adapter card—or just about any other component in your computer—gets too much of this heat, it expands. Over time, that can cause integrated circuit chips to pop loose and stop working. Don't stack your computer components or keep them in that nook with Southern exposure. Also, although those of you who are budget conscious might not want to turn on air conditioning when you're sweltering in the summer's heat, you should do what you can to keep your computer cool.

TIP If you suspect a network adapter or other printed circuit board of failure, before ordering a new one, try pressing all the integrated circuit chips on the board down into their sockets. Over time, thanks to corrosion and the phenomenon known as chip creep, in which the chips work their way out of their sockets, they may lose contact with the socket. A gentle push can correct the problem.

Dust A buildup of dust can interfere with airflow from a fan, creating damaging pockets of heat that can cause your computer or network to fail sporadically or completely. In addition, dust can short out circuits. Keep computers clean and cool by making sure all adapter card endplates are installed and vents are clear.

Electromagnetic interference Noise and crosstalk can come from a variety of sources, including other network traffic and poorly insulated electric appliances such as television sets. If a hub, computer, or other device suddenly stops working when you switch on a nearby lamp, suspect interference and move the appliance or the cable away until the interference stops.

Static electricity A spark that you can barely feel can easily blast holes in electronic circuits that are less than a thousandth of an inch wide. That's why you should handle NICs and other circuit boards only by their edges and always ground yourself by touching metal before working on the insides of your computer.

Stopping Static

You can generate a static electric discharge of 1,000 volts by merely lifting your foot. Computer components, meanwhile, can be ruined by a 30-volt spark. What's particularly tricky is that static damage usually doesn't cause immediate failure, but will, over time, create intermittent breakdowns that can be maddeningly difficult to fix. You can ease your networking life by following these rules:

- Always turn off the power when you work on the inside of your PC.
- Use the wall outlet cover plate as a grounding point for added safety when you remove the power cord from your PC.
- Use a wrist strap or a static mat when working on computer parts.
- Don't let anyone come up and touch you when you are working on a PC.

Continued

CONTINUED

- Never touch the electrical leads on integrated circuit chips.
- Use static-shielding bags to carry and store circuit boards, disk drives, and other parts.
- Never place a circuit board, chip, or other part on a metal or other conducting surface.

Static problems are much more likely to occur when humidity is low. So, if you're really serious about untracking static electricity, you should see that the humidity in your home is kept at 50 percent to 70 percent when you are working on electronic components. Or, you could just avoid attempting repairs on those cloudless, cold days when conditions are best for static discharges.

Computer viruses   Malicious programs that aim to infect, destroy, corrupt, steal, or otherwise damage your computer data or system can bring down a network in a hurry. Conscientious use of antivirus software will help minimize this risk.

 NOTE   See Chapter 20, "Network Security," to learn how to protect yourself from computer viruses.

Human error   This is the biggie. Whether we're talking about somebody driving a nail into a network cable while trying to hang a picture, or a user forgetting their password, simple mistakes are the cause of most network problems. Patience, training, and tact are the answers here.

To go with these known risks are the mysterious problems ascribed to gremlins or bugs. Everybody who has used computers much has experienced the odd system hangup or crash that occurs once and never or rarely again, seemingly without any cause. You shouldn't assume that just any network failure is one of these non-repairable bugs—odds are that you can get and keep your network running on your own or with a little help—but it's also a good idea to remember that no network is perfect. There is always a little unscheduled downtime.

Diagnosing Problems

Troubleshooting your network is the process you will go through whenever a problem crops up, such as a workstation suddenly can't connect to the network. Although troubleshooting can be a frustrating, time-consuming experience, there are quite a few tricks to ease the job. And there's nothing that satisfies in quite the same way as the feeling you get when the Windows' Network Neighborhood network browser starts showing all your networked computers, or a formerly lifeless network printer starts spitting out documents. It starts with accurately diagnosing the problem.

Diagnosis is most of the cure when it comes to network problems. If you can figure out precisely what's wrong, you are well on the way to fixing the network. The first thing to do when you have a network problem is to make sure you actually have a problem. Or, to put it another way, make sure the problem is the network, not a user.

Human factors, also known as *operator error*, are easily among the primary causes of network difficulties. It's more likely that users who complain of not being able to log on have forgotten their passwords or are mistyping, rather than that the password file has inexplicably disappeared or been corrupted. When somebody reports a network problem to you, look first at human factors. This will often require some diplomatic skill and effort at exercising your tact. But it's worth it. Network users who are willing to come to you to report trouble are less likely to make the problem worse by trying to fix it on their own. Keep this in mind when you're questioning someone about a reported network difficulty.

 NOTE The importance of human factors applies to network administrators as well. Anytime you are having a network problem, ask yourself seriously whether it's a mistake you are making, such as letting the printer run out of paper, or whether there is truly something wrong.

Once you've verified that there is a problem, it's time to gather information. Grab a piece of paper—don't try to remember all the information you'll need—and jot down the following:

- A general statement of the problem, such as: "Mom's PC can't connect to the Internet anymore."

- Any error messages that appear when the problem reveals itself.

TIP Verbatim transcriptions of error messages, down to the exact filenames or memory addresses reported in the error, are enormously helpful when using online troubleshooting databases. Often, you can search for the exact error message in such a database, and be rewarded with a help file addressing your specific problem.

- Any ideas you might have about what could be wrong and how to fix it, such as: "Probably that loose connector in the attic again."

After you've identified the problem, you are ready to locate the solution. Take the following steps and you're on your way to being a true network administrator:

TIP When you're deciding how to proceed to remedy a network problem, go for the quick fix first. Anything you can attempt with a few keystrokes gets first try. Wait until you are out of options before you decide to order a new part or ship something off for repair.

1. Check with the experts. There are many resources available for people experiencing network problems. These may range from a savvy neighbor to a friendly technician at your local computer store. Online resources are among the most powerful and useful. These will be discussed more in the "Calling For Help" section later in this chapter.

2. Try to isolate the problem. This may mean testing a network printer from other computers on the network to see if it refuses to work with all of them or only one. Or, it might mean swapping suspect network cables or adapter cards with known good units, to narrow down the problem to a specific part.

TIP The most valuable piece of troubleshooting advice you could get is: Take notes. Computers and networks are complicated systems. If you try to remember what happened when you tried one solution and how that affected something else, you will quickly get lost. Odds are, you will wind up making things worse. If you take notes, on the other hand, you will not only find it much easier to zero in on the problem and likely solution, you will have something to refer to in the event that a similar problem crops up some day.

3. Do the repair. Once again, it's important to write down exactly what you are doing, as well as the result, including any new error messages. This will allow

you to put things back the way they were, in case it still doesn't work. It will also keep you from trying things that you already experimented with unsuccessfully.

4. Make sure it's really fixed. After you've found a fix that seems to work, try to make the problem happen again. Print the same document to the same printer or try to access the same shared disk. Verifying the repair will keep you from dragging your tools and manuals out again to work on something you thought was already fixed.

Ping

Ping is a venerable network testing utility that sends a small chunk of data—32 bytes, to be precise—to another computer on the Internet. The other computer then responds to the message. Ping has several uses. With Ping:

- You can tell whether a computer is connected to the network and turned on by whether it responds to the ping.

- You can see how good your connection is between computers by measuring the time between the sending and receiving of the ping—the ping time.

- You can check the quality of your connection by seeing how many, if any, packets of data are lost in transit.

 TIP Since Ping only works with Internet Protocol addresses, you'll need to have the TCP/IP protocol installed to use it. If TCP/IP is installed and Ping does not work, you should reinstall TCP/IP.

If you can ping a computer successfully, odds are you can connect to it via the Internet. Here's how to use Ping:

1. Click Start ➤ Programs ➤ MS-DOS Prompt.

2. At the MS-DOS prompt type "ping hostname" and press Enter, where *hostname* is the name of a host computer. In Figure 21.1, for example, it's `ftp.cdrom.com`.

```
MS-DOS Prompt                                                    _ □ ×
Auto    ▼    □ 🗎🗎    ⊠    🗂🗐    A

C:\WINDOWS>ping ftp.cdrom.com

Pinging wcarchive.cdrom.com [209.155.82.18] with 32 bytes of data:

Reply from 209.155.82.18: bytes=32 time=94ms TTL=241
Reply from 209.155.82.18: bytes=32 time=100ms TTL=241
Reply from 209.155.82.18: bytes=32 time=121ms TTL=241
Reply from 209.155.82.18: bytes=32 time=109ms TTL=241

Ping statistics for 209.155.82.18:
    Packets: Sent = 4, Received = 4, Lost = 0 (0% loss),
Approximate round trip times in milli-seconds:
    Minimum = 94ms, Maximum =  121ms, Average =  106ms

C:\WINDOWS>
```

3. You should get a screen displaying the output of Ping, as in Figure 21.1. This information includes the IP address of the server you pinged, and various statistics including the time in milliseconds (ms) it took for a reply to be received.

 NOTE   Four pings, generating four responses, is the default setting for the Windows version of the Ping command. The first ping may take longer than subsequent pings. The size of the ping time may range from 500 or more milliseconds for a connection through a 28.8Kpbs modem down to as little as 1ms if you are hooked to the Internet backbone through a speedy T-3 line.

Any ping time at all indicates at least that you are connected to the Internet and things are working properly.

Ping also generates error messages when something goes wrong:

• "Unknown host" probably means you typed in the hostname incorrectly. It may also mean that the host you're trying to ping does not exist on the Internet.

 NOTE   To protect against hackers, who have been known to overload Web sites by flooding them with pings, an increasing number of Web sites will not respond to a Ping command. You may have to try a number of sites before you can find one that will respond. It's a good idea to write down the IP addresses of any responsive sites you find. That way, you'll have some known responders to use when testing with Ping in the future.

- "Request timed out" means the computer you pinged didn't reply or took so long to do it that Ping gave up waiting. It may mean there is a problem with the host's connection, or that it is behind a router or firewall that blocks ping commands.

You can use Ping to check whether you have a good connection to the Internet as well. Inability to get a good ping from a host that you have been able to ping successfully in the past may indicate you have a bad cable, loose connection, or other problem between you and your modem.

 NOTE Ping has been around a long time and is available for many different operating systems, including Macintosh, Unix, Linux and all versions of Windows. There are also a number of add-ons and elaborations to the standard ping utility. Windows CyberKit, for example, is a network utility for Windows machines that combines Ping and several other tools in a graphical user interface. You can learn more at www.cyberkit.net.

Using Ping, you can also test an internal networked computer—if your system is using the TCP/IP protocol. Follow these steps:

1. At the computer you suspect of causing the communication failure, type **WINIPCFG** at the MS-DOS command prompt, and hit Enter.

2. You will see a dialog box with an Adapter drop-down list. Check to see that the Network Adapter card is selected. Record the IP Address listed in the center of the dialog box.

3. Next, go to any other computer on your internal network and ping the address you just recorded.

If the ping works, you know that both computers can communicate with each other and the suspected problem is elsewhere. To pinpoint the trouble spot, try pinging the recorded address from different locations on your network.

Printing a System Summary Report

One of the most valuable tools you can have for any troubleshooting session is a printed list of all the devices, resources, and settings for the computer on which you are working. Fortunately, Windows 98 has a way to generate one of these almost automatically. Here's how:

1. Click Start ➤ Settings ➤ Control Panel.

2. Select the System icon in Control Panel and press Enter or double-click.

3. In the System Properties window, as shown in Figure. 21.2, click the Device Manager tab.

4. Click Print and, when the Print dialog box is displayed, click the radio button next to All Devices and System Summary, as shown in Figure 21.3.

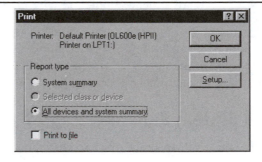

5. Click OK.

FIGURE 21.4

A System Summary printout provides lots of helpful information when troubleshooting network problems.

```
******************** IRQ SUMMARY ********************

IRQ Usage Summary:
  00 - System timer
  01 - Standard 101/102-Key or Microsoft Natural Keyboard
  02 - Programmable interrupt controller
  03 - IRQ Holder for PCI Steering
  03 - CMI8338/C3DX PCI Audio Device
  04 - Communications Port (COM1)
  05 - CMI8338/C3DX PCI Audio Legacy Device
  06 - Standard Floppy Disk Controller
  07 - Printer Port (LPT1)
  08 - System CMOS/real time clock
  09 - SiS 7001 PCI to USB Open Host Controller
  09 - IRQ Holder for PCI Steering
  10 - IRQ Holder for PCI Steering
  10 - NETGEAR FA310TX Fast Ethernet PCI Adapter
  11 - Lucent v.90 Modem
  11 - IRQ Holder for PCI Steering
  12 - PS/2 Compatible Mouse Port
  13 - Numeric data processor
  14 - SiS 5513 Dual PCI IDE Controller
  14 - Primary IDE controller (dual fifo)
  15 - Secondary IDE controller (dual fifo)
  15 - SiS 5513 Dual PCI IDE Controller
```

The resulting printout will provide you with a considerable amount of information about how your system is set up. In addition to the IRQ assignments summary shown in Figure 21.4, this includes the following:

- An I/O port summary showing how various input/output devices—such as the network adapter, modem, keyboard, printer port, etcetera—are using memory addresses.

- An upper memory usage summary showing how devices such as the motherboard and network adapter are using upper memory.

- A DMA usage summary showing how direct memory access channels are allocated to floppy disk controllers, audio cards, and the like.

- A memory summary showing how much extended memory the system has in addition to the 640KB conventional memory.

- Information about your floppy drive, hard disk drive, and CD-ROM, including the capacity, number of cylinders, and heads, sector, and track information.

- Information including drivers, manufacturer name, and IRQ settings for all the devices attached to the system, including Universal Serial Bus controllers, scanners, COM ports, printers network adapters, and modems.

The system summary printout tells you your current status; it doesn't tell you what to do or how to do it. Check your card's manual for details on appropriate IRQs and other settings, as well as instructions on how to change them. You may need to physically change jumper settings on the card's printed circuit board, or you may be able to alter these settings using software provided with the card. Most newer cards are software-configurable, meaning you won't have to open your computer's case or monkey with jumper switches to change settings.

Troubleshooting with NIC LEDs

Many network interface cards have one or more lights, called *light emitting diodes*, or LEDs, on the back that indicate the card's status. Those little lights provide helpful information when you're trying to troubleshoot a network problem. They may indicate:

- The speed of the connection
- Whether the connection is a two-way or duplex connection
- Whether there is any connection at all

Figure 21.5 shows a typical card with three LEDs indicating network speed and duplex status. Reading these LEDs is generally easy. They may be on, off or, in some cases, blinking. Some LEDs may show different colors, as in green for a good connection and yellow for not-so-good. The documentation that comes with the NIC explains the exact condition of each LED when the network is working properly. Checking your NIC's LEDs can help you rule out hardware trouble, or indicate that a card or connector has failed.

FIGURE 21.5

You can learn a lot about whether and how well your network interface card is working by checking the LED lights on the back of the adapter.

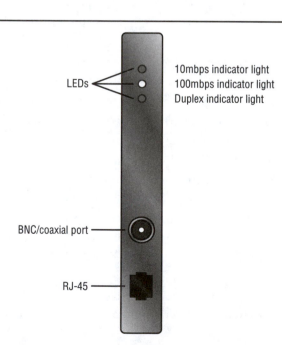

LEDs

10mbps indicator light
100mbps indicator light
Duplex indicator light

BNC/coaxial port

RJ-45

TIP Before network adapter LEDs can help with troubleshooting, the adapter has to be connected to the network and you must have network drivers installed.

Identifying Common Problems

Of all the things that can go wrong with a network, a relatively small number of troubles make up most of the actual instances of failure. Here are some of the most common problems that you're likely to face, along with diagnoses:

- A computer that is supposed to be connected to the network doesn't show up in Windows' Network Neighborhood. This is more commonly due to a problem in the software configuration of the network connection or, less commonly, to an unplugged connector or faulty cable.

- You can't access shared hard drives on another computer on the network. The most likely cause of this problem is that you don't have file sharing set up properly in your network configuration.

- You can't print to a network printer from one or more workstations on the network. Probably, you have incorrectly set up printer sharing in your network configuration.

- You can't connect to the Internet from one or more of the computers on the network. You don't have TCP/IP set up properly in the network configuration, or the modem has become unplugged from the network.

These common problems and others typically fall into one of the following categories:

- Hardware trouble, caused by a faulty network adapter card, a damaged cable, or a loose connection.

- Software configuration error, caused by a mistake in configuring your network, such as failing to set up Microsoft file- and print-sharing on a computer with a hard drive that you want to be able to access from elsewhere on the network.

Connectors

Networks aren't anywhere without connections and, unfortunately, connectors are prime sources of trouble. That's especially true if you're using coaxial cable, since BNC connectors are somewhat trickier to install correctly than the RJ-45 connectors used with Category 5 cables. However, an inadvertent push down on the plastic spring that holds in RJ-45 connectors can result in these becoming loose enough to cause trouble, as well.

One of the things that makes connector problems maddening is that they often crop up only occasionally when, for instance, a slightly loose connector gets bumped, a cable receives a slight pull, or even normal heating and cooling causes the connector or cable to expand or contract slightly. Here are things to check if you suspect a cable problem:

- Check to make sure connectors are inserted firmly into the network adapter cards on the back of your networked PCs. These may be exposed to bumps while installing peripherals or cleaning behind the PCs. If the plastic spring that holds in RJ-45 connectors is damaged or broken, replace the RJ-45 connector or the cable itself.

- Check your hub to make sure the connectors are fully inserted into it as well. Hubs may be located in closets or other out-of-the-way places where a loose connection doesn't get noticed. Also, check to see that the power source to the hub is unobstructed.

- If you're using coaxial cable, make sure the terminators are properly installed at both ends of the cable, and only one terminator end is grounded.

- Also if you're using coaxial, check the crossbars of T-connectors for tightness and straightness.

 TIP If you're using a phoneline network, double-check any duplex jacks or splitters you are using to connect two cables into one line. These are subject to being pulled loose if someone picks up a telephone connected to one of the lines. They also tend to be too heavy or bulky to easily insert in a proper manner. That's especially true when a splitter is plugged into close confines at the back of a network adapter card.

Cables

Cables used to be a bigger problem than they are now. That's partly because the coaxial cable that formerly was the standard for networking computers is relatively frail compared to the Category 5 cable that is now nearly universal for small networks. An overly sharp bend in the cable or even something as simple as a desk chair rolling over the cable can cause a coax-based network link to go down. Cat 5 media is much sturdier; you can bend it quite sharply and subject it to all sorts of indignities without risking a break in your connection.

There's another reason that diagnosing and fixing problems with cables is easier for most home networkers than it's ever been—easier even than it is for many business network administrators. That's because the star topology, as shown in Figure 21.6, is the most popular physical design for home networks and also the easiest to troubleshoot when it comes to cable problems.

FIGURE 21.6

The star physical network topology makes it relatively easy to find and fix problems with the network cable.

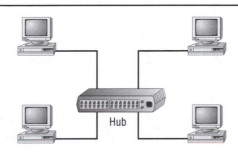

Hub

Isolating cable problems

The great thing about the star topology is that each computer on the network has its own connection to the hub. This greatly simplifies the task of isolating the problem to one cable. If one of the computers on your network suddenly can't connect to the rest, therefore, you should suspect the cable connecting that computer to the hub. Swap out the cable and, if the computer now can connect, you know the problem is in the old cable.

 TIP It's not a bad idea to keep around a spare length of cable long enough to span your longest wiring run so you can perform swap-out tests. You might also want to keep a spare hub so you can swap it out if you suspect a faulty hub. You don't have to buy an expensive spare hub; even a 4-port stripped-down model will suffice for testing.

With coaxial cable, it's much more involved. Since coaxial networks commonly employ the bus physical topology, where all the computers are connected in a line, you can't isolate the problem as easily, as shown in Figure 21.7. If a workstation can't connect, you will need to split the network into equal segments. Then, using a technique called *binary testing*, you'll need to test each half for problems. You can do this by trying to connect to the network using different spans of cable and different PCs that you know are able to connect to the network. After determining which half of the cable is experiencing problems, you may need to split that segment in half and test it as well. This way, you can slowly zero in on the problem segment.

PART

V

Networking
Housework

FIGURE 21.7

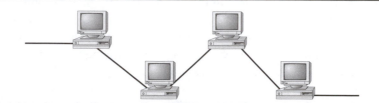

A bus physical topology that connects computers in a line makes it more difficult to troubleshoot cable problems.

Network Testing Tools

If you're really serious about keeping your network up and running, you can outfit yourself with the tools of a professional network troubleshooter.

- A digital voltage meter measures the electrical continuity of a cable. It tells you if the cable has a short in it. You can buy these for $20.00 or so at many hardware and electronics stores. Be sure you get a digital model, however, as the less expensive analog versions emit voltages that could damage computer parts.

- A cable tester is a somewhat more sophisticated device that can check for proper continuity, shorts, and cross wiring, and provide information such as the assignments of pins on a connector. You can get one of these for $75.00 or so.

- A time domain reflectometer measures the way signals reflect from the ends of a network cable. This can tell you how functional a cable is and provide details about the location of cable faults. At around $2,000.00 and up, this is a tool for pros only, however.

- A network analyzer, also called a protocol analyzer, is another tool with a four-figure price tag, used to decode and resolve problems with the various layers in a network protocol.

- Understandably, you may not care to invest thousands of dollars in network testing and repair equipment. However, it's not a bad idea to get an inexpensive computer repair toolkit, available at any computer store, to help you with any necessary fix-it projects. Mid-priced kits, costing from $40.00 to $70.00, typically include such electronic repair necessities as miniature non-magnetized screwdrivers, insulated tweezers, 3-pronged parts retrievers, chip extractors, anti-static wrist bands, parts clamps, and even miniature vacuums with canned compressed air for cleaning.

Repairing cable problems

Fixing a cable problem usually involves simply replacing the unsound piece of cable. This can be tricky, however, if you have a hidden cable run through a wall or attic. Make it easy on yourself by being sure to attach a wire or cord to the cable before you pull it out of the wall or crawlspace. That way, you will probably be able to simply attach the new cable to the cord and pull it back through to complete the installation.

 NOTE In rare instances, you will opt to patch or splice the cable. You may want to do this if, for example, you accidentally cut an exposed section of a cable that would be very difficult to replace in its entirety. As a general rule, however, the best idea is to get a new cable.

Protecting Cables

The best thing you can do with regard to cable problems is keep them from happening in the first place. Protecting cables starts with installing them with an eye to preventing future trouble. Here are a few pointers to keep in mind when running cable to set up your network:

Avoid bending cables sharply.

- Don't stretch cables, and leave a few turns of extra wire in case you want to move your computer later on.

- Be careful not to place cables in locations where they are likely to be damaged later on, for instance, by someone driving a nail to hang a picture.

- Don't run cables over fluorescent light fixtures or across electric motors, as these can create electromagnetic interference.

- Even the best cable installation could eventually experience problems. You can make it easier to repair any trouble that does crop up by trying to install your cable so that cable runs are as accessible as possible. Be particularly vigilant about installing cable where it is likely to be covered up by a construction project later on. Before you floor your attic, for example, reroute any cables that would be covered so you can get to them if you need to.

Troubleshooting Network Adapter Cards

Network adapter problems are usually configuration problems. So, if you think a NIC is causing difficulties, the first thing to do is check in network configuration to see if everything is set up properly. Here's how:

1. Click Start ➤ Settings ➤ Control Panel.

2. Select the Network icon in Control Panel and press Enter or double-click.

3. Check the scrolling list in the Network Configuration window, as shown in Figure 21.8, to see that all the clients, adapters, protocols, and services that should be there are present.

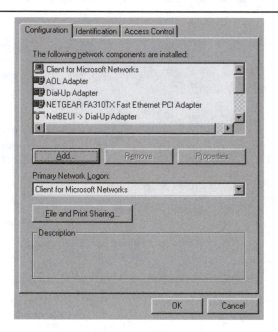

 NOTE As a general rule, at a minimum you should probably have installed Client for Microsoft Networks, an adapter for the NIC in your system, the NetBEUI protocol for that adapter, and the enable File and Print Sharing for Microsoft Networks. See Chapter 1, "Understanding Computer Networks," to learn more about network protocols and related topics.

4. Click OK to close the Network configuration window.

If all the needed items appear to be present, you can try removing and reinstalling the driver for the adapter you suspect of causing trouble. Here's how:

1. Click Start ➢ Settings ➢ Control Panel.

2. Select the Network icon in Control Panel and press Enter or double-click.

3. Select the suspect adapter in the scrolling window in the Network Configuration window, as shown in Figure 21.9, and click the Remove button.

FIGURE 21.9

Remove a suspect adapter preparatory to reinstalling it in the Network Configuration window.

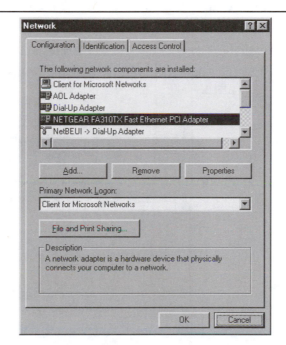

4. Click OK and, when prompted, click OK again to restart Windows.

If your card is a Plug 'n' Play device and you're running Windows 98, you will be prompted to install the driver for it when Windows restarts.

NOTE For more on installing network adapter drivers, see Chapter 6, "Ethernet Networks."

PART

V

Networking Housework

In the event that removing and reinstalling the driver for your adapter doesn't work, you can remove everything but the bare minimum you need to use the card with your network. This means removing all clients, adapters, protocols, and services except for the adapter's driver, the protocol you need to get on the network (usually NetBEUI), and a client service, such as Client for Microsoft Networks. Try using the card with the network again after stripping the system down to the bare minimum network components.

You remove clients, adapters, protocols, and services the same way you removed the adapter driver in this section, using the Remove button in the Network Configuration window. Here's how to reinstall, using the TCP/IP protocol suite as an example:

1. Click Start ➢ Settings ➢ Control Panel.

2. Select the Network icon in Control Panel and press Enter or double-click.

3. Click the Add button in the Network Configuration window, as shown in Figure 21.10.

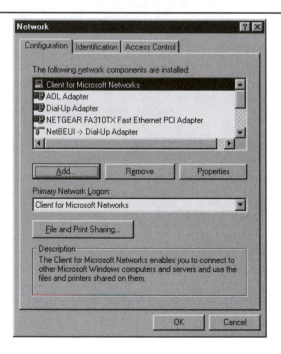

FIGURE 21.10

Click the Add button in Network Configuration to begin adding a client, adapter, protocol, or service.

4. Highlight the network component you want to add, a protocol in this case, as shown in Figure 21.11, and click Add.

FIGURE 21.11

Choose the component you are adding from the list in the Select Network Component Type window and click Add.

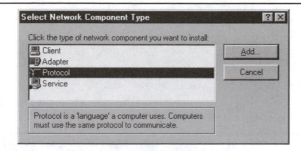

5. Select Microsoft in the Manufacturers list and TCP/IP in the Network Protocols window, as shown in Figure 21.12, and click OK.

FIGURE 21.12

Choose Microsoft in the left window and TCP/IP in the right window and click OK to install the TCP/IP protocol.

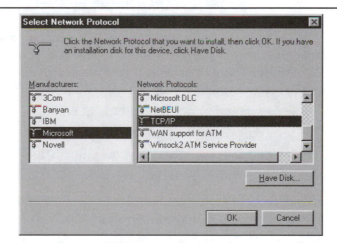

6. Check the Network Configuration window to make sure the component you have added is present, and click OK.

If, after twiddling your network configuration—keeping careful notes of what you are doing and what happens—your network adapter still won't operate properly, you may need to check and change its Interrupt Request (IRQ) settings or memory address assignments. To start with, you should generate a system summary report, as described in the next section.

PART

V

Networking
Housework

Troubleshooting Network Printers

It's second nature to glance at a printer next to your desk to see if the ready light is burning before trying to print on it. It's not so easy to know whether a printer at the other end of the house is up and running. Often, the first indication that the printer you are trying to use is not working is an error message like the one in Figure 21.13.

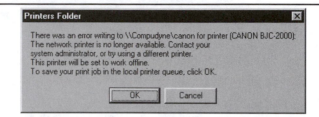

The first thing to do if your print job fails doesn't have anything to do with networking, per se. You just need walk over to the printer to make sure that it is turned on and ready to print. Sometimes it's the simplest problems that we just don't think of when something goes wrong. You know what to check:

- Make sure the on switch is in the right position.
- See if the printer's ready light is lit.
- Look for any error messages on the printer's display, if it has one.
- Check to make sure the printer has paper.
- Look for a paper jam.
- Check the ink cartridge or toner cartridge.

If none of these does the trick, you may need to press the printer's reset button, if it has one, or simply turn it off and on.

 TIP Sometimes restarting the Windows computer you are trying to print from will also get the printer driver up and working properly. You can usually exit and reboot Windows without losing print jobs. Instead, you'll get a message at restart saying that you have some print jobs in the queue and asking if you want to print them.

Even more common than trying to print to a turned-off printer is trying to print to a printer that is connected to the network through a turned-off computer. Even if the printer is turned on and ready to go, most have to be connected to the network through a computer (with a few exceptions for printers that have their own built-in network interface cards). If that computer isn't turned on, you won't be able to access the printer.

Surfing for Help

A typical computer user has mounds of manuals for all kinds of computer gadgets old, new, and in between. In all this confusion, it can be difficult if not impossible to find a current telephone number or Web site address to get technical support. Older manuals, even if they can be found, may not have Web sites for online support.

When you've gone through all your hard copies without finding what you need, check out www.supporthelp.com. This is a nerve node for technical support, listing over 5,000 major hardware and software vendors. You can search a database of tech support resources by keyword, company, or product. A search on the keyword "home" in the network category, for instance, produced 71 hits. A click on any vendor name provides detailed information including links to Web sites, tech-support e-mail addresses, phone and fax numbers, and dozens of user support groups. These groups, with their online message forums, let you post questions and problems for other users to help you with.

Using Online Help Files

Online help is one of the best things to happen to network troubleshooters. Using a computer connected to the Internet, you can tap into all sorts of instantly available, comprehensive, custom-tailored advice. No matter what your networking problem is, it's almost certain that someone, somewhere has had the identical difficulty, found the solution, and placed it somewhere on the Internet.

The manuals for most computer products sold today carry a URL for the manufacturer's Web site where you can get free online help. This help often takes the form of lists of Frequently Asked Questions and answers, Knowledge Bases, or e-mail submission tools. Each of these is described below, along with some of the other online help sources and tips on how to find and use them:

- FAQs, or lists of Frequently Asked Questions and answers, contain concise solutions to commonly posed problems. They are often maintained by knowledgeable and highly motivated private individuals, rather than professional support personnel working for a company. This doesn't mean they're not extremely useful, however. FAQs are often posted regularly to Usenet discussion groups dealing with the subject matter. For instance, the Usenet newsgroup `alt.os.windows95` is devoted to the Windows 95 operating system.

- User group discussions contain many answers to questions that don't appear in the FAQs. Monitoring user group messages over time, or searching archives of past messages can produce very informative tips and tricks for solving all kinds of issues.

 TIP   Deja.com, at www.deja.com, is a good place to start searching for newsgroups to help you with a particular problem or interest.

- Knowledge Bases are searchable indexes of common problems and solutions, technical documents, installation manuals, and other helpful documents. Many manufacturers of networking equipment maintain Knowledge Bases on their Web sites. To use them, know your networking product model and number, the revision number of your driver, and have in mind some keywords to search for. For instance, if you are getting a particular error message, you might search the Knowledge Base for terms from that error message.

- Driver updates can solve many problems with networks. You can download and install updates to drivers for network devices, such as adapters. Check your device's manufacturer site for a section labeled Downloads or Drivers. The files are usually small and easy to install. It's a good idea to save a copy to a floppy, in case you need to reinstall it later on.

- E-mailed questions to a vendor's support desk can provide you with a precise answer to your specific question. Many vendors offer free support by e-mail, with the drawback that answers may take a day or two to arrive, and may be brief and short on details.

 TIP   Faxed help documents may seem a little old-fashioned, but they can work as well as online help if you're patient. You can find fax numbers for vendor help desks in many product manuals. The main problem with faxed help documents is that you are likely to have to go through a long process of listening to lists of options and punching in codes on your phone keypad before you can determine which document you need and get it sent to you. You also, of course, need to have access to a fax machine. But if the network problem you are having is preventing you from reaching the Internet, fax help may be the next best option.

Using Telephone Help

Telephone help is, in many ways, the best kind of help. You have a trained technician all to yourself, not to mention the computerized help desk system the technician is likely to be sitting in front of. You are also in front of your computer so you can reboot it and check error messages to see if the technician's recommendations help. However, you can make telephone support even more useful if you address the following issues:

- Check your system, software, or peripheral's warranty to check the duration of your no-cost telephone support. For instance, you may receive free phone help for 90 days after purchase or, in some cases, until sometime after the next version comes out. If there's some nagging issue that you want to correct, try to call before the free time is up.

- Try to call first thing in the morning, before all the other network troubleshooters are up and about.

- Don't call at what are likely to be peak times, such as late Friday afternoon, lunchtime, or Monday morning.

- If you can't call a help desk about your home network during working hours because you are, understandably, at work, take advantage of time zones. That is, try to call during hours when the help desk is open, but at least some of the people in the country are at work. If you're on the East Coast or on Central time, this probably means in the early morning or just after you get off work. If you're on Mountain or on Pacific time, you may have to call late in the evening to avoid the crush.

- Have something to read or work on nearby, so you aren't completely idle and bored while you wait.

- Have details of your system, the problem, and what you've done to try to correct it, as well as any user registration number you may need to have to obtain support.

Summary

As discouraging as network problems can be, there are ways to solve them. With discipline, resourcefulness, and patience, you can usually work out how to get balky connectors working, frazzled cables communicating, and confused network adapters straightened out. And if you can't figure it out, there are many helpful resources where you are almost certain to find an answer.

What's Next

In a topic as vast as networking, there's always more to be learned and applied. The following appendices include information on where to find additional online resources for home networking, how to use networking consultants and sign up for home networking classes, as well as a glossary of home networking terms.

APPENDICES

APPENDIX <u>A</u>

Online Home Networking Resources

Overview

The Internet is the best thing that ever happened for home networkers. It's not just that high-speed Internet access is one of the prime motivations for people to network their home computers. Even if you have other reasons for getting into home computer networking, such as playing games or running a home-based business, the Internet will make the experience far more enjoyable and productive.

The main reason the Internet is so great for home networking is the expansive selection of resources you can reach from any Internet-connected computer. There are countless networking-oriented Web sites, user groups, FAQs, articles, and software downloads you can access with a few clicks. Although you can't take delivery of hardware such as cables and hubs over the Internet, you can easily order what you need. And the ability to comparison shop among many vendors by using the Internet greatly increases the chances that you'll not only get what you need to set up your network, you'll also get a good deal on it.

The availability of all this information, advice, assistance, and software online is indisputably a great thing. But, with the number of Web pages stretching into the billions now—not to mention the many gigabytes of message board postings and e-mail communications—it can be tough to find exactly what you need. Even a seasoned online researcher would be hard-pressed to claim knowledge of all the home networking resources on the Internet. However, as with most things, you can tap into the vast majority of the Internet's home networking resources by being aware of only a handful of the more useful sources.

Internet Search Engines

A lot of heavy Internet users have a favorite search engine that is the first one they turn to when they have a question or problem. That's understandable, because while search engines all aim to accomplish basically the same task, each one is a little different from all the rest. Some are indiscriminate indexers, some make recommendations from a select list of preferred sites, some are focused on particular niches, some allow natural-language questions, some prefer queries phrased in Boolean logic, and all combine these traits and others in ways that are probably unique. In addition, they use different underlying technologies, employ different search and indexing strategies, and certainly offer widely differing interfaces to their services.

NOTE If you find yourself using the same search engine repeatedly, why not make that page your home page? Do this in Microsoft Internet Explorer by clicking the menu bar item for Tools ➢ Internet Options. In Internet Explorer version 4.0, you will choose View instead of Tools. Type the Web address for your favorite engine into the Address text box in the Home Page section located at the top of the window. Then click OK. If you are already at the search engine home page, you can click Tools (or View in Internet Explorer 4.0) ➢ Internet Options ➢ Use Current ➢ OK.

One effect of the different approaches to Net searching is that a question that stumps one search engine might be a cinch for another. So, instead of invariably using the same one, it's a good idea to have a few you use regularly so that you learn their ins and outs. That way when you're trying to find information about a home networking issue, no matter how arcane the subject, it's unlikely that the Internet will be able to refuse to yield up its bounty. Here are selected Web search engines and tools, one or more of which can make up at least a part of a regular Internet search kit for home networking:

Google   Located at `http://www.google.com`, Google takes a completely different tack from Yahoo, Infoseek, Excite, and the other online portals. Rather than cluttering the interface with a hundred links to news articles, shops, directories, and other searches, it's nothing but a search engine. When you go to the Google site, you're presented with a box to type your search term into, and very little else. Nonetheless, it's an extremely fast search engine with an uncanny ability to locate exactly the resource you're looking for.

Hotbot   Located at `http://www.hotbot.com`, Hotbot offers excellent flexibility in the way you can tailor your searches. In addition to mundane keyword and phrase searches, you can tell Hotbot to filter sites by date, language, and whether or not they contain various types of multimedia files. Hotbot's advanced search options let you zero in even more precisely on the information you're after, which is a valuable capability in the rapidly expanding chaos of the World Wide Web.

Ask Jeeves   Located at `http://www.askjeeves.com`. If you prefer to ask questions in plain old English, and get answers that consist of more than a list of URLs, Ask Jeeves is the place for you. As an added bonus, you can click on a button to see what questions other Ask Jeeves users are asking at that moment. (And you thought you had unusual interests.)

WebFerret   Located at `http://www.Webferret.com`, WebFerret is not a search engine. Rather, it is a program you download and install on your computer that lets you search numerous engines simultaneously and display the results. The great thing about WebFerret is that you can use precise key phrases, such as "Networking Linux and Windows 98" and get back only sites with that exact phrase. Because so many search engines are being queried, you can often get listings with just a very few sites, making it easy to home in on exactly what you're looking for. In addition to WebFerret, you can download NewsFerret for free. NewsFerret searches for Usenet articles using AltaVista, DejaNews, and InfoFerret, which search published articles and other news resources.

Search for an Available Domain Name at Register.com

Register.com isn't intended to be a search engine. It's a place where people can register names for World Wide Web domains. If you want a personal domain called www.myname.com, you could go to www.register.com. After searching to see if myname.com is taken, you fill out some forms, pay a fee of $70.00 for the first two years, and you are the owner of a domain name.

Register.com is mentioned in a section on search engines because it's actually a pretty good one. Since theoretically it indexes all the domain names, it finds things other search engines might miss. If you use Register.com's search tool to look for, say, www.homepcnetworks.com, you'll be directed straight to the HomePCNetworks site, rather than seeing a selection of hits, some of questionable value, as you will if you use one of the general-purpose search engines. Plus, Register.com gives you the name of the person or business owning the domain, along with an address, telephone number, and e-mail address.

Computer Information Search Engines

When you're looking for information on, say, NICs, you don't want to be directed to a bunch of pages for Nick at Nite, or nickel collectors, or even Network Information Centers. That's why it's handy to use search engines that specialize in information about computers and nothing but computers. Here are a few of the better ones:

CNET.com   Located at http://www.cnet.com, CNET's site is actually a network of sites containing a massive amount of product reviews, technical articles, help files, and more. The information, while generally from experts, is typically written for the average layperson. If you have virtually any kind of problem with computers or networking hardware or software, this is a good place to start.

IEEE   Located at `http://standards.ieee.org/catalog/index.html`, the Institute of Electrical and Electronic Engineers is the primary standards-setting body for computer networking. If you want the authoritative details on any IEEE standard, such as the 802.3 Ethernet standard, you can get it here, searchable by keyword and other methods. One problem: It will cost you. The IEEE charges a subscription for accessing its standards online.

RFC Editor   Located at `http://www.rfc-editor.org/rfc.html`, RFC stands for *Requests for Comments*, which are a series of notes about the Internet that go back to 1969, when it was called the ARPANET. These notes cover networking protocols as well as many other aspects of computer communications. They are often informal and, not infrequently, humorous, but can represent an important source of information for the puzzled networker. You can search the RFCs through a number of means, including the number assigned to each RFC, keyword, contents, and other search terms at the RFC Editor Site. In addition, you can also look though numerous other RFC indexes, to which you can link from the RFC Editor Site.

Virus Bulletin   Located at `http://www.virusbtn.com`, the Virus Bulletin is a technical journal about computer viruses and antivirus products. It's the last word in what's new in the world of viruses. That includes both what is threatening your network and what you can do about it. Especially useful are the sections on current alerts and virus hoaxes.

Webopedia   Located at `http://www.webopedia.com`. There's no doubt about it—networking has its share of jargon and more. Webopedia is a quick way to cut through the thickets of verbiage with its online dictionary. You simply type in the term that's puzzling you and click to get a concise definition. Plus, Webopedia provides links to related terms, as well as other sites with more information on the topic.

General Home Networking Resources

Even big computer-oriented information sources are likely to seem a little thin when it comes to the special problems of networkers. Fortunately, there are a number of Web sites devoted specifically to networking, and even home networking.

homePCnetwork.com   Located at `http://www.homepcnetwork.com`, this site, as shown in Figure A.1, is a general-purpose, comprehensive site for all kinds of home networks. Detailed and authoritative product reviews cover software and hardware for Cat 5, phoneline, wireless, and powerline networks. There are FAQs on topics from Why home networks are useful to Wiring a home with network cable. Links connect you to recent news articles on home networking, step-by-step instructions for networking Macs and PCs, and more. There are also user forums where you can post questions and help others with their problems.

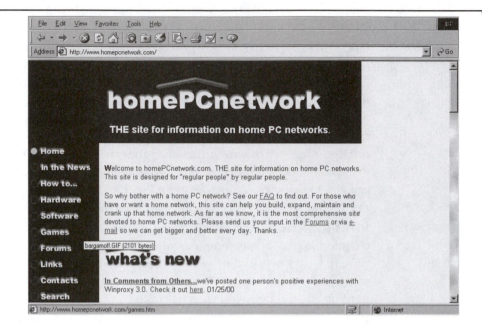

homepcLAN   Located at `http://www.homepclan.com`, homepcLAN is for owners of Microsoft Windows 95/98 and NT computers who are trying to set up or run home or small-office networks. As shown in Figure A.2, The site contains numerous how-tos on everything from setting up Interrupt Requests on network adapters to sharing Internet connections using proxy software. The site also features an online store where you can purchase computer and networking products. Still, its how-tos often recommend shareware or freeware solutions.

Networking Macintosh Computers   Located at `http://www-commeng.cso .uiuc.edu/nas/nash/mac.html`, this site is maintained by the University of Illinois at Urbana-Champaign and is primarily aimed at helping Mac-using students hook up to the UIUC campus network. However, it's as good an independent guide to general Mac networking as you'll find, with many FAQs and how-tos on connecting to AppleTalk networks and more, along with links to other sites.

FIGURE A.2

The homepcLAN site is focused on home and small office networking for Windows 95/98 and NT machines.

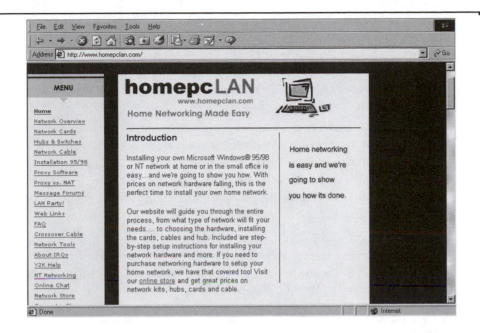

MacFixit   Located at `http://www.macfixit.com`, MacFixit is a general-purpose Mac troubleshooting site. However, you'll find plenty of reviews, articles, news, FAQs, how-tos and—especially useful—message boards here on networking with all kinds of Macintoshes.

Linux Networking Overview HOWTO   Located at `http://www.linux.org/help/ldp/howto/Networking-Overview-HOWTO.html`, Linux networkers are blessed with a rich selection of how-tos, FAQs, and even mini how-tos on virtually all facets of using Linux. This networking overview should be enough to get you started networking with Linux. It also includes a short but excellent list of additional links for more information.

General Home Networking Resources from Manufacturers

Companies that sell home networking hardware and software have a vested interest not only in helping people understand how to use their products, but also with getting people to generally appreciate and feel comfortable with home networking. They also have the resources and motivation to put together some really comprehensive and, especially, easy-on-the-eyes presentations of the material. It's unlikely that you'll see a manufacturer really objectively assess its own products, much less recommend a competing product. Still, some of the better online resources out there come from manufacturers.

Farallon Computing Located at `http://www.farallon.com/homenet`, Farallon makes popular Macintosh networking software, so its home networking site focuses on Macs. However, there is plenty of information on PC-to-Mac connections as well.

Asanté Technologies Located at `http://www.asante.com`, Asanté makes lots of networking cards, switches, hubs, and other gear for Windows PCs, but it has a stronger Mac focus than most sites. You can go here to download network drivers for the latest release of the Mac OS as well as diagnostic software to help you puzzle out Apple networking issues. There are also lots of technical how-tos and product specifications.

 NOTE Asanté has a free e-mail newsletter on networking that you can sign up for to help you keep abreast of networking news and trends. Learn more at `www.asante.com/corporate/c_e5.html`.

Linksys Located at `http://www.linksys.com/support/faqs/howbuild/default.htm`, this is a pretty good how-to on networking from a maker of popular network adapters, hubs, and other home networking gear.

3COM Home Networking Page Located at `http://www.3com.com/client/pcd/homeconnect/homenetworking/index.html`, 3COM is one of the largest commercial networking suppliers in the world, with a large interest in home networking. The sophistication and depth of its site on home networking reflects that, with extensive information on why and how to set up a network of home PCs.

Intel Home Networking Page Located at `http://www.intel.com/anypoint/home.htm`, Intel's site on home networking is focused on its AnyPoint phoneline networking technology. However, it contains a good number of how-tos on sharing Internet access as well as providing online support, including downloadable software, for AnyPoint users.

 TIP You can sign up to receive a free Intel-sponsored e-mail newsletter on home networking at `www.intel.com/anypoint/news/nwsltr/index.htm`.

Microsoft Home Networking Page   Located at http://www.microsoft.com/ HOMENET, Microsoft doesn't miss too many bets when it comes to backing computer technologies with mass appeal. Its site for home networking reflects an intense interest in providing consumers with the information and assistance they need to successfully network home computers. This goes beyond software solutions, although there is of course a good bit on the networking capabilities of the various Windows operating systems. Microsoft includes much on home automation, as well as links to many vendors of hardware for home networking.

NOTE   While you're surfing the net looking for home networking information, check out Merloni. This washing machine maker is working on an appliance that will connect to the Internet with a Bluetooth short-range wireless hookup to call a technician if it needs service. Learn more at www.merloni.com.

Netgear   Located at http://www.netgearinc.com, Netgear is the home networking unit of telecommunications behemoth Nortel and, as such, its site features an impressive array of both technological sophistication and sharp focus on home networking. Netgear is perhaps a little too sharply focused on its own products; there's a dearth of general-interest how-tos. But if you are interested in learning about one of the broadest and best product lines for home networkers, this is the place to go.

Phoneline Networking Resources

Networkers tend to divide along technological lines, with the Ethernet/Cat 5 group on one side and the wireless, phoneline, and powerline folks occupying three other ramparts. To be sure, the issues are different with each technology, which makes it fortunate that phoneline networkers, in particular, can find lots of online resources from manufacturers and others to help them with their networking problems.

Home Phoneline Networking Alliance   Located at http://www.homepna .org. At the Home Phoneline Networking Alliance's site, you can find the latest information on standards and developments in the phoneline networking field.

HomePNA.com   Located at http://www.homepna.com, this site is a commercial phoneline networking information and sales site. It's not to be confused with the industry association described above. However, that doesn't mean it's worthless. Far from it. In fact, it's generally more useful than the HPNA's site.

Its content of news, reviews, FAQs, how-tos and more, as shown in Figure A.3, is about as good a place to learn about phoneline networking as you'll find. Plus, there's a free e-mail newsletter you can sign up for.

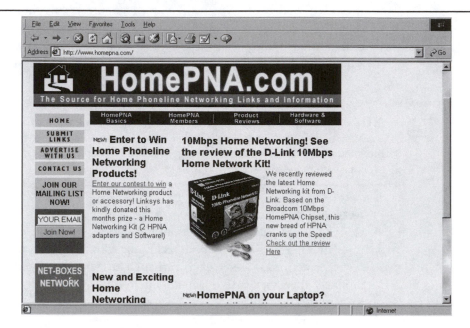

Tut Systems   Located at `http://www.tutsys.com`. Tut Systems developed the phoneline networking technology used by consumer network equipment vendors. But Tut doesn't sell its products to home networkers. Instead, it focuses on the market for apartment buildings and other large customers. Still, if you're interested in the background of phoneline networking—or maybe you have an apartment you're trying to network—Tut's page provides some useful information.

Diamond Multimedia HomeFree   Located at `http://www.homefree-networks.com`, Diamond Multimedia's HomeFree phone networking kits have done as much as anything to bring this technology to the masses. That hasn't happened without a lot of sales pressure from this subsidiary of S3, and the site reflects a strong product focus. However, if you're still in the very early stages of networking, take a look at Diamond's unique online decision tree for selecting a networking technology.

Powerline Networking Resources

Powerline is the networking technology that, so far, hasn't quite taken off. This is partly because of performance issues compared to faster Ethernet, phoneline, and wireless solutions. It may also be partly because there seems to be a finite need for alternative networking technologies. However, if you're already using powerline, or you would like to learn more about it, here's the place to go:

Intelogis   Located at www.intelogis.com. At this writing, Intelogis was in the process of changing its name to Inari Corp. and dropping its end-user products in favor of selling powerline networking it pioneered to other equipment makers. However, the Intelogis site remains the best powerline source for home networkers. It contains numerous FAQs, white papers, downloads, how-tos, and specifications relating to this technology.

Wireless Networking Resources

Wireless is generating as much buzz as anything in home networking, and you'll find no shortage of news articles and press releases on the topic flowing over the Internet and appearing in general interest business, consumer, and technology publications. But if you want the latest, most authoritative information and assistance on wireless networking, it's best to go straight to the companies that sell it and the groups that set the standards.

Home Radio Frequency Working Group   Located at http://www.homerf .org, the Home RF Working Group is the place to find the latest on the Shared Wireless Access Protocol (SWAP) that is supporting all the development in wireless networking. Although there's not much in the way of how-tos, you can see a slide presentation describing the technology behind SWAP and check news about recently introduced wireless-enabled networking products.

Proxim Wireless   Located at http://www.proxim.com/symphony/index.htm, Proxim is a longtime leader in wireless networking for businesses, now branching out into the home market. One interesting feature is the interactive step-by-step configurator that helps you prepare a shopping list for a wireless home network. It may not tell you anything you didn't know, but it never hurts to go through the process.

Aironet Wireless Communications   Located at http://www.aironet .com, Aironet has been making lots of waves with its 11Mbps RF networking products that can match the performance of regular Ethernet without the wires. This is cutting-edge stuff for high-speed wireless, complete with product specifications, backgrounds, FAQs, technical white papers, market evaluations, and more.

Networking Resources for Game Players

Gamespot PC Workshop   Located at `http://www.gamespot.com/features/ pc_workshop7/index.html`, Gamespot, one of the leading sites for computer gamers, has done everyone a service with its PC Workshop series of how-tos on setting up and running a game-playing computer. Workshop number seven is on networking, specifically. It focuses on Windows peer-to-peer networking, but includes, appropriately, information on using the IPX protocol that many games rely on, as well as the general-purpose TCP/IP protocol.

Western Pennsylvania Network Gaming Group   Located at `http:// trfn.clpgh.org/wpngg/network/index.htm`. If you like your information on gaming with networks presented in informal fashion, this is the resource for you. The WPNGG covers the bases—including some few other network sites do, such as networking with IPX protocols under DOS—in an easygoing manner that sounds like nothing so much as some helpful tips from a friend who's been there before.

Miscellaneous Networking Resources

Cablemodemhelp   Located at `www.cablemodemhelp.com`, Cablemodemhelp has lots of help for people who are having trouble sharing cable modems over a home network as well as general cable modem FAQs and how-tos.

TimHiggins.com   Located at `http://www.timhiggins.com.` Tim Higgins is an expert on sharing Internet hookups via home network whether you're using cable modem, dial-up line, ISDN, DSL, Windows PCs, or Macintoshes. Plus, he's willing to share his advice as well.

Gibson Research Corporation   Located at `www.grc.com`. Steve Gibson is primarily known as the author of some very handy disk utilities, but this site has information, tips, tricks, and software concerning security issues involving the Internet and Windows-based home networks that you won't find anywhere else. If you want a surprise, click on the Shields Up! icon on the opening page to find out just what you may be revealing about yourself every time you access a Web page.

APPENDIX B

Home Networking Consultants and Courses

Overview

Home networking is getting easier, but it's still not the simplest project you'll ever take on. Even the savviest techies may wind up needing some outside help in order to install, configure, maintain, or expand a home network. When and if that time comes, you have a selection of home networking consultants and courses to choose from. The first group of resources, consisting of home networking consultants and technicians, promises to provide a remedy for you, although at what's likely to be a fairly steep cost. The second group of resources, consisting of the many courses on networking that you can take, offers to teach you to provide your own remedy. Each solution has its advantages and its disadvantages, as well as a few tricks you can use to make the experience more satisfying, no matter which one you employ.

Home Networking Consultants

If you ever really get stuck with a home networking problem—or if you can't quite summon up the resolve to even get started—the ultimate assistance is probably only a phone call or two away. There's no substitute for having a knowledgeable, experienced, and dedicated network professional there to help. There are thousands of such consultants, in every major city and most smaller towns. They provide a wide enough variety of special expertise, pricing, and services that odds are good you can find just the right one you need, if and when the need arises.

Choosing a Consultant

Generally speaking, a home networking consultant is somebody who gives advice on designing a home network, selecting the equipment, installing it, and configuring it. However, not all consultants are created equal. Some consultants provide only advice, others may also install and service a home network. Some consultants work primarily as network troubleshooters, coming out to help repair a balky network. Consultants may also sell networking hardware or software in addition to selling advice and services.

The way you deal with a given consultant depends on the type of consultant you are dealing with. For instance, consultants who also sell equipment will tend to recommend you use the type of equipment they sell. Depending on your circumstances, this may mean that you don't wind up with the best network for your needs. On the other hand, you may be able to get a better deal on equipment when you buy it from a consultant, whom you are also paying for advice, than if you purchased it at a computer store. Always try to figure out what kind of consultant you are dealing with before you attempt to do business with them.

TIP Keep in mind that hardware and software make up only about 40 percent of the investment you'll make in your network. The rest will be related to service—installation, configuration, and maintenance. So look for a service-minded consultant.

Finding a Networking Consultant

If you want to quickly get a list of possible home networking consultants, check your Yellow Pages. Look under "Computer Networking". Most of the businesses you find there will be specialists in business networking. That's true even if you're using the consumer edition of your local Yellow Pages. You should be able to identify the ones you don't want by looking for such terms as "WAN" and "Fiber Optic" in the descriptions of the services these firms provide. Wide Area Networks and Fiber Optic cabling are technologies commonly employed in business networks, but are rare in the home. Instead, look for networking companies that specialize in small networks or, at best, home installations.

 TIP You may not be able to find a home networking specialist in your local phone book. But that doesn't mean you shouldn't call a couple of the firms specializing in business networking, looking for information and referrals. Even if consultants don't handle your type of job, they are quite likely to be able to refer you to someone who does.

Don't limit yourself to the phone book when you are looking for a home networking consultant. Along with or instead of checking the Yellow Pages, you can tap the following resources:

Personal referrals   If you know anyone with a home computer network, ask them if they've ever used a consultant.

Computer stores   Some retail computer stores have service departments that can help with installing and servicing networks.

 TIP Salespeople at computer stores that don't have service departments may still be aware of and able to recommend consultants that specialize in home networks.

User groups   Local computer user groups are excellent places to seek out referrals to home networking consultants, as well as other networking resources.

TIP To find a user group, check your local newspaper's weekly listings of computer clubs and other computer organization meetings.

Advertisements Many daily newspapers now have display advertising sections, usually in the daily business or weekly technology sections, listing consultants for many types of computer-related services, including home networking.

 TIP It's a good idea to check with your local Better Business Bureau to see if a consultant has a good business record before hiring him or her.

Another place to look is the Web site for the Independent Computer Consultants Association, at www.icca.org. The St. Louis-based ICCA has nearly 1,500 members and chapters in many major cities. Its Web site has a Find a Consultant tool that lets you search for consultants that specialize in the skill you need so you can find consultants in your city or state. The ICCA skill keyword closest to home networking is "Network Design."

Networking Certifications

Networking isn't like medicine or law. Anybody can hang out their shingle and claim to be a networking consultant without running afoul of any laws or governing bodies. However, there are some specific credentials—the networking equivalent of an M.D. or J.D.—that are a little harder to come by. Networking credentials to look for include the following:

- The gold standard of certificates for networking with Windows computers is the Microsoft Certified Systems Engineer (MCSE). Learn more at www.microsoft .com/train_cert.

 NOTE MCSE focuses on Windows NT, which differs in important ways from Windows 95/98, so an MCSE may not always be the best choice for a home Windows network.

- Certified Novell Administrator, or the more advanced Certified Novell Engineer, are certifications to look for when dealing with NetWare networks. Learn more at http://education.novell.com/cne.

- Apple Solution Experts are consultants, resellers, and others specializing in Apple products. Learn more at http://aspn.apple.com.

- In keeping with the wide-open world of Linux, there are a number of certification options for Linux networking experts. Red Hat Software, one of the leading vendors, grants several levels of Red Hat Certified Engineer (RHCE) certification. Learn more at www.redhat.com.

Certificates show you that a networking consultant has had some exposure to networking a classroom environment. They don't say much, if anything, about that consultant's ability to solve real-world networking problems. The best networking consultant will have a mix of classroom instruction and on-the-job training.

NOTE The most important requirement for a home networking consultant is skill at communicating. No amount of experience or quantity of credentials will replace being able to listen and talk to you about networking issues and options in language you can understand. If your candidate for consultant seems proficient only in techno-speak, and is unable to tone down the jargon even when you indicate you don't understand, keep looking.

What Consultants Cost

Networking consultants don't come cheap. Like plumbers and electricians, most charge for their services by the hour. Quoted rates may range from $40.00 an hour to $175.00 an hour. You'll probably be asked to pay a figure in the middle of this range.

The range of fees is explained by variations in the individual consultant's experience, level of skill, education, certifications, specialization, and, of course, market factors. That is, consultants in large cities with lots of home networks may get more money per hour. Also, consultants who work for large companies that have lots of overhead tend to charge more. Often, independent consultants, including moonlighters from large corporations who work out of their homes at nights and weekends, may turn out to be the best deal for you because they have good skills and low overhead.

Hourly rates aren't the only issue to bring up when discussing prices. In addition to asking consultants what the hourly pop will be, include questions about the following:

- Can you get an initial meeting without having to pay for it?

- Will you be charged for travel time? (If so, you may be better off with a local consultant who charges a higher hourly rate.)

TIP Get it in writing. Include rates of pay, estimated time to completion or, if appropriate, the flat rate you've agreed upon. A written document may only provide a basis upon which to alter the agreement later, but it's better than nothing.

- What kind of terms are offered? Some consultants may expect a deposit, and then bill you the full amount when the network job is finished.
- Is there any guarantee? If so, what is being guaranteed and what happens if the network doesn't operate properly? For example, will you get all of your money back?
- Who pays for expenses, such as long-distance phone calls to suppliers, that the consultant incurs in order to execute your job?

Does the fee include any extra services such as telephone support?

 TIP The best way to maximize the value of a consultant is to make sure you tell the consultant what you want, not how to do it. In other words, specify the problem, not the solution. Let the consultant figure out how to solve it. That's what you're paying for, after all.

Home Networking Courses

Why depend on others to fix your problems? With a little training, you can go far beyond even the treatment afforded by a book such as this, and personally acquire the knowledge and skills to install and manage your own home network. Networking courses are widely available at computer stores, community colleges, and technical training centers.

Choosing a Course

When you're going for training in Windows networking, the best bet is a course offered by a Microsoft Certified Technical Education Center. These centers can be found around the world and each offers Microsoft's official curriculum for Windows computers. A good second choice would be a non-Microsoft certified course offered by a community college, continuing education center, or other accredited learning institution.

Going Further

The time may come when you get so interested in networking that you decide to be more than a hobbyist. If you get to that point, you'll doubtless be pretty experienced at dealing with your own network, and confident that you can handle most of the network problems you're likely to see. But there's a lot to be said for formal education when it comes to networking. In fact, the key to making the most of your networking experience—including, perhaps, making it into a career—is getting the official credentials of a professional networker.

Achieving Professional Certifications

If you want to get off to a fast start as a networking professional, you can't beat the effects of obtaining one of the professional certifications. While having a certificate doesn't guarantee you success in a career as a networking expert, it does get you off to a good start.

There are certifications to match networking specialties based on the major operating systems, hardware platforms, and network operating systems. These programs are, for the most part, open to the public, meaning anyone who wants to take on the study and other requirements can obtain a certificate.

Microsoft Certified Systems Engineer   Obtaining an MCSE certificate is a serious course of study that may require a year or more of study and test taking to complete. Classroom study is not required, however. You can learn everything you'll need from books such as the series published by Sybex.

 TIP Learn more about the Sybex MCSE study guides at www.sybex.com.

Whether you study in a classroom or a bedroom, you'll have to pass a minimum of six technical exams on networking and other tasks. To receive the MCSE+I—standing for MCSE Plus Internet—designation, you have to take even more tests (a total of nine), to demonstrate your knowledge of the Internet and World Wide Web, in addition to local area networks.

Tests are given by Microsoft-certified exam centers and typically cost $100.00 each to take. If you sign up for a classroom course that will take you from newbie to MCSE, the cost will run several thousand dollars. The good news is that consultants with MCSEs earn an average of over $90,000.00 a year. Learn more at www.microsoft.com/train_cert or http://www.mcpmag.com/.

APP

B

Home Networking
Consultants and
Courses

Certified Novell Administrator   Certified Novell Administrator (CNA) is the first level in the Novell Netware certification hierarchy, suitable for a person whose assignment includes planning, installing, configuring, troubleshooting, and upgrading networks. Next up is Certified Novell Engineer, which signifies an expert capable of supporting a large networked workforce and solving high-level network problems. The elite Novell certifications are Master Certified Novell Engineer and Certified Directory Engineer, for top-shelf networking professionals.

In addition to seeking different levels of Novell certification, you can specialize in one of several areas, including NetWare 5, intraNetWare, NetWare 3, and Novell's GroupWise 5 and GroupWise 4 groupware products. Learn more at `http://education .novell.com/cne`.

Apple Solution Experts   Apple Solution Experts don't have to undergo the rigorous training that some other network certifications require. To get an ASE, you must be a consultant or reseller of Apple products. You also have to register with Apple Computer Corporation, pay a $495.00 fee, and provide at least three business references. Learn more at `http://aspn.apple.com`.

Red Hat Certified Engineer   Red Hat Certified Engineer (RHCE) certification comes in levels corresponding to network users, network operators, network administrators, and network engineers. The RHCE course consists of 4 days of intensive training including, as with most certification programs, lots of hands-on workshops with real-world configuration and administration problems and tasks. To get the diploma, you have to pass a certification exam the last day. All these courses, of course, employ the Red Hat distribution of Linux. Learn more at `www.Redhat.com`.

Helping Others with Home Networks

The considerations about hiring consultants to help with a home network apply—in reverse—when you're thinking about helping someone else with a home network.

- If you're doing the job for pay, make sure price and terms are clearly spelled out in a contract that both of you sign.

- Have a solid, mutual understanding in writing of what the network design, installation, upgrade, or repair is supposed to accomplish.

- Don't take on a project you can't handle, whether the problem is lack of time, shortfall in expertise, or another issue.

- Do good work, on time and, if possible, under budget. This will ensure that your efforts generate good word-of-mouth, which is the best kind of advertising.

APPENDIX <u>C</u>

Glossary

10BaseT

A standard for transmitting *Ethernet* at 10 megabits per second over *twisted-pair* cable.

10Base2

A standard for transmitting *Ethernet* over *coaxial* cable.

100BaseT

A standard for transmitting *Ethernet* at 100 megabits per second over *twisted-pair* cable. See also *Fast Ethernet*.

2.4GHz

A section of the radio frequency spectrum used in some wireless home networks.

802.11

The *IEEE* committee responsible for setting standards for wireless *local area networks*. Its standard is known as the 802.11 standard.

802.3

The *IEEE* standard for *Ethernet* networks.

802.5

The *IEEE* standard for *token ring* networks.

900MHz

A section of the radio frequency spectrum used by some cordless telephones and wireless home networks.

A

ACAP

Abbreviation for *Application Configuration Access Protocol*.

Access method

A collection of rules and policies determining which node on a network has access to the network at any given moment.

Access Point

A wireless networking device that provides access to the wired network.

Address

The unique number identifying a node (host connection) on a network.

Address mask

An address, expressed as a four 8-bit numerals separated by periods, that masks the part of the IP address used by all the computers on a particular *subnetwork*. The most common is 255.255.255.0. This address mask means the first 24 bits are shared by all the computers on this subnetwork. The last 8 bits contain the addresses to specific machines. Also called *subnet mask*.

ADSL

Abbreviation for *Asymmetric Digital Subscriber Line*. See also *Digital Subsriber Line, DSL*.

Advanced Research Projects Agency Network

Original name for the *wide area network* that became the *Internet. ARPANET* was established in 1969 by the U.S. Department of Defense to link researchers at UCLA and the Stanford Research Institute.

Alphanumeric

Consisting of letters, numerals, and sometimes other characters such as spaces, punctuation marks, etcetera. Commonly specified for use in creating passwords for network user accounts.

Analog

A method of representing data that constantly changes in either amplitude or frequency. Compare to *digital*.

Anonymous FTP

A technique for using the *file transfer protocol* to access a computer over the *Internet* without a password.

AppleTalk

Apple Computer's proprietary networking software.

Application Configuration Access Protocol

Client/server protocol which allows a software application, such as an e-mail program, to retrieve configuration settings from a central server. Abbreviated *ACAP*.

ARPANET

Abbreviation for Advanced Research Projects Agency Network.

Assembly language

The programming language that is just above *machine language*.

APP

C

Glossary

Asymmetric Digital Subscriber Line

Technology that allows more data to be sent over existing copper telephone lines. *ADSL* supports data rates from 1.5 to 9Mbps when receiving data, and from 16 to 640Kbps when sending data. See *Digital Subscriber Line, DSL*.

Attachment Unit Interface

A 15-pin socket used in Thicknet Ethernet networks to connect cables and other devices to the back of a computer. Abbreviated *AUI*.

Attenuation

The tendency of a signal to decrease in power or fade out as distance from the source increases. The opposite of amplification. Usually measured in decibels.

AUI

Abbreviation for *Attachment Unit Interface*.

B

B Channel

The Bearer channel in an *ISDN* connection. B channels operate at 64Kbps and can be bonded together for increased *bandwidth*. See also *D channel*.

Back Orifice

A set of programs that can let hackers access and control computers running Windows 95/98 and NT.

Bandwidth

The total available transmission capacity of a network. Expressed in *Hertz* or *Megahertz*.

Binary testing

A technique for isolating cable problems in coaxial-wired networks by splitting network segments in two and testing each separately.

Bluetooth

A technology for small, low-cost, short-range radio links between mobile PCs, mobile phones, and other portable devices. See also *Piconet*.

Bridge

This is a device that connects two *LAN* segments and moves frames of data from one segment to the other.

Broadband

Refers to high bandwidth networks capable of two-way delivery of multimedia content and services. Broadband uses *xDSL*, cable and satellite systems.

BNC connector

A type of connector used in thinnet coaxial cable networks. Also commonly used for video connections, including connecting a television set to a cable television service.

Bus topology

A network design with all devices connected to a central cable, called the bus or backbone.

C

Cable modem

A *modem* device capable of delivering *high-speed Internet access* over a cable television *coaxial cable* system.

Cable tester

A network troubleshooting device used to check for proper continuity as well as shorts, cross wiring, and other problems.

Cache

An area of memory or disk space used for temporarily storing data that may be used again. For example, Web pages that a surfer has viewed may be stored in a cache on the computer's hard drive so that the pages can be viewed more quickly, since they don't need to be downloaded again.

Cat 5

Abbreviation for *Category 5*.

Category 5

The classification of *twisted pair* cable used for *Fast Ethernet* networks. (Regular *Ethernet* networks use Cat 3 cable.) Abbreviated *Cat 5*.

Central office

The local switching centers used by telephone companies to route calls the *last mile* to homes. Abbreviated *CO*.

Central Processing Unit

The main computing chip (i.e., Pentium). It is also known as the processor or central processor of the computer. Abbreviated *CPU*.

Channel Bonding

A technique for joining two or more *modems*, transmission lines, *network adapters,* or other communications devices or channels to achieve higher *bandwidth*.

Changemac

A hacking program designed to make a hacker appear to a network to be an authenticated user.

Checksum

An error-detection scheme calling for the sender to add up all the binary values for each byte, word, or other data item, and then transmit this sum along with the data. On the receiving end, the sum is computed again and the result is compared to the checksum. A difference indicates an error during transmission. See also *Cyclical Redundancy Check, CRC*.

Client

A computer that uses the resources of a *server* on a *client-server* network.

Client-server

A *network* that has a computer designated as a *server* that provides services to other computers, called *client* computers, on the network. Specific kinds of servers include *file servers, mail servers, printer servers,* and *database servers*.

CO

See *central office*.

Coaxial cable

Type of networking cable that has a center wire that is surrounded by a layer of insulation and a braided shield to counter interference. Varieties include *thicknet* and *thinnet*.

Collision Sense Multiple Access with Carrier Detection

The network access method used in *Ethernet* networks. Abbreviated *CSMA/CD*.

Compile

To process a computer program's source code into a machine-readable form that the computer can use.

Concentrator

See *hub*.

Convergence

The melding of two or more separate technologies, such as TV and computer technologies.

CPU

Abbreviation for *Central Processing Unit*.

CRC

Abbreviation for *Cyclic Redundancy Check*. See also *checksum*.

Crossover cables

Network cables specially wired to perform the work of a hub in simple networks.

CSMA/CD

Abbreviation for *Collision Sense Multiple Access with Carrier Detection*.

Cyclic Redundancy Check.

An error-checking method used by nearly all modern communications protocols. Abbreviated *CRC*. See also *checksum*.

D

D Channel

The Data channel in an *ISDN* connection. The *D channel* handles signaling and control of *ISDN* features. See also *B channel*.

Database servers

A computer designated to provide database management and access services to *client* computers on the network.

DBS

Abbreviation for *Digital Broadcast System*.

Deceit.C

A hacker's program that attempts to foil an otherwise secure network by tricking network users into disclosing their passwords to hackers.

Denial of service attack

An attempt by a hacker to render a network temporarily inoperable, often by overloading it with meaningless messages.

DHCP

Abbreviation for *Dynamic Host Configuration Protocol*.

DHCP Server

A computer set up to use the *Dynamic Host Configuration Protocol* to allocate *Internet Protocol* addresses to computers on the network.

Dial-Up Connection

Connecting to a network using the regular dial-up telephone network.

Dial-Up Networking

A tool in Microsoft Windows used for making dial-up connections.

Dial-Up Networking Server

A feature in Microsoft Windows 98 and Windows NT that can be used to make a connection to your network using a modem.

Digital

A way of representing data as a stream of 1's and 0's. Compare to *analog*.

Digital Broadcast System

A term for home satellite television systems. Abbreviated *DBS*.

Digital Satellite System

A method of broadcasting that sends information, such as TV programs and Internet data, directly from a satellite to a dish antenna on a building's roof or other location. Abbreviated *DSS*.

Digital Subscriber Line

A high-speed data line provided by telephone companies. Abbreviated *DSL* or, sometimes, *xDSL*.

Digital voltage meter

A network testing tool used to find shorts in cables by measuring the electrical continuity of the cable.

Distribution server

A network computer on which software, such as an operating system, resides and which is used to install that software to other computers on the network.

DNS

Abbreviation for *Domain Name Service*.

Domain

A Windows NT or Windows 2000 network with centralized security and administration.

Domain name

The address of a computer on the Internet. Usually consists of two parts, separated by a period, as in domain.com.

Domain Name Service

A distributed database used in *TCP/IP* networks, such as the *Internet*, to translate individual computer names into *Internet Protocol* addresses.

DSL

Abbreviation for *Digital Subscriber Line*. See *ADSL*.

DSS

Abbreviation for *Digital Satellite System*.

Dynamic Host Configuration Protocol

A system that allocates *Internet Protocol* addresses to computers in a network. Abbreviated *DHCP*.

E

End User License Agreement

The type of license used for most software. Abbreviated *EULA*.

Ethernet

An industry-standard *local area network* that supports data transfer rates of 10Mbps. It is one of the most widely implemented LAN standards.

Ethernet adapter

A *Network Interface Card (NIC)* designed for an *Ethernet* network.

Ethernet address

A unique 48-bit identification number given to each *Ethernet adapter* by its manufacturer. The *IEEE* assigns blocks of addresses to manufacturers to hard-wire into their cards.

EULA

See *End User License Agreement*.

F

FAQ
Abbreviation for *Frequently Asked Questions*.

Fast Ethernet
A standard for Ethernet networks that provides transmission speeds up to 100Mbps.

Fiber optic cable
A networking cable that uses glass threads to transmit data on light waves.

File server
A computer in a network that is designated to provide file storage to other *client* computers on the network.

File Transfer Protocol
The *TCP/IP* protocol used to *logon* to a network, list files and directories, and transfer files.

Firewall
A system consisting of hardware and software or, sometimes, software alone, that is designed to keep unauthorized users from accessing a network. Firewalls are frequently used to prevent unauthorized Internet users from accessing private networks connected to the Internet, especially intranets. All messages entering or leaving the intranet pass through the firewall, which examines each message and blocks those that do not meet the specified security criteria.

Firewire
See *IEEE 1394*.

Fractional T1
A transmission service that provides one or more channels of a T1 line, offering more flexible performance at a lower price than a full T1. Fractional T1 lines are usually sold in increments of 56Kbps, with the 8Kbps per channel used for data management. See also *T1*.

Frame
The name for a *packet* (package) of network data.

Frame relay
Network access method used in some *wide area networks* that transmits *frames* of variable length.

Frequently Asked Questions

Files of questions commonly posed about newsgroups, online services, software, and other technical commodities that are posted online to help information-seekers. Abbreviated *FAQ*.

FTP

Abbreviation for *File Transfer Protocol*.

G

Gateway

A combination of hardware and software that connects two different types of networks.

Gigabit Ethernet

A technology for transmitting data at 1000Mbps, or a billion bits per second, over *Ethernet* networks.

GUI

Abbreviation for *graphical user interface*.

Graphical user interface

A computer interface, like the ones in Microsoft Windows and the Macintosh, that uses buttons, icons, and windows, as well as pointing devices like trackballs and mice, to control the computer. Abbreviated *GUI*.

H

Hertz

A unit of measurement used for measuring frequencies. One hertz equals one cycle per second. Usually abbreviated *Hz*.

High-speed Internet access

Any Internet access offering data transfer rates in excess of the 56K limit of standard analog modems.

Home automation

The process of automating different systems in the home, such as lighting, temperature, and other functions.

Home Networking

Connecting multiple computing and information devices through a collection of technologies and services.

HomeAPI

Home Application Programmer Interface.

HomePNA

Home Phoneline Networking Alliance. A group of companies that supports and sets standards for home networking using existing phone lines. Also called HPNA.

Home RF

Home Radio Frequency. A group that supports and sets standards for using radio transmission in home networking.

HPNA-compliant

Descriptive term referring to networking equipment that conforms to the *HomePNA* specifications.

Host

A user accessing a computer system from a remote location. The host is the system that contains data, and the computer is referred to as the remote terminal.

HTML

Abbreviation for *Hypertext Markup Language*.

Hub

A device joining communication lines at a central location in any network, providing a common connection to all devices on the network.

Hypertext Markup Language

Abbreviated HTML. The computer language used to create pages on the *World Wide Web*.

Hypertext Transfer Protocol

The language used for Web servers and browsers across the Internet.

Hz

Abbreviation of *Hertz*.

I

IDE

Abbreviation for *Integrated Drive Electronics*.

IEEE

Abbreviation for the *Institute of Electrical and Electronic Engineers*.

IEEE 802.X

A set of specifications for *local area networks* from the Institute of Electrical and Electronic Engineers (*IEEE*). Most wired networks conform to *802.3* for *Ethernet* networks or *802.5* for *token ring* networks.

IEEE 1394

A standard for a high-speed serial bus that provides high bandwidth and provides a universal interface for a variety of devices. Also called *Firewire*.

Industry Standard Architecture

A personal computer bus design that has been widely used since IBM introduced it in 1984 with the PC/AT. Abbreviated *ISA*.

Institute of Electrical and Electronic Engineers

An important group for setting standards for networking and communications. Abbreviated *IEEE*.

Integrated Drive Electronics

A widely used standard for personal computer hard-drive interfaces.

Integrated Services Digital Network

A service that offers high speed communication over phone lines. Abbreviated *ISDN*.

Internet

A global network of networks that connects millions of computers and includes, but is not limited to, the *World Wide Web* and newsgroups.

Internet Connection Sharing

The software for sharing Internet access bundled with Microsoft Windows 98 Second Edition Update.

Internet Protocol

Part of the *TCP/IP* protocol suite that tracks internet addresses, routes outgoing messages, and receives incoming messages. Abbreviated *IP*.

Internetwork Packet Exchange

Part of the standard protocol used in Novell NetWare networks.

IP

Abbreviation for *Internet Protocol*.

APP

C

Glossary

IPX

Abbreviation for *Internet Packet Exchange*.

ISA

Abbreviation for Industry Standard Architecture.

ISDN

Abbreviation for *Integrated Services Digital Network*.

ISM

An unlicensed band of the radio spectrum used for Industrial Scientific Medical purposes.

J

JPEG

Abbreviation for *Joint Photographic Experts Group*.

Joint Photographic Experts Group.

A standard for compressing images. It can reduce files sizes to about 5% of their normal size, although some detail is lost. Abbreviated *JPEG*.

K

Kbps

Abbreviation for *kilobits per second*.

kHz

Abbreviation for *Kilohertz*.

Killer app

An extremely popular personal computer software application or, more generally, any use of a technology that is so powerful and helpful that few people can resist it.

Kilobits per second

One thousand bits per second. A measure of data transmission speed. Abbreviated *Kbps*.

Kilohertz

A measurement of frequency. One thousand hertz, or cycles per second. Abbreviated *kHz*.

L

LAN
Abbreviation for *local area network*.

Last mile
The term used to describe the distance between a local telephone customer's premises and the telephone company central office serving that customer.

Latency
The amount of time it takes a message to travel from source to destination and referred to as a delay. Latency and *bandwidth* together define the speed and capacity of a network.

Leased line
A high-speed data line leased on a monthly basis from a telecommunications provider.

LED
Abbreviation for *Light Emitting Diode*.

LILO
Abbreviation for *Linux Loader*.

Light Emitting Diode
A small, bright light used as a status indicator on *network interface cards*, *hubs,* and other network devices which is used to indicate power or activity. Abbreviated *LED*.

Linux
The name for a popular freeware operating system primarily developed by Linus Torvalds.

Linux Loader
The standard utility used for booting computers running the *Linux* operating system. Abbreviated *LILO*.

LIZARD
Abbreviation for the Linux wizard installation program that allows installation of the Linux operating system with a point-and-click graphical interface.

Local Area Network
A network that connects computers and other devices in a single building or group of buildings located near each other. Abbreviated *LAN*.

APP

C

Glossary

Local Computer
The computer on the network that you are using at the moment.

LocalTalk
The cabling scheme used in Apple's proprietary *AppleTalk* networks.

Login
See *Logon*.

Logoff
To end a session of using a computer, network, or online service by sending a message notifying the system that you are signing off. Logoff is a preliminary step to turning off the computer. Also referred to as *Logout*. See also *Login*.

Logon
To establish a connection to a computer, network, or online service. Also referred to as *login*. See also *Logoff*.

Logout
See *Logoff*.

Loopback address
An *Internet Protocol* address that refers to the local computer. *IP* addresses beginning with 127, such as 127.0.0.1, are reserved for the local computer.

M

Machine language
The programming language that computers can actually read. All computer programs must be translated into machine language in order to run. See also *assembly language*.

Mail server
A computer in a network that is designated to provide electronic mail services to other *client* computers on the network.

Mapping
Assigning a drive letter on the local computer to a shared folder on a remote computer.

Master Boot Record
The first sector (track 0, head 0, sector 1) on a PC hard disk, usually contains the partition table, but on some PCs may only contain a boot sector. Abbreviated *MBR*.

Mbps

Megabits per second. One million bits per second. A measure of data transmission speed.

MBR

Abbreviation for *Master Boot Record*.

Mean Time Between Failure

A term, usually expressed in hours or days, that specifies how long a computer or computer component will last before it fails. Abbreviated *MTBF*.

Mean Time To Repair

Average time it takes to repair a network, computer, or peripheral problem. Abbreviated *MTTR*.

Media

In a network, the cables linking *workstations* together. Examples of media include *twisted-pair, coaxial,* and *fiber optic cable*.

Megahertz

One million cycles per second.

MHz

Abbreviation for *Megahertz*.

MIME

Abbreviation for *Multipurpose Internet Mail Extension*. See also *UUENCODE*.

Modem

Short for *MOdulator-DEModulator*. A device that converts digital signals to analog and vice versa. Modems allow data to be transmitted over voice-grade telephone lines.

Moving Pictures Experts Group

An industry standards group set up to develop and maintain formats for compressing and transmitting digital video files. Abbreviation for *MPEG*.

MPEG

Abbreviation for *Moving Pictures Experts Group*.

MTBF

Abbreviation for *Mean Time Between Failure*.

MTTR

Abbreviation for *Mean Time To Repair*.

Multihoming

Allowing one computer to connect to more than one network domain by, for example, installing two network interface cards in the computer.

Multipurpose Internet Mail Extension

An encoding technique that allows people to send formatted documents, photos, sound files, and video files attached to e-mail messages. Abbreviated *MIME*.

N

NAT

See *Network Address Translation*.

NetBEUI

An enhancement of the NetBIOS networking protocol. *NetBEUI* is the most appropriate and commonly used networking protocol for home networks.

NetBIOS

Abbreviation for *Network Basic Input/Output system*.

Network

Collection of computers, printers, routers, switches, and other devices that are able to communicate with each other over a transmission medium.

Network Adapter

See *Network interface card*.

Network Address Translation

A method for sharing Internet connections between networked computers. Abbreviated *NAT*.

Network Basic Input/Output System

A very popular networking protocol for PC-based *local area networks*. Abbreviated *NetBIOS*.

Network Interface Card

A printed circuit board that installs in a computer's expansion slot, allowing the computer to be connected to a network. Abbreviated *NIC*. Also called a *Network Adapter*.

Network Neighborhood

A function built into Windows 95 and Windows 98 that provides access to the other computers on your network.

Network Operating System
The operating system software that runs the network. Abbreviated *NOS*.

Network protocols
An agreed-upon format for transmitting data between two computers. A set of rules and procedures used to make network communication work smoothly.

Network scanner
A hacking program that automatically scans networks looking for unprotected servers that can be easily hacked.

Network analyzer
A sophisticated network testing tool used to decode and resolve problems with the various layers in a network protocol. Also called *protocol analyzer*.

Newsgroup
A bulletin board–type discussion group on the Internet.

NIC
Abbreviation for *Network Interface Card*.

Node
A computer hooked up to the network.

Noise
Interference that corrupts or damages the integrity of signals in a network. Noise can be caused by poor cable connections, radio waves, nearby electrical wires, lightning, and other causes.

NOS
Abbreviation for *Networking Operating System*.

O

OEM
Abbreviation for *Original Equipment Manufacturer*.

Original Equipment Manufacturer
Manufacturers that produce the end products sold to consumers with their brand name (i.e., Sony) displayed. Abbreviated *OEM*.

Open Source Movement

A trend toward making widely available a computer program's original *source code*, a policy at odds with almost all commercial and some non-profit software publishers.

P

Packet

A small self-contained parcel of data sent across a computer network. Each packet contains a header giving addresses for the source and destination, as well as data- and error-detection information.

Packet Switched Network

A network on which each *packet* carries its own routing information and can be routed to its destination independently of other packets in the same message.

Partition table

A data structure, 64 bytes in length, that defines the way a PC hard disk is divided into logical sections known as partitions.

Password sniffers

Hacking programs designed to snag passwords as they go by in network traffic.

Patch cable

A short (usually 25 feet or shorter) networking cable with connectors on both ends.

PCI

Abbreviation for *Peripheral Component Interconnect*.

Peer network

See *Peer-to-Peer networking*.

Peer-to-Peer Networking

A network architecture that allows all computers on the network to be used as both clients and servers by all other users on the network. Also called *peer network*. Peer-to-peer networks may have dedicated servers, but they are not required as in a *client-server network*.

Peripheral Component Interconnect

A high-speed local bus connecting a personal computer's central processor with peripheral devices such as network adapter cards, video adapters, and disk drives. See *Plug 'n' Play*. Abbreviated *PCI*.

Piconet

A small, personal-sized network, usually between devices using *Bluetooth* technology.

Pine

An e-mail editor for Linux computers.

Ping

A tool for testing networks. It sends a special data packet to a designated computer on the network, requiring the terminal to respond.

Ping of Death

A malicious use of the Ping tool—a tool normally used to test networks—by hackers. The Ping of Death can stall or crash a computer or an entire network by tying up the system with pointless tasks. See also *Ping*.

Ping time

The amount of time that elapses between the time a *ping* is sent to a networked computer and a response is received.

Plug 'n' Play

A capability that automatically configures PC adapter cards, including *PCI* cards, when the PC is started. See also *Peripheral Component Interconnect*.

Point-to-Point Protocol

The protocol used to accomplish most long-distance Internet connections. Abbreviated *PPP*.

Port

An interface on a computer to which devices such as disk drives, mice, and keyboards are attached.

Port sniffer

A device that searches a network for machines connected to the network. A port sniffer may be built for network diagnostic purposes, or by criminals looking for poorly defended computers to invade.

POTS

Plain Old Telephone Service. Analog data being sent down the phone wire.

PPP

Abbreviation for *Point-to-Point Protocol*.

Print servers

A computer designated to provide printing services to other *client* computers on the network.

Protocol

An agreed-upon standard for transmitting data between two computers. It can be implemented either in hardware or in software.

Protocol Analyzer

A sophisticated network-testing tool used to decode and resolve problems with the various layers in a network protocol. Sometimes referred to as a network analyzer.

Q

QIC

Abbreviation for *quarter-inch cartridge*.

Quarter-inch cartridge

A popular standard for media (tapes) used in tape data backup drives. Usually abbreviated as QIC-80, etcetera.

Queue

A temporary list of items awaiting service, such as documents in line to be printed.

R

Redirection

Technique used by Novell NetWare to allow workstations to use server hard drives as if they were local drives.

Remote Computers

The other computers on the network, as seen from your local computer.

Repeater

A device that regenerates or replicates a signal on a network. A *bridge* that connects two segments to get around limits on the maximum separation between segments, such as the 100-meter limit on *Ethernet* segments.

RFC

Abbreviation for *Request For Comment.*

Request For Comment

A series of notes and comments about the Internet that date to the Internet's beginnings as *ARPANET* in 1969. Abbreviated *RFC.* RFCs are often precursors to Internet standards

Ring topology

A network design with all devices connected in a closed loop, with each device directly connected to the two devices on either side.

RJ-11

A connector with either four or six wires used to connect U.S. telephone equipment and, less commonly, network devices. Abbreviation for Registered Jack-11.

RJ-45

A connector with eight wires, popular for connecting computers to networks. *RJ-45* is similar to but larger than the *RJ-11* connectors that are used to connect telephone equipment and some network gear. Abbreviation for Registered Jack-45.

Root account

Linux user account reserved for the system administrator. Also called *superuser* account.

Router

A piece of networking hardware that connects one or more *local area networks.*

S

Samba

A free software package that adds Windows-like file- and printer-sharing features to a *Linux* server.

Segment

Part of a network that is separated from the rest of the network by a *bridge* or a *router.*

Server

A computer or device on a network that manages network resources. The server is dedicated to storing files, and, with proper permissions, any user on the network is able to store files on the server.

Server Message Block

The protocol Windows networks use for file- and printer-sharing. Abbreviated *SMB*.

Sharing

Making available a local computer's drives and printers to other computers on the network.

Shielded twisted pair

Cable with a pair of twisted wires surrounded by a metal shield to protect the signal from electrical interference. Compare to *unshielded twisted pair.* Abbreviated *STP*.

Shopping Agents

Web sites that search a number of online vendors and compare prices for specific products.

Shopping basket

An electronic list of the goods a shopper has selected to purchase from an online vendor.

Simple Mail Transfer Protocol

The *TCP/IP* protocol for sending electronic mail. Abbreviated *SMTP*.

SMB

Abbreviation for *Server Message Block.*

SMTP

Abbreviation for *Simple Mail Transfer Protocol.*

Smurf attacks

A type of hacker attack that can overwhelm a network by sending and requesting vast floods of echoed data packets.

Snail mail

Regular mail delivered by the postal authority.

Sneaker Net

Transferring files between computers by physically carrying floppy diskettes between machines, usually by walking.

Source code

A computer program in its original form, as it was written by the programmer, and before it has been compiled into machine language.

Spam

Unsolicited Commercial E-mail, especially mail containing commercial messages.

Spam filter
Software that helps to block or filter out *spam* e-mail messages.

Spread spectrum
A radio technology that spreads transmissions over a wide bandwidth to improve interference tolerance.

Standards
A definition for something such as a programming language, data formats, or communications protocol that has been approved by a recognized standards organization.

Star topology
A network design with devices connected to a central hub.

STP
Abbreviation for *shielded twisted pair*.

Subnet mask
Synonym for *address mask*.

Subnet
The section of an *IP* network identified by a particular *address mask* or *subnet mask*.

Superuser
See *root account*.

Syn Flood
A type of hacker attack that floods network ports with so many false requests for connections that they can no longer communicate.

Syntax
The options, switches, and other elements of a command given to a computer.

T

T1
A high-speed transmission link with a data rate of 1.544Mbps. A complete T1 carrier contains 24 channels, each of which provides 64Kbps. See also *Fractional T1*.

T3
A very high-speed transmission link with a data rate of 45Mbps.

APP

C

Glossary

TCP/IP

See *Transmission Control Protocol/Internet Protocol*. The networking protocol used on the Internet and other *wide area networks*.

Terminal

A combination of a keyboard and display screen that lets you communicate with a computer or host.

Terminal Adapter

Hardware used to connect a computer or network to an *ISDN* line. Essentially, an ISDN *modem*.

Terminator

Device placed on the end of a *coaxial* network cable to keep network signals from reflecting after reaching the end of the cable.

Terms of Service

A document describing the rights and responsibilities of a user of an online service, and the conditions under which the service is offered. Abbreviated *TOS*.

Thicknet

A heavy, stiff type of *coaxial cable* used in some networks. Rarely found in home installations.

Thinnet

A type of coaxial cable, resembling the *coaxial cable* used in cable television connections, used in some home networks.

Thin client

A stripped-down PC in a *client-server* network that is designed to rely on the data processing power of the server.

Thin servers

Radically stripped-down PCs that can be hooked up to a home network to do, typically, a single job, such as provide security, store files, or control printers.

Time domain reflectometer

A network troubleshooting tool that measures the way signals reflect from the ends of a network cable.

Token passing

A network *access method* that circulates an electronic token among *workstations* to determine which workstation can use the network at any given moment.

Token ring

A network that uses a *ring topology* and an *access method* employing *token passing*.

Topology

A description of the design of a network, as in *bus topology, star topology,* and *ring topology.*

TOS

Abbreviation for *Terms of Service.*

Transceiver

In *thicknet* networks, an adapter that taps into the *coaxial cable* running between *workstations.* In networking Apple Macintosh computers, refers to an adapter that fits into the *AUI* port on the back of the Mac, allowing the computer to be connected to *Ethernet* networks using an *RJ-45* connector.

Transmission Control Protocol/Internet Protocol

The networking protocol used on the Internet and other *wide area networks.* Abbreviated TCP/IP. See also *Internet Protocol.*

Tree

Windows 2000 network consisting of a group of domains.

Twisted pair

Networking cable with two insulated wires twisted around one another. Only one wire carries the signal. The other is grounded and protects against interference.

U

UCE

Abbreviation for *unsolicited commercial e-mail.*

Uniform Resource Locator.

An address identifying a page of information on the *World Wide Web.* Abbreviated *URL.*

Universal Serial Bus

A port for connecting peripherals to personal computers that supports data transfer rates of up to 12Mbps, and allows up to 127 devices to be connected to a single PC. Abbreviated *USB.*

Unshielded twisted pair

A type of wiring used for *Ethernet, 10BaseT,* and *100BaseT* networks. See also *Shielded twisted pair.*

APP
C

Glossary

Unsolicited Commercial E-mail

Electronic mail sent for the purpose of selling or promoting a product or service to people who have not requested it. See also *spam*. Abbreviated *UCE*.

Uplink port

Port on an *Ethernet hub* that is used for attaching additional *hubs, cable modems,* and other devices to the network.

URL

Abbreviation for *Uniform Resource Locator*.

USB

Abbreviation for *Universal Serial Bus*.

Usenet

A huge bulletin board–type network that is part of the *Internet*, and provides user news and e-mail discussion forums for many thousands of topics. An abbreviation of *USEr NETwork*.

Username

A name assigned to a person using a network for purposes of identification, security, access control, e-mail delivery, etcetera.

UTP

Abbreviation for *Unshielded twisted pair*.

UUENCODE

An encoding technique that allows people to send formatted documents, photos, sound files, and video files, along with e-mail messages. See also *MIME*.

V

Vampire tap

A device used to connect to a *thicknet Ethernet* cable.

Virus

A dangerous or destructive program that alters stored files and programs and copies itself to other computers and diskettes.

W

WAN
Abbreviation for *wide area network*.

Web
Abbreviation for *World Wide Web*.

Wide Area Network
A network that extends beyond a single building. Compare with *local area network*. Abbreviated *WAN*.

Windows Internet Naming Service
A system that determines the *IP* address associated with a particular computer name. Abbreviated *WINS*.

WinGate
A popular software program used for simultaneously sharing a single modem and Internet service account among two or more networked PCs.

Winhack Gold
A hacker program for Windows that scans blocks of network addresses, looking for shared files that anyone can access.

WINS
Abbreviation for *Windows Internet Naming Service*.

Wireless Node
A computer with a wireless network interface card.

Workgroup
Term for a small Windows 95, 98, 2000 *peer-to-peer network*.

Workstation
A personal computer, other than a *server*, connected to the network.

World Wide Web
System on the Internet that allows information to contain text, images, audio and video clips, and links to other pages. Abbreviated *WWW* and *Web*.

Worm
A computer virus-like program than can spread working copies of itself to other computer systems, usually through a network. Unlike viruses, worms don't necessarily attach themselves to a host program.

WWW

Abbreviation for *World Wide Web*.

X- Y - Z

X-10

A powerline networking technology used in home automation systems.

X.25

The network access method used in *packet switched networks*.

xDSL

See *Digital Subscriber Line*.

ZIP file

A file containing data that has been compressed using the *ZIP* format.

Zone

A division used in AppleTalk networks for organizing the services available on a network similar to a workgroup.

APPENDIX <u>D</u>

The Companion CD

Overview

Almost any time you alter or upgrade a computer system, you will need some additional software to get the full benefit of the improvement. Networking is no exception. There are thousands of network-ready versions of popular mainstream programs you can use on your network, as well as many utilities and applications that are of interest only to networkers. The CD accompanying this book has more than a dozen of the most useful programs around, including games, applications, and utilities. Each will enhance your enjoyment of a home network by making it more fun and useful.

Following are brief descriptions of the programs on the CD. To learn more about them in person, you can install them directly from the CD. Descriptions also include Web sites you can visit to learn about the uses and latest versions of the programs.

123 Free Solitaire

123 Free Solitaire is a highly rated freeware card game that comes with the popular solitaire variations Klondike, Pyramid, Easthaven, FreeCell, Fourteen Out, and Four Seasons. Published by TreeCardGames, Inc., it has digital sound effects, a variety of choices of background and card decks, and numerous options to improve gameplay. It's a scaled-down version of the even more highly rated commercial SolSuite 2000 game. Learn more at www.123freesolitaire.com.

Acrobat Reader

Adobe's Acrobat Reader is one of those programs that belong on every computer. The reason is, it lets you read and use files that are in the portable document files (.PDF) format, which is a popular format for software and hardware documentation, instruction manuals, technical white papers, and many other documents. To create PDF files, you need the full-fledged and expensive Adobe Acrobat program. But to read them, all you need to do is install Acrobat reader. Learn more at the Web site of the publisher, Adobe Systems Inc., at www.adobe.com.

Backup Exec Desktop Edition

The version of Veritas' Backup Exec Desktop Edition 4.2 on the CD is a trial edition of the well-done commercial backup software. It's an excellent choice for backing up data on Windows 95, Windows 98, and Windows NT Workstation 4.0 computers. It's fully network-compatible, so you can back up any disk, tape, or other drive on the network. A flexible scheduling tool makes it easy to back up when it's convenient to you. Note that Backup Exec will not run on Windows 2000. This trial version is good for 30 days from the time you install it. Learn more from Veritas Software's Web site at `www.veritas.com`.

CoreSave v.2.0

CoreSave v.2.0 is a Windows utility that saves your system configuration and lets you quickly restore it in the event your system freezes and you get the chilling *blue screen of death*. You can select what system configuration information should be saved, such as printer information or Internet settings. Then, when a system freeze occurs, you can use a quick restore button to recover from disasters or malfunctions without losing any data or more than seconds of time. CoreSave wisely won't allow you to restore old registry data over an operating system that has been upgraded or patched with a service release update. CoreSave 2.0 runs only Windows 95/98 systems, although the publisher, Innovative Softwave, Ltd, says Windows NT Workstation and Windows 2000 updates are in the works. Learn more at `www.innovativesoftware.com`.

Essential NetTools

Essential NetTools is a sort of Swiss Army Knife of software for network administrators. Its arsenal of helpful utilities includes NBScan, a NetBIOS scanner that can give you a graphical look at all the computers on your network that are offering file sharing. There's also NetStat, which graphically displays all of a computer's inbound and outbound network connections. The version on the CD is a 30-day evaluation edition. Learn more from the TamoSoft Inc. Web site at `www.tamosoft.com`.

Eudora Light

Eudora Light is the freeware version of Eudora for Windows, one of the most popular e-mail programs around. This version of Eudora Light is a 30-day evaluation version for Windows 3.x, 95, and NT only—it won't run on Windows 98 systems. Learn more from the QualCOMM, Inc., Web site at `www.qualcomm.com`.

ImageCast IC3

ImageCast IC3 lets you copy a hard drive, including the boot track, partitions, registry settings, and applications, onto other machines on your network. This means you can clone multiple Windows 95/98/NT/2000 machines very quickly and easily so that all the machines on your network will have up-to-date software and configuration information on their hard drives. This evaluation version lets you try out the software for 30 days. Learn more at the Web site for Innovative Software, Ltd., at `www.imagecast` `.com/enter.htm`.

Internet Explorer 5

Internet Explorer 5.0 is the latest version of Microsoft's standard-setting Web browser software. It's available free for the downloading, of course, from Microsoft's' Web site at `www.microsoft.com`. The advantage to having it on the CD is that you don't have to wait for the entire 78MB or so to trickle through your Internet connection.

McAfee VirusScan 4.02

McAfee's VirusScan 4.02 is a full-featured antivirus program able to detect and remove virtually all known viruses in lab tests, including boot sector, file, stealth, polymorphic, encrypted, and macro viruses infecting Word and Excel. This is a trial version for Windows 95/98 PCs from McAfee.com Corporation at `www.mcafee.com`.

Netscape Communicator 4.7

Netscape Communicator 4.7 is the latest version of the Web software suite that revolutionized the Internet. This version includes the Navigator browser, Messenger mail software, AOL Instant Messenger 3.0, Netscape Radio, RealPlayer G2, Winamp, PalmPilot Synch tools, and more. Learn more from Netscape Communications Corporation at `www.netscape.com`.

VyPRESSS Messenger

VyPRESS Messenger lets you send and receive text messages over home networks and the Internet using the TCP/IP protocol. It supports group messaging, so you can send the same message to every computer on your network, and it operates instantaneously, so that messages pop up on their recipients' screen as fast as you can send them. The program comes in four languages: English, German, French, and Russian. Learn more from VyPRESS Research, at `www.vypress.com`.

WebFerret

WebFerret is a powerful and convenient way to ransack the Web for just the information and software you need. You can choose to search all or any of a group of popular search engines, selecting the number of hits you want to see and ranking results by relevance and other traits. Despite its flexibility, it's simple and straightforward to use. You enter your search words and choose from four radio buttons: All keywords, Any keyword, Exact phrase, or Boolean Expression, then click Find Now. Learn more about this useful freeware at FerretSoft's Website, `www.ferretsoft.com`.

WinGate

WinGate 3.0 is one of the most popular third-party Internet sharing programs available. It is easy to set up, runs on Windows 95/98 and Windows NT computers, and also functions as a filter to screen out inappropriate Web sites. Learn more from Deerfield.com, WinGate's US distributor, at `www.wingate.deerfield.com`.

Using the CD

The most convenient way to use the CD accompanying this book is through the Sybex CLICKME interface, which is included on the CD. This should start automatically and pop up when you insert the CD. If it doesn't, you can start it by double-clicking the CLICKME.EXE file in the CD's root directory.

The CLICKME interface makes it easy for you to select and install individual programs from the CD. You don't have to use the interface, however. You can also install programs individually by reading the installation instructions for each program in the CD's Readme file. In any event, you should take a look at the readme.txt file on the CD.

Using Freeware

Freeware is a type of software that the author gives away for free. That means anybody can use it, without having to pay anything ever. A key distinction with freeware is that the author keeps the copyright and, often, imposes some restrictions on its use. Typically with freeware, users are not allowed to sell the software. Other prohibitions may include altering the software and passing it on, or passing the software on to anyone else without giving credit to the program's author.

Public domain software, on the other hand, is freeware that is not copyrighted. Anyone can use and modify this type of software without restriction. An example of public domain software is the original version of the Ping networking utility, which was written for Unix by Mike Muuss in 1983 and released for others to use and modify without restriction. The public domain Ping utility has been modified for use with many operating systems, such as Windows, and included in countless commercial products. You can learn more about freeware, as well as obtain freeware programs, at one of the many Web sites devoted to freeware, such as Freeware32 at `www.freeware32.com`.

Using Shareware

Like freeware, shareware is distributed without charge. Unlike freeware, you are supposed to pay a registration fee if you continue to use shareware after looking it over. Shareware could, therefore, be described as commercial software that is distributed on the honor system. The registration fee, which is usually a small fraction of the sum commercial software publishers might charge for similar products, typically entitles you to extras such as a printed manual, technical support, and updates to the program.

You are usually allowed to pass along copies of shareware to other people, as long as you don't attempt to sell the software. Some shareware programs remind you to register the program from time to time. (This type of shareware is known as *nagware*, in recognition of the reminder function.) But even if there are no reminders, legally you must register any shareware you use regularly. Most shareware is produced by a single programmer, who keeps the price low by not charging for fancy packaging or advertising. Many shareware programs rival commercial products in quality and features, and not a few sizable software companies had their beginnings as shareware publishers. You can learn more about shareware at the Web site of the Association of Shareware Professionals, `www.asp-shareware.org`.

Using Trial, Demo, and Evaluation Software

The practice of providing potential customers with trial, demonstration, and evaluation versions of commercial software packages is growing rapidly in popularity. It's a great idea: You get to download a working demonstration version of the commercial product, try it out and, if you like it, buy it.

There are differences between shareware and evaluation software. Evaluation software is more likely to be crippled, or missing important functions, to encourage you to buy the full-fledged program. It's also likely to be much more expensive than shareware. In exchange, you'll usually get a more sophisticated and polished product, with the resources of a larger software company behind it. Many evaluation programs are also set up so that they will no longer work after a certain number of days have passed since they were installed and run for the first time. Whether you end up buying the evaluation software or not, you must comply with the restrictions in the publisher's end user license agreement before installing and using it.

INDEX

Note to the Reader: Page numbers in **bold** indicate the principle discussion of a topic or the definition of a term. Page numbers in *italic* indicate illustrations.

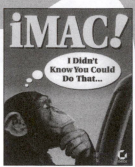

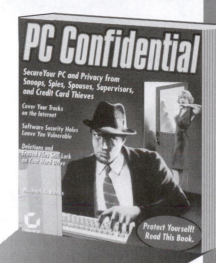

What's on the CD

To help you get the most out of your home networking experience, the CD accompanying this book has more than a dozen useful programs, including games, applications, and utilities.

Network Utilities

Just having a network isn't enough—you need utilities that help protect, enhance, and maintain your network. Here are trial versions of numerous utilities.

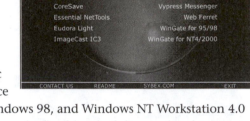

Backup Exec Desktop Edition

This trial edition of Veritas' Backup Exec Desktop Edition 4.2 is an excellent choice for backing up data on Windows 95, Windows 98, and Windows NT Workstation 4.0 computers. It's fully network-compatible, and a flexible scheduling tool makes it easy to back up when it's convenient to you.

CoreSave v.2.0

CoreSave v.2.0, from Innovative Software, is a Windows 95/98 utility that saves your system configuration and lets you quickly restore it in the event your system freezes.

Essential NetTools

Essential NetTools from TamoSoft Inc. includes NBScan, a NetBIOS scanner that can give you a graphical look at all networked computers, and NetStat which graphically displays all of a computer's inbound and outbound network connections.

ImageCast IC3

ImageCast IC3, from Innovative Software, lets you copy a hard drive, including the boot track, partitions, registry settings, and applications, onto other networked machines.

McAfee VirusScan 4.02

McAfee's VirusScan 4.02 is a full-featured trial version antivirus program able to detect and remove virtually all known viruses in lab tests.